Death Ground

Other books by Daniel P. Bolger

The Battle for Hunger Hill
Savage Peace
Feast of Bones (a novel)
Americans at War
Dragons at War

DEATH GROUND

Today's American Infantry in Battle

Daniel P. Bolger

PRESIDIO

BALLANTINE BOOKS • NEW YORK

A Presidio Press Book
Published by The Ballantine Publishing Group

Copyright © 1999 by Daniel P. Bolger

www.ballantinebooks.com

Library of Congress Cataloging-in-Publication Data

Bolger, Daniel P., 1957–
    Death ground : today's American infantry in battle / Daniel P. Bolger
        p.   cm.
    Includes bibliographical references and index.
    ISBN 0-89141-671-4 (hardcover)
    ISBN 0-89141-720-6 (paperback)
    1. United States. Army—Infantry. 2. United States. Marines—Infantry. 3. United States—Armed Forces—Combat sustainability. 4. United States—Armed forces—Operational readiness. I. Title.
UA28.B65   1999
356'.1'0973—dc21   98–37216
                                                        CIP

Printed in the United States of America

This edition printed in 2000

For America's infantrymen—past, present, and future

Contents

Preface

I love the infantry.

That passion came to me honestly. It started long before I joined the United States Army in 1978. My father, John W. Bolger, served in the Korean War with Company M, 3d Battalion, 31st Infantry Regiment, humping recoilless rifles and .50-caliber machine guns up and down the steep mountains of that peninsula. He learned about the hard face of war. Although my dad never boasted of his year in combat, I knew that he was proud of being an infantryman, of doing things that few others could do and doing them well.

That's the essence of the infantry experience, having the combination of brains, stamina, reflexes, and willpower to get out on the ground, face-to-face with your enemy. It's no accident that the root word for infantry is the Latin *infans,* for baby. Only the young can tolerate the squalid living conditions and long odds that often mark the infantryman's lot in warfare. Surprisingly, some thrive on the challenges. The same manly ethos that motivated primitive hunting parties and contemporary college football teams also energizes rifle platoons. Although it may not please those of tender sensibilities, this volatile brew of high spirits, raging testosterone, and youthful optimism when disciplined to serve the common purpose proves exceedingly appropriate in confronting the grim butchery of ground combat. Small-group expectations make young men do difficult and dangerous things rather than lose face with their comrades. Grunts do not let their brothers down. They bring back their wounded and their dead. They get the job done. Their pride comes from belonging to a small team that does what few others can do.

This book is about those happy few, today's American infantry. I have written other books that describe the U.S. Army and the armed forces as a whole. The present volume focuses much more narrowly on a single fighting arm, the infantry. Modern warfare is a team effort, of course. All soldiers do their part, and to look closely at one part of the force in isolation can obscure that vitally important point. Infantry does not fight alone—far from it. But its kind of war remains very traditional, very personal, and very dangerous. It merits special attention. If this modest work tells more about today's infantry, it has served its purpose.

A few comments on style are in order. As much as possible, I have steered clear of the acronyms that serve as the professional shorthand of our military. Those used have been defined within the text. With regard to measurements, although the U.S. armed forces have largely embraced the metric system, the reading public has not. Accordingly, to make these descriptions more understandable, I have translated almost everything to English measures, such as feet, miles, gallons, pounds, and tons. The one exception involves certain weapons commonly known by their bore size in millimeters, as in the 25mm chain gun carried on an M-2A2 Bradley fighting vehicle. I have also used the twenty-four-hour clock to define times, all local to the action unless otherwise noted. This matches American military practice.

No book writes itself; in the present case, I benefited from lots of quality help. I am particularly grateful to the fellow military professionals who shared their views on the recent battles and present roles of American infantry. Along these lines, special thanks go to Jim Antal, John Antal, Ronald Britt, Dennis Chapman, Kurt Fuller, Frank Hancock, Rich Hooker, Ken Keen, John Lock, Tom Maffey, Doug McCallum, John Partin, Mike Scaparotti, Joe Smith, Dan Stempniak, and Jerry Vevon. As always, the good counsel of Col. Walter B. Clark must be acknowledged. Patient and tolerant editor E. J. McCarthy also deserves due appreciation, along with the wonderful staff at Presidio Press. Finally, the greatest debt of all is owed to my wife, Joy, son Philip, and daughter Carolyn, whose unconditional love and understanding make all things possible.

Prologue: A Few Good Men

> *In difficult ground, press on;*
> *in encircled ground, devise stratagems;*
> *in death ground, fight.*
>
> —Sun Tzu, *The Art of War*

Everybody expected shooting, serious shooting. Tension, bad karma—bad *juju* indeed, to use the local lingo—hung in the humid evening air, as strong as the sweet tang of rotting garbage, as pervasive as the dull stench of lingering human waste, as unnerving as the strong aroma of drying animal blood. Yes, somebody was definitely going to get it this time. The only question involved exactly when and where.

Nobody bothered to ask why. That was obvious, given the antagonists. Put U.S. Marine riflemen and Haitian paramilitary toughs at close quarters, and a clash could be expected sooner or later. It had always been that way in and around the squalid port town of Cap-Haitien. Both sides knew the deal.

The two groups were supposed to be working together to keep order. Clever men in tailored suits back in Washington cooked up this scheme, but they missed some rather important realities out among the dusty shanties of Haiti. It might sooner be expected that Marines and Imperial Japanese soldiers would cooperate in policing Iwo Jima in 1945. No, the Marines knew their enemy. They had always known. The Haitian gunmen knew, too. As they used to say in western movies, the town just wasn't big enough for the two of them.

It only made sense. After all, the Marines had been gearing up for months to storm ashore in Cap-Haitien, the island republic's second city, with orders to destroy the *Forces Armées d'Haiti* (FAd'H) and their police auxiliaries. Embarked aboard the amphibious assault carrier USS *Wasp* and the big landing ships USS *Nashville* and USS *Ashland*, the young riflemen prepared to go ashore via old, rattling CH-46E Frog helicopters and the ungainly, slab-sided, armored, clanking amphibious assault vehicles (AAVs, sometimes called amphibious tractors, or amtracs), which were capable of swimming in to the beaches fronting Cap-Haitien. Rehearsed, briefed, rerehearsed, rebriefed, definitely anxious to get going, the men waited for the traditional, fateful predawn command: "Land the landing force."[1]

The order never came. Or, to be more precise, it came in an entirely different manner. Things changed. There would be no forced entry into Haiti, no Inchon, no Saipan, and, thank God, no Tarawa—not this time. The bad guys knuckled under, and they had the good form to do so in the nick of time.

Just as American Marine and Army assault forces moved into position to deliver an overwhelming blow, Haiti's Lt. Gen. Raoul Cédras and his junta cracked. Rather than take their chances trying to oppose U.S. firepower, the military clique agreed to step down without fighting and turn over authority to Haiti's elected president, a thoroughly unpredictable yet undeniably charismatic defrocked priest named Jean-Bertrand Aristide. Americans would land anyway, to ensure that Cédras and company kept their bargain.

Like attack dogs with leashes jerked tight just before they slipped from the cages, the American contingents responded to their masters in Washington, and they definitely showed some teeth. In full battle array, armed and dangerous, Marines and soldiers landed unopposed on 19–20 September 1994. Rather than destroy Haiti's armed forces and paramilitary echelons, now the Americans intended to cooperate with the FAd'H to keep a lid on things in the Haitian streets until Cédras and his associates departed and Aristide and his entourage arrived. Anywhere else, that handover would have happened within hours. But this was Haiti. Nothing ever moved that fast there, except bullets.[2]

So for more than three weeks, Americans were expected to work with the inept Haitian FAd'H troops to keep the country functional—no mean task in Haiti, which barely functioned even in normal times. The bulk of the populace welcomed the American "intervasion" but chafed under the continued presence of hated FAd'H bullyboys.[3] The FAd'H seemed like a supporting cast from a Marx brothers production—ill organized, sloppily attired, unloved, and incompetent. But they knew how to crack heads, and their ample suite of firearms was only too real. In and around the sprawling capital of Port-au-Prince, U.S. soldiers tried to work with the FAd'H to keep a semblance of order, to make this shotgun marriage function for the short time it needed to do so. It wasn't easy. From their arrival, light infantrymen of the 10th Mountain Division found challenges aplenty. Made up of a good number of veterans of brutal city firefights in Somalia the year before, the 10th Mountain men faced an endless string of "incidents": wild mob scenes, beatings of Haitians by the FAd'H, bellicose confrontations with khaki-clad local police, random hostile gestures, and stray gunshots aplenty. Not surprisingly, the American soldiers and their erstwhile local partners spent as much time watching one another as quelling overly boisterous crowds.[4]

The Marines faced a different, more difficult situation, if only because they wore the famous globe and anchor. The Corps had been to this party before, and neither side had much enjoyed it. In 1994, Marines landed with a reputation built on nineteen years of aggressive and successful counterinsurgent operations conducted throughout Haiti. Two generations of "Old Corps" Marines cut their teeth chasing the elusive, deadly Haitian *cacos* (guerrillas). Along with numerous superb sergeants and young officers who led the Corps across the Pacific in World War II, future generals, legends such as Smedley D. Butler, Lewis B. "Chesty" Puller, Alexander A. Vandegrift, and Herman "Hard Head" Hanneken, all served in the restive republic.[5] It happened in another lifetime, another era really, way back in 1915–34, in a thankless "banana war" ignored by the American public then and now. But the Haitians remembered.

In the oral tradition that characterizes this illiterate land, every Haitian heard stories of the mighty U.S. Marines, the de facto rulers of their country from 1915 until 1934. When Haitian nationalists talked about American evils and gringo imperialism, they meant Marines, the awful bogeymen, the big men who stalked their grandfathers and great-grandfathers to their deaths in the hills, the relentless, pitiless Yankee Marines. Those same great warriors built the roads, taught sanitation, supervised elections, and, in the style of authoritarians everywhere, made the trains run on time. Indeed, anyone driving the crumbling Highway 100 from Port-au-Prince to Cap-Haitien traveled thanks to Marine Corps construction efforts.[6] Yet for all their prowess and achievements, the Marines weren't Haitians. They were interlopers, uninvited and unwanted self-appointed guardians in a proud, defiant island state that had thrown off its French overlords in 1804 and never looked back. The Marine occupation stood as a blemish on an otherwise clean record of independence. In a country without much else, that meant something.

And now, with a United Nations mandate in hand, the Marines were going back into the streets of ramshackle, seaside Cap-Haitien, just like old times. As in those bygone days, like their *caco* forefathers, a good number of armed Haitians didn't like it. Not all were happy to see Cédras and his FAd'H go away, especially in willful Cap-Haitien, where being different from Port-au-Prince sometimes became an end in itself. Whatever happened down south in the capital carried only so much weight. The people of Cap-Haitien, as usual, would choose their own way.

The crowds seemed happy enough as the Americans appeared, but anyone could sense a ripple of discontent, a potential for the lid to blow off. After all, this was Haiti, land of the machete. Knowledgeable U.S. Army civil affairs specialists summarized conditions without any sugar coating: "Jungle law in effect."[7] In this lethal cauldron, this dark, cramped urban jungle known as Cap-Haitien, the FAd'H could stage one shocking event and play it out to the tune of a good number of dead gringos. Let that go down, especially on a live news camera feed, and all bets were off. It had happened that way in Somalia less than a year before, hadn't it?

Colonel Thomas S. Jones, the Marine commander, fully expected that brand of trouble. Given a populace of some 75,000 to placate, and facing some 400 to 500 FAd'H trigger pullers and an equal number of affiliated militia types none too happy about the turn of events, Jones brought ashore a task force totaling less than 1,900, built around the 2d Battalion, 2d Marine Regiment.[8] With Port-au-Prince cooking away, Tom Jones anticipated no reinforcement from the 10th Mountain Division for at least a week, maybe longer.

With only a few hundred Marine riflemen at hand, Jones and his chain of command drew on the strong heritage of America's most traditional armed forces.[9] The commander consciously built on the Corps' reputation in Haiti, including symbolic measures such as calling his task force's region of responsibility Area of Operations Hanneken, after the Medal of Honor winner. Jones took time to remind his young fighters of what their predecessors did back in 1915–34. As in that distant campaign, Colonel Jones and his task force emphasized gaining and maintaining popular support, just the way the Old Corps had done their business in Haiti, Nicaragua, the Dominican Republic, and elsewhere during the era of gunboat diplomacy.[10] These ideas resonated, both with the Marines and with their foes.

But Tom Jones went beyond tradition. He took a hard look at the Haiti of 1994. After a careful study of his mission and the situation, the Marine commander determined that the FAd'H in Cap-Haitien did not plan to respond to Cédras in the capital. "Reported to be led by one of the most disciplined, hard-line commanders," Jones wrote later, "these forces had discarded their uniforms, pledging to resist U.S. intervention."[11] You couldn't play nice with these characters, not if you wanted to retain the support of the citizenry, who had endured indignities, beatings, torture, and death from this pack of FAd'H hard cases. In the words of a Marine historian, the colonel explicitly "ruled out joint operations with the FAd'H."[12] From the start, the Marines wore their war faces, making no secret that they considered the FAd'H as adversaries, unsavory thugs better dead than alive.

This tough approach manifested itself right from the start. After a delay of about a day to recock amphibious timetables and turn off preassault fires, the Marines prepared to land at 0700 on 20 September, using essentially the same scheme of maneuver rehearsed for the original invasion plan. In the only concession to the Cédras agreement, the Marines did not carry out their previously rehearsed slate of preemptive attacks on the Haitian military and police units. But everything else went just as the numerous practice runs had.

Teams of SEALs (Sea Air Land, Navy special operators) reconnoitered and marked the landing sites in the surf. Other reconnaissance elements marked helicopter landing zones near the Cap-Haitien airfield. Some also watched the FAd'H barracks, just in case that bunch elected to interfere. With all in readiness, and the tropical sun coming up, Colonel Jones's Marines went in. Armed AH-1W Cobra attack helicopters flew cover, with loaded 70mm rocket pods in evidence. Beneath the Cobras, a wave of big, cumbersome amtracs roared over the beach, carrying the riflemen of Company G; it was followed by a light recon company aboard more nimble, wheeled light armored vehicles bristling with 25mm autocannons. They secured the dilapidated piers and pilings that marked the port of Cap-Haitien. Company E, the floating reserve, came in later in the day to reinforce the mechanized elements. Most of the FAd'H watched and waited, stunned by the speed and scale of the Yankee buildup.

Confronted by a few dazed Haitian policemen on one particular wharf, Company G's lead rifle squads dismounted from their big amtracs. With a minimum of fuss, the Americans handily disarmed the befuddled Haitians. Later that day, the Marines had to return the weapons. But the point had been made.[13]

Simultaneous with the operations around the port, a heliborne assault seized the local airstrip almost two miles south of the waterfront. Company F and Battery B/10th Marines (employed without howitzers as a provisional infantry outfit) rapidly consolidated on initial objectives. Here, the FAd'H stood aside completely, clearly outclassed. In his account of the day's efforts, Tom Jones put it this way: "The rapidity of movement ashore, coupled with the variety of landing means and sites occupied, overwhelmed and psychologically dislocated the 'former' enemy forces."[14]

With their combat echelon ashore, the Marines began to exert their authority, especially over the people Jones pointedly referred to as the enemy. Each company expanded its area of influence, pushing detachments and patrols throughout the towns to gather information, win popular support, and keep track of the stunned FAd'H forces. The words of a Marine captain from 1915 applied just as well to Colonel Jones's men in 1994: "Squads of Marines patrolled the city to prevent any disorder. We went on patrol as soon as we got there."[15]

The Marines walked the streets with loaded weapons, taking advantage of rules of engagement (ROE) that permitted Americans to use "necessary force," including "deadly force," against "persons committing hostile acts or showing hostile intent" in order to "protect lives/property and accomplish [the] mission."[16] In plain English, the rules let Marines shoot anyone threatening them or their buddies or interfering with the mission. Because Jones interpreted protection of innocent Haitian civilians to be fundamental to the Marine mission, they, too, would be defended to the death. Although not exactly a hunting license, these ROE left a lot of discretion to young corporals and sergeants. Trained to deal with such knotty situations, the Marines plunged into the twisted, dirty streets of Cap-Haitien.

To get closer to the action, Company E moved to a vacant girls' school a few blocks west of the town center and began conducting scheduled patrols. Crowds of locals collected around dozen-man foot patrols or trailed Marine Humvee (high mobility multipurpose wheeled vehicle, HMMWV) trucks, chanting pro-Aristide slogans or mocking the FAd'H and their henchmen. On Wednesday, 21 September, a joyful throng of Aristide supporters following two U.S. Humvees grew especially excited in response to the messages blaring from loudspeakers mounted on the American trucks. This episode finally spurred the seething Cap-Haitien police to act. Wading into the revelers, Haitian security men whacked wildly with long, flexible black batons, whipping down women and children indiscriminately. Some khaki-clad policemen fired into the crowd. The demonstrators scattered.[17]

Apprised of this clash, Tom Jones went to FAd'H headquarters to lay down the law. In blunt terms, he warned Lt. Col. Claude Josephat, the same man he described as a FAd'H hard-liner, to get control of his men—or else. To underscore that directive, and to protect the defenseless inhabitants of Cap-Haitien, Jones began to place squads of Marines in front of FAd'H facilities, with orders to keep Josephat's surly crew from beating or killing their fellow Haitians.[18]

So it had come to this, just as both sides knew it would all along. Some of these cards had been dealt as far back as 1915. Now Tom Jones and his Marines were deep in the concrete jungle, as surely as Smedley Butler or Herman Hanneken had ever been. Determined to protect the civilians, the Marines pushed the Cap-Haitien FAd'H into its lair. Shorn of political power, reviled by the mob, unmanned by the cocky Americans, its future existence measured in mere days, the FAd'H snarled and scrapped like a wounded, desperate animal. And in this urban jungle, as in any real one, cornered beasts lash out.

Those desiring a showdown couldn't beat the situation developing along 20th Street in Cap-Haitien toward sunset on Saturday, 24 September 1994, in front of the city's main police barracks, a nondescript two-story building that took up the entire west side of a city block. Across the street stood a run-down apartment complex, with more than a few occupants leaning out open windows to watch the fun. The street was barricaded at either end to hold back rowdy, anti-FAd'H multitudes milling about to the north and south. The local citizenry gathered at these barriers—hooting, jeering, chanting spectators anxious for some action. It all made for a nice, neat rectangular arena, suitable for street theater. Or, as a participant more accurately described it, the place looked all too much "like the O.K. Corral."[19]

To the west, men of Cap-Haitien's 1st Military Police Company watched activities from in and around their barracks. The senior officers were somewhere inside the unremarkable yellow structure, doing something to occupy their time now that the Yankees barred them from the streets. In front of the structure, facing east and flanking the central doorway, stood two guards in khaki uniforms. The one to the north, to the right of the door as seen from the street, carried an Uzi submachine gun. His partner sported a holstered pistol. The pair kept up appearances, if nothing else.

The rest just hung out, sullen and listless, whiling away the hours. Strung up and down the block, some two dozen Haitian policemen and soldiers stood around or sprawled on the crumbling sidewalk. Some played cards or dominoes. Others talked and smoked. Most wore civilian dress. Almost all carried weapons and eyed their unwelcome companions uneasily across the pavement.[20]

There, a mere seven or so yards away, third down and long in an average football game, stood a rifle squad from 2d Platoon, Company E, 2d Battalion, 2d Marine Regiment, looking all too alert. They stood with their backs to the apartment wall, legs spread, rifles hang-

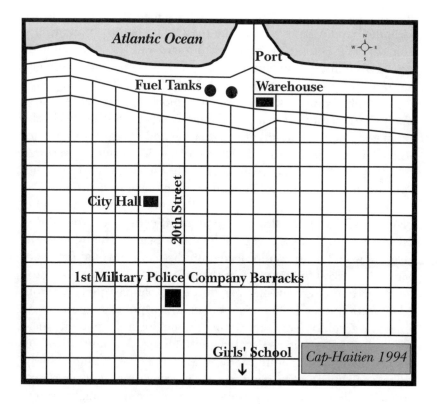

Cap-Haitien 1994

ing with barrels down, eyes searching their Haitian counterparts for any false moves. These young Americans were enforcing Tom Jones's concept, keeping this clutch of Haitian police in their hole, separated from the raucous, surging bands of city people cavorting around the barricades and steadily taunting the paramilitary men.

The rifle squad should have totaled thirteen Marines. It should have been led by an experienced sergeant. But, of course, the actual composition here on the ground deviated from the tables of organization found in Marine Corps manuals. As usual, the variation reflected some deficits from the textbook scheme. There is never more, only less. This particular squad contained only eleven men, and its leader was a corporal named Kyle Todd.

The squad's mission looked like bad business—an evening in Indian country. So Corporal Todd did not go alone. The platoon commander, 1st Lt. Virgil Palumbo, joined the patrol, bringing along his radioman and a sailor who spoke the Creole patois. In many circumstances, a lieutenant and his entourage would be as welcome as cancer. By definition inexperienced and at the same time holding a key rank, the green, incompetent lieutenant is one of those stock figures of military lore, like the wise old senior sergeant, the guy normally charged with keeping such immature young officers in check. But a good lieutenant, full of imagination and energy yet willing to listen before he talks—well, that breed of youthful leader is welcome in any squad, anytime. Like so much in the face-to-face world of the rifle-bearing infantry, it all depended on the man in question.

This man was the right one. Virgil Palumbo graduated from the Naval Academy and, following the usual officer schools, joined the 2d Marines just before the Haiti operation began. The twenty-four year old would be the senior leader on the scene. If something bad happened, it fell to him to make the call.

It's worth noting that when generals and diplomats quote Karl von Clausewitz and send riflemen out to conduct "political intercourse, carried on with other means,"[21] they are talking about turning matters over to folks such as Virgil Palumbo, Kyle Todd, and a handful of well-disciplined, painfully young Marines. These fellows rarely grow familiar with a Prussian theorist's musings, but they become extremely skilled in those ugly, essential "other means." Tonight looked like a night for that kind of dirty work.

The squad's earlier movement to the police barracks set the tone for the evening. With their platoon commander and his team along in the formation, Corporal Todd and his men left Company E's commandeered girls' school just after 1600 and headed north on a five-and-a-half-block route. The men formed into an open tactical column, with point, flank, and trail security, and headed slowly toward the police barracks. Each Marine watched his assigned area and kept his loaded weapon at the ready. This late afternoon shimmered with typical heat and humidity. The streets teemed with loud, jostling people, as usual. Burdened by sweltering flak vests on their torsos, coal-scuttle, German-style Kevlar helmets, a full brace of ammunition, canteens brimming with tepid water, and a good dose of justifiable apprehension, the squad took a while to get to the police station.

Every foot patrol in Haiti reminded all involved that they were not in Kansas anymore. Sensations engulfed the Americans: a strong stink of decay, the lingering whiff of disease and death, garbage strewn in the gutters, and half-clad children playing in oily puddles. Above it all, like a sound track from one of Dante's lower levels of the underworld, cranked the steady, driving, rhythmic din of tens of tuneless melodies assaulting one another and their listeners. Much of the loudest, most annoying music emerged in steady shrieks from rattletrap little trucks weaving slowly through the cramped streets, each shuddering, overloaded "tap-tap" decorated with brightly colored, intricately painted holy icons and religious verses, many in fractured English. "Abandon all hope, ye who enter here" would have been a perfect sentiment. Some Haitian wiseacre had probably thought of it, too.

Fronting the bustling streets on both sides leaned an unending jumble of pathetic wooden shacks, interspersed with a few more substantial cement-block buildings older than any of the Marines. Every hovel featured one or more yawning black openings, presumably windows and doorways, screened by waving dirty curtains. Forget glass panes or wooden doors. Each aperture could conceal anything and often did. Checking every one was not possible. Instead, as the squad moved along, individual Marines watched specified slices of the area around the U.S. formation, searching for the glint of a blued gun barrel emerging from the unseen depths, the telltale motion of a Haitian with a grim mission of his own. Every dark hole promised a game of "the lady or the tiger," played for keeps with live rounds.

This afternoon, pressed all around the fourteen Americans was a sea of sepia brown faces, white teeth, clutching hands, and chattering in the high, lilting Haitian Creole, a kind of bastardized high-school French with old African borrowings tossed in to sweeten the mix. Moving through this human coagulation threatened to disrupt the Marines' practiced patrol drills, separating squad members, blocking lines of sight and lines of fire. Yes, the locals all seemed spirited and happy, but which one had the pistol or the grenade? Which one was scouting for a hidden sniper? You never knew.

Journalist Bob Shacochis perfectly illustrated the atmosphere on such a patrol. Although he wrote about an Army rifle element in

Port-au-Prince at about the same time, this same story was lived by Kyle Todd and his fellow Marines.

It is an odious honeycomb of colorless blocks connected by a grid of dirt alleys, where lethal games of hide-and-seek are a nightly occurrence. My level of apprehension is modest compared to what we now observe on the faces of a platoon of U.S. soldiers, one of the first foot patrols dispatched into the city, fly bait trying to walk down the street. Escorted by the noisy crowd—hundreds of people—the soldiers rotate their bodies like automatons, some walking backward, some straight ahead, their eyes stark with fear, their rifles leveled for firing.[22]

That was the picture, all right, the trail security pivoting to clear the rear arc, upper bodies constrained by inflexible flak jackets, all shooting irons steadied for use. In fact, Bob Shacochis misstated only one thing. Those eyes weren't wide with fear but with vigilance. It's what you don't see that can kill you. So the trick is to see it all, to see it first, to be quick, quick, quick, and thus never dead. In this style, Palumbo, Kyle, and their squad arrived at their destination about 1700, working their way around the southern roadblock to arrive opposite the 1st Military Police Company's building. Then, with little discussion, the squad deployed.

At each corner, down near the barricades with their unruly, howling mobs, Todd placed a Marine carrying the Belgian-designed M-249 squad automatic weapon (SAW). A baby machine gun able to spit out eight hundred high-velocity 5.56mm bullets a minute, the aptly named SAW could certainly cleave a path through a lot of people, should that become necessary. Between the SAWs stood the squad's other men, including Todd, evenly spaced and all with M-16A2s, the latest variant of the familiar Vietnam-era assault weapon. A few Marines also had a little black pipe, a 40mm M-203 grenade launcher accessory, hooked below their rifle barrels. Every rifle and SAW was "locked and loaded," ready to shoot as soon as its owner flicked off the safety catch and pulled the trigger.

Conscious of the need to set the example and be in position to make the right things happen, Lt. Virgil Palumbo centered himself directly opposite the main doorway. He looked straight into the blank faces of the two Haitian sentries. His radioman and translator stood beside him, as did Cpl. Kyle Todd. The leaders passed the word up and down the line: "Pick fields of fire."[23]

Repetitive training kicked in. It was just like all those long afternoons on the firing range. "Firers, watch your lanes." Each American chose a strip of the yellowing headquarters, identifying targets from street level to the roof. The SAW men also scoped out their adjacent street intersections, in case the mobs erupted in something more than joyful noise. The U.S. squad knew that if shooting broke out, their rounds must count. There was absolutely no place to hide on the long, naked wall.

In novels or movies, our brave lads often spend the next few minutes lamenting the need to shed blood, feeling guilty and uneasy over preparing to take human lives. But this scene was only too real, not some hackneyed Hollywood plot. If any of the young Marines with Virgil Palumbo and Kyle Todd wanted to express regrets, they saved it for much later, when they had the luxury to do so. For now, the thin line of Americans stood, backs literally to the wall, counting on one another to shoot fast and true. The dictates of hours spent "snapping-in" under the broiling sun of Parris Island or Camp Lejeune weighed far heavier than pangs of conscience. Those guys over there would kill you if you hitched or halted, if you gasped and fretted instead of squeezing up the trigger slack and firing away. Professional warriors, disciplined Regulars, schooled riflemen—brave terms those, and now these Marines had to live up to them, and do it instinctively the first time.

Their targets, the FAd'H police, at first appeared to ignore the stoic line of Marines. But gradually, Marines noted more and more of the Haitians laying down their dominoes, standing up, fingering their pistols and rifles, staring back at the brazen gringos. At either end of the block, surging crowds shouted and cheered, screaming anti-Cédras epithets and pro-Aristide rallying cries. The SAW gunners noted armed Haitians in the crowd—how many males in this damned town carried weapons?—and glanced back nervously at their squad leader and platoon commander, sending that unnerving report man to man.

The two leaders stood as impassive as granite. The officer had the radio handset in his ear, listening. The Haitian gunmen were looking serious now, measuring ranges, checking angles, sizing up potential victims. "Everyone knew something was going to happen," commented LCpl. Baldemore Brown. "It felt like they were surrounding us."[24] American fingers were edging to the safety levers, just in case.

Nothing felt right, not a bit of it. Intelligence updates radioed from higher predicted a FAd'H-initiated ambush sometime after 1800. Friendly Haitian civilians at the cross blocks shouted warnings. Of course, the closely packed masses that were clustered around the barricades yelled incessantly, and alerts to the Marines made up only a fraction of their repertoire. Most of the hollering insulted the police, and a steady cadence of slogans poured from both ends of the street. Palumbo's U.S. Navy boilerman-cum-linguist, Francis José Joseph, supplied the platoon commander with a running translation: "Down with Cédras!" "Take the guns away from these dogs!" "Long live Aristide!" One worthy even tossed a bag of garbage at a cluster of FAd'H security men. In the barracks windows, more and more shadows flitted back and forth. Something was going on in there.

Behind the police barracks, as the western sky flared into a spectacular, blood red tropical sunset, the Marines heard the cracking echo of gunshots. The Marine radio net carried messages about the incident. A couple short blocks away, some pro-FAd'H sniper had popped off a few rounds into a demonstration of Aristide supporters. Two civilians appeared to go down before the panicked mob scattered. Another Marine team raced to the scene and nabbed the shooter.[25] This fracas started around 1845 and, to hear the radio traffic, seemed to consume the attention of everyone senior to Palumbo.

Just after 1900, with all the street in shadows, Palumbo and his men heard the telephone ringing inside the darkening police headquarters. Like the rest of Cap-Haitien, the station had no electrical power. Obviously, the phones still worked. The ringing began again a few minutes later. In the gathering twilight, just inside the guarded center door, the lieutenant saw four Haitians in animated conversation. One gestured emphatically. Then all four looked out, glaring directly at 1st Lt. Virgil Palumbo, USMC.

At the same time, the two uniformed Haitian sentinels stiffened. The one to the right began to raise his Uzi. His buddy fumbled for his pistol.

Crack!

The police *pistolero* jerked back and crumpled.

Crack!

Now the Uzi bearer pitched over, too, down and out as surely as if poleaxed.

His rifle muzzle smoking, Virgil Palumbo shot without thinking. *Just like at Quantico, Mister.* Beside him, the radio operator was calling for the quick reaction force (QRF), the speedy, light armored vehicles with their wicked, unforgiving 25mm chain guns and teams of onboard riflemen. Palumbo could barely hear the force through the roar of gunfire echoing all around him.

That was because the instant their lieutenant shot, Kyle Todd and his squad opened up. It was straight infantry stuff. *Follow me. Do as I do.* Both SAW gunners and all the riflemen methodically worked through their designated sectors. The Marines expended about a thousand 5.56mm slugs, mostly from the hammering SAWs, which chewed and chipped a few of the rectangular windows into ragged ovals. Some Haitians went down. Many, those who could, dropped their firearms and ran. A few clambered back into the barracks, scuttling through ground-floor windows. Red tracers pinged and spattered after them.

With tremendous volume and execrable accuracy, Haitian policemen shot back. They fired from the roof, from windows, from the street, even from out of the wild-eyed, screaming, running crowds dispersing madly from either end of the block. Bullets from Uzis, old M-1 rifles, revolvers, and God knows what else pocked apartment walls or skipped off the uneven asphalt pavement, the ricochets sparking in the gathering gloom. Most of the Haitian shooting went well high, the sure sign of poor marksmen. All in all, the initial exchange, the one that did all the damage, lasted about fifteen seconds. Then, the firing trailed off into odd shots and unaimed bursts.

By the time the U.S. QRF rumbled up, only four minutes later, at least eight Haitians lay dead in and around the barracks' ground floor. Over the next three hours, with the Marine battalion commander in charge at the scene, the QRF coaxed out five prisoners, found two more dead, and recovered a badly wounded FAd'H man. Not a single Cap-Haitien civilian was hit. The Marine marksmen had been right on target, and the Haitian police cadres bowled over before they could light up the defenseless locals.

In the sole friendly injury, linguist Joseph suffered a flesh wound in the leg. A ricochet had probably struck him. The sailor refused evacuation, translating for the Marines until the standoff ended and the QRF withdrew.[26] That ended it for the night and, as it turned out, for the campaign.

Stunned by the brutal Marine riposte, the FAd'H melted away, first in Cap-Haitien, then, within days, across the entire benighted country.[27] Although there were a few other shooting episodes during U.S. operations in Haiti, they represented isolated, random, unfocused banditry. Organized opposition ended in fifteen violent seconds on 20th Street in Cap-Haitien. Despite all the U.N. and U.S. rhetoric, the majestic aircraft carriers offshore, the flights of powerful aircraft overhead, and the big amtracs in the streets, the final outcome depended, as usual, on a few good men.

A few good men—it's a well-used Marine Corps recruiting line and a popular movie title. But it means more than that, a lot more. Out there, engulfed in the tropical stink, the pressing alien throngs, the snipers and ricochets, the terrible, swift sword of American warpower comes to a pretty damn small point. There alone stand America's few good men, the Regular infantry.

Infantrymen really have no place in polite civil society. Only two sorts of people hunt other people with the express intent of killing. The first are criminals, and we do all we can to keep a lid on them. The others, our infantry, are kept at the fringes of day-to-day life, clustered on a few faraway, rustic Army posts and Marine bases, garrisoned overseas, or loaded aboard ships. This distance helps civilians avoid thinking about infantry and what they do. We talk ourselves into clean, remote, rapid push-button warfare, forgetting that even our smartest weapons are not as selective as a shooter such as Virgil Palumbo. So we dress it all up in euphemisms about "deadly force" and "defense policies" and try to forget about the whole thing.

Sure, when something goes haywire out in the wide world, we want somebody to gun down those bad guys. And if we're personally threatened in some Third World horror show, we damn sure want our men in green to break down the door and save us. But as for doing such things ourselves, in heat and darkness, face-to-face with some enraged terrorist shooter or determined guerrilla gunman— well, better leave that to somebody else, to some experts, but we want them to do only the bare minimum absolutely necessary to complete this dirty work.

Those who fight on foot for America are few, surprisingly few when they line up and count off. An infantry battalion organized for battle, such as the 2d Battalion, 2d Marines, in Haiti, will at most include a thousand men. Often, there are far fewer, about five hundred or so. Whatever the final accounting, it must include necessary medical corpsmen (in Marine units, attached sailors), artillery forward observers, forward air controllers, combat engineers, air defense gunners, signalers, intelligence teams, frontline mechanics, and others who are infantry in all but name. With 91 active-duty infantry battalions (67 Army, 24 Marine) and the Army Special Forces, Navy SEALs, and Air Force combat control teams who also fight up close and personal, there are about 100,000 infantry types in the entire armed forces.[28] That's the sharp point, those 100,000 Regulars.

Some may argue for considering the Army National Guard or the Marine reservists, who combine to contribute a similar number of battalions when fully mobilized and trained. These part-time warriors reflect the best of the American militia tradition, but they are not manned, equipped, trained, disciplined, or led to the standards of the Regulars. Perhaps in the days when preparing for battle meant grabbing a squirrel gun off the mantel and learning a few parade-ground evolutions, the armed forces could get by with that caliber of soldier. But those days are long gone, if indeed they ever existed at all. Close combat demands professionals, and even they have plenty of trouble. Not many of us would trust a heart bypass to "reserve" surgeons doing their two weeks in the hospital operating room, nor would most folks want their house wired by an electrician who spent only thirty-nine days a year at his craft and the rest of his time selling used cars. No, today's complex world demands schooled, full-time experts. That's as true in infantry combat as in anything else. America has about 100,000 professionals skilled for this dangerous stuff. Even 100,000 sounds like a lot until you look at the bigger picture. Among 260 million or so American citizens, the infantry barely shows as a blip—a green line so thin as to be almost transparent—on the demographic radar screen. Indeed, based on current census data, you would be much more likely to encounter a post office worker (791,992), a lawyer (777,000), a prison inmate (444,584), a news reporter (266,000), a librarian (195,000), a musician (174,000), an amusement park attendant (161,000), a public relations associate (155,000), a professional author (139,000), or a Department of Agriculture employee (128,324) than a serving Marine or Army rifleman.[29] Certainly those figures suggest several curious stories, not the least involving a country where convicts outnumber librarians by more than two to one. But each of these categories of people, and many more classes and groups of professionals and craftsmen, far outstrip the strength of Uncle Sam's infantry.

That's as it should be, given that the country has not mobilized for a major war since Vietnam, discounting the short-lived Persian Gulf crusade. Blessed is the nation in which the postal service (791,992) exceeds the Regular Army (499,145) and the Marine Corps (172,434) put together, and paid entertainers (2,026,000) total more than the entire active armed forces (1,493,391).[30] Keep these statistics in mind when people talk about America's "large" standing military establishment. In an absolute raw head count, it's big enough. But relatively speaking, the individuals playing *Rambo* and *G.I. Jane* well outnumber the legitimate articles. The infantry, in particular, gets lost in the statistical shuffle out there.

Even within their own milieu, the infantry constitutes a distinct minority. The armed forces field 1.4 million men and women. Doing the math tells its own tale. For every rifleman or machine gunner, there are thirteen guys doing something else. Some fly jets, fire missiles, or drive tanks, all impressively capable engines of destruction that are vital to the country's defense. Most of the others fix and feed those mighty war machines that compose the U.S. air, sea, and land fleets. Even in the Army, which exists to fight and win on the ground, there are three times as many administrators and logisticians as there are infantrymen. Add in the rest, and the infantry sinks to some 12 to 15 percent of all soldiers. This proportion has held true since the early days of World War II.[31] When it's high noon, time to face the badniks with a hand weapon and a camouflage-cloth shirt, the crowd really thins out.

That 12 to 15 percent—those 100,000 soldiers, Marines, and special warriors that make up the infantry—certainly amount to only a few of the whole. Accordingly, they had better be good, the second ingredient in that popular "few good men" formulation. Today's Regular infantry is all good, arguably the best man for man and battalion for battalion ever put into the field. By World War II standards, every active battalion is an elite body. That's a real change from as recently as the Vietnam era. It's why the country gets by with so few.

Starting in World War II, the United States chose not to organize particularly large numbers of infantry. Infantry regiments pay the majority of the human costs in modern combat, thanks to the efficiency of hostile artillery, air bombardments, and machine guns. Serving a democracy, with access to living memories of the carnage of the Civil War, the World War II military leadership displayed a humane and understandable determination to prevent U.S. casualties. Men such as Gen. George C. Marshall (himself an infantry officer) watched U.S. Army and Marine rifle companies chewed up in the Meuse-Argonne campaign, which concluded the Great War in 1918. More than 120,000 Americans fell in seven weeks.[32] The horrific French losses at Verdun and the British martyrdom at the Somme and Passchendaele demonstrated how much worse things could have been. Trying to fight and win a modern industrial-age infantry war cost bodies. No American wanted that, then or now.

Not surprisingly, the United States chose a different way of war, a style that used only a relatively small number of rifle troops. Drawing on the might of their economy's burgeoning industrial base and tapping the country's rivers of wealth, American military leaders intentionally and systematically substituted firepower for manpower. The phrases describing this methodology became ingrained, maxims for war in the age of guns. "There can never be too many projectiles in a battle." "The larger the piles of shells fired, the smaller the piles of our corpses." "Spend shells like a millionaire and live like a pauper." "The thing we value most deeply is not money, but men." Or, in the simple formula that says it all, "Send a bullet, not a man."[33] The United States prefers to invest in things, not infantry.

This method, pursued from 1941 through the present, produced several consequences, not all intended. The first has already been mentioned. The country doesn't use much infantry. At the line of contact, U.S. infantry has been and will continue to be outnumbered. This seems to fly in the face of popular images of an American juggernaut rolling over hapless Germans, Japanese, North Koreans, Chinese, North Vietnamese, and Iraqis. That certainly happened, but not much thanks to U.S. infantry. The Yankee colossus was mostly about flying hot metal and ear-shattering concussions, not men.

Even at the height of World War II, the United States generated only 95 divisions (67 infantry, 16 armored, 6 Marine, 5 airborne, and 1 mountain) and a few independent regiments, a pittance compared to allies and foes. By 1944, the Soviet Union employed more than 500 rifle divisions. In that same year, Germany struggled to man nearly 284 divisions.[34] By contrast, the United States settled on a small frontline force and backed it up with extraordinarily responsive close air support and exceptionally accurate and devastating artillery firepower, not to mention the greatest Navy and Air Force ever assembled. The Germans repeatedly cursed the wide-ranging *verdammte jabos* (the damned fighter-bombers), and both they and the Japanese dreaded the ferociously efficient American artillery barrages, especially the massed fires of multibattalion time-on-target strikes.[35] Firepower worked.

In Korea, too, the United States made do with a fairly small number of rifle troops. The Eighth Army was made up of 7 divisions and a separate airborne regiment, not much by the standards of 1945. Even these were not fully manned. Four United Nations allied brigades, 9 national battalions, and 12,718 individual Koreans augmented the ranks of the U.S. infantry. The bulk of the U.N. ground strength came from the embattled Republic of Korea (South Korea), to the tune of 10 infantry divisions, for a total of 17 allied formations of divisional strength. Against this, the North Koreans and Chinese employed 64 divisions (41 Chinese, 23 North Korean), brimming with light infantry. Again, the United States evened the odds with fire-power, routinely ravaging enemy rifle regiments with bombs, straf-ing, and pounding artillery. Enemy prisoners and captured docu-ments testified to the slaughter inflicted by American shells and bombs.[36] As before, firepower did the job.

During the Vietnam War, the comparative numbers get a bit squishier, given that there have been lawsuits, acrimony, squabbles, and bile aplenty—not to mention a war lost—revolving around just how many bad guys came to fight. On the American side, the num-bers are known. At maximum strength in 1968, the United States re-lied on the usual 15 percent of its 536,000 in country: about 80,000 close-combat troops organized into some 81 Army and Marine in-fantry battalions and various smaller Special Forces elements. Allied contributions included 22 Korean, 9 Thai, and 2 Australian battal-ions and, of course, more than 188 South Vietnamese battalions, these of dubious quality. Communist rolls at the height of the war ran between a low estimate of 70,000 men in 222 regular and Viet Cong main force battalion equivalents and a high peg of 140,166 in 309 battalions. In any event, out in the bush, small U.S. outfits rou-tinely bumped into bigger enemy units. Firepower ensured a lop-sided body count, usually (but not always) in favor of the Americans. As always, the opposition hated the results, especially the earth-quaking punishment delivered by unseen B-52 bombers and the ac-tive, incessant, deadly shells of the artillery.[37] Once more, firepower "worked," in the sense that it reduced American casualties and took out many hostiles.

It also lost the war. Using a hammer failed to make the problem into a nail. Vietnam proved to be utterly unlike Normandy or Ko-rea. The war in Southeast Asia did not fall neatly into any conven-tional pattern, at least during the most active period of U.S. inter-vention. Thanks to sending bullets, not men, Americans never really destroyed any Viet Cong or North Vietnamese organizations. Sure, Uncle Sam's lavish use of munitions bloodied more than one enemy regiment, killed many, and wounded even more. But the far-flung American battalions, often operating by detachments in trackless wilderness, lacked the strength and agility to trap their often more numerous foes and thereby really finish battles. The Communist side routinely disengaged and withdrew, often to cross-border sanctuaries. Thus, every opposing marker stayed on the board—defiant, reinforced, and soon ready for more.

Just as disconcerting, the ceaseless Niagara of explosives beat large segments of South Vietnam into a moonscape, making it the most heavily bombed and shelled country in history.[38] Local civilians died or fled for their lives, and the opposition was never squeamish about compelling battles among the innocents. Americans blazed away in their usual style. Killing your allies is not usually the best way to win hearts and minds. When the Americans left, the discredited South Vietnamese regime succumbed quickly to Communist forces.

Vietnam taught many lessons. Here is one. In some conflicts, the enemy is not susceptible to aerial bombardment of his homeland or overly concerned about casualties. And if you care about popular support, let alone adherence to the customary laws of war, you must be very careful about those uninvolved civilians hanging around the countryside. To do the job, you need fine infantry—good men willing to close in and fight. Ammunition by the ton cannot do it all.

Vietnam exposed a weakness in the firepower-intensive American way of war, a flaw well known to many American professionals and their enemies in World War II and Korea. Historian Eric M. Bergerud studied both World War II and Vietnam at the tactical level. His work illuminates why American riflemen relied so much on firepower.

In other words, when contact was made, especially if it was made by American infantry, our forces would pull back and allow their powerful supporting arms to have a shot at the other side. It was a controversial tactic then and still is today. The *most highly skilled soldiers advocated rapid maneuver and quick assault when contact was made.* Any delay, they believed, allowed the enemy to withdraw or wait out the storm in his field fortifications. On the other side of the coin, most soldiers believed there was no such thing as too much firepower. Skilled and experienced fighting men are always a rare commodity, and *the normal citizen-soldier, regardless of personal fortitude, did not have the split-second timing required for fire and movement to work as planned.*[39] [Emphasis added.]

Bergerud captures the essence of an unintended consequence of sending bullets, not men. Rightfully impressed with their firepower, American leaders discounted the value of the small amount of infantry they did send into action. From 1940 to 1973, the military tried to get by on the cheap. In the words of Russell F. Weigley, one of the most sympathetic chroniclers of the U.S. wartime experience, most infantry units were filled with the military's "least promising recruits, the uneducated, the unskilled, the unenthusiastic," drawn from "those left over" among the citizen draftees. Infantrymen were often undersized, not overly bright, ill trained, and poorly led.[40] Smart, tough characters went elsewhere, encouraged by the system to avoid, if they could, the doughboy, Sad Sack, dogface, Willie and Joe, grunt world of the poor, bloody American infantry.

The results were predictable. Mediocrity ruled. "You would always end up with a good sergeant or a good officer and three or four men doing all the work," remembered one rueful infantry commander. "Unfortunately," he continued, "the rest contributed to the casualties." This led the same officer to a sobering, common-sense observation, borne out by substantial evidence: "The average man, like nine out of ten, or eight out of ten, does not have an instinct for the battlefield, doesn't relish it, and will not act independently except under direct orders."[41] During the time of the draft, despite their low relative strength in the overall military, American line infantry battalions contained too many of those 80 percent or 90 percent, those average men, and some below-average ones, too.

Training rarely made up the deficit in native skill and motivation. Draftee infantry training followed standard, prescribed programs: thirty hours of rifle shooting, six hours of first aid, seventy-two hours of the platoon day attack, and so forth. Units hit the stations of the cross with little regard for quality or realism. "The learning function was obscured and secondary to the scheduling function," recalled one battlewise commander. "Few took training seriously," he concluded.[42] It all looked good on paper, though.

Concerns over letters from American mothers, hectoring congressmen, and a determination to provide the best quality of life for "our boys"—especially those unwillingly impressed into rifle companies—engendered uncertainty, the use of dangerous weapons and explosives, and overly stylized, unrealistic training exercises that were long on displays and movement and short on rigor. Flocks of safety officers and noncommissioned officers (NCOs) rigidly directed stateside live-fire problems, sometimes steering soldiers with hands on their backs, all to prevent accidents. In a 1956 interview, a discouraged George Marshall lamented "a completely mistaken illusion that infantry was easy to train. It's been easy to badly train, and it's been badly trained in every war we've had."[43] As it turned out, many U.S. units were retrained by the Germans and Japanese using real bullets, a hard education.

Serious tactical consequences followed from indifferent manning and unimpressive training. Although many good men, enough to make a difference, made it into every battalion, and American draftee units learned quickly in action, in general the standard rifle units tended to be cautious, slow, and unwilling to close for battle. "We let the arty fight the war as much as possible," recalled an officer of the 12th Infantry Regiment in 1944.[44] The job of the infantry seemed to be to guard the artillery forward observers and air support spotters, find the enemy, hang on during the rain of U.S. supporting fires, then occupy what the gunners and pilots had cleared, just as Eric Bergerud described. As for the gruesome knife-fight class of encounters, the night engagements, clearing hedgerows, blowing bunkers, seizing trenches, taking buildings—well, they got done, but always at a cost and almost always with a lot of supporting firepower.

This situation did not improve much in Korea or Vietnam. If anything, things got worse. American citizen-soldiers just weren't screened or trained to standards high enough to make a difference in death ground, to move fast enough through a hail of lead to get eye to eye with Chinese burp gunners or North Vietnamese regulars. They could have been so picked and taught, but they were not. Leaders settled for less: many sloppy victories and some reverses in World War II, a gory stalemate in Korea, and, finally, a brave but doomed effort in Vietnam. At a certain point, even rich, technologically advanced America had to be willing to pick and school its sons to kill their enemies up close and personal.[45] America's infantrymen may be few, but they must be good.

The alternative was there all along during the draft years of 1940–73. There were natural riflemen in the United States, all right, a lot of them, given the wide population base from which to choose. These men never made it into the mass of conscript line battalions. They joined volunteer elite formations: the Marines, the airborne, and the Rangers, for example. Such outfits trained hard, using extensive live fire and physically demanding courses to teach assault skills suitable for going straight into death ground, taking defended beaches, clearing drop zones at night, or raiding fortified targets. Because these men had volunteered, the leaders pressed them to push themselves physically, to demonstrate initiative, to solve problems in unorthodox ways, to *do something now* rather than just sit there, almost always the best answer in combat.[46] Those who did not measure up left, often washing into the ranks of the "other," nonelite infantry.

Not surprisingly, this brand of American volunteer assault battalion always fought more aggressively. Some of their draftee colleagues sneered at them for taking more casualties, as in fact they did on occasion. But invariably, Marine, airborne, and Ranger infantry demonstrated the will to close with their foes and the skill to make that maneuver decisive.[47] Coupled with the same firepower available to the less aggressive majority of America's conscript infantry, these picked, well-trained organizations displayed that "split-second timing" and high degree of battle savvy that Eric Bergerud rightly observed separate good infantry from the rest. That comes from tough selection standards and uncompromising training before, during, and after battle. This was true from World War II through Korea and into Vietnam. It is true today.

Changes made after Vietnam greatly affected U.S. infantry for the better. The draft ended in 1973, so, by definition, everyone after that was a volunteer. As a result, men chose to be in the infantry rather than ending up there as the unlucky losers in a grim personnel classification lottery. This single aspect, electing to fight, meant more than the high-school graduation or high mental testing scores often referenced by military authorities as proof of better troop quality.[48] A man willing to join the infantry had made a commitment already. Willingness to submit to hardships, tough discipline, lack of personal freedoms (including intrusive drug testing), and dangerous training represented long steps toward being willing to pull the trigger and blow a hole in some adversary. With only the usual small American infantry force to man and ease in removing those who wanted to

U.S. Infantry Battalions

	1938	1968	1998
Infantry	100[1]	58	0
Air Assault	0	9[3]	11
Airborne	0	26[4]	11
Light	0	15[5]	18
Marine	18[2]	33	24
Mechanized	0	59	24
Ranger	0	0	3
TOTAL	**118**	**200**	**91**

1. All were understrength. Of these, seventy-two served in three-battalion regiments; the remaining twenty-eight were in two-battalion regiments. Some issue of trucks had begun.
2. Six understrength regiments existed.
3. Heliborne assault infantry was known as "airmobile" in 1968.
4. Many airborne battalions in 1968 found it difficult to recruit parachute-qualified volunteers and accepted non-parachutist draftees. By late 1968, all battalions in the 101st Airborne transitioned to airmobile (air assault) configuration. Other battalions remained "airborne" in name only.
5. Vietnam-era light infantry resembled a standard foot infantry battalion, except they had fewer heavy trucks. By midwar, the distinctions between light and standard infantry had largely disappeared; all gravitated toward an organization specifically modified for the war in Vietnam.

Sources: James A. Sawicki, *Infantry Regiments of the U.S. Army* (Dumfires, Va.: Wyvern Publications, Inc., 1981), 10; Capt. Shelby L. Stanton, USA (Ret.), *Vietnam Order of Battle* (Washington, D.C.: U.S. News Books, 1981), 260–63, 340–41; Col. David M. White, *Office of Infantry Proponency Overview* (Fort Benning, Ga.: Office of Infantry Proponency, 1994), 4; International Institute of Strategic Studies, *Military Balance 1996–97* (Oxford, U.K.: Oxford University Press, October 1996), 23, 26.

leave, every American rifle contingent gained the same selection advantages long enjoyed by the Marine Corps, the Rangers, and the airborne, where failure to meet standards caused separation. The ones who could not cut it were cut loose, back to civilian life. With more willing learners, American infantry necessarily became much more serious about training. Largely rote classroom instruction, undue emphasis on completing the schedule, and preprogrammed demonstrations gave way to demanding, continuous force-on-force, free play field exercises using a militarized version of laser tag to determine who shot John. These involved extended, exhausting mock battles engaging units up to regimental-brigade scale, pitted against wily opposing forces taught to use the tactics and weapons of likely U.S. enemies. Additionally, live-fire training became serious; it did away with the ubiquitous white-helmeted safety NCOs and canned ranges to create realistic assault problems focused on trench clearing, bunker busting, and house-to-house fighting. As in war, the chain of command took charge of safety. Finally, all training events featured time carved out for after-action reviews (AARs)—self-criticism sessions involving all ranks in the best tradition of Maoist guerrillas, a conscious adoption of a technique used by the other side in Korea and Vietnam.[49] Constant training built up those skills, that split-second timing, allowing the volunteer rifle troops to execute the tough maneuvers under fire that the draftee infantry often eschewed in favor of waiting for more artillery.

The force structure folks took advantage of these important changes in selection and training. Commencing in the mid-1980s, all U.S. infantry became elite in nature. Remaining battalions of generic line infantry converted to light or mechanized configurations, each with specialized training and tactics. These joined the existing airborne, air assault, Ranger, and Marine types. The ninety-one battalions in the Regular force retain all the ability to tap firepower that characterized their brothers in World War II, Korea, or Vietnam, now complemented by the close-combat will and skill often absent in mass-produced draftee infantry outfits.

Designations of "airborne," "Marine," or "Ranger" mean something. They are not won cheaply. Each of the six types of infantry—airborne, Marine, Ranger, air assault, mechanized, and light—distinguishes itself by its means of insertion, and there are notable variances in how each fights. All are capable under certain circumstances, and all can shape matters to their own ends under some conditions. The study of recent operations offers opportunities to examine the makeup, methods, and combat effectiveness of each of the categories of infantry that now compose the Regular establishment. To understand what happened at Cap-Haitien on 24 September 1994, and, moreover, to understand why it went the way it did, you must go beyond the specific narrative of that evening and look at how Marine infantry fights. The same is true of the Army varieties. Each brings its own culture to battle.

There is one other break with the practice of the recent past. Regardless of how they get there, U.S. riflemen today expect, and even seek, to start the action already in close combat, in death ground, locked in mortal contests with a more numerous enemy committed to drawing American blood. Skip the preliminaries and get right to the killing. The success of U.S. foreign policy in counterinsurgency, peace enforcement, evacuations of U.S. nationals, and all those ugly imbroglios that T. R. Fehrenbach labeled "this kind of war"[50] often depends on this kind of infantry.

The United States ended the Cold War in 1989 with this kind of infantry, limited in number but sound in quality, typified by Kyle Todd and Virgil Palumbo. America's new model rifle corps emerged as a hidden benefit from the suspension of the draft. United States Marine and Army riflemen of all types have proven extremely versatile and useful over the last few years, as able with massive fires as without. And there's one other thing, the most important of all. In death ground, these few good men will fight.

Notes

The epigraph is from Sun Tzu, *The Art of War,* ed. and trans. by Brig. Gen. Samuel B. Griffith, USMC (Ret.) (Oxford, U.K.: Oxford University Press, 1963), 131.

1. Captain John F. Quinn II, USMC, "Marine Expedition to Haiti: September–October 1994," *Marine Corps Gazette* (July 1995), 51, 52. The Army's 82d Airborne Division, Rangers, and various special operations forces also had major roles in the planned invasion.

2. Major Mark S. Martins, USA, et al., *Law and Military Operations in Haiti, 1994–95, Lessons Learned for Judge Advocates* (Charlottesville, Va.: Center for Law and Military Operations, 11 December 1995), 15–20. American paratroopers were already en route before Cédras and his followers accepted U.S. demands. The airborne forces sometimes jokingly call the mission Operation U-Turn. Cédras departed on 10 October 1994. Aristide returned on 15 October 1994.

3. Adam Siegel, *The Intervasion of Haiti* (Alexandria, Va.: Center for Naval Analysis, August 1996). Siegel coined the term *intervasion* (*inter*vention + in*vasion*) to describe the combination of forced entry and permissive entry schemes that characterized U.S. operations in Haiti in 1994–95.

4. Ibid., 25.

5. Ivan Musicant, *The Banana Wars* (New York, N. Y.: Macmillan Publishing Co., 1990), 158–59, 202–3, 213–15. Major General Smedley Butler won two Medals of Honor, the first in Veracruz, Mexico, in 1914 and the second in Haiti in 1915; as a general, he led U.S. forces in North China in 1927–29. Lieutenant General Lewis B. "Chesty" Puller started as an enlisted man, then rose to command a battalion at Guadalcanal (1942–43), the 1st Marine Regiment at Peleliu (1944), and the same regiment again in Korea (1950–51), including the Inchon landing and the fighting withdrawal from the Chosin Reservoir. General Alexander A. Vandegrift commanded the 1st Marine Division on Guadalcanal (1942–43), where he won the Medal of Honor. Later, he became the commandant of the Marine Corps. Herman Hanneken, who started as an enlisted Marine and won the Medal of Honor in Haiti, also commanded a battalion on

Guadalcanal and eventually the 7th Marine Regiment. He ended up a brigadier general.

6. U.S. Headquarters Marine Corps, Marine Corps Intelligence Activity Detachment Quantico, *Haiti Handbook* (Quantico, Va.: Defense Printing Service Office, 1993), 1-12, 1-13; Bob Shacochis, "The Immaculate Invasion," *Harper's* (February 1995), 47. Shacochis does a superb job of capturing the ambience surrounding the American intervention.

7. U.S. Company E, 96th Civil Affairs Battalion, *Haiti* (Fort Bragg, N.C.: 96th Civil Affairs Battalion, 1993), 16.

8. William Booth, "Marines Defend Shooting of Haitian Gunman," *Washington Post* (29 September 1994), A32; Col. Thomas S. Jones, USMC, "Review the Ingredients: Commander's Insights from Cap-Haitien," *Marine Corps Gazette* (July 1995), 56; Quinn, "Marine Expedition to Haiti," 50–51. The FAd'H openly employed civilian auxiliaries, known as attachés. Additionally, the Cédras regime's political allies formed the Revolutionary Front for Alliance and Progress in Haiti (Front Révolutionnaires *pour l'avancement et le progress de Haiti*, FRAPH), a right-wing extremist party prone to street violence. Indeed, almost all Haitian parties resort to street violence. Some are merely better armed and organized than others.

9. Thomas E. Ricks, *Making the Corps* (New York, N.Y.: Scribner's, 1997), 266.

10. Quinn, "Marine Expedition to Haiti," 51, 54. Colonel Jones's actions in Haiti were in accord with U.S. Marine Corps traditions and practices in similar circumstances. These views are best expressed in U.S. Headquarters Marine Corps, *Small Wars Manual* (Washington, D.C.: U.S. Government Printing Office, 1940), especially on 2-2. The entire manual offers a wonderful distillation of Marine experience in counterinsurgency, and it has a modern flavor. The *Small Wars Manual* is still one of the best single sources for professionals dealing with interventions in poor countries wracked by civil unrest. Its tenets of pacification were used in Vietnam. The manual was reissued in the late 1980s.

11. Jones, "Review the Ingredients," 56.

12. Quinn, "Marine Expedition to Haiti," 52.

13. Ibid., 52–53; Siegel, *The Intervasion of Haiti*, 25; Thomas E.

Ricks, "U.S. Troops Send Clear Message in Haiti, but Ambiguities Remain," *Wall Street Journal* (26 September 1994), A16. Ricks tells the story of the incident at the docks.

14. Jones, "Review the Ingredients," 56.

15. Musicant, *The Banana Wars*, 180. The speaker was Capt. Frederic "Dopey" Wise, commander of the 6th Company in 1915. Wise saw extensive action in Haiti.

16. Martins, et al., *Law and Military Operations in Haiti, 1994–95*, 213–16. In the Army zone in and around Port-au-Prince, soldiers took a narrower interpretation of their ROE and watched Haitian factions beat one another to death in some cases. Rules of engagement cards issued on 23 September 1994 explicitly directed all U.S. troops to use force, including deadly force, "to defend U.S. forces, U.S. citizens, or *designated foreign nationals* (emphasis added) against attack or threat of imminent attack."

17. Booth, "Marines Defend Shooting of Haitian Gunman," A32; Eric Schmitt, "Disorders Follow Clash in Haitian City," *New York Times* (26 September 1994), A10.

18. William Booth and James Rupert, "Marines Kill 9 Haitians in Battle at Police Station," *Washington Post* (25 September 1994), A1; Jones, "Review the Ingredients," 57; Schmitt, "Disorders Follow Clash in Haitian City," A10. Booth and Rupert mentioned that Marine squads outposted all four Cap-Haitien police stations, beginning on 21 September 1994, a decision also discussed in Jones's own article.

19. Eric Schmitt, "How a Tense Standoff in Haiti Erupted Into Deadly Shootout with the Marines," *New York Times* (27 September 1994), A16. The speaker was twenty-two-year-old LCpl. Jerry Acton, USMC.

20. Schmitt, "Disorders Follow Clash in Haitian City," A1, A10.

21. Karl von Clausewitz, *On War,* ed. and trans. by Peter Paret and Michael Howard (Princeton, N.J.: Princeton University Press, 1984), 87.

22. Shacochis, "The Immaculate Invasion," 46. The author of the present book experienced street operations in Port-au-Prince in November 1995. Shacochis has it right.

23. Schmitt, "How a Tense Standoff in Haiti Erupted Into Deadly

Shootout with the Marines," A16; Booth, "Marines Defend Shooting of Haitian Gunman," A32. For weapons characteristics, see U.S. Department of the Army, *FM 7-8 Infantry Rifle Platoon and Squad* (Washington, D.C.: U.S. Government Printing Office, 22 April 1992), B-1. See also Tom Clancy, *Marine* (New York, N.Y.: Berkley Books, 1996), 69–71, 82. Clancy puts the cyclic rate for the SAW at 725 rounds per minute; the U.S. Army says 800. The targets don't much care.

24. Schmitt, "How a Tense Standoff in Haiti Erupted Into a Deadly Shootout with the Marines," A16.

25. Schmitt, "Disorders Follow Clash in Haitian City," A10; Schmitt, "8 Haitians Killed by Marine Patrol," *New York Times* (25 September 1994), I-1.

26. This account draws most heavily on Schmitt, "How a Tense Standoff in Haiti Erupted Into a Deadly Shootout with the Marines," A16. See also Booth, "Marines Defend Shooting of Haitian Gunman," A32, and Quinn, "Marine Expedition to Haiti," 53. Both the U.S. Navy translator and the wounded Haitian were later treated aboard the USS *Wasp.*

27. Martins, *Law and Military Operations in Haiti, 1994–95,* 21.

28. Colonel David M. White, USA, *Office of Infantry Proponency Overview* (Fort Benning, Ga.: Office of Infantry Proponency, 1994), 4; International Institute of Strategic Studies, *Military Balance 1996–97* (Oxford, U.K.: Oxford University Press, October 1996), 23, 26.

29. U.S. Bureau of the Census, *The American Almanac: Statistical Abstract of the United States* (Austin, Tex.: The Reference Press, Inc., 1994), 215, 346, 407–9.

30. Ibid., 346, 407–9; U.S. Department of Defense, "Defense Almanac 96," *Defense* (15 September 1996), 17.

31. James A. Sawicki, *Infantry Regiments of the U.S. Army* (Dumfries, Va.: Wyvern Publications, Inc., 1981), 668; White, *Office of Infantry Proponency Overview,* 14, 35A, 39A.

32. Russell F. Weigley, *The American Way of War* (Bloomington, Ind.: Indiana University Press, 1977), 203.

33. These quotes offer a small sample of a much more numerous selection. The first is from World War II, in Gen. George S. Patton, Jr., *War As I Knew It* (New York, N.Y.: Pyramid Books, 1970), 307. The

next is a shortening of a longer Korean War message by Gen. Matthew B. Ridgway, as found in Walter G. Hermes, *Truce Tent and Fighting Front* (Washington, D.C.: U.S. Government Printing Office, 1992), 227. The two that follow come from the Vietnam War. The first is from then Col. Sidney B. Berry, as discussed in Lt. Col. Andrew F. Krepinevich, Jr., USA (Ret.), *The Army and Vietnam* (Baltimore, Md.: Johns Hopkins University Press, 1986), 198; the second quotes Secretary of Defense Robert Strange McNamara, as found in Robert Pisor, *The End of the Line* (New York, N.Y.: W. W. Norton & Co., 1982), 56. The final phrase has been heard many times by the present author and can be found in a similar form in Krepinevich, *The Army and Vietnam*, 6.

34. Chief Warrant Officer E. J. Kahn, Jr., USA, and TSgt. Henry McLemore, USA, *Fighting Divisions* (Washington, D.C.: Zenger Publishing Co., Inc., 1946), xi. In World War II, the so-called 1st Cavalry Division was actually a dismounted infantry formation, as it was in the Korean War. By Vietnam, the 1st Cavalry had become a heliborne airmobile infantry division. It fought in the Gulf War as an armored division. For Soviet Army strength, see John Erickson, *The Road to Berlin* (Boulder, Colo.: Westview Press, 1983), 429. For German Army strength, see Matthew Cooper, *The German Army, 1933–1945* (New York, N.Y.: Stein and Day, Publishers, 1978), 489.

35. Major Michael D. Doubler, USA, *Closing with the Enemy* (Lawrence, Kans.: University Press of Kansas, 1994), 41; Lt. Col. Keith E. Bonn, USA (Ret.), *When the Odds Were Even* (Novato, Calif.: Presidio Press), 3; Eric M. Bergerud, *Touched with Fire* (New York, N.Y.: Viking Press, 1996), 192–93, 199. The first two books, written by experienced Regular Army officers, offer the best tactical analysis of the 1944–45 campaign in Western Europe. Tanker Doubler examines U.S. combined-arms tactics from Normandy until the German surrender. Infantryman Keith Bonn concentrates on the nature of Seventh Army's fight in the Vosges Mountains. Together, these works greatly advance the scholarship on the question of how American ground forces fought the war in Europe. For the Pacific war, the comparable work is equally impressive. Eric Bergerud also gets at the details of how the war was fought in the South Pacific.

36. Hermes, *Truce Tent and Fighting Front*, 57–59, 76–80; Lt. Col.

Roy E. Appleman, AUS (Ret.), *Ridgway Duels for Korea* (College Station, Tex.: Texas A & M University Press, 1990), 155, 507, 527, 561.

37. Captain Shelby L. Stanton, USA (Ret.), *Vietnam Order of Battle* (Washington, D.C.: U.S. News Books, 1981), 268, 270–75, 333; Lt. Gen. Phillip B. Davidson, USA (Ret.), *Vietnam at War* (Novato, Calif.: Presidio Press, 1988), 382; Eric M. Bergerud, *Red Thunder, Tropic Lightning* (Boulder, Colo.: Westview Press, 1993), 45–47, 63, 133. In 1967–68, Davidson was the J-2 (senior intelligence officer) for Military Assistance Command, Vietnam, the U.S. headquarters that ran the war in country.

38. Krepinevich, *The Army and Vietnam*, 197; Thomas C. Thayer, *War Without Fronts* (Boulder, Colo.: Westview Press, 1985), 57, 79.

39. Bergerud, *Red Thunder, Tropic Lightning*, 133.

40. Russell F. Weigley, *Eisenhower's Lieutenants* (Bloomington, Ind.: Indiana University Press, 1981), 27; Doubler, *Closing With the Enemy*, 26–28.

41. General Paul F. Gorman, USA (Ret.), *The Secret of Future Victories* (Fort Leavenworth, Kans.: Combat Studies Institute, February 1992), II-78. The officer, William E. DePuy, fought from Normandy into Germany with the 90th Infantry Division and rose to command a battalion. A key senior leader in Vietnam, he formed the Army's Training and Doctrine Command in 1973 and retired as a full general. Similar thoughts underscore the classic study of small-unit combat found in Brig. Gen. S. L. A. Marshall, AUS (Ret.), *Men Against Fire* (New York, N.Y.: William Morrow, 1964). Marshall's research methods have been questioned. His conclusions have not.

42. Gorman, *The Secret of Future Victories*, II-73. The speaker is General DePuy, commenting on stateside training in World War II. His 90th Infantry Division ran through the program twice and also trained in England before D day. It sputtered miserably in the Normandy hedgerow fighting, losing 100 percent of its rifle strength and 150 percent of its junior officers, often failing to carry assigned objectives.

43. Ibid., II-71–72, III-6.

44. Weigley, *Eisenhower's Lieutenants*, 28.

45. This case is most elegantly made in T. R. Fehrenbach, *This Kind of War* (New York, N.Y.: Macmillan Company, 1963), 426–43. Fehrenbach led combat troops in World War II and Korea.

46. Bergerud, *Touched with Fire,*156–61, discusses the Marines; Clay Blair, *Ridgway's Paratroopers* (Garden City, N.Y.: The Dial Press, 1985), 32, 36, 61–62, 234–35, describes airborne infantry training programs; Michael J. King, *Leavenworth Paper No. 11, Rangers: Selected Combat Operations in World War II* (Fort Leavenworth, Kans.: Combat Studies Institute, June 1985), 8, comments on Ranger training.

47. To be fair, the Marines have, now and then, resorted to draftees. But their volunteer ethos and standards have not been compromised. Two excellent descriptions of the effectiveness of such picked, well-trained units can be found in Bergerud, *Touched with Fire,* 153–61, 182, and Michael Herr, *Dispatches* (New York, N.Y.: Avon Books, 1978), 23–28, 101–4, 155–56. Herr's descriptions are extremely critical, but they capture the very real capabilities of airborne, Marine, and airmobile forces.

48. Troop quality statistics must be weighed carefully, given that high-school diplomas today often indicate nothing other than some modicum of attendance, and military test scores can be adjusted as necessary (and have been) to prove whatever needs to be proven. For a good critique of presumptive quality measures of recruits, see Col. William Darryl Henderson, USA (Ret.), *The Hollow Army* (Boulder, Colo.: Westview Press, 1990), 1–10, 29.

49. Gorman, *The Secret of Future Victories,* III-35–38.

50. Fehrenbach, *This Kind of War,* 3–6.

Chapter 1: Death from Above

"All okay, jumpmaster."

Four voices, shouting in near unison, four separate hands, fingers joined, pointed like a knife edge toward a single dark, bulky, helmeted figure standing on the dim red-lit deck. All four hands, all four voices told the same story: The other twenty-five to thirty men behind each of the four stick leaders were ready to go.[1] The four lines stood shoulder to shoulder, facing the rear of the C-141B Starlifter. Centered between the two jump doors, still closed, was the primary jumpmaster, who nodded slightly. An Air Force sergeant with a headset called forward to the flight deck, then gave a thumbs-up to the jumpmaster. Everything was right on time, a welcome change after all the screwing around in the freezing sleet and ice scud back in North Carolina.

Almost as soon as the leading foursome reported ready, the pilots up in the cockpit commenced "slowdown procedures," U.S. Air Force talk for decelerating the big, four-engine C-141B so that the 110 men on board could survive their exits. Descending in a shallow glide, tracking with the other seven jet transports in the formation, the Starlifter throttled back from its cruising speed of nearly 500 miles per hour down to about 140 miles per hour, close to the aircraft's stall threshold. With a heavy slug of paratroopers in its belly and a drop zone (DZ) dead ahead, it took some cool customers to keep the big bird in the sky at all, let alone on the right glide path.

In the back, it felt the way it always felt at this stage of the flight— as if the plane had run into a vertical pillow the size of Long Island, bounced slowly backward, and hence was slipping out from under the numb, cold, booted feet of 110 tense Americans waiting to end their flight the hard way. The big aircraft tilted steadily downward by the nose, as if urging the jumpers to back away from the doors that would soon swallow them all. Soldiers leaned backward, staggering to keep their feet, jostling, bumping, and bouncing, holding one another up. As in many training jumps, the paratroopers were rigged with full combat loads, including the deadweight of hefty radio batteries, lots of small-arms ammunition, plenty of hand grenades, and a good selection of mortar rounds. This inevitable, unforgiving mass of cumbersome gear made the entire five-hour flight crammed into tiny nylon bench seats bad enough. But it made these last few minutes standing upright especially agonizing.

Each man wore a coal-scuttle Kevlar helmet on his head, a main parachute the size of a robust knapsack on his back, and a weapons case tied to his left leg. The case protruded up under the left arm, the hard rifle butt end sticking up like the top of a crutch. Some weapons containers proved particularly awkward. Those saddled with the versions for carrying M-60 machine guns, mortar tubes, and antitank weapons endured roughly the equivalent of being strapped to an outboard boat motor. Small reserve chutes the size of full plastic grocery bags sat athwart each man's upper stomach, to be used if the main chute failed to open. Swelling rucksacks packed full of ammunition and water hung across each jumper's knees, tied off beneath the reserve chutes. Under all of this, the paratrooper wore his combat webbing, which included a canteen and small-arms magazines. All the gear was "mission essential," of course, although the experienced sergeants and the long-suffering privates had their own views on that.

Most men wore ensembles that equaled their body weight. Many, especially leaders who carried heavy secure-voice radios, carried gear that outweighed them. The book cautioned: "Regardless of rank or grade, parachutists should jump in extra LAWs [light antitank weapons], antitank mines, MAWs [medium antitank rounds], or radio batteries."[2] You never knew when, if ever, resupply might show up. So like Boy Scouts, airborne forces believe in being prepared. As a result, these jumpers rocked and rolled in the crimson twilight, swaddled and sweating in green camouflage equipment. Their mottled green and brown face paint smeared as beads of sweat formed and dripped from brows and noses.

The parachutists balanced on leaden feet, their canvas-sided jungle boots dampened and chilled by the drenching ice storm back at Fort Bragg–Pope Air Force Base. Handholds were few along the outer hull of the C-141B. Many steadied themselves by grabbing the upper edges of the stowed, flimsy bench seats made of taut red nylon stretched over light aluminum tubes, some kind of USAF version of cheap lawn furniture. No longer needed, the seats were tied off neatly with Velcro strips to the exposed airframe ribs. Others held on to transverse frames and bracing spars. There were enough of those. The Starlifter granted nothing to comfort or style. All of the jetliner's bundles of wires and pipes and cables stood exposed on the gray-green inner fuselage, barely identifiable in the red night-lighting. Soundproofing wasn't a priority on this kind of flight, so along with the meat-locker temperature of high altitude and decor akin to a steam plant, the airborne troopers endured the steady roar of the plane's four Pratt & Whitney TF-33-7 turbofans.[3] Some paratroopers used foam earplugs. Some did not; it wouldn't matter after a few more minutes.

The steady jet-engine pitch kept changing, growing alternately deeper, then higher, pulsing as the crew goosed the throttles. The big jet bled off speed and altitude, sloping downward. In a few minutes, they would level off for the final run over the drop zone. The eight-plane formation tightened and settled into a staggered column for the delivery. They were committed, heading inexorably toward the Pacific coast of Panama, toward the reason for all of this miserably taxing activity.

With their conveyance losing airspeed and height, the four swaying lines of overloaded paratroopers strained to stay upright. Besides having odd touchpoints along the plane's unadorned innards, the airborne people all had one sure handhold. Like subway riders holding overhead straps in a crowded car, with a tight fist each soldier grasped a bright yellow static line. Above each man's fist, at the end of this tether, was a strong metal clip, locked onto one of four anchor line cables, every cable a quarter inch of twisted steel sagging gently under the pull of more than two dozen intent jumpers. The yellow line stayed in the plane when the jumpers exited; it stayed attached until then. If everything went right, no paratrooper needed to pull a ripcord by hand. The yellow line served that function. Thus, this line, at least, remained "static."

The nonstatic part of the static line hung below each jumper's fist. First came a small loop of slack, enough to keep it clear of a soldier's arm. If the yellow line somehow wound around an arm, a neck, or a weapon, the forces of gravity and buffeting wind guaranteed gory results on exit: muscles stripped off bones like filleted fish, impromptu amputations, strangling, battering against the side of the moving transport jet—all bad outcomes, to be sure. Keeping control of excess yellow line prevents these horrors. Jumpers don't have to be told twice.

Its bight of excess firmly grasped, the line then snaked into the main parachute pack tray, held in place for the present by rubber bands. In the chute, the line hooked to the main canopy. When pulled by a great mass, such as a falling, overloaded body clearing the jet, the line yanked the canopy out of its bag, handily splitting away the rubber-band tiedowns. The line then split away, flapping on the outside of the plane, still clipped to the stout anchor line. The paratrooper drifted down to battle. That was the idea, at least.

Battle there would be. Thanks to an onboard satellite transceiver, the word had already been passed. It wasn't good. The phrases turned over in the mind as the Starlifter started to square up for its final approach: "The Rangers have not secured the drop zone . . . the DZ is hot . . . one pass and one pass only."[4] All aboard knew what this meant.

With a roar, both doors slid open and rose up the curving tracks toward the pipes and conduits overhead. Warm, humid air washed through the plane, dank and foul like a crowded locker room after a big game, mixed with a touch of sea salt. A few men gagged: a bad sign, because once one nauseous guy vomited, the chain reaction would not be pretty. Almost everyone worked cold toes on the frigid metal deck, letting the welcome warmth soak in. Those not already sweating profusely under their burdens started the waterworks. And with less than three minutes to go, all eyes locked on the brightest red lights in the plane, little half globes over the howling jump doors.

"Stand by," came the command. Nobody heard it, but the first few soldiers saw the dark arm point at the yawning gap. Everyone began pushing for the door, "assholes to elbows," as the sergeants liked to put it. The push for the exits told all aboard that they were close, really close.

Hooked up, the jumpmaster at the door held his outboard stick of thirty in check. His counterpart at the other door did likewise. The two inboard lines of twenty-five waited, ready to push once the outside streams cleared. With a DZ of just over five hundred yards, and no go-arounds to drop those who didn't get out, nobody dared hesitate. When those hard red lights turned Christmas green, it would be a stampede through the door, propelled by a green-clad human piston. Everybody was going.

"One minute," came the shout. The warning moved back down the rows as hands not on the static line held up an index finger. The lead jumpers in the door were physically holding their men back from the maw.

The first few jumpers could see green streaks and flashes in the black rectangles beyond the doors, a real fireworks show. Everyone could hear what sounded like pebbles popping against the airframe. But those lights outside weren't skyrockets, and the things hitting the fuselage weren't pebbles.[5]

"Thirty seconds." Each man passed the information, hoarsely shouting in the blast of hot air and making the sign of a thumb and forefinger an inch apart. It was that close.

Two men in the center rows made the sign of the cross.

All eyes watched the shining red light, waiting for the green.

It didn't come.

Instead, they heard the big turbofans accelerate and saw the jumpmaster and his assistant back away from the open doors. A hand across the throat signaled "no drop."[6]

It was like a balloon deflating, with curses all around. Many of the heavily loaded men dropped to a knee or leaned onto the hull struts, groaning under their equipment. The Starlifter gained a little altitude for what would be a painful, twenty-minute oval back to the drop zone. So much for one pass and one pass only. It happened this way enough in training, but in combat, too? Welcome to shooting war. Friction reigned supreme.

Thanks to the trusty satellite link, the full story moved down the long rows of perspiring paratroopers. The heavy drop cargo birds were still over the DZ, thirty-one more Starlifters dropping all kinds of big weapons and containerized supplies, including eight M-551 Sheridan light tanks, four 105mm howitzers, and some seventy-four Humvees of various descriptions.[7] The ice storm had not delayed them, but they were a little late anyway, so these unmanned cargo pallets were still dropping at 0155 when the eight C-141Bs from Bragg-Pope showed up. Had the paratroopers realized that the Rangers were hotly engaged around the DZ, and that their flight crews were having trouble finding that featureless black quadrilateral on the eastern fringe of the contested Omar Torrijos International Airport, all might have been more grateful for the short delay and the dry run.

But that logic ignored the psychological impact of walking literally right to the brink, then pulling back, *combatus interruptus* in the worst way. The keyed-up paratroopers wanted to get the show going. The jump would also free them of some of their crushing personal baggage, no small matter as all were sweating freely now. Muscles ached from standing erect with the suffocating equivalent of another guy wrapped all around you. In the words of Sgt. Roy E. Burgess, "Let's go. The heck with the fighting. Let's get out of here."[8]

Again, the big jet slowed, this time only a bit, and the men fell back toward the cockpit, again only a small amount. The eight transports shook themselves into a staggered column over the Pacific and steadied on course. Once more, the Starlifter straightened up, and the jumpers swayed in their hellish subway tube, hands in death grips around their sweat-slimed static lines.

"Stand by," came the well-known command. Again, the men pressed for the open doors. The countdown started, just as before.

"One minute."

The now-familiar display of flashing and sparking started outside. Small-arms rounds or shell fragments or something else unwelcome began skipping off the Starlifter's thin aluminum hull.

"Thirty seconds."

Hands tensed on the yellow cords. Boots shuffled toward the door. Green light.

"Go! Go! Go!"

The rows raced out like a rope through a smoking capstan, stepping into the tracer-cut blackness. The manuals said it took a second per parachutist, but every planeload beat that time.

As each jumper waddled diagonally through the opening, the clawing black slipstream sucked his feet right out from underneath him, pulling him out. Static lines yanked away, and the round, light green T-10 parachute canopies blossomed with a series of *whoompf* sounds audible even over the drone of thirty-two whining jet engines. Dropped from five hundred feet, men had time to look up to see that their chutes had opened, look down at a sea of tall, waving grass rippling in the light breeze, and drop their bulging rucksacks to dangle fifteen feet below them. *Keep feet and knees together,* thought many, as they had learned at Fort Benning's jump school and perfected at Fort Bragg.

And then they were down, feet, calves, thighs, buttocks, upper backs—just like in school—plus heads, elbows, knees, and faces, just like in real life. Most men landed in fifteen-foot-tall swamp grass, in squishy, stinking mud and slop. Few could see anything but the swaying sawgrass towering above their heads.

Above, the departing, empty airplanes motored off into the distance. Around the men on the ground, gunfire crackled from all directions. Tracers arced up on the horizon. Green were enemy. Red were American, although maybe not, as this time, the enemy used quite a few weapons made in the United States.

No time to worry about that. Automatically, as in numerous training drops, practiced hands popped off the tight chute harnesses (blessed relief). Weapons containers were opened, and rifles with magazines were slid out. Along with the din of shooting on the nearby Ranger objectives, the characteristic click of M-16A2 bolts slamming rounds up the barrel, ready for action, echoed across the wide marsh. Machine gunners and mortarmen got out their pieces and loaded them up, too, then went looking for their team members. Leaders screwed in radio antennas and keyed hand mikes, trying to check in, to get a communications net going. Then, with their tools of the trade in hand, men shouldered their heavy rucksacks and moved out. They intended to find their brothers, to assemble, to get to work.

Little groups of paratroopers (LGOPs)—that was what they were called at Fort Bragg.[9] The very act of jumping ensures that although almost nine hundred men can be put on the ground in a few minutes, they get scrambled up like pieces from a child's puzzle tossed into the air. So step one was always identical: Get organized. That sometimes took fighting. Once more, as in Sicily, as in Normandy, as in Holland, the 82d Airborne's LGOPs began to coalesce out in the darkness.

The drop into Panama by the 1st Brigade, 82d Airborne Division, demanded more from the LGOPs than most. As planned, the 1st Battalion, 75th Ranger Regiment, would jump at 0100 to seize the Torrijos civilian airport and the adjacent Tocumen military airfield.

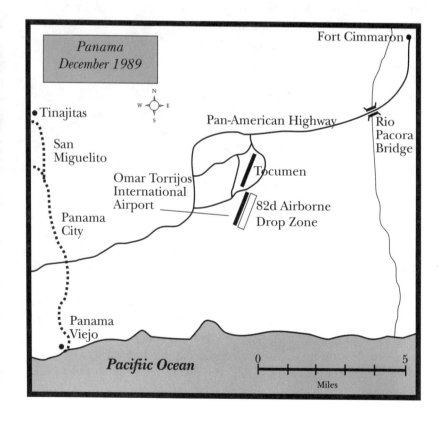

Panama
December 1989

N
W — E
S

Tinajitas

San
Miguelito

Fort Cimmaron

Pan-American Highway

Rio
Pacora
Bridge

Omar Torrijos
International
Airport

Tocumen

82d Airborne
Drop Zone

Panama
City

Panama
Viejo

Pacifiic Ocean

0   5

Miles

Then, starting with a heavy drop at 0135 and a troop jump ten minutes later, the All-Americans of the 82d were due to insert in the grassland east of the Torrijos airstrip. Normally, an airborne assault force likes to hit right on its objectives, as the Rangers did at Torrijos-Tocumen. Given the confusion built into any parachute drop, especially at night, it made sense to face reality and inflict your chaos on the befuddled, surrounded, infiltrated nests of bad guys. You land right on the opposition's heads and come up shooting.

But the 82d took a risk and intentionally tried to go beyond that kind of conventional use of airborne infantry. In doing so, they recalled the memorable words of Bernard Fall, who had seen plenty of French paratroop operations in Vietnam in the 1950s. "A parachute," Fall cautioned, "is merely a means of delivery, but not a way of fighting."[10] For the All-American troopers, the jump simply got them there in one clump. All the fighting came later. And the scheme for that combat was definitely ambitious.

After forty-five minutes allotted for assembly, the airborne brigade would stage its three battalions for pickup by helicopters already in Panama. Each battalion was bound for a critical enemy outpost, going one after another in rapid succession, like bullets shot out of a revolver. The 2d Battalion, 504th Parachute Infantry Regiment, expected to form at the south end of Torrijos and launch first, bound to defeat the Panamanian Defense Force (PDF) garrison at Panama Viejo, a seaside PDF compound. Next, the 1st of the 504th, gathering in a central pickup zone (PZ), would lift off to take on another PDF element, a reinforced heavy weapons company at Tinajitas. Finally, 4/325 expected to assemble at the north end of the strip and go third. Its destination was Fort Cimmaron, home of the PDF's premier mobile force, Battalion 2000. All three missions would be finished before the sun rose over the green hills of the Panama jungles.

These three successive air assaults, using the airborne contingent just dropped from Bragg, would complete the neutralization of Gen. Manuel Noriega's PDF, taking the last of the twenty-seven key objectives designated for Operation Just Cause before dawn on 20 December 1989.[11] With its insistence on defeating, indeed decapitating, the foe in a single night's stroke, the Just Cause scheme resembled few other American military undertakings before or since. There were to be no front lines, no big arrows, no long power drives, no large-scale flanking maneuvers other than from the top flank, the night sky. It was one big takedown, landing right on the objective, a classic airborne profile inflicted not on an isolated airfield or fortress but on an entire small country. Multiple U.S. task forces worked to appear simultaneously out of the darkness right atop every key PDF facility in and around Panama City. Whether or not the nefarious Noriega survived the first blow, his PDF would not.

Indeed, though few might have wanted to discuss the parallel for obvious political reasons, the U.S. intervention in Panama resembled the Soviet Union's lightning "liberations" of Hungary (1956), Czechoslovakia (1968), and Afghanistan (1979), especially the latter two.[12] Like the Soviet assaults, the American version drew on in-country friendly units, including special operations forces (SOF) and airborne, rapidly reinforced by even more airlifted SOF and paratroopers. Politically odious though they might be, from a military standpoint, the 1968 Czech takedown and the even more effective initial takeover in Afghanistan in 1979 demonstrated how to shock, paralyze, and assume control of a hostile country. In Operation Just Cause, Lt. Gen. Carl Stiner and his Joint Task Force (JTF) South team outdid these Soviet adventures, and with a much better outcome for the indigenous people, to say the least.

In keeping with the thoroughly unconventional tone of Just Cause, the 82d Airborne role did *not* rely on its airborne skills, save to get there and get organized. In what would surely surprise—and hopefully shock and overwhelm—its PDF opposition, the 82d borrowed a leaf from its Screaming Eagle brothers of the 101st Airborne Division (Air Assault) and devised three swift, daring heliborne descents to complete the demise of the PDF. This would have been a hell of an effort for the 82d even if everything went exactly as planned.

It did not.

Unseasonably wretched freezing rain pelting the Fort Bragg–Pope Air Force Base complex slowly shredded the carefully sequenced drop. Only eight of twenty Starlifters launched on time from the frozen-over Pope Air Force Base, a direct result of the limited deicing gear available to the ground crews. The aircraft were just late enough to cross airstreams with the thirty-one heavy drop aircraft coming in from Charleston Air Force Base in South Carolina. The resultant wave-off delayed the initial jump until 0211, a mere nineteen minutes before the first air assault on Panama Viejo had been due to start. So much for that idea.

This was bad enough, but even worse, the C-141Bs were not the first eight planes in the planned pattern but birds 1 through 6, 9, and 10.[13] Given habitual airborne cross-loading procedures, no one plane had men from only 1/504, 2/504, or 4/325. To prevent catastrophic effects on any one unit if a plane went down, and to assist in assembly on the ground, each load consisted of a mixed bag, with 2/504 teams at the rear of the planes to jump first for the southern stretch of the elephant grass, 1/504 in the middle headed for the center of the spongy DZ, and 4/325 at the front end, destined to go out last, bound for the marsh just east of the north end of the Torrijos main runway. Perfected over years of jumping, and coupled with the very low drop altitude that limited dispersion, cross-loading worked, but only if enough troops arrived to get going on the air assaults.

Had all twenty C-141Bs arrived at 0145, or had more of them showed up together, all three fighting battalions might have shaken out quickly. Instead, hobbled by deicing back in North Carolina, the drop of the All-Americans dragged on through the wee hours of the morning: two C-141Bs at 0350, three at 0400, another pair at 0455, and the rest at 0515, three and half hours late. This series of partial formations and dribbling follow-ups guaranteed trouble. Units never quite assembled before the next batch of jumpers floated down. This resulted in incomplete, screwed-up units unready to conduct any air assaults at all, let alone commencing at 0230.

The air assaults might have gone off even later had not the 82d Airborne's senior commanders insisted on getting key leaders onto the 0211 drop serial.[14] As a result, enough commanders got in early enough to get the three battalion PZs established, saving some time as their trigger pullers slowly arrived. The designated assault helicopters waited at a distant refueling site, marking time as the cover of night steadily ebbed away. With every passing minute, it became more obvious that the All-Americans were doomed to make daylight helo landings against alerted opposition. All the LGOP guts in the world couldn't solve that problem, imposed by war's iron laws of time, distance, and friction.

The DZ imposed its own nagging costs on the hurrying paratroopers. Dumped into the high reeds, slowed by viscous mud, bewildered by the black of night, and bearing crippling loads of weapons and gear, the jumpers took longer than usual to link up and move out to their PZs. One radioman who landed within eighty yards of the runway found himself almost immobile. "It was so bad that I could only take three steps and fall down," he said. Worse, "in the dark, I couldn't tell if the man only three feet away was a good guy or a bad guy, so I would lay very still until he went away."[15]

There was another problem, the PDF. Their 2d Company's barracks lay at the Tocumen end of the double airdrome, and they had come out fighting when the Rangers hit them at 0100. Although the 82d's commander, Maj. Gen. James H. Johnson, later told researchers that his men "did not engage a single PDF troop" as they gathered for their air assaults, the situation looked a little different down at the private level. Several jumpers drifted north into the Tocumen complex, smack into a major firefight between the Rangers and Noriega's supporters. Others in the grass down near Torrijos reported sniper fire and shot back. Roy Burgess recounted his thoughts as he moved to his linkup point: "I could hear weapons going off in the near distance, but I didn't know whose they were."[16] Floundering at night to breast the sticky, thick cane grass, some 82d men might have been shooting at one another, but there were no casualties attributed to friendly fire. Nobody moved too quickly in this maze of dark canebreak.

Casualties from the jump itself turned out to be light. In a training drop, the 82d anticipates a 4 percent rate; in Panama, only 1.38 percent (thirty men) suffered injuries. The equipment did not survive as neatly. About two-thirds of the heavy drops smacked into the deeper quarters of the boggy DZ, though USAF graders adjudged the drop 90 percent effective. (Scoring somehow looks better back at a safe, air-conditioned air base.) Most of what fell could not be found until after daybreak and so contributed almost nothing to the initial three air assaults. One Sheridan tank was a total loss. Another was nearly so and became a source of parts to keep the rest going.[17]

The human and material costs of the drop did not turn out to be great. But the minutes and hours that slipped away exacted their own hard price.

The sky shaded to pearl gray well before the first helicopter chattered onto the Torrijos runway at about 0610. The brigade commander, Col. Jack Nix, led his key staff onto the command and control (C2) ship, which allowed for an aerial post to oversee the upcoming attacks. Rigged with extra-long-range radios, the UH-60A C2 Blackhawk was piloted by Lt. Col. B. Howard Bornum, commander of Task Force (TF) Hawk, the composite aviation element programmed to carry the All-Americans into battle. Bornum and his flight crews had already carried out a tricky night insertion at Fort Amador at 0100, drawing plenty of ground fire and losing a small scout chopper. That done, the aircraft of TF Hawk then refueled and waited at a remote site.[18] Having already lost a man and an aircraft at night on a surprise landing, the TF Hawk pilots knew only too well what flying in daylight meant, especially against an aroused foe.

With Colonel Nix and his C2 bird in an overwatching orbit, the 2d Battalion, 504th Parachute Infantry Regiment, departed at 0645, destined for Panama Viejo. The first of the day's three 82d Airborne air assaults found a dry hole, with most of the enemy long gone. But the remnant elected to make the gringos bleed. Between eighteen and twenty-five energetic hostile stay-behinds opened fire on the landing zones (LZs) and managed to wound a few Americans. Slogging through tidal mudflats and more of the high sawgrass, 2/504 took until 1155 to declare their objective secure. At least the tired soldiers grabbed a large arsenal for their troubles.[19] Thankfully, the human price was small for this marginal outcome.

The helicopters of TF Hawk took it on the chin, however. It might have been worse had not an accompanying AH-1F Cobra gunship chased off the gunners on a Soviet-made ZPU-4 quad-barreled anti-aircraft gun. Small-arms fire badly damaged two of the seventeen lift UH-60As. Those aircraft diverted for repairs.[20] Pocked by a few bullet holes, the other fifteen flew back to Torrijos for round two.

Arriving after 0730, TF Hawk found Lt. Col. Renard H. Marable's 1st Battalion, 504th Parachute Infantry Regiment (Red Devils), lined up for loading in PZ Center. The paratroopers faced a tough target at Tinajitas, home of the PDF 1st Infantry & Fire Support Company, *Los Tigres* (Tigers). Intelligence assessed the Tigers with 184 men, 4 big 120mm mortars, 6 mortars (81mm), 3 mortars (60mm), and another one of those ZPU-4 quad flak guns.[21] Nobody knew how much of 1st Company would still be there by now, but given the experience at Panama Viejo, Marable and his rifle companies prepared for a firefight. They were not disappointed.

Tinajitas Barracks was a tough nut to crack, thanks to some brutal terrain. The PDF compound stood in the middle of a saddle between a pair of sheer five-hundred-foot hills. The only decent landing zone—LZ Leopard—lay at the foot of the ridge that held the twin hills, leaving 1/504 troopers with almost a half-mile climb up the steep, foliage-choked slope to get at their prey. Even this six-ship LZ had problems, such as a dirty little creek called Rio Matias Hernandez flowing to the south, the busy Trans-Isthmus Highway to the west, and a basket weave of telephone wires and power lines hanging all over the place to the north. In addition, shanties and shacks full of poor Panamanian civilians choked the whole area except for the hilltops and garrisons proper. Many of them carried AK-47s courtesy of Manuel Noriega's Dignity Battalion (Digbat) civil militia program. Some would use them.[22] It looked bad, all right.

In true airborne fashion, Marable and company might well have gone in atop the barracks parade ground and gently angled metal building roofs, right onto the objective at Tinajitas. Though this would require a rain of fire to get the paratroopers to ground, it would concentrate on the bad guys and avoid moving through the surrounding residential neighborhoods. Plus, there is something to be said for just kicking in the door, especially with an alert enemy. The audacity alone might have helped generate some degree of local surprise.

Such a dangerous direct descent certainly could not have been any tougher than what the 1/504 commander chose to do, landing 800 yards away at LZ Leopard and crashing uphill through the undergrowth. To protect this advance, the Red Devils relied on attack helicopters to deliver covering fires. In addition, Ren Marable decided to fly in a mortar squad with a heavy, tripod-mounted, .50-cal-

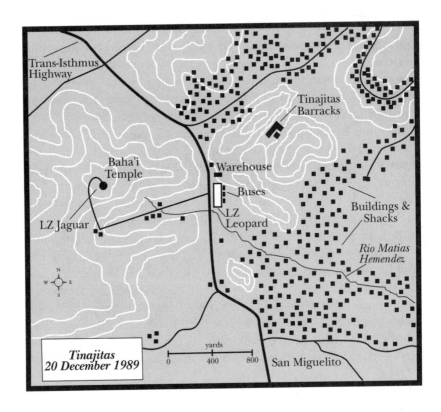

Trans-Isthmus Highway

Baha'i Temple

LZ Jaguar

Tinajitas Barracks

Warehouse

Buses

LZ Leopard

Buildings & Shacks

Rio Matias Hemendez

Tinajitas
20 December 1989

yards
0   400   800

San Miguelito

iber machine gun. While everything else went in through LZ Leopard, that group planned to get out at miniscule LZ Jaguar, an open slash of ground near a Baha'i temple sited on a commanding 650-foot hill about 1,500 yards southwest of the PDF buildings. From the map and aerial photographs, the temple mount appeared to dominate Tinajitas and offer a good firing post. Taking this high ground would also ensure that the hostile PDF did not use it for their own purposes.

With the attack aviation and the powerful .50 caliber in support, Marable stuck with the scheme of maneuver prepared and rehearsed back at Fort Bragg. It would be Company A swinging east to take one of the looming hills, Company C pushing west to secure the other hill, and Company B right up the gut.[23] This would isolate the PDF in their garrison.

Therein lay the other reason that the Red Devils of 1/504 did not pounce right onto their target. Ren Marable developed his maneuver concept in accord with ideas originated by JTF South's General Stiner, the overall commander of Just Cause. Stiner envisioned surrounding each PDF garrison, broadcasting an appeal for surrender, then beginning to employ precision fires to coerce the enemy to quit. Normally, the ill-disciplined opponents quit long before the Americans brought full firepower to bear. That suited Stiner well. After all, the goal was to retake Panama from Noriega's goons, not slaughter every living member of the PDF, let alone the innocent citizenry of Panama City. This exact method had been used quite well at Fort Amador.[24]

But that had been at H hour, in the darkness at 0100 in the morning, before the bad guys knew what had hit them. After a night of wide-ranging attacks, after the Panama Viejo assault, exposed in the full light of day—well, maybe Stiner's slow squeeze method didn't make sense anymore at Tinajitas. Indeed, with the PDF shattered and on the run, maybe the entire landing at Tinajitas deserved reconsideration. But nobody in 1/504 thought that way. That was way above their pay grade. At their level, they prepared to execute, to do what infantrymen do best and make the leap into death ground.

The small, uneven LZ known as Leopard forced TF Hawk to proceed in two flights, each with two serials. Just to add to the complexity, the tail Blackhawk on the second serial needed to divert to the Baha'i temple, to unload the .50-caliber machine-gun team at LZ Jaguar. Whereas the plan back at Bragg counted on twenty UH-60As, now there were only fifteen. There were no extra C2 craft, no designated medevac birds, no spare lift ships, no dedicated search and rescue teams, just these fifteen Blackhawks, several already sporting nicks and holes from their adventures at Fort Amador and Panama Viejo. With no margin for error, the airborne hoped to get in without losing an aircraft, banking on the durability of the Sikorsky Company's Blackhawks, the nerves of some good Army fliers, bad shooting by frightened, half-trained PDF and Digbats, and the courage and skill of airborne infantrymen. One rocket-propelled grenade or shoulder-fired heat seeker pumped into an overloaded UH-60A, one blazing fireball, and then all the bills would come due, a blood debt of corners cut, big chances taken, and lives in the balance. It was very risky business, an air assault on the cheap, low, and slow under the shining tropical sun.

So be it. Paratroopers live with adversity. They train for it. Now they would fight under it. Men loaded up, packing aboard to make up for the five helicopters not there. Up to twenty-six sweating, grim-faced troopers, bowed by heavy rucksacks, shoehorned themselves into the waiting choppers. With nothing to hold them in but a green canvas nylon retaining strap strung across each open door, the first nine took off at 0815, followed within a few minutes by the second six.

Meanwhile, someone was checking out LZ Leopard and the Tinajitas Barracks, sniffing around for *Los Tigres*. A pair of AH-64A Apache attack birds and an OH-58C Kiowa scout trolled across the San Miguelito slums, looking for trouble. They found it.

Just east of the PDF barracks, northeast of LZ Leopard, about a dozen uniformed PDF types opened fire on the three U.S. aircraft. Using a big machine gun, the enemy poured it on. They blew holes through the little OH-58C, which broke away, leaking fuel. More impressively, they tore up the lead Apache, wrecking one of its two engines and dislodging the 30mm under-nose cannon, rendering it useless. The shot-up chopper broke for nearby Howard Air Force Base, out of action. The other Apache pulled off, protecting its battered wingman. This was great shooting by the PDF.

Unfortunately for the Panamanian gunners, they quit firing a little too soon. They also had the bad timing to open up just as their targets had been about to trade out with a new team of two Apaches and a new scout ship. Covering the withdrawal of their injured mates, the next two Apaches came on station. The lead gunner, CWO John Flankey, marked the target by laser pulse at almost 3,000 yards. His craft then reared up, its 30mm cannon swiveling. Flankey looked right at the hostile squad, and the gun followed along, guided by the warrant officer's helmet sight. In the distance, the PDF team recognized the hovering AH-64As on the horizon. They started to run, but it was too late. With a rasping roar, the U.S. Army chopper spat out 160 big 30mm rounds, finishing off all but one survivor. He dropped his weapon and fled into the brush fronting the cleared hilltop.[25] That scratched off about ten opponents, but it also left no doubt that the 1st Company at Tinajitas was ready and waiting.

Flying in an oval pattern slightly offset from the main U.S. approach routes, Col. Jack Nix and the men in his C2 bird also saw plenty of armed Panamanians in and around LZ Leopard and the Tinajitas compound. Opposition elements took up positions along the edge of the landing zone. Additionally, attracted by the diving Apache gunfight and the orbiting C2 ship, a large crowd gathered in the dusty streets and along the Trans-Isthmus Highway. The neighbors of San Miguelito were going to see this show. Mixed in among them, civilian-clad Digbat activists hunted for good ambush spots. As for separating these bad actors from the innocent bystanders—well, no UH-60A door gunner or Apache driver wanted to try that kind of surgery. Somebody besides American and PDF soldiers looked sure to get hurt this morning. Helicopter weapons just aren't very discreet.

The first six helos swung out across the Pacific, then turned inland, crossing the coastal highway and Panama City proper. Below, smoke from earlier attacks along the Panama Canal itself and downtown billowed in the bright morning sun. Many civilians waved white handkerchiefs and cheered as the green-black American helicopters crossed over their apartment buildings.

The cheering stopped as the decent offices and apartments gave way to the ghetto of San Miguelito. Local Digbats, some of them women, opened fire as the string of American aircraft passed over. The TF Hawk pilots had to slow down and flare to land, threading a needle of fire and overhead wires to worm their way into little LZ Leopard. Slugs tore through aircraft hulls, wounding men in the last two helos. Even so, young door gunners held their fire, clutching bouncing M-60D flexible-mount machine guns. They could have made short work of these AK-47 shooters, but they would certainly have hit many civilian gawkers. In doing so, they followed the directive of Maj. Gen. James H. Johnson of the 82d Airborne Division: "We put our soldiers at risk in order to minimize casualties and damage to the Panamanian people and their country."[26] So the frustrated helo gunners held their triggers, taking the beating as their craft sank slowly (too damn slowly) toward the high elephant grass covering LZ Leopard.

One door gunner got a clear target and an okay to fire from TF Hawk commander Howard Bornum. With two bursts of 7.62mm rounds, every fifth bullet a red tracer, the soldier blew three Digbat autoriflemen out of the bed of a pickup speeding up a rutted trail paralleling the Trans-Isthmus Highway. Two accompanying AH-1F Cobras and the Apache team waded in to engage, but they broke off. There were too many civilians intermixed. To clear LZ Leopard meant grunt work, sending men, not bullets. It was going to be necessary to wade in and clean them out with rifle, grenade, and bayonet—*mano-a-mano*, Red Devils versus *Los Tigres*.

The first half dozen choppers settled into the blowing waves of tall swamp reeds. As they did, enemy automatic fire erupted from a warehouse to the north, just past the low-hanging electrical wires. Most of it whipped way overhead, well above the whirling rotor disks but rising right into the teeth of the next three inbound birds. One lucky 7.62mm round smacked into the flight lead's left windscreen, wrecking the instrument panel and opening a bloody scalp wound on Capt. Tom Muir, the Blackhawk pilot. Muir's face exploded, ripped by metal and glass fragments. The impact came just as he tried to get his helo down into the thrashing elephant grass. Thinking fast, Muir's copilot, CWO Neal Vandenhoovel, wrestled to gain control of the ship and get his twenty-six paratroopers onto the ground. Dazed, his visage a bloody mask, Muir stayed conscious.

The chief somehow got the helo down, and the Red Devils rolled out. A few reached back for tripods and rucksacks. The rushing howl of helicopter turbines, the steady whacking of the rotor blades, did not mask the unbroken stuttering of enemy small arms. With the north end of the LZ already sparking with fire, now the east flank opened up. Hostile gunmen engaged from inside a row of three rusting bus carcasses. The ill-disciplined, poor-shooting Panamanians evidently learned the virtues of the L-shaped ambush, because they were inflicting one on the Red Devils of 1/504 and their assault pilots.

The volume of enemy gunfire escalated as the paratroopers cleared the aircraft. On one UH-60A, three paratroopers slumped back, hit as they tried to get out. On another, a helicopter door gunner staggered back, a hole in his arm, his M-60D machine gun dangling useless as he slumped into his gray nylon seat. Then, led by the bleeding Tom Muir's battered Blackhawk, the six helos took off, skirting the swinging power lines above the enemy-held warehouse.

They had been on the ground an average of ten seconds. Blood smears, gunpowder stains, and gaping holes told their own tales. Spent brass cartridges, flashlights, batteries, canteen caps, the jetsam squashed from men crowded rucksack to rucksack, all rattled around the damaged, empty insides of the helicopters as they sped back to PZ Center at the airport. They had another lift to bring in.

On the ground, the paratroopers found themselves entangled in the same fifteen-foot-tall brand of thick, wet grass that had dogged assembly at Torrijos-Tocumen. Getting bearings was hard. The carefully briefed attack plan did not help much here. With the helicopters gone, and another three on short final approach, all attracting fountains of fire, soldiers quickly sensed where the enemy had holed up. When a Cobra flashed overhead, gunning the warehouse that the men could not see, several teams turned that way. Others focused on the shooting coming from the bus hulks to the east.

It was like the drop on Torrijos-Tocumen all over again, only in the light of day. The Red Devils wanted to conduct a quick, tight air assault. Instead, it seemed that a typically chaotic airborne operation had broken out. But that was not bad news at all. After all, these men knew well how to exploit that kind of confusion and friction. On LZ Leopard, it was LGOP time.

It was up to them to do what the door gunners and attack aviators could not, to clean off the fringes of this rotten little LZ. There had been little preparatory attack helo fire, no AC-130 Spectre flying gunship, no mortars, no artillery, no rain of ruin to pave the way. No, this one counted on the good old little groups of paratroopers. At least the pilots had some minor armoring on their craft, and swift rotor blades to take out the aircrews. The men of 1/504 had only camouflage-fabric shirts and guts to protect themselves. And they would not be leaving until they took Tinajitas. There was no turning back.

The time was 0830. The next set of Blackhawks floated down, three fat targets headed to ground. But already, the LGOPs were having an effect. The M-249 SAW guns were snorting away, and grenades were going off. A few NCOs, a clutch of privates, and some tough young officers saw the enemy and went after them, just the way they had been taught. Staff Sergeant Joseph Sedach, platoon leader of 1st Platoon, Company B, described it this way: "The soldiers fought just the way they practiced back at Fort Bragg, but with a difference. Usually, the live fires we had at Fort Bragg are only one way."[27] Sedach's platoon did not have an officer or a sergeant first class, as the approved table of organization said it should. But it had Sedach, a tough, smart, young NCO. With his example, the guys knew what to do.

This time, ground fire hit only one chopper, and that on the tricky egress over the warehouse. Aviator 1st Lt. Lisa Kutschera said later, "Whoever planned that LZ gave the PDF an easy shot at us as we departed the area. We couldn't go under the wires because of a shorter set running alongside the tall set."[28] When the helos climbed up and away, showing belly, the opposition punched holes in the bottom of the airframes.

Now the PDF threw another card on the table. Mortar rounds started to burst on the LZ. They landed in twos and threes, randomly popping out in the long grass. The paratroopers pressed against the warehouse and buses. Their best chance involved getting belly to belly with these PDF defenders. Staying out on the LZ meant death. Indeed, a mortar shell killed two men from Company B, both under care at an impromptu aid station for gunshot wounds suffered on landing. The attending medic also went down, injured.[29]

The next rack of five helicopters descended, enduring another gauntlet of fire from the buses and warehouse, plus mortar rounds spewing hot fragments all about. A sixth helo broke off from that flight and veered into cramped LZ Jaguar, up at the Baha'i temple hill. All the aircraft got out, punctured but without casualties. Now, if only that .50 caliber might uncork and hose down these bastard mortarmen. The rifle companies would take care of the tormentors in the buses and the warehouse.

With parts of all three rifle companies down, Lieutenant Colonel Marable gradually imposed order on his industrious LGOPs. He sent Capt. Gordon Gidumal's Company A up toward the southeastern hill. They skirted the fire nest in the buses, pressing for that summit. Company B went for the buses. Hell, the LGOPs were already there, the PDF down or fleeing. Company C drew the warehouse. That took some time to clean out. All expected the second lift shortly, minus Muir's smashed-up Blackhawk.

The fight at LZ Leopard ended quickly, within a half hour. Like the Viet Cong of legend, the Panamanians proved ghosts, mere handfuls turning up dead or wounded when the rifle squads finally got into their positions.[30] Had the rest melted away into the slums of surrounding San Miguelito? Or had there been no others, merely these diehards with lots of ammunition?

Whatever the reason, the Red Devils' immediate assault from the doors of their helos broke the back of the resistance at LZ Leopard. It had not been pretty or neatly choreographed, but it had certainly been violent and relentless, short-range grunt work. Although the second lift of helicopters still took sniper fire, they all got in and out with only bullet holes, no casualties or major damage. Thanks to all of the shooting on the first trip, the door gunners did not hestitate. Indeed, one overzealous crewman stitched 7.62mm bullets right across the base of the hill, accidentally catching the lead platoons of Company A laboring up the rise. One All-American collapsed, shot in the leg by the misguided burst. In a better-coordinated bit of aerial firepower, a Cobra loosed six Hydra-70 rockets (2.75 inch), peppering a corner of the Tinajitas garrison. That largely ended the hail of mortar rounds that had been coming from that spot up there.[31]

The .50-caliber machine-gun element at the Baha'i temple turned out to be a big nothing. The ground did not quite match the map. Regardless of what all had been told, the gun crew could not see the PDF barracks on the neighboring hilltop. By the time they set up to shoot at where they thought it stood, the rest of 1/504 had humped halfway up the hill. Not that it mattered. The .50-caliber gunners had no targets up there anyway by now. Unschooled in tactics, *Los Tigres* and their Digbat buddies did not know the value of high ground. The ones inclined to resist evidently decided to fight it out on the rim of LZ Leopard. With those characters killed, wounded, or run off, with the enemy mortar teams scatttered by Cobra rockets, there was nobody shooting back from Tinajitas proper anymore.

It took the Red Devils several hours to establish that fact. To the east, Company A made their way carefully, thanks to advice from its experienced senior NCO, 1st Sgt. Johnny R. Oliver. The rifle platoons rotated their point men to break the lush green foliage. They also reconnoitered, and found a covered draw. This twisting crack, though encrusted with heavy vegetation, led them slowly right to their designated objective, the eastern hill.[32] It took time, but the company got there without further loss. Company B, which took the brunt of the fire on the LZ, faced the toughest climb. Specialist Andrew Slatniske of 1st Platoon called it "the longest seven hundred meters [760 yards] I ever did—up that hill in that elephant grass."[33] But with the relentless SSgt. Joe Sedach leading, 1st Platoon bent their backs and kept moving, Slatniske included.

The adrenaline rush of the LZ cross fire drained away, sapped by the hot sun, the unyielding jungle, and the crushing burden of those same hundred-pound rucksacks that had pressed the men into the marsh mud after the jump the night before. Had it really been less than twenty-four hours since they left Fort Bragg, cursing the chill winds, longing for the warmth of the tropics? Well, now they had warmth in spades, heat to the nth degree, a hot flight in, a hot LZ, a hot gunfight in the old buses, and now this endless march. Occasional sniper rounds snapped overhead. But the sun was the enemy now. It proved more persistent than the PDF.

The steep hillside took its toll. Eyes clouded by sweat; men stumbled. Their monstrous backpacks sent them tumbling. At times, entire trudging files crept along on hands and knees, clutching root knobs and vines. Men had not slept the night before, or much the night prior to that, back at Bragg. Few had eaten much; a full stomach makes for ugly abdominal wounds. Now, lack of water and dwindling energy began knocking men down. Six troopers keeled over, one after another, some out cold with heat prostration.[34] Far more surprisingly, almost four hundred men kept going, up and up, crusty white sweat rings crisscrossing their sodden camouflage uniforms. Still, they labored onward.

Company A got there first, then Company C, and finally Company B. At 1433, Ren Marable declared Tinajitas secure. In a search of the abandoned garrison, the men found a litter of PDF uniforms, racks of rifles, and boxes of ammunition, as well as all kinds of discarded service equipment. They also found three 120mm mortars, two aimed at LZ Leopard and one at the U.S. facility at Fort Clayton.[35]

They would fire no more rounds in anger. Like Panama Viejo, the garrison itself turned out to be a dry hole. But the Red Devils had certainly done their part to dry it up.

The third All-American air assault inserted 4/325 near Fort Cimmaron. By that time, PDF's will to fight back had largely dissipated. The landings were unopposed. The airborne infantrymen had several sharp small-scale engagements later, to include a major fracas at the Battalion 2000 barracks with a few PDF holdouts. Shooting went on most of the night. An AC-130 Spectre flying gunship helped settle that affair. By 0730 on 21 December 1989, 4/325 declared Fort Cimmaron to be secure.[36] Once again, the mass of the enemy fled long before the U.S. paratroopers attacked.

In fact, Fort Cimmaron stood empty for a good reason. Before the 82d Airborne even jumped into Torrijos-Tocumen, Fort Cimmaron's elite Battalion 2000 had been ravaged trying to cross the Rio Pacora Bridge. It was an "on-the-fly" mission passed to Company A, 3d Battalion, 7th Special Force Group (Airborne), in response to late-breaking intelligence. Manuel Noriega's shock troops had started moving; even without the weather delays, the 82d would not get there in time to stop them. So the Special Forces drew the task.

Between 0045 and 0300 on 20 December, as the Rangers and 82d fought it out at Torrijos-Tocumen, two dozen Green Berets and a supporting Spectre gunship stopped and wrecked an eight-vehicle Battalion 2000 convoy full of heavy weapons. In a tough fight that lasted all night, they killed or wounded thirty-six PDF troops and snagged twenty prisoners.[37] No wonder that in the encounter on 21 December, the few still willing to fight in the Battalion 2000 barracks reconsidered once 4/325 again brought the hated Spectre overhead.

During the battle of the Pacora Bridge, twenty-four Special Forces men and a Spectre did more physical damage to the PDF than the 82d Airborne's three air assaults on 20 December, and at no cost to the Americans. By contrast, following a jump strung out and bollixed up by bad weather in North Carolina, the All-Americans had taken three largely empty PDF compounds. In the toughest of the three engagements—Tinajitas—they lost two paratroopers killed and seventeen wounded, plus three wounded aviators. An Apache and a

Kiowa scout were knocked out of action, and fourteen of the fifteen Blackhawks took a beating, one sufficient to render the aircraft unflyable for the rest of Operation Just Cause.[38] It could have been worse, and probably should have been, except the enemy's morale had cracked before sunup on 20 December.

Essentially, all of the 82d's disappointments related to timing. In an unconventional lightning strike such as Just Cause, speed is life. There is only one chance to surprise the foe, and you had better be there in his face or be ready to pay. The All-Americans certainly got there, and they hit every objective—but too late. They paid in blood and pain to verify victories already won.

Hindsight allows that unobstructed view, but things were not so clear on the morning of 20 December. At that point, launching the 82d Airborne's three air assaults made military sense. In Lt. Gen. Carl Stiner's command post, the situation at the time looked pretty dicey. Noriega himself had fled, and his rabid *Radio Nacional* kept broadcasting prerecorded appeals to take to the streets, jungles, and mountains and fight on against the hated gringos. Combat continued in and around the PDF headquarters at *La Commandancia* in downtown Panama City, with surrounding neighborhoods afire and sniper rounds going off like firecrackers. Would the PDF regroup and go into insurgent mode? Were the thousands of American civilians in country in danger? What about the support of the local populace? Nobody knew, not really.

In that light, the U.S. forces had to take the last three known enemy garrisons, if only to clamp hands on their arms caches. Under the PDF program called *Operacion Montana*, a pro-Noriega guerrilla movement counted on taking the heavy weapons from Panama Viejo, Tinajitas, and Fort Cimmaron.[39] In the former two urban locations, seizing the garrisons would also send an unmistakable signal to the people of Panama. The Americans had the initiative. When the men of 1/504 went in hard at Tinajitas, the spectators got the message—these Yankees would not go home.

In the war on the PDF's will, the meager returns on the daylight air assaults meant less than the fact that tough All-Americans took on, and took out, the last three major enemy nodes of resistance. Manuel Noriega's bluster about guerrilla warfare turned out to be hollow. The three 82d Airborne attacks underlined and ensured that outcome. They were a part of the whole, and it is hard to say that they were unnecessary. Only the PDF leadership knew that for sure, and their view had been relayed incoherently. It all happened too fast. In that important way, the paratroopers did their job well.

That acknowleged, the airborne infantry experience in Panama deserves more consideration, particularly in light of the confusing jump and the difficult daylight air assault at Tinajitas. But that did not happen as well as it should have. Hungry for a victory, the American public and military accentuated the positive. The courage and capability of the paratroopers certainly earned welcome praise. Then the war with Iraq erupted, and the Panama operation faded away, its fifteen minutes of fame long gone. One afternoon and evening in Somalia in October of 1993, though, it all came rushing back in technicolor blood and fire. There's not much future in flying helicopters full of men across enemy gun barrels in broad daylight.

But that was still in the future as the country applauded the heroes of Just Cause. Proud Americans in uniform nearly broke their arms slapping backs and exchanging high fives. This came right from the top, when General Stiner told a group of reporters that, "in my judgment, there were no lessons learned on this operation. I don't think that I or my commanders or our armed forces learned a single lesson." That got quoted repeatedly, implying that all went exactly as planned. Mostly, it did.

Less often did folks hear Stiner's next sentence, an important qualifier: "But we did validate a lot of things."[40] That's military terminology for relearning old lessons. Friction, the enemy, freezing rain, ubiquitous swamp grass, hot sun, and human nature all played their parts. There were obvious miscalculations in time and space. In the internal military trade journals and documents, that validation process did start, although truncated by the Gulf War.

Taking Stiner's lead, some in the armed forces have airbrushed Just Cause into some kind of simultaneous blitzkrieg, ignoring the important nuances of the 82d's late entry on the field of action. The self-described "keystone document" of the armed forces, *Joint Publication 3-0: Doctrine for Joint Operations,* uses Just Cause as a prototype for a forced entry. No argument there; this nonlinear "takedown" campaign was truly revolutionary and worthy of emulation. But in an unexpected nod to George Orwell, readers of *Joint Pub 3-0* learn that the JTF "simultaneously attacked twenty-seven targets" at H hour (0100 on 20 December 1989), which is not true. The last three targets were not even due to be hit until 0230, ninety minutes after H hour. In reality, of course, these air assaults dragged on throughout the morning of 20 December. Perhaps *simultaneous* means something different to doctrine writers.

Worse, the 82d Airborne's troubled drop gets explained away thusly: "One large formation experienced delays from a sudden ice storm at the departure airfield—its operations and timing were revised in the air."[41] Well, that's one way to put it.

Incensed by this kind of material, some sideline experts relooked at the 82d Airborne's role in Just Cause, then overreacted. They argued that the airborne jump made no sense.[42] These critics think that the 1st Brigade should have landed at the twin airports like any other airline passengers (albeit a lot faster). Although superficially attractive, this idea makes a hash of reality.

Start with the basics. To land big transport jets at Torrijos-Tocumen, the entire area must be secure. It's one thing to pass over in the night sky. It's another to land, taxi, and park. Air Force Starlifters lack armor, and a few well-placed tracer rounds or an RPG could turn the parking ramp into a barbecue scene. One such explosion would end airlanding very quickly.

Next, the runways must be clear of battle debris. A few spent cartridge cases or a ditched parachute promised mayhem if sucked into a C-141B's screaming turbofans. In mortal combat from the minute they landed, the Rangers had little time to police up the trash of war. Days after the initial assault, a special ops MH-6 Little Bird helicopter vacuumed up a crumpled parachute and beat itself to death.[43] And that was after the airport runways had supposedly been cleaned off.

Even if they could navigate through the PDF gunfire and the military detritus, it takes a while for USAF jets to land and off-load troops. By comparison, an airdrop takes minutes to get thousands of boots on the ground, plus lots of heavy gear. That all happened, too, if not as elegantly as preliminary plans suggested. As late as the

82d was, it would not have formed until early on the morning of 21 December had it landed inside its jet transports, a delay of twenty-four hours or more. The division leadership tried that in Grenada, and it took days to build combat power, which delayed resolution of the fighting.[44] In Panama, they went with the jumps and took their lumps.

No, the jump wasn't the problem, although it caused it. The problem was the follow-on air assaults. That concept simply did not fit into the prevailing scheme, and through no fault of the 82d Airborne, either. Even if the airdrop had gone off like clockwork, the air assaults were guaranteed to go off one after another, not simultaneously, due to a shortage of Army aviation in country. There just weren't enough helicopters allocated.[45] For added trouble, the JTF South planners wanted to start ninety minutes after the rest of the party, which might well have ensured trouble no matter what. Once the flights slid back into daylight, it is impressive that things went as well as they did.

Focusing on the air assaults misses the real benefit of the 82d's big drop. In a few hours the American effort in Panama brought in a full fighting brigade, to include heavy equipment. This increased the line battalions in country by 25 percent in one swoop. Coupled with the Ranger jumps on Torrijos-Tocumen and distant Rio Hato, the airborne insertions doubled American infantry strength overnight.[46] Although their triple air assault landed no knockouts, the 82d Airborne was in place by daybreak to handle the myriad of 911 calls that soon flooded into Stiner's JTF South.

These started almost immediately. On 20 December 1989, after taking Panama Viejo, 2/504 dispatched a force to secure endangered American civilians at the Marriott Hotel. Following their seizure of Tinajitas, the Red Devils of 1/504 began civic action in San Miguelito, utterly defusing the Digbat presence by medical aid and distribution of meals. The men of 4/325 went into the Punta Patilla Airfield on 22 December. In addition, the 82d Airborne took over Torrijos-Tocumen to clear the runways for the arrival of follow-on troops from the 7th Infantry Division (Light).[47] This freed the Rangers for additional missions, too. And those kept coming, as the Americans mopped up across the country.

That's what makes the airborne infantry useful and unique. They arrive in bulk, right from America. Unlike any other conventional unit shipped from the U.S. homeland, the paratroopers can fight their way in. That capability made a difference in Panama, and promises to do so again some day.

On the face of it, the airborne battalion looks pretty much like any other dismounted infantry outfit in the U.S. Army. The 1st Battalion, 504th Parachute Infantry Regiment, is typical. When they went into Tinajitas, the Red Devils drew their assault echelon from three rifle companies, an antiarmor company, and a headquarters unit.[48] The total strength on paper is 697 men, not particularly strong. Few battalions run at full strength, though in the 82d Airborne, most are close.

Within the rifle companies, each of the three rifle platoons has three nine-man rifle squads and a nine-man weapons squad. Split into two fire teams of four, the rifle squad has the usual mix of M-16A2 rifles, SAW light machine guns, and M-203 40mm grenade launchers. The weapons squad packs M-60 machine guns, big old 7.62mm models based on the World War II German MG-42 series. On paper, the weapons guys also carry M-47 Dragon antitank missiles, but few units bother with these big, weak, obsolescent items. A radioman, platoon sergeant, and lieutenant round out this basic fighting unit.

Three such platoons make a rifle company, designated by the letters A, B, and C. Along with a captain, a lieutenant executive officer, and a first sergeant, there's a handful of others: a supply sergeant; an armorer to fix weapons; a chemical defense NCO, who often does anything but that; and a few more radio operators. A six-man squad carrying 60mm mortars provides readily responsive firepower. In Panama, the ROE prohibited using these mortars except under very restrictive conditions, with all sorts of permission required.[49] So the company mortar sections usually acted as an extra rifle squad, often securing the company first-aid post.

The antiarmor company, Company D, consists of five platoons of four Humvees each. Aboard the Humvees can be mounted a mix of TOW (tube-launched, optically tracked, wire-guided) antitank missile launchers, Mk-19 automatic grenade launchers (40mm), or the

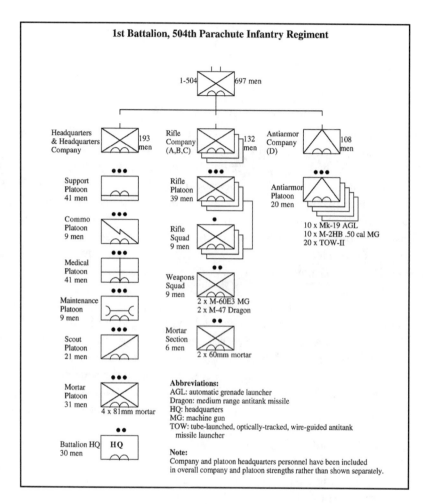

1st Battalion, 504th Parachute Infantry Regiment

1-504 | 697 men

Headquarters & Headquarters Company | 193 men

Rifle Company (A,B,C) | 132 men

Antiarmor Company (D) | 108 men

Support Platoon 41 men

Commo Platoon 9 men

Medical Platoon 41 men

Maintenance Platoon 9 men

Scout Platoon 21 men

Mortar Platoon 31 men
4 x 81mm mortar

Battalion HQ 30 men | HQ

Rifle Platoon 39 men

Rifle Squad 9 men

Weapons Squad 9 men
2 x M-60E3 MG
2 x M-47 Dragon

Mortar Section 6 men
2 x 60mm mortar

Antiarmor Platoon 20 men
10 x Mk-19 AGL
10 x M-2HB .50 cal MG
20 x TOW-II

Abbreviations:
AGL: automatic grenade launcher
Dragon: medium range antitank missile
HQ: headquarters
MG: machine gun
TOW: tube-launched, optically-tracked, wire-guided antitank
missile launcher

Note:
Company and platoon headquarters personnel have been included
in overall company and platoon strengths rather than shown separately.

ever-popular M-2HB .50-caliber heavy machine gun. The platoons regularly mix this potent arsenal, with some TOWs, some grenade launchers, and some .50 calibers. The Humvees have Kevlar-hardened cabs and can be dropped by parachute. About half of the battalion's firepower resides in Company D.

In Headquarters and Headquarters Company (HHC), along with the staff, the communicators, and the supply, maintenance, and medical men, a platoon of scouts and a platoon of four 81mm mortars offer dedicated reconnaissance and fire support for the battalion commander. At Tinajitas, Ren Marable used his mortarmen to bring in the .50-caliber machine gun at the Baha'i temple. It wasn't exactly their assigned job, but not far out of line with firing their mortars to suppress enemy positions and allow the battalion to advance. It also got around the ROE restriction rather neatly. Unfortunately, the ground around Tinajitas did not allow this clever technique to work out.

There are also habitual attachments. Some of the medics from HHC always split out to the rifle platoons. Outside assistance also comes routinely. The artillery battalion that supports 1/504 gives the battalion a team of forward observers, enough to send one to every rifle company and rifle platoon. The U.S. Air Force sends forward air controllers to call in laser bombs and Spectre gunships, along with just plain old high explosives, but this small team stays at battalion level. Loudspeaker teams and Spanish linguists accompanied the Red Devils in Panama. Engineers or air defenders might have also gone if needed.

In the 82d Airborne Division, all of these characters came ready to jump and fight. The real steel of 1/504 came from its men, not its organizational diagram. Everyone in an airborne infantry battalion jumps and fights, led by the lieutenant colonel. All graduate from Fort Benning, Georgia's demanding three-week basic airborne course. All meet the standards of the 82d's own challenging training program.[50] Leaping out of airplanes already says something about a man's willpower. If you can get a guy to do that, over and over, such schooled bravery translates well into charging enemy machine guns and sticking bayonets into badniks. It all creates an aggressive attitude that pays off when things go on the fritz, as in the opening round at Tinajitas.

Airborne infantry is at its best when dumped right on the enemy, preferably at night. With AN/PVS-7B goggles on their faces and AN/PAQ-4A laser spotters on their weapons, paratroopers can see and shoot in the dark,[51] although goggle fighting is like dodging through a football game looking through two toilet paper tubes. It takes a lot of training to get good with night gear. Many foreign armies have the toys, but only a few bother to learn to fight with them. The 82d Airborne Division has learned. It is a fearsome advantage for a force that prefers to start its war amongst the bad guys.

As far as air assaults, patrolling, infiltration, defense, and all the other aspects of the grunt art, those necessarily get attention *after* parachute infantrymen master the exceptional perils of a mass night drop right into death ground. That central function takes a lot of time and effort. Sometimes, the All-American riflemen could use work on ground movement or heliborne operations.[52] A few of those gaps showed at Tinajitas. But the United States has other infantrymen to do these tasks. We do well not to forget that, among conventional forces, only the 82d can go straight into battle from stateside. If you want a parachute assault, call America's Guard of Honor, the 82d Airborne Division. They deliver.

Real deliveries have been pretty rare. Since World War II, the 82d has made one combat drop—Torrijos-Tocumen. They almost made another in Haiti in September 1994. But that makes two nights of work since 1945. We maintain and train our airborne infantry at great expense, and have for decades, although we use it sparingly indeed.

Aside from Panama, there have been four other American parachute assaults in the years after World War II. Two came during the Korean War, carried out by the 187th Airborne Infantry Regimental Combat Team. Both drops attempted to cut off enemy forces. In both cases, most of the opposition slipped away. In Vietnam, the 2d Battalion (Airborne), 503d Infantry, jumped in 1967 as part of Operation Junction City. It had some aspects of a stunt in that unexpectedly successful friendly forces had already secured the drop zone.[53] Airborne battalions fought bravely in many engagements in Korea and Vietnam, as well as leading interventions into Lebanon (1958) and the Dominican Republic (1965–66). They did not jump, though.

Army Rangers, not airborne infantry, took the Point Salines runway in Grenada in 1983, the fourth post-1945 American drop aside from Just Cause. Rangers have made airfield seizures into a fundamental mission, and so drew the nod in Panama, too. The 82d came in on top of them at Torrijos-Tocumen, bound for other business. Had the 1994 Haiti assault occurred, the 82d would have dropped in anger, but that almost happened in Grenada, and even in Santo Domingo back in 1965, too. A strong plea also arose for a jump into

Iraq in 1991 during the Gulf War.[54] None of these came to pass. Does close count?

Apparently, it does. Those facing the 82d are the main reasons it rarely jumps. Here's a case in point. Raoul Cédras and the rulers of militant Haiti discounted every U.S. threat until they received definitive word that the 82d Airborne was in the air, coming to drop waves of tough LGOPs all over the Haitian strongmen and their tinpot army. American envoy Gen. Colin Powell told Cédras face-to-face: "They are already in the air. The entire division is on the way."[55] Cédras threw in the towel. The 82d turned back, mission accomplished without firing one shot.

That is real fighting power.

It's the reason America pays to keep the Red Devils of 1/504 and all their brothers fed, watered, and walked, on the leash, just in case. Transcontinental forced entry offers a terrific tool for senior commanders and the civilian political leadership. But in the end, it works because bad guys don't want to be on the ground some night when Andy Slatniske and Joe Sedach drop in, along with a couple thousand of their closest friends.

Notes

The epigraph comes from Robert A. Heinlein, *Starship Troopers* (New York, N.Y.: Ace Books, 1987), 4, 208.

1. All descriptions of the jump sequence have been checked against the methods found in U.S. Department of the Army, *FM 57-220 Static Line Parachuting Techniques and Training* (Washington, D.C.: U.S. Government Printing Office, 19 August 1996), especially 5-1 to 5-11 (jump commands), 10-1 to 10-10 (jumpmaster duties), and 16-13 to 16-23 (techniques specific to the C-141B Starlifter).

2. Ibid., 28-4.

3. Ray Bonds, ed., *The U.S. War Machine* (New York, N.Y.: Salamander Books, 1983), 188–89.

4. Lieutenant General Edward M. Flanagan, USA (Ret.), *Battle for Panama* (McLean, Va.: Brassey's [U.S.], Inc., 1993), 173.

5. Noris Lyn McCall, "Assessing the Role of Air Power" in Bruce W. Watson and Peter G. Tsouras, *Operation Just Cause* (Boulder, Colo.: Westview Press, 1991), 117.

6. David Maraniss, "A Trooper's Four Days in Battle," *Washington Post* (28 December 1989), A1, A29. This recounts the story of Sgt. Roy E. Burgess, Jr., of the 4th Battalion, 325th Airborne Infantry Regiment, who jumped from one of the first eight 82d Airborne transport planes to reach Panama. His account forms the basis for the opening segment of this chapter, supplemented by details discussed in Flanagan, *Battle for Panama,*171–76. See also Thomas Donnelly, Margaret Roth, and Caleb Baker, *Operation Just Cause* (New York, N.Y.: Lexington Books, 1991), 201–4.

7. Flanagan, *Battle for Panama,* 172. It took twenty-eight C-141Bs to carry the vehicle and equipment drop platforms, and three more to provide a variety of small supply containers loaded with food, ammunition, and spare parts.

8. Maraniss, "A Trooper's 4 Days in Action," A29. Interview with Lt. Col. Thomas C. Maffey, USA, Carlisle Barracks, Pa., 9 November 1997. Tom Maffey commanded Company B, 1st Battalion, 75th Ranger Regiment, during the Panama intervention. He witnessed the 82d Airborne drop on Torrijos-Tocumen.

9. Tom Clancy, *Airborne* (New York, N.Y.: Berkley Books, 1997), 23.

10. Quoted in Lt. Col. Robert D. Ramsey, III, USA, "Airborne Operations: Seizing and Holding the German Bridges at Arnhem, September 1944" in Rojer J. Spiller, ed., *Combined Arms in Battle since 1939* (Fort Leavenworth, Kans.: U.S. Army Command and General Staff College Press, 1992), 9.

11. Ronald H. Cole, Joint History Office, *Operation Just Cause: The Planning and Execution of Joint Operations in Panama, February 1988–January 1990* (Washington, D.C.: U.S. Government Printing Office, 1995), 18–24.

12. David C. Isby, *Weapons and Tactics of the Soviet Army* (New York, N.Y.: Jane's Publishing, Inc., 1988), 129, 387, 389–90.

13. Malcom McConnell, *Just Cause* (New York, N.Y.: St. Martin's Press, 1991), 95.

14. Flanagan, *Battle for Panama,* 171.

15. Ibid., 174.

16. Maraniss, "A Trooper's 4 Days in Action," A29; Donnelly, et al., *Operation Just Cause,* 203; 1st Sgt. Johnny R. Oliver, USA, "Paratroopers Aren't Troopers until Surrounded," *Army Times* (12 February 1990), 25. First Sergeant Oliver served with Company A, 1st Battalion, 504th Parachute Infantry Regiment.

17. Flanagan, *Battle for Panama,* 172, 174, 175; Donnelly, et al., *Operation Just Cause,* 202. According to Flanagan, the airmen made a much tougher appraisal with Army representatives present, critiquing the "featureless" approach and "black hole" of a DZ, almost impossible to find. After recounting various flying errors, the USAF review ended this way: "Bottom line: crews not trained for this."

18. Lieutenant Colonel Douglas I. Smith, *Army Aviation in Operation Just Cause* (Carlisle Barracks, Pa.: U.S. Army War College, 1992), 47–49, 59. A commander for several of the Just Cause air assaults, Smith offers firsthand insights and an objective look at all aviation missions conducted during the U.S. intervention.

19. Donnelly, et al., *Operation Just Cause,* 219; U.S. Department of the Army, Center for Army Lessons Learned (CALL), "Operation Just Cause Lessons Learned" in *CALL Bulletin 90-9* (October 1990), I-9.

20. Smith, *Army Aviation in Operation Just Cause,* 61.

21. Flanagan, *Battle for Panama*, 192.
22. Dolores DeMena, *Operation Just Cause/Promote Liberty Supplement to U.S. Army South Annual Command History, 1 October 1989 to 30 September 1990* (Fort Clayton, Panama: HQ, U.S. Army South, 1990), 262.
23. Oliver, "Paratroopers Aren't Troopers until Surrounded," 25; Flanagan, *Battle for Panama*, 194; Donnelly, et al., *Operation Just Cause*, 223.
24. *Army Times* staff, "The Architect of 'Just Cause,'" *Army Times* (12 March 1990), 68. This article reproduces a lengthy 26 February 1990 briefing given by Lieutenant General Stiner to a group of reporters. For an account of the action at Fort Amador, see Maj. Samuel S. Wood, Jr., USA, "Joint Fire Support in Low-Intensity Conflict," *Military Review* (March 1991), 16–17.
25. McConnell, *Just Cause*, 210–11; *Army Times* staff, "The Architect of 'Just Cause,'" 18.
26. Donnelly, et al., *Operation Just Cause*, 223; Smith, *Army Aviation in Operation Just Cause*, 61–62. For a discussion of female Dignity Battalion fighters, see Edilma Icaza, "I Want to Relive the Invasion with You" in Independent Commission of Inquiry on the U.S. Invasion of Panama, *The U.S. Invasion of Panama* (Boston, Mass.: South End Press, 1994), 52.
27. Flanagan, *Battle for Panama*, 194.
28. Ibid., 194.
29. Donnelly, *Operation Just Cause*, 225.
30. Cole, *Operation Just Cause*, 41. Quoting JTF South and Pentagon report logs, Cole gives the total reported enemy losses as 5 dead and 22 wounded for the assaults at Panama Viejo, Tinajitas, and Fort Cimmaron. Most of these enemy died or fell wounded at Tinajitas. There may have been others. The official estimate of hostile dead for the entire conflict totals 324, but only 50 identified PDF bodies were recovered. Enemy dead for all of Just Cause may have been as low as 53. See Lt. Col. Lorenzo Crowell, USAF (Ret.), "The Anatomy of Just Cause: The Forces Involved, the Adequacy of Intelligence, and Its Success as a Joint Operation" in Bruce W. Watson and Peter G. Tsouras, *Operation Just Cause* (Boulder, Colo.: Westview Press, 1991), 95.

31. Oliver, "Paratroopers Aren't Troopers until Surrounded," 25; Donnelly, et al., *Operation Just Cause*, 225.

32. Oliver, "Paratroopers Aren't Troopers until Surrounded," 25.

33. Flanagan, *Battle for Panama*, 194.

34. Center for Army Lessons Learned, *Operation Just Cause Lessons Learned*, I-19.

35. McConnell, *Just Cause*, 215.

36. Smith, *Army Aviation in Operation Just Cause*, 63–65; Flanagan, *Battle for Panama*, 207–8.

37. Flanagan, *Battle for Panama*, 77–80; Kenneth J. Jones, Roberta G. Jones, Israel Aguedas, Indira Williams, and Veronica Villanueva, *The Enemy Within: Casting Out Panama's Demon* (Panama City, Panama: Focus Publications, 1990), 81.

38. Smith, *Army Aviation in Operation Just Cause*, 129–31, 134–35. The aircraft that went out of action was not the one carrying Capt. Tom Muir but another one that took extensive tail damage from the PDF-Digbat soldiers firing from the rusty bus. Another heavily damaged aircraft was the C2 bird, which took fifteen hits all over the fuselage and in one rotor blade.

39. Flanagan, *Battle for Panama*, 41.

40. *Army Times* staff, "The Architect of 'Just Cause,'" 14.

41. U.S. Department of Defense, *Joint Publication 3-0: Doctrine for Joint Operations* (Washington, D.C: U.S. Government Printing Office, 1 February 1995), IV-11. For another example, see U.S. Department of the Army, *FM 100-5 Operations* (Washington, D.C.: U.S. Government Printing Office, 14 June 1993), 6-7–8, which also says that U.S. units "simultaneously hit targets in 26 separate locations." It is unclear why the Army field manual discussed only twenty-six targets; all other sources agree on the number twenty-seven.

42. There are many examples of such criticism. See Tacitus (pseudonym), "Few Lessons Were Learned in Panama Invasion: Just Cause Victory Came Despite Ineptitude," *Armed Force Journal* (June 1993), 54–56; McConnell, *Just Cause*, 192–93; Flanagan, *Battle for Panama*, 231. Bob Woodward, *The Commanders* (New York, N.Y.: Simon & Schuster, 1991), 165, recounts that the chief of naval operations, Adm. Carlisle Trost, "was pretty certain this was all designed to make sure that the maximum number of troops received their combat

jump badges." It was a source of "much private amusement" for the senior naval officer.

43. Smith, *Army Aviation in Operation Just Cause*, 133.

44. De Mena, *Operation Just Cause/Promote Liberty Supplement*, 23. For an account of the 82d's airlanding in Grenada, see Peter M. Dunn and Bruce W. Watson, ed., *American Intervention in Grenada* (Boulder, Colo.: Westview Press, 1985), 104. It took more than twenty-four hours to bring all three infantry battalions of the 82d's lead brigade into Grenada.

45. Task Force Hawk consisted of elements drawn from in-country Army aviation and crews and aircraft brought in from 7th Infantry Division (Light) at Fort Ord, California. Another battalion-sized aviation task force carried out air assaults at H hour at Cerro Tigre, Madden Dam, and Renacer Prison. Attack choppers from the 82d Airborne Division and 7th Infantry Division made up TF Wolf. A fourth aviation force from the 160th Special Operations Aviation Regiment (Airborne) conducted all rotary-wing special operations missions.

46. Prior to H hour, American infantry in country totaled six battalions [1-508th Airborne, 5-87th Infantry, 6th Marine Expeditionary Battalion, 4-17th Infantry, 3-504th Airborne, and 4-6th Infantry (Mechanized)]. The 75th Ranger Regiment dropped two battalions (less one company) at Rio Hato and one battalion (plus one company) at Torrijos-Tocumen. The 1st Brigade, 82d Airborne Division, brought in three battalions. By late 20 December, five more infantry battalions began arriving, part of the 7th Infantry Division (Light).

47. Flanagan, *Battle for Panama*, 183–91, 208; Center for Army Lessons Learned, *Operation Just Cause Lessons Learned*, II-23.

48. The organizational details here and following come from U.S. Department of the Army, *FM 101-10-1/1 Staff Officers' Field Manual Organizational, Technical, and Logistical Data, Volume 1* (Washington, D.C.: U.S. Government Printing Office, October 1987), 4-46–53, 4-138–139, and U.S. Department of the Army, *FM 7-8 Infantry Rifle Platoon and Squad* (Washington, D.C.: U.S. Government Printing Office, 22 April 1992), A-2. Over time, assigned strengths of airborne infantry battalions (as with all units) vary. The total has ranged from 650 to 700 in recent years. The 697 strength was in use during Operation Just Cause.

49. Wood, "Joint Fire Support in Low-Intensity Conflict," 15.

50. Clancy, *Airborne*, 63–77; Hans Halberstadt, *Airborne* (Novato, Calif.: Presidio Press, 1988), 34–55.

51. Clancy, *Airborne*, 97.

52. Observer-controllers at the U.S. Army's Joint Readiness Training Center at Fort Polk, Louisiana, see every dismounted infantry battalion in the force as they rotate through on exercises. Most of these experienced officers and NCOs note that the 82d Airborne paratroopers and their helilifted 101st Airborne brothers are absolutely overwhelming on the initial forced entry missions but are often less skilled in infantry fieldcraft compared to lightfighters from the 10th Mountain and 25th Infantry Divisions.

53. On the Sukchon-Sunchon operation, see Clay Blair, *The Forgotten War* (New York, N.Y.: Times Books, 1987), 361; for the Munsan-ni drop of 1951, see Lt. Col. Roy E. Appleman, AUS (Ret.), *Ridgway Duels for Korea* (College Station, Tex.: Texas A&M University Press, 1990), 383. Regarding the 2/503 Airborne assault, see Lt. Col. Andrew F. Krepinevich, USA (Ret.), *The Army and Vietnam* (Baltimore, Md.: Johns Hopkins Uinversity Press, 1984), 191.

54. Lawrence A. Yates, *Leavenworth Paper #15: Power Pack: U.S. Intervention in the Dominican Republic* (Washington, D.C.: U.S. Government Printing Office, July 1988), 69. As in Haiti and Grenada, the 82d headed for Santo Domingo rigged to jump. For the 82d's near jump in Grenada, see Sgt. Patrick J. O'Kelly, USA, "So I Gave It a Shot" in Kesharu Imai, ed., *D-Day in Grenada* (Tokyo, Japan: World Photo Press, 1984), 82. On the decision not to parachute-assault in the Gulf War, see Rick Atkinson, *Crusade* (Boston, Mass.: Houghton Mifflin Company, 1993), 146.

55. Clancy, *Airborne*, 194–95. Of course, General Powell exaggerated a bit. Even with nearly 150 C-130E/H model Hercules and C-141B Starlifter transports, only the division's assault echelon could jump. This consisted of the trigger pullers and just enough headquarters and service strength to get through the forced entry. The Rangers also had a major jump scheduled.

Chapter 2: Stormbringers

One moment it's peaceful; the next moment they've got a whole brigade on them.

—Cmd. Sgt. Maj. Jim Arrabondo

Lieutenant Colonel Frank Hancock knew something bad was hiding on the objective. The more the intelligence types said otherwise, the more he became convinced that the Iraqi Army would be there, dug in and ready to fight. All the bombing, the leaflet drops, and the prisoner interrogations suggested otherwise. And all of that meant exactly nothing if these particular bad guys missed muster on the intell scoreboard, then decided to duke it out. The brigade S-2 promised him: "Sir, there's no enemy in Cobra."[1] But it was like the Force in *Star Wars*. Hancock had a bad feeling about this. He just knew.

On the morrow, in the predawn gloom, Hancock's 1st Battalion, 327th Infantry Regiment, would join three other similar infantry outfits from the 1st Brigade, 101st Airborne Division (Air Assault), to kick off the ground phase of Operation Desert Storm. They would be among the first Americans to enter Iraq with the intention of staying. Planners billed it as the largest, deepest mass heliborne attack in history. If it worked out, these Screaming Eagles would fly some sixty miles into Iraq, hurdling over the enemy's border guards and frontline units. The men of the Always First Brigade intended to establish Forward Operating Base (FOB) Cobra, a giant desert fuel and ammunition dump. Its location had been chosen based on three factors: the range of the CH-47D Chinook heavy hauler helicopters, the suitability of the soil to handle lots of rotary-wing aircraft without killer dust clouds, and the distance to the next set of objectives.[2] The big patch of desert floor known as Cobra met all those criteria.

Once up and running, the big service station at FOB Cobra permitted follow-on maneuvers to cut the main Iraqi reinforcement and withdrawal route, Highway 8 along the Euphrates River. It would also put Screaming Eagles within striking distance of Baghdad, Saddam Hussein's capital, center stage in his web of political-military power.[3] If done right, it could wrap up the entire campaign with a few decisive giant steps.

That all hinged on taking Cobra, which depended on Frank Hancock and his fellow air-assault infantrymen. Brought in by helicopters, they had to do the job way out there, well beyond the phalanxes of crawling tanks, past the reach of the long guns, even outside the arc of the shrieking multiple launch rocket system (MLRS) volleys already known as Steel Rain on both sides of this war. But if the weather went to hell, or the American-led Coalition ground attack stalled, or the Iraqis were on FOB Cobra and ripped up the 1st Brigade—if any of that, or several other equally horrible things (chemicals, for one) happened—the Screaming Eagles would be stuck out there in Indian country, surrounded and in mortal peril.

A French Army liaison captain saw the risk instantly. Briefed on the operation, he responded, "I think your plan is like the movie, you know, *A Bridge Too Far*."[4] He referred to a film recounting the great Allied airdrop of 1944 in Holland, drawing on Cornelius Ryan's superb book of the same title. In it, three airborne divisions jumped and glided down to take a series of bridges to allow British armored regiments to race into northern Germany and thus end the war in Europe. The drops worked. But the armored linkups did not. Assailed by swarming German forces, many of whom were discounted or missed by Allied intelligence experts who were certain that their enemy's morale had broken, the airborne divisions were carved up. The tank relief force stalled and sputtered against strong resistance. Badly bloodied American 101st and 82d troopers took their bridges and held on until the ground forces finally arrived. The British 1st Airborne Division took its objective, too, the great highway bridge at Arnhem that spanned the Rhine River. But the British paratroopers and glidermen succumbed to relentless German counterattacks and lost the bridge and 7,758 of 10,005 men, including most of the 1st Polish Airborne Brigade as well.[5] The armored forces just could not get through to that last bridge.

Would Cobra be the same?

It could be. The same "ifs" held sway: weather, enemy on the objective, the pace of follow-up armored attacks, the enemy will to resist. A few wrong guesses and 1st Brigade might share the fate of the British at Arnhem. Everyone in the 101st knew that they had done all the proper calculations, carried out the right reconnaissance, sent enough fighting power. And yet, Field Marshal Bernard Law Montgomery had done the same in 1944, hadn't he? It wasn't a comforting thought.

The intelligence picture did not look as clear then as it looks now. We all know that the Iraqi Army folded like a house of cards in the face of the Coalition ground offensive. Because we remember how the Gulf War ended, we sometimes forget that none of that was preordained. True, the aerial bombing wreaked tremendous damage, especially to enemy morale. But until Americans met Iraqis in close combat, we did not know for sure how the war would turn out.

In the 101st Airborne area, the rather murky view matched the warnings of Karl von Clausewitz, a pretty good S-3/G-3–operations sort long before he became the revered author of *On War*. Having put up with enough of the usual half-baked guesstimates of enemy activities in the Napoleonic Wars, Clausewitz drew a hard line. "Many intelligence reports in war are contradictory," he warned, "even more are false, and most are uncertain."[6] That doesn't leave much room for accuracy, does it?

Karl would not be surprised by the picture painted for Frank Hancock and his Bulldogs of 1-327th. The Iraqi 45th Infantry Division defended this chunk of Iraq, including what Hancock and his men knew as FOB Cobra. Made up of Iraqi reservists recalled for the war, the 45th disposed four fighting brigades: the 841st, 842d, 843d, and 17th Border Guards, backed by two artillery battalions, the 642d (152mm towed howitzers) and 951st (with 130mm field guns) and the 54th Tank Battalion, with its old T-55 models.[7] Most of that seemed to be over in the west, in the zone of the French 6th *Division Légère Blindée* (light-armored division). But who really knew?

The intelligence community trusted imagery, all kinds of pictures, good old hard data. Seeing is believing, say the G-2 folks. These views

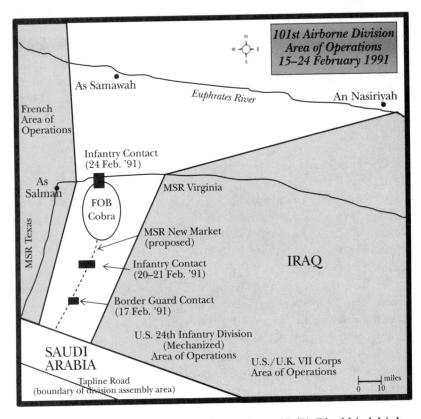

101st Airborne Division
Area of Operations
15–24 February 1991

As Samawah

Euphrates River

An Nasiriyah

French
Area of
Operations

Infantry Contact
(24 Feb. '91)

As
Salman

MSR Virginia

FOB
Cobra

MSR New Market
(proposed)

MSR Texas

Infantry Contact
(20–21 Feb. '91)

IRAQ

Border Guard Contact
(17 Feb. '91)

U.S. 24th Infantry Division
(Mechanized)
Area of Operations

SAUDI
ARABIA

U.S./U.K. VII Corps
Area of Operations

miles

Tapline Road
(boundary of division assembly area)

0   10

filtered down from satellites and streaking SR-71 Blackbird high-altitude recon jets, not to mention soaring U-2R/TR-1 spy planes, plus a bunch of other even more secret electronic eyes and ears floating in orbit or nibbling at Iraqi airspace. Analysts delighted in showing incredibly detailed views of individual enemy tanks and trucks driving or parking. Stories went around about being able to read license plate numbers or count ammunition round by round. Even the privates in the rifle squads heard about this impressive reconnaissance. And why not? Hollywood productions routinely depict the capability, so it must be true. With this imagery, picking out the stuff in and around FOB Cobra should have been a simple matter.

Well, reality does not exactly match intelligence officer hype or movie screenplays. As Marine general Joseph P. Hoar remarked later, "You don't have to be a rocket scientist to figure out when the imagery comes through."[8] In other words, we had showed Iraq enough of our pictures during their 1980–88 war against Iran. They knew how to track our collectors and hide from our surveillance systems. And they did.

Above Frank Hancock's level, lots of guys were sifting around for Iraqis in the overhead photographs procured by division intelligence. Some items looked interesting. Trained interpreters haggled over possible bunkers, potential trenches, and suspected trucks. To most soldiers, the photos might just as well have showed the floor of Death Valley, a microscopic close-up of a parking lot, or the back side of the planet Mercury—all cracks and hardpan and minor rollovers of rock, seemingly devoid of life. But that 45th Infantry Division was out there somewhere. The photo gurus could not find it.[9] So the Screaming Eagles started hunting Iraqis the only sure way—with men, just like Jeb Stuart in the Civil War. Helicopters stood in for horseflesh, but the idea was as old as combat itself.

Just after midnight on 17 February, patrolling attack aircraft located "something" on a fold of ground about a third of the way between the Saudi-Iraqi border and what would become FOB Cobra. In the dark, the AH-64A Apaches saw flashlights and bodies. It could have been Bedouin nomads—that seemed probable. But just in case, another Apache flight went forward at dawn, with instructions to "develop the situation," Army verbiage meaning find out what was really there. That often entailed shooting.

This time was no exception. Two AH-64As sighted what looked like bunkers on an escarpment, near the grid coordinates of the night contact. It was hard to tell. The Iraqis rivaled the mythical Mole Men of *Flash Gordon* fame. They burrowed deep and hid well. One pilot later commented, "You could fly right over a bunker complex and not even know it." As for all those high-tech satellite views, "We get absolutely zilch on intelligence."[10] So the fliers resorted to the tried and true method, cavalry style. They made their own. One bird aligned a likely smudge in the sights and popped off a Hellfire missile. The thing zipped into the hole and blew off a dirt-covered lid. A pall of dust hung in the early-morning air.

That brought a reaction, all right. One, two, three figures scrambled up, finally ten in all, several frantically waving white rags. One Hellfire was enough. They wanted to surrender.

Of course, how could a pair of two-man Apache attack helos handle this?

It took a platoon of Pathfinders—teams of infantry assigned to the aviation forces and specially schooled to mark LZs—to streak in aboard two UH-60A Blackhawks and make the pickup. The prisoners turned out to be a captain and his headquarters from 2d Company, 2d Battalion, 17th Border Guard Brigade. These characters proved pretty talkative, volunteering the news that there were other elements of their parent 45th Division in the 101st Airborne's zone, including line battalions of the 841st and 843d Infantry Brigades.[11] The first ten Iraqis sure looked harmless, and they hadn't even been bombed by the Coalition air armada. One Hellfire shot broke their will like a dry stick.

Later that day, more 101st choppers flushed thirty-one more prisoners. They gave up after a single pass of Apaches firing 30mm rounds. This time, the aviators called in riflemen from Company C, 3d of the 502d Infantry, to herd the dispirited hostiles aboard Blackhawks.[12] Also from the 17th Border Guard Brigade, they, too, told of more battalions due north, loosely grouped around the town of As Salman. That collection of cinder-block hovels formed the major objective for the French division to the west, so the friendly light armor promised to engage most of these bad guys. But if the loquacious Iraqi border guards were right, one of these enemy ground units might be smack on the north end of FOB Cobra, squatting on 1-327th's LZs.

Further scouting unearthed one of the missing Iraqi battalions about halfway to FOB Cobra; it was positioned properly according to Iraqi doctrine, right behind the border guard screen. With some of that screen in Screaming Eagle POW cages spilling the beans, it took the division another day to pinpoint a much larger set of bunkers, numbering an unlucky thirteen. Army aviators saw some fifty vehicles, both military and civilian, plus mortars, generators, and two or three ZPU-4s—wicked black four-barreled 14.5mm antiaircraft guns. Reports from passing Air Force pilots agreed with this assessment. These targets demanded immediate attention, and not just to take another strip off the unlucky Iraqi 45th Division.

In the bigger scheme, once FOB Cobra went in, American engineers planned to create main supply route (MSR) New Market to link the Saudi assembly areas with the new airhead. That would allow huge fuel trucks to trundle north and feed the 101st's fleet of thirsty aircraft. But the only decent route went directly through this fortification. Due to rocky outcrops and soft sand, going right or left wasn't an option. No, this bunch of enemy had to be crushed now, before the air assault started.

Here, the 101st Airborne had to be careful. Up in Gen. H. Norman Schwarzkopf's U.S. Central Command headquarters, the idea was to convince Saddam Hussein's minions that the main ground offensive would come straight up the coast into Kuwait. Then, as Baghdad fixated on the Kuwaiti shoreline roads, the entire weight of the U.S. XVIII Airborne Corps and VII Corps would boil up far to the west, swinging around an unguarded enemy flank that dribbled off into the desert, tailing down to isolated, slipshod reserve outfits such as the 45th Infantry Division. To date, the Iraqi high command showed no knowledge of the multiple U.S. Army formations that had moved west to get in place for the great wheeling attack. A lot of preliminaries way out west in 101st territory sort of spoiled the surprise. It might even tip off the Iraqis to shift their Republican Guard mobile forces.[13] Much as the Screaming Eagles wanted to reach north and eliminate the inhabitants of the thirteen bunkers, they could not launch a major push and take the ground. No, it had to be the old in-out, an aviation strike, so it might look akin to the rest of the air war currently ripping the innards out of the Iraqi military.

After finally getting approval from XVIII Airborne Corps, the division sent in a daylight raiding party on 20 February. Built around an AH-1F Cobra attack battalion optimized for day fighting, the task force also included some Apaches. Two pairs of U.S. Air Force A-10A Thunderbolt II Warthogs joined the lineup. These ungainly armored ground-attack jets carried big loads of 30mm cannon rounds, racks of cluster bomblet dispensers, and good old Mk-82 five-hundred-pound bombs. Standing by in Saudi Arabia on division pickup zones, a psyops broadcast section on a UH-60A Blackhawk and a POW guard and interrogation team aboard four CH-47D Chinooks waited to be called forward. Finally, the aviators also had a rifle company (Company B, 1-187th Infantry) and affiliated Blackhawks on alert at a Saudi PZ, to go in and clear bunkers the old-fashioned way, if necessary.[14]

It proved necessary. The Iraqis of 1st Battalion, 841st Infantry Brigade, were not border guards but real infantry, veterans of the war with Iran and counterinsurgent scraps with the Kurds. They hung in there for six hours, despite teams of Cobra and Apache helicopters sweeping over at will, punching off dozens of TOW and Hellfire missiles, hundreds of 70mm unguided rockets, and thousands of cannon shots. Directed by Army fliers, the Air Force Warthog drivers dropped bomb after bomb, some right into bunker apertures. The bunker complex spat up fountains of sand and dirt. Several erupted in secondary explosions. There was even some disjointed return fire—and no sign of surrender.

The 101st aviators upped the ante. Ceasing fire, they called in the psyops team, which buzzed the silent, smoking Iraqi trench lines. The chopper dumped bundles of leaflets and tried to use a backpack loudspeaker to ask the Iraqis to quit. This produced nothing. Maybe the Iraqis could not even hear the Arabic words over the rotor wash. So the Blackhawk pulled away and settled down on a nearby ridge. The scattered surrender leaflets blew across the bunkers, unheeded. The 101st attack birds hovered just out of range, waiting to restart the deadly deluge.

The speaker team dismounted from the helicopter, set up beyond the whirling rotor disk, and began a live announcement.[15] A head popped up out of the dirt, then another, then more. Arms raised, white cloths waving, dozens of Iraqis came out of their holes. Within minutes, there were hundreds of Iraqis above ground, weaponless, ready to give up.

The aviators brought in their infantry, the 1-187th, and that's when the fun started. The riflemen landed and it became pretty clear that about forty or so Iraqis weren't keen on giving up. Masked by the flock of prisoners, these diehards fought back. It took a bunker-to-bunker fight to clean them out. This eventually required all three rifle companies from Lt. Col. Hank Kinnison's infantry battalion. "Those hard-core guys clearly did not want to surrender," Kinnison remarked later.[16] So the air assault grunts convinced them with aimed fire and a few hand grenades. Four Iraqis were wounded in this sharp skirmish. Ominously, the prolonged aerial barrage had not scratched a single Iraqi soldier.

Even so, the raid was a real coup. The division hauled out 423 prisoners and went back the next day and found 13 more, plus four ZPU-4 guns, six 120mm mortars, and all the rest of the Iraqi battalion's impedimenta. Coalition airpower had missed this battalion until the 101st Airborne found it. The enemy position told an interesting story, all right. Iraqi resupply came intermittently, but nobody was starving and the equipment worked. Every weapon had a liberal stock of ammunition. The bunkers were sound and cleverly built. These soldiers had the means to fight.

But for most, the will was lacking. When questioned, the Iraqi leadership, including the battalion commander, painted a sorry picture. Although the unit was deployed with 618 men in November 1990, desertions, disciplinary executions, and a few casualties from disease had sapped its strength down to the 436 captured on 20–21 February 1991. The unit had been pretty much cut off from its parent brigade since late January due to the destruction of Baghdad's military communications network by relentless Coalition air strikes. Ground couriers had to resort to civilian trucks to avoid rampaging American fighter-bombers. This lack of information, more than anything else, ruined the battalion's morale. Rumors ran wild, few of them good. The reserve officers joined the grumbling. Nobody trained or sought action. Instead, they became soft, squishy tunnel dwellers—Mole Men—and showed about as much fight as those rodents when finally struck by people who meant business.

Abandoned by their higher headquarters, the majority of the Iraqi officers and men showed no stomach for close combat with Americans. One fifty-four-year reservist sergeant spoke for many: "I myself fought for eight years during the war against Iran, where I was wounded four times. In that war, all of my seven sons were sacrificed for Saddam, for nothing. I would gladly kill Saddam myself for what he has done to Iraq."[17] So much for the vaunted "battle-hardened" rank and file of the "fourth largest army in the world."

Hearing these kinds of reports, so out of whack with the capabilities portrayed by the intelligence experts before now, 101st commander Maj. Gen. J. H. Binford Peay III checked these prisoners himself. He talked to the battalion commander and several others. He was unimpressed. "This wasn't the NVA [North Vietnamese

Army] in front of us," he decided. Peay called another division commander and opined that "this thing will roll a lot quicker than we thought" because "the will to fight was not there."[18] Well, so be it. Maybe this would be a cakewalk.

Perhaps Frank Hancock should have quit worrying. The bad guys might just cave in. But he knew about the forty or so who didn't knuckle under. What if they had a few shoulder-launched antiair missiles or a ZPU-4 full of ammo? What then? All those TOWs and Hellfires and bombs killed exactly nobody. The rifles and machine guns did the damage. At the General Peay level, it all came out in the wash. At the Frank Hancock level and below, his men would be going into those bunkers and trenches, eye to eye in the dusty gloom.

And there looked to be some of that in store, too. Aerial recon over FOB Cobra proper disclosed another one of those suspicious escarpments, a low brow sloping down to overlook MSR Virginia, that grandiosely named strip of macadam road that rimmed Cobra's northern boundary. Surveying this dominant high ground, some of the Apache pilots thought they saw bunkers and trenches. Others disagreed. The intelligence people came down squarely on both sides and called it a "possible" position. That sounded typically vague. For sure, though, the Apache videotapes revealed some kind of "log [logistics] site" about two miles north of the "possible" trench-bunker area.

That did it for Lt. Col. Frank Hancock. Something was there that shouldn't be there. Intelligence expertise be damned, thought the infantry leader. After all, the smart, confident, young analysts would not be getting out of Blackhawks within rifle range of this problem. They could afford to be smug.

If the Bulldogs of 1-327th stuck with the plan as briefed and rehearsed, the battalion's Company A intended to land within a few hundred yards of that possible rack of emplacements. As Hancock's own intelligence people put it, "The Iraqis would not have constructed the trench line without some plan of occupying it."[19] To land as planned appeared to ensure a gunfight right from H hour, with all the attendant pain. The Screaming Eagles had plenty of desert to play with; FOB Cobra spanned almost 125 square miles. Why not back off a few miles and give the 1-327th some room to fire and maneuver? One stretch of Iraqi hardpan pretty much equaled another.

That sounded smart to Frank Hancock and his men. But one echelon higher, at 1st Brigade, it did not seem like such an obvious answer. The entire 1st Brigade—four complete infantry battalions, hundreds of chopper crews, artillerymen, engineers, signalers, and scores of supply soldiers bearing fuel apparatus—all knew the FOB Cobra landing scheme by heart. They had walked through it, run through it, and refined matters over and over. Now, on the eve of battle, a battalion commander wanted to jack everything around, reshuffling LZs, supporting fire schedules, and maneuver laydowns based on a hunch.

It fell to the brigade commander, Col. James T. (Tom) Hill, to make a hard choice. He could follow his own intelligence staff's (and division's) optimistic forecast and go as planned, leaving the great blueprint undisturbed. Or he could go with his gut instinct, born of service in Vietnam as a young officer in this same 101st Airborne Division. Hill had heard the same reports as Hancock. Back the staff or trust a commander's judgment? Hill made the tough call.

Together, Hancock and Hill moved 1-327th's northern landing zone (LZ 1) about a mile and a quarter south.[20] Here, the innate flexibility of air assault forces paid great dividends. They train for exactly these kinds of bold shifts. Working from a solid air mission checklist, the brigade's aviators and infantrymen made the necessary corrections to accommodate the altered landing plan and got the word out to all concerned. Well-known landing patterns and off-loading drills needed only minimal adjustments; flight routes were tweaked accordingly, and the supporting fire scheme got updated.

All this work kept leaders busy that last night before battle, but it seemed worth it to get a clean landing, out of enemy small-arms range. Once down and set, let the badniks take their shots and launch their counterattacks. But then, they would fight on Screaming Eagle terms, on death ground of American choosing.

Of course, in daylight, any opposition in that trench could still get some clear shots at Frank Hancock's Company A coming in on LZ 1. But luckily, the great air assault into FOB Cobra would launch at 0520 local, landing before first light at 0600. The Bulldogs of 1-327th would be among the Iraqis before the sun rose.[21] Flying at night made it all workable.

Like their All-American brothers en route to Panama in Just Cause, the Screaming Eagles played hell with weather at the moment of truth in Desert Storm. A dense fog arose from the chill desert floor and hung like a shroud over the flight routes that connected PZs to LZs. Scout choppers struggled aloft after midnight, feeling their way slowly across the border. At 0330, an OH-58D Kiowa Warrior bounced into a dune, wrecking the aircraft and injuring all three aboard. Although Apache pilots could see through the murk using their trademark forward-looking infrared (FLIR) eyepieces, Blackhawk crews using more conventional image-intensifying night-vision goggles reported "no fly" conditions. So General Peay delayed dispatching his Pathfinders and attack choppers for an hour, which automatically bumped H hour from 0600 to 0700. The fog remained as thick as ever, and the time slid to 0800.[22] Like the 1-504th Red Devils at Tinajitas, the 1-327th Bulldogs would be moving in broad daylight.

Few of the riflemen in Lieutenant Colonel Hancock's battalion had been under fire. They spent the night near their helos, many talking quietly, most too keyed up to sleep. The more experienced soldiers knew what the fog meant as soon as it rolled over the PZs. The word came down: Back off one hour. Then, after another stretch, they were told to wait another hour. The men fingered their weapons and exchanged glances. Forget about the cover of darkness. Iraqi gunners would see them coming tens of miles out, and the range of a ZPU-4 quad-barreled or DShK heavy machine gun ran to more than four miles (ouch). If the enemy got serious, a lot of birds would get hit. It might get pretty grisly.

The Bulldogs knew they'd go anyway. "It turned up the tension a notch or two," deadpanned Capt. John Russell, whose Company A faced the prospect of cleaning out those possible positions to the north.[23] Send a bullet, not a man. The bullets had all been sent. Now, it was time for the men.

The great air assault finally began at 0720, two hours late, but now unhampered by the clearing banks of fog. Assembling like a World

War II bomber formation, the great flying flotilla shook out into strings of like aircraft, each set of three to five following its flight leader. Once aligned, the birds headed north, led by heavily armed AH-64A Apaches and nimble Kiowa scouts. It was an awesome spectacle. Ground troops waved and showed thumbs-up as dozens of black-green choppers roared overhead, bound for battle.

The view from inside this flying array was no less exciting. "After we crossed the border escarpment," recalled Cmd. Sgt. Maj. Robert Nichols, "our Blackhawks flew around ten feet over the desert. I looked out of the bird. As far as the eye could see to our left, right, and rear, more than 300 helicopters were flying north into Iraq." Although Bob Nichols exaggerated a bit on altitude (they were not quite that low) and numbers (he overestimated by a factor of two), he surely got the atmospherics dead right. In training, such a mass heliborne lift happened at night, and the average soldier saw the guys next to him only after the aircraft touched down. But now, in the opening round of Desert Storm, the division took a risk and launched in daytime. All in all, the 101st Airborne committed sixty-six Blackhawks and thirty Chinooks. The goal was to land four infantry battalions and all the rest smack on FOB Cobra, the biggest of big footprints.[24] Turning back was not an option. Like the 82d at Tinajitas, they were going in, Iraqis or no Iraqis.

Aboard the aircraft, the men knelt, squatted, and sprawled, wedged in atop one another like an especially squirming brand of cordwood. They rode without seats, a cramping agony with an average of fifteen trigger pullers per UH-60A. For the Bulldogs of 1-327th, this first wave went aboard twenty-four Blackhawks, eight per rifle company. It took some ingenuity to cram in these men with their hundred-pound rucksacks, bulging with the usual water and ammunition, a nod to their paratrooper heritage. (Their 82d Airborne brothers would understand and sympathize.) In addition, each bird carried three full five-gallon water cans and a grunt home bunker kit: 750 empty sandbags, 8 long metal pickets to shore up walls and roofs, 8 sheets of plywood to put on the pickets, and 4 shovels and picks to dig, dig, dig. The Bulldogs intended to defend FOB Cobra against any Iraqi counterattack. They brought the right tools. But it made for a very uncomfortable ride. More than one man literally ached to land.

Not everything fit in the Blackhawks. The battalion's antiarmor firepower rode on eight armed Company D Humvees gingerly backed into four twin-rotored CH-47D Chinooks. On landing, these hard-shelled trucks would bounce out the helo's back ramp and provide TOW antitank missile fires on the outer perimeter. Two communications Humvees flew in similar style on another Chinook, and an ambulance full of medical supplies went alone in another. Normally, trucks going in with CH-47Ds dangle on sling ropes, hooked below the aircraft's belly. On this initial assault, though, going inside made a lot of sense; it increased the Chinooks' airspeed, cut fuel consumption, and reduced dust brownout when the Chinooks hovered to release their external loads. In addition, the loads were not exposed to fire. Without the protection of darkness, it seemed like a smart decision.

The tough choice, unlikely except under the pressures of combat, came at a cost. Peacetime safety concerns did not allow it, but after all, the 101st Airborne was at war, and some chances had to be accepted. Like astronauts on the launchpad, the drivers and crews got sealed into their vehicles before takeoff. There was no room to get out of a Humvee once it had been shoehorned into a Chinook.[25] Plus, the men could not see much beyond the green inside hull of the aircraft, and that only through the windshield of the truck. Claustrophobes need not apply. If one of the big double-rotored birds went down—well, nobody wanted to think about that. These men did not enjoy their ride into Iraq either. They longed for escape, for the blessed ground, home of the happy infantryman.

What awaited them up at Cobra? The intelligence staffers said not much, or nothing.

They got that wrong.

Vietnam veteran Bob Nichols, aboard the third Blackhawk in the formation, picks up the story.

As we flew closer to our touchdown point, we were given "fifteen minutes . . . ten minutes . . . five minutes . . ." We could see the horizon, black with smoke from explosions. Our Apache helicopters were attacking an Iraqi battalion in the target sector. Fears, hopes, and dreams flash through a soldier's mind within moments of combat.[26]

The bad guys were there, all right, and in battalion strength, just north of the 1-327th area. And they sure did not seem to be surrendering, either.

Not that they lacked for persuasion; the AH-64As and Air Force A-10A Warthogs spun and dove over the escarpment fronting MSR Virginia, pummeling the Iraqi defenders. The Frank Hancock nightmare scenario had come to pass; but thanks to the altered landing scheme, the Americans held most of the leverage. True, as feared, Iraq's 2d Battalion, 843d Infantry Brigade, held the high ground north of FOB Cobra, snuggled in on the reverse slope leading down to the roadbed. The Iraqis obviously wanted to stick it out. American aviators definitely had a tiger by the tail. An Apache staggered out of the fight, clipped by a ZPU-4. But the attack birds did the job

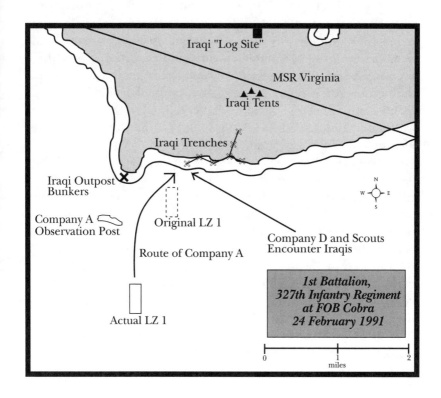

Iraqi "Log Site"

MSR Virginia

Iraqi Tents

Iraqi Trenches

Iraqi Outpost Bunkers

Company A Observation Post

Original LZ 1

Route of Company A

Company D and Scouts Encounter Iraqis

1st Battalion, 327th Infantry Regiment at FOB Cobra 24 February 1991

Actual LZ 1

0   1   2
    miles

and kept the Iraqis busy as the American riflemen landed to the south.[27] Smoke, tracers, and darting U.S. aircraft marred the northern sky.

For Hancock's Bulldogs of 1-327th, touchdown happened quickly, smoothly, almost without warning. This is the crucial juncture of an air assault, the moment when the entire venture hangs in the balance. The riflemen must dismount speedily, in thirty seconds or so, and get oriented as they do so. When they land on an objective, they may rush out a single door and go straight into the familiar fire and maneuver drill, that leapfrogging minuet of shooting and moving that constitutes the business end of infantry attacks through death ground. The fight at Tinajitas went this way.

But in other cases, as at FOB Cobra, the enemy does not effectively oppose the landing. Here, the rifle squads simply spill out both doors, race past the circle of the spinning rotors, and plop down, facing outward. Once the helos empty, the pilots gun their turbines and spring away. Then the infantrymen get up and get going, linking up with the other aircraft loads as they move swiftly off the LZ. At night, in tall grass, or under fire, it gets confusing. Assembly breaks down. Sometimes, things go completely nuts, and an airborne operation breaks out, stark chaos among the bad guys. In that case, the air assault grunts revert to heritage and go with the same kind of ad hoc LGOP tactics as their parachute infantry comrades.[28] Men simply join with the nearest friendlies and move out for the closest assault objectives, and it all gets sorted out in the morning—if ever.

All of that might have happened in Iraq on 24 February 1991, but it did not. Instead, clearly visible on the flat, stony ground, Bulldog riflemen tumbled out of their aircraft. Some dragged their bunker kits, others yanked water cans, and a few pulled on one another as the Blackhawks increased power, then tilted forward and departed. "I really thought the LZ would be hot," John Russell said. "It wasn't."[29] But one look to the north told him that he had work to do. With battalion S-3 Maj. Tom Dempsey and the battalion scout platoon accompanying them, Russell and his men saddled up for the long hump to that escarpment, the beckoning death ground.

For Lt. Col. Frank Hancock, the situation demanded some decisions. Certainly, Company A had to get a grip on the bad guys, then direct fires to destroy them. But the real threat might well be to the west, toward As Salman, where the Iraqis reputedly kept the 45th Division's mobile tank reserves. So Hancock could not turn off more than Company A to deal with that troublesome trench line. The overloaded 11B10 riflemen of Companies B and C, plus the antiarmor trucks of Company D, took up their assigned perimeter, facing west and northwest. As the men are taught from day one, the mission comes first. The hostiles in the north weren't going anywhere. But a counterattack force from As Salman could ruin the entire fuel and arming activity developing at FOB Cobra.[30] So Hancock remembered his priorities and made his deployments.

The battalion commander had no idea that the enemy outnumbered his 360-man assault echelon, but he did know how to even the odds: firepower. Because the riflemen had a walk to get there, why not while away the time by sending some bullets, the smarter the better? Hancock failed to get hooked up with the Apache crews, radio communications being maddeningly flaky at this critical juncture. But by 0830, the Apaches handed off to the AH-1F Cobra outfit, and these Vietnam-era birds rapidly reported in on the 1-327th net. This provided the first definite report of what was on the escarpment, tucked neatly behind the rollover: nearly a mile of trenches—two miles or more counting all the satellite redoubts—lots of bunkers, heavy machine guns, and oodles of enemy shooting back. Behind the escarpment, about two miles to the north, stood that supposed supply dump, which Hancock now guessed to be the enemy battalion's command post (CP), and perhaps the site of the local counterattack force.[31] The entire complex would easily tie up—indeed, eat up—all the 1-327th.

And that could not happen, not today. The defense of FOB Cobra took priority. So Frank Hancock told his S-3 and Company A commander to get a patrol as close as they could immediately, to direct fires with precision, then to bring the rest of the company up for a ground assault. Laboring under their packs, the grunts could not get there before midmorning. For now, the Cobra pilots and the Air Force occupied the Iraqis' full attention.

Hancock himself did the fire coordination, talking directly to the Cobra drivers and allowing his Air Force liaison officer (ALO), Capt.

Mark Reister, to guide in the USAF war birds that began to show up on station about 0845. The Army Cobras pulled off, and two racing F-16C Fighting Falcons roared in on cue. Each jet planted a two-thousand pounder on the enemy resupply–command post to the north of the trenches and bunkers. The Cobra drivers said the Air Force pilots had put both eggs right into the target area.

As the air strike finished, the AH-1F Cobras rolled back in. Meanwhile, Capt. Joe Best flew his attack chopper to Hancock's tactical CP, near Company B's LZ 2. Best found a cluster of a dozen men and radios huddled on the desert floor within a few hundred yards of where they had landed. As air battle captain, the aviation officer had the opportunity to orchestrate the various fires on the enemy trenches, and he wanted to get it right. After dismounting, the Cobra leader compared maps with the infantry commander and decided on a plan. With a 105mm howitzer battery up and ready to fire now, they could alternate Cobras, air strikes, and artillery. Until Dempsey and Russell got close enough, the attack guys would call in all fires through Hancock, who would then let his artillery fire support officer relay them to the guns. Best understood.[32] He reboarded his helo and soared away.

The firefight certainly attracted attention beyond Frank Hancock's purview. To the east, the 3-327th had already taken a small position and captured eleven bewildered Iraqis near one of the American LZs. But other than that brief encounter, only 1-327th had a battle to win. With the rest of the landing proceeding unopposed, and Hancock's fight the only game in town, strong incentive existed for Col. Tom Hill at brigade, and General Peay at division, to intervene. But they did not. "I felt he [Hill] had it [had the situation under control]. He was asking all the right questions. Lieutenant Colonel Frank Hancock was moving his forces around correctly. Hill was ensuring that the battalion commander had the right forces in there."[33] Fully conscious that high-level meddling can screw things up, the Vietnam veteran senior commanders backed off. This fight belonged to Hancock and his Bulldogs, plus their Cobra aviator companions.

The alternating artillery, helicopter, and air-strike drill started at 0922.[34] As John Russell and his patrol worked forward, followed by the main company column, Joe Best and the Cobra fliers called in artillery missions. First, they plastered the resupply-cum-headquarters site, then the trench line. As the shells ceased bursting, Best's Cobra company again charged in, with rockets, 20mm cannons, and a few TOW missiles. They focused on the trench network.

About 1000, the lift helicopters returned, depositing Hancock's second wave, twenty-four more Blackhawks and six more Chinooks full of men and trucks, respectively. The UH-60As came in without a problem. But the Chinooks had some adventures.

The Chinook pilots flew with external loads this time. A flight of three of the big birds vectored toward the towering cloud of dust hanging over the Iraqi emplacements along MSR Virginia. Maybe they thought it marked an LZ. An Apache battalion commander, Lt. Col. Dick Cody, saw the wandering Chinooks. Without figuring out call signs, he broke in on the aviation radio net: "Three hooks [Chinooks], northbound over EA [engagement area]—turn around!" The big birds responded in their wallowing fashion, slowly banking to land their swinging loads back inside FOB Cobra. Green enemy tracers chased the trio back inside friendly airspace.[35]

The Chinook odyssey botched the 1-327th landing plan, plopping down two platoons of Company D Humvees almost five miles off their proposed LZ. Hancock wanted to use those hard-back armed Humvees to help in the impending assault on the escarpment.[36] Their heavy weapons could do a job on bunkers. Now the Bulldog commander had to wait while Capt. Allen Gill motored into position to bring his TOW missile launchers to bear on the hostile bunkers.

At about this juncture, John Russell and Tom Dempsey called in. They and their patrol had reached a vantage point that allowed a clear look down into the Iraqi emplacements. With an artillery observer in hand, they wanted to take over directing the fires on the enemy. Hancock willingly passed the baton.

The gunners back at Battery C/2d Battalion, 320th Field Artillery, fired two more battery missions. This time, the forward observation post allowed better adjustment of fall of shot. Every round did damage. Airbursts popped above the open trenches, and some shells used delayed fusing to penetrate the bunker tops. A few hits touched off secondary explosions. The Cobra crews, with Captain Best reporting, judged these rounds to be effective. Aviators do fine work; but in placing supporting fires, skilled ground force observers really get the job done.

Now the Air Force rejoined the fray. Around 1030 or so, a pair of A-10A Warthogs appeared overhead, carrying Mk-82 five-hundred-pound bombs and some cluster munitions. The 1-327th leadership held off on the cluster bomblets; they tend to leave behind some nasty grenade-sized duds, and those guaranteed trouble when the Bulldogs started clearing trenches. But the five-hundred pounders would do nicely. The AH-1F Cobra commander, Joe Best, had the best view of the trench line, so, with Hancock's okay, he guided the Warthogs on their runs. Marching in open order toward the hostile western flank, Company A went to ground as the twin-engined jets swooped down to deliver their ordnance. In their forward observation post, John Russell and his team took cover.

The Air Force jets cut loose their deadly cargo. Falling true, the bombs smashed into the lip of the escarpment. Pillars of dirt shot skyward, mixing with the oily black smoke already hanging over the bunker complex. As soon as the Warthogs pulled off, bomb racks empty, Russell and his artillery observer called in another "battery three" of artillery. Eighteen 105mm rounds arced in, a mixture of aboveground detonations to spray hot fragments and burrowing charges to turn dirt. Cobra pilots reported a slackening in ground fire, and fewer green tracers stabbed up out of the drifting smoke and dust.

Meanwhile, Company A's riflemen, up and moving under their big rucksacks, broke out into assault formation to the southwest of the Iraqi trench line. Captain Russell asked for another dose of artillery. He got it, along with a warning: After this mission, each howitzer had only one round left.[37] With no more air strikes, almost no more artillery, and the Cobras down to 20mm cannon and a few rockets, the fight now went over to John Russell and his riflemen—his nineteen-year-old 11B10s—and their will to close with the enemy. They had it in spades.

Watching from farther away, Cmd. Sgt. Maj. Bob Nichols saw the assault begin. "Our ground infantrymen were charging uphill toward the Iraqi trenches like Gettysburg," he said. The artillery rained in again. In Nichols's words, "Their airbursts over the bunkers and trenches helped to turn the tide. The Iraqis ceased to fight."[38] As the clouds of dust from the last artillery barrage rose, a few white flags showed along the enemy trench. The Iraqis had broken.

Hancock checked his watch: 1102. He had been on the ground about two and a half hours.[39] It had been both the fastest and slowest two and a half hours he had ever spent. So far, so good. Now he had to get the endgame right.

Here, the armed Humvees of Company D proved their worth. Under his battalion commander's orders, Capt. Al Gill rode forward to pick up the scout platoon, then push on toward the Iraqi position, now silent in the drifting smoke. It took a few minutes to mount up the scouts; most hung on atop the hard-backed Humvees like Russian storm troops riding tanks in old World War II newsreels.

A few more minutes dragged by as the little group of five trucks pushed slowly up the hillside. Above them, the Cobra attack birds swung in low, lazy circles, no longer firing. A few gunshots echoed, audible above the throaty Humvee diesel engines. Spread in a ragged line, the vehicles slowed. As the trucks approached the crest, the Americans looked down. Before them lay the smoking reverse-slope position, its Iraqi earthworks shrouded in yellow dust. The scouts dismounted and took up security positions, rifles trained on the curiously empty trench cuts.

Gill saw only one white flag as he dismounted. An Arab linguist with a bullhorn hopped out to stand at the captain's side. Gill smelled a trap—one of those false surrender deals, such as the Japanese on Okinawa back in 1945. He hestitated, taking it all in for a minute or so. Bunkers and trenches zigzagged down the entire slope. Not an Iraqi showed his head. The dust slowly settled. What were they up to this time?

Scouts waited for some enemy reaction. With sights trained on selected Iraqi bunkers, vigilant gunners in TOW missile trucks watched their commander. Overhead, Cobra helicopters hovered in menace. For good measure, Al Gill drew his pistol, as if that mattered; maybe it steadied his nerves. The linguist started his speech, the equivalent of "come out with your hands up." The melodic Arabic syllables echoed down the gentle incline.

A few rifles cracked, their aim off target but clearly defiant. Scouts tensed to fire back, but Gill stayed their hand. On the captain's call, a Cobra chopper overhead rippled off a series of 70mm Hydra rockets.[40] The shattering impacts rocked the hollow. That did it. Honor had been satisfied. The Iraqis scrambled out, a captain among the first dozen or so. Gill recognized him as an officer and, through the linguist, told the Iraqi leader to get the rest to quit. He did.[41] Within minutes, the emplacements above brimmed with swarthy men, hands up, minus helmets and firearms.

Hancock himself arrived on the scene by helicopter at about this time, taking advantage of a UH-1H Huey offered by brigade commander Hill. The Bulldog commander thought maybe he could haul prisoners in the aircraft. Little did he know just how many POWs he had captured.

On landing, Frank Hancock met his counterpart, Maj. Samir Ali Khader, commander of the Iraqi Army's 2d Battalion, 843d Infantry Brigade. "This was a new experience for me," recounted Hancock, "as I wasn't sure how to act—magnanimous or like a mean bastard. Since I was sure we had not captured all the Iraqis in the area, I chose the latter demeanor." Hancock knew that the enemy still held the alleged logistics site to the north. He wanted those bad guys, too.

Turning to the linguist, Hancock resorted to grunt-speak, blunt and unmistakable. "You tell this son of a bitch that he better surrender everyone or I'll bring the aircraft back and bomb them again," he barked. Even before the translation, Maj. Ali Khader got the message.[42] He willingly accompanied Maj. Tom Dempsey to the northern position, which surrendered without resistance.

The haul of enemy proved to be substantial: 339 able-bodied prisoners, 25 lightly wounded or in shock, 6 seriously injured, plus a trove of weapons, including antiaircraft guns, mortars, and small arms, not to mention 8 tons of ammunition.[43] By eliminating the Iraqi battalion, 1-327th allowed Cobra to open for business unmolested. That solid foothold permitted the 3d Brigade to air assault to the Euphrates River the next day, cutting off Iraqi retreat and imperiling Baghdad itself.

The Bulldog victory at FOB Cobra represented the commanders' victory rather than the soldiers' triumph. The latter often occurs when the chain of command succumbs to friction or guesses wrong, and then the 11B10s sort it out with their courage, skill, and blood. The soldiers certainly did everything asked, but this time their leaders—Peay, Hill, and especially Frank Hancock—made the right calls time after time. As Pfc. Ronald Guminksi of 3d Platoon, Company A, observed, "The way they were dug in, it would have been hard to take and hard to fight. It would've cost a lot of casualties."[44] He and his comrades would have been in the middle of it. But that did not happen.

Instead, Hancock and company brought down the storm on the heads of the hapless Iraqis. Shifting their LZ to "hit 'em where they ain't," the battalion got in smoothly. Then, alternating the various destructive means in the air assault inventory as his men maneuvered, Hancock and his leaders pinned and finally snapped the Iraqis. Had the enemy shown the gumption, there can be little doubt that a bunker fight would have been just as one-sided. The Iraqis bore up for hours under shot and shell but folded rather than face the grim-faced riflemen of Company A. That about says it all.

The fight at FOB Cobra stands as a prototype of air assault infantry in action, minus the finish fight, of course. Indeed, although the men of 1-187th had a decent skirmish on their 20 February raid, and several 3d Brigade companies fought some knotty ambush actions along the Euphrates highway, only the 1st of the 327th's engagement reflects the strengths—and the weaknesses—that make air assault infantry unique. Former 101st Airborne cavalry squadron commander, G-3 (division operations officer), and assistant division commander Lt. Gen. Gary Luck, who commanded XVIII Airborne Corps during the Gulf War, summed it up rather neatly: "a classic operation."[45]

What made the escarpment fight a classic? To know that requires an understanding of air assault infantry.

Although they wear the same "airborne" tab over their Screaming Eagles as the paratroopers of the 82d, the men of the 101st represent the fulfillment of the other half of the airborne heritage. In World War II, airborne meant parachutists and glider troops. Each had their utility.

The American soldiers thought of as today's airborne came from the parachute regiments of 1941–45. Paratroopers leaped into almost any open area, and some not so open. Conveyed by fixed-wing transports, they spanned vast distances. The jumpers came down intermixed, off target, and armed with whatever they could carry, plus the contents of a few cargo bundles. Like their modern descendants of the 82d Airborne, they worked best in World War II when dropped right on the objective, preferably at night. A roiling ball of confusion by nature, a parachute assault does its best work on the initial jump, mainly by imposing that same chaotic friction on the stunned enemy below. From World War II until now, this kind of warfare has demanded carefully selected and superbly trained units.

Glider soldiers brought in organized planeloads of men and equipment, including cannons, jeeps, and even some experimental light tanks by 1945. These units did not come in snarled up and scattered but landed by squads and sections, ready to get to work. They had sufficient cohesion to carry out follow-on tasks beyond simply grabbing the drop zone. With less energy expended getting organized, glider forces had a better chance to exploit a surprise descent in the enemy rear area. So went the theory.

In practice, World War II glider units proved to be only a little better than paratroopers. Because they moved at foot speed once down, they, too, did their best work when placed directly on the objective. When the assault went well, these kinds of units sailed intact into key locations and grabbed them by bold coup de main. To make the best of this capability, the Germans and British understood that gliderborne troops needed the same kind of rigorous selection and training as the parachutists. So organized, their glider infantry did yeoman service throughout World War II. The Germans at Fortress Eben Emael in May 1940 and the British at Pegasus Bridge in June 1944 took key objectives by relying on silent wings and well-chosen men.[46] They made the investment and reaped some rewards, getting about as much as they could out of their glider teams.

Contemporary U.S. leaders tried a different tack with significantly less success. Enthralled by the thought that in gliding, the towing aircraft crew and glider pilots did all the skill work, American infantry leaders wanted to use average line battalions for these kind of assaults. This logic suggested that any old guys could be packed into these engineless craft and turned loose in the things, thereby gaining most of the benefits with a minimum of extra fuss. With a typical trust in technology, the U.S. Army chose to rely on a novel wood contraption. The grunts aboard amounted to passengers. Anyone would do.

Accordingly, America's first glider riders were not carefully selected—far from it. Paratroopers chose from volunteers. Glider troops got draftees. Parachute units got specialized training, heavy on live fire and mock airborne drops. At first, glider outfits did not get any such opportunities. "No flight pay. No jump pay. But never a dull moment," as the barracks smart alecks put it.[47] Eventually, glider troops transitioned to the same selection, training, and privileges as their paratrooper brothers. But in the American airborne world, the glider gang—even brought up to high training standards—remained second-class citizens.

The real problem involved the gliders themselves. True, they brought in formed units. But there is something disquieting about starting combat by a crash. Too many gliders pancaked in, flipped over, smacked into trees, or shredded in flight. Plus, once the glider infantry touched down, they joined the parachutists in advancing at walking speed. Like paratroopers, glider fighters represented a one-shot capability. They had better be placed well, because they could not fly back out and recock for a second try. Not surprisingly, only a few U.S. infantry units actually assaulted by glider in World War II, although artillery batteries had to rely on the engineless wood crates to get their snub-nosed 105mm howitzers into action.[48] After 1945, every major power gave up on these shaky, dangerous excuses for real airplanes. Airborne came to equal parachute jumps from legitimate transport aircraft—period.

But the good things about glider tactics demanded further development. Spurred by wartime paratrooper Lt. Gen. James M. Gavin and cavalryman Lt. Gen. Hamilton H. Howze, Army aviation enthusiasts began to see a new role for the collection of light helicopters that had been doing utility duties since the Korean War. A sufficiently powerful helicopter could not only bring in assault troops, evacuate casualties, and observe supporting fires, it might also fight alongside the ground battalions, sort of like a flying tank. Gavin titled his persuasive article on the subject "Cavalry, and I Don't Mean Horses."[49] Thanks to a new concept called "airmobility," the heirs of the glider riders were about to graduate to real war steeds. The transition came in time for the Vietnam War. Technology cooperated, too. In the new UH-1 Iroquois, soon known to all as the ubiquitous Huey, airmobility found its wings. This powerful, sturdy, turbine-engined bird formed the backbone of the U.S. airmobile brigades that carried the war into the hinterlands of Vietnam from 1965 to 1973. Its direct progeny, the UH-1H, carried Frank Hancock forward to the Iraqi trenches on 24 February 1991 even as its cousin, the AH-1F Cobra, rode shotgun overhead. The UH-60A Blackhawk and AH-64A Apache carried on the roles pioneered by the Huey series in Vietnam. Rounding out the team, the CH-47D Chinook filled the same role as its earlier models did in Southeast Asia—assured heavy lift.

Airmobile infantry sprang directly from the parachute force. Indeed, the pioneering 1st Cavalry Division (Airmobile) formed around the core of the 11th Airborne Division, kept its 3d Brigade on jump status, and went to Vietnam under the command of Maj. Gen. Harry W. O. Kinnard, Screaming Eagle G-3 at the epic siege of Bastogne in 1944–45. When the expanding war in Vietnam required a second airmobile division, the 101st Airborne converted in country during 1968.[50] This conscious unity of paratrooper ethos and Army aviation kept the Viet Cong and North Vietnamese regulars on the run. If the war had been winnable, these guys might have won it.

The technique worked so well that all American and allied battalions tried airmobile operations. By midwar, everybody had access to helicopters, but not everybody knew how to use them effectively. For most American 11B10s, the chopper delivered them to battle and snatched away the wounded. Sometimes, gunships joined a firefight. But by and large, most line unit riflemen fought on their own, out in the bush. Only in the 1st Cav and 101st, and to a lesser extent with the Marines, did the partnership of grunt and aviator come to full fruition. There, the aviation fought alongside the infantry "all the way," as the airborne community says.

After the war, the 1st Cavalry Division gradually metamorphosed into a conventional armored formation. Not so the 101st; there, air-mobility took root and flourished. Under aggressive Maj. Gen. Sidney B. Berry, the division resurrected Harry Kinnard's original title for heliborne tactics, "air assault." Airmobile sounded like a good name for a flying bus. But air assault—well, as they say in the backwoods, "Them's fightin' words."

Berry also introduced the equivalent of airborne school to imbue his soldiers with the right values. Built on the model of jump school, the 101st's air assault course has been called the "Ten Toughest Days in the Army." It teaches new Screaming Eagles how to plan and carry out night combat assaults, how to sling-load trucks and other cargo, and how to exit aircraft by rappel ropes, like mountaineers bounding down a rock face. Lately, the soldiers also learn to slide down thick, springy ropes, sort of like flexible fire station poles, which get boots on the ground quickly, even in congested cities or among closely spaced trees. Between the instruction, there are long runs, speed marches, pushups, and obstacle courses, all of the usual strainers used by the Army to separate the players from the pretenders. At the end, each air assault graduate receives his coveted wings, a silver device modeled on the parachute badge, with a head-on view of a Huey replacing the traditional parachute.[51]

Unlike the jumpers in the 82d, nobody in the 101st earns any hazardous duty or proficiency pay for being air-assault qualified. In fact, officially, the badge is not even mandatory in the 101st Airborne. But in a volunteer military, peer pressure builds up. Screaming Eagles know the deal, and those who don't soon find themselves on orders to less demanding outfits. Most infantry battalions run about 90 percent qualified, with only the newest arrivals lacking their wings.

The air assault mind-set inculcated in the school teaches all division soldiers to be aviation minded. Blessed with a fleet of almost three hundred helicopters (reinforced to nearly four hundred in the Gulf War), the 101st integrates these aircraft into every operation. Grunts and aviators live cheek to jowl, and the same fliers habitually back the same ground battalions. It's worth noting that Frank Hancock passed control of fires to Cobra pilot Joe Best as willingly as he delegated it to John Russell of 1-327th's Company A. The same close relationship links Blackhawk and Chinook crews to their infantry brothers. Both groups know that the other will come. This explains why the division is not an infantry oufit with a bunch of aircraft. In the 101st Airborne, aviation holds an equal status with the rifle units. In some circumstances, the fliers take the ball; in others, the infantry has the starring role. At FOB Cobra, both parties worked well together, assisted by supporting arms, to shock and overwhelm the Iraqi defenders. That is the great strength of air assault infantry.

Borne on rotary wings, backed by speedy gunships, sustained by an aerial train, air assault riflemen go deep in force. They aim to disembowel their foes by tearing out service support facilities and command posts thought safe behind enemy lines. Intervening mountains, rivers, and cities do not impede a heliborne contingent, which skims along largely independent of the ground. Once on the LZ, the Screaming Eagles can do it again, and again, ninety-plus-mile thrusts night after night in brigade strength. Few enemies can stand up to that.

The Iraqis certainly could not. As Maj. Ali Khader told Tom Hill and Frank Hancock, he had been prepared to fight a conventional foe. But as head of the 45th Infantry Division's backstop unit, he expected contact four to five days into the ground war. The pace and ferocity of the 101st's attack bowled him over. The Americans came in too fast and too strong. Unaccustomed to the speed, violence, and scale of the U.S. air assault firepower, Ali Khader capitulated.[52] But not all enemies are so accommodating.

Air assault infantry is not invincible. Its symbiotic embrace of Army aviation inflicts several major weaknesses. Although these showed in Iraq, the enemy there lacked the willpower and skill to exploit these vulnerabilities. But some shortcomings remain and must be considered.

First, helicopters cannot press the fight in close combat. The finicky aircraft simply have too many delicate moving parts. With the aerodynamic stability of an average air conditioner, rotary-wing aircraft do not degrade gracefully when damaged. If smacked hard, they tend to beat themselves to death, along with all aboard. Even heavily armored craft such as the AH-64A Apaches cannot shrug off hits to tail rotors, instruments, or engines. Lighter Blackhawks can take some pounding; stately Chinooks can tolerate somewhat less. Speed, altitude, and terrain masking all give great protection. But when helicopters flare to land or hover to fire, they become vulnerable. True, modern choppers take batterings and survive. But they do not continue their missions very long, because engines blow out and blades shred. The birds might spare their crews and passengers, but they cannot trade bullets in death ground. Someday, maybe—but not yet.

This great weakness means that air assault infantrymen cannot blithely descend on heavily defended targets. Because that method often makes tactical sense, particularly in a raid, the grunts need to work around their aviation partners' figurative glass jaw. So air assaults almost always occur at night. The great flight to FOB Cobra became etched in many minds not only because of its import but because it happened in daylight, and the participants saw more than the aircraft or rucksack in front of them. Against the likes of Iraqi reservists, that may work. But it remains risky to go in during daylight. Frank Hancock might have found out why had he not moved his northern LZ.

To pounce in hard atop a strongpoint, air assault forces must use overwhelming, accurate firepower. The Cobras and Apaches play their parts, but the Air Force, Navy (both jets and warship cannons), Marine air, artillery, and mortars also have roles. Spotters have to get the rounds right on target—hard enough under the sun but extraordinarily tough at night, laser range finders and thermal viewers notwithstanding. When landing on a defended objective, sending bullets, not men, becomes a necessity. Unless the bullets are effective, the men in their fragile helicopters can never close the range. Even with lots of fire, it's straight death ground. Both men and helicopters will pay.

If the price appears too high, air assault infantry resorts to the measure adopted by Frank Hancock's Bulldogs and lands away from the designated target. This also works well if intelligence cannot tell pretty clearly what's up there. If you don't know, it makes eminent sense to land in a safe spot and go in on the ground, like any other light infantry formation.[53] The aerial firepower can still back you up when you make contact. That on-call attack aviation makes for a powerful equalizer in any firefight.

A related problem involves avoiding, suppressing, or destroying the opponent's air defenses. Thanks to the skill of U.S. Air Force, Navy, and Marine fighter jocks, the enemy's aircraft do not factor into the equation. Our fliers dominate the skies. Because bad guy soldiers cannot count on any air-to-air help, they use their own weapons to hit back at U.S. airpower. America's foes invest heavily in antiaircraft guns and missiles of all types. Some big weapons have their own radars. Others depend on keen-eyed men. Either type can tear up helicopters, which tend to move at relatively slow speeds and at low altitude. The Iraqis never did a good job at this kind of unit air defense, but the Vietnamese Communists and the Somali militias proved avid learners.

With this vulnerability in mind, every air assault requires a concerted effort to deal with hostile air defenses. Going in at night offers by far the surest way to obviate the whole nasty array. Day or night, staffs plan flight routes that cut through enemy weak points, skirt around hummocks and ridges to confuse and block enemy radars, and avoid known hostile antiaircraft nests. For those opposing air defenses that must be confronted, heliborne units rely on various means to get through. Electronic jammers blank out enemy radars. Aircraft, artillery, naval guns, and Apaches may hit troublesome sites, either enough to kill them or, more likely, just enough to keep their heads down and let the Americans slip past. In either case, the suppression effort never gets everyone. True, the spoofers and shooters can and do blind or knock out the big radar-slaved guns and sophisticated missiles, but they cannot hope to blast every last enemy ground unit.[54] Any run-of-the-mill batch of soldiers carries machine guns and often shoulder-fired surface-to-air missilery. They bite back at anyone who comes too close. So flying at night, as fast and low as possible, ensures a fleeting aim point for annoyed badniks below.

Air assault commanders learn how to compensate for their aviation's inabilities to enter death ground or transit hostile air defenses without bloodbaths. Other shortcomings allow fewer workarounds.

No matter how many tactical tricks you conjure, some things simply defy solutions. You simply endure them.

For openers, you need a landing zone. It must be free of trees, poles, electrical wires, and other obstructions. The ground cannot slope more than about 15 percent (fifteen feet of rise for every hundred feet of run), lest the rotor blades dig turf as the crew attempts to set down.[55] The problems with hostile direct fire have already been mentioned. It's not a welcome feature.

When searching for LZs, the bigger, the better, say aviators. Although a UH-60A Blackhawk can land on an average convenience store parking lot, threading the needle with one ship hardly brings in the kind of massed fighting strength needed for most missions. With seats out, a flight of five Blackhawks can carry an entire rifle company at once. Five is also a safe, compact formation size for lift helos flying at night. Landing five Blackhawks takes a forty thousand-square-yard flat, clear strip. Such open spots can be found most anywhere. In thick woods or jungle, air assault forces may even create them, using 15,000-pound BLU-82 Daisy Cutter earthquake bombs to knock down pesky trees.[56] But finding the right LZ deserves attention. A Blackhawk cannot land just anywhere.

Smart enemies know this. They read our books and do the math. In densely wooded terrain or in towns, the few good LZs glare up at you. The hostile units stake them out and wait. If the Americans go to the obvious sites, they get spanked. It happened often enough in Vietnam. In any helicopter assault, regardless of the intelligence picture, the grunts go in ready to fight, just in case they and the opposition have selected the same LZs.

Even if good landing zones can be found in abundance, the fliers must get there in one piece. Weather extremes ground aircraft. Gale-force winds, blowing dust, lightning, heavy snow, low clouds, fog that obscures the passive night-vision goggles, thermal inversion that blanks out the Apache FLIR by rendering all temperatures depressingly uniform—any of these can halt an air assault in its tracks, as happened in the opening hours of the Gulf War's ground campaign.[57] Army aviators know how to make it through pretty hairy weather. In fact, sometimes, flight formations pop through breaks in thunderstorm cells or breast heavy rains, so never say never. But, in general, storms and fog banks make night formation attacks impossible. Many enemies see their opportunities and act accordingly.

Even in ideal weather, air assaults can go only so far. Although the precise combat radius of an air assault varies by what the aircraft carry, planners recognize that the shortest-legged U.S. Army lift aircraft remains the CH-47D Chinook. The Blackhawk can carry a useful load farther; the Apache, much farther. In the contest with Iraq, local environmental conditions, fuel supply, and flight characteristics kept Chinooks within 93 miles if they had to return to the PZ.[58] That provides a good rule of thumb. It's a long way to go in one crack, especially when the helos can blow through or vault across the enemy frontline divisions. No tank division or foot infantry can do that; they get bogged down trying to smash through enemy defenses. Air assault brigades simply hop over all that mayhem, in 93-mile legs, 186 miles if the helos can stay where they land. It's more than enough to disrupt most enemies.

That kind of mobility works well once the aircraft are in the theater, but therein lies the rub. Unless we have designs on Caribbean neighbors, as we sometimes do, air assault forces must move into the war zone by air (fast) or sea (slow). They need a safe spot—an intermediate staging base (ISB)—to get the helicopters unloaded and reconfigured for flight. Ferried by USAF aircraft capable of aerial refueling, the 82d Airborne can go into action anywhere in the world directly from its North Carolina garrison. Without a flight to a secure ISB, the 101st Airborne can reach only Indiana or Alabama from its home at Fort Campbell, on the Kentucky-Tennessee state line.

Activities at the ISB focus on getting Army aviation ready to fight. It takes a couple hours to unfold blades and check out UH-60A Blackhawks or AH-64A Apaches, fairly new designs intended for compact air shipment. The big CH-47D Chinooks, however, reflect 1960s technology and do not disassemble or reassemble easily. Once stripped for transport, these large twin-rotored craft go back together in about a day, a painful process that resembles outright reinvention.[59] Once back intact, the aircraft must be fueled and armed for battle. The infantry and their affiliated engineers, artillery, and the like move from USAF airlifters and align to assault by helicopter.

Once grunt and flier unite, the Eagles really go forth. No parachute unit does this, not without some handily prepositioned choppers, as in Panama. (Helicopters cannot be air-dropped.) But air assault forces train to go deep from the outset. Starting from the ISB, the heliborne troops commence a series of those 93-mile giant steps. The drill ends when the enemy collapses. So goes the concept.

The number of those giant steps depends on fuel. During Desert Storm, the 101st's aircraft burned JP-4, and they needed a lot of it—about 350,000 gallons daily.[60] Because conventional Army helos cannot refuel in the air, all those gallons must be brought forward. Helicopters refuel on the ground, with hoses and pumps, just like filling the family car down at the gas station—only with guys shooting at you. The huge stock of fuel comes forward by sling-loaded rubber blivets—Air Force C-130 "bladder birds" rigged to dispense fuel—and 2,500-gallon fuel trucks lumbering along the MSRs. Just to add to the fun, the huge fuel trucks cannot be carried under Chinooks, either. But the helos need JP-8, pilot lingo for "gas," although it is more akin to high-grade kerosene.[61] Whatever it is, the aviators need it by the gross. The fuel war paces the air assault war.

Accordingly, spotting fuel becomes a big job for air assault forces. The urge for gas underlies the entire purpose behind seizing FOB Cobra. It's worth noting that in the four-day ground war against Iraq, the 101st Airborne Division carried out four brigade-scale operations. Two of these involved taking FOBs—in other words, big gas stations. (The other two closed the Euphrates River highway and shot up the escape routes from Kuwait, both key maneuvers that broke the back of the Iraqi Army.[62]) So taking ground for gas is important. The aviators like to say that it's the reason the 101st keeps all that infantry hanging around. Somebody has to grab the next fuel point.

Of course, the Screaming Eagle infantry does a lot more than snatch turf for gas stations, although taking an FOB serves as a baseline skill. Just as the 82d Airborne works most often on a night brigade drop to seize an airfield, a unit such as Frank Hancock's 1st Battalion, 327th Infantry Regiment spends the bulk of its training on tasks related to a brigade-sized night air assault to secure an FOB. No unit can do everything, not even an air assault battalion. So like their paratrooper brothers, the air assault troops focus on their core competency—taking key terrain from those who do not want it taken. That means working in death ground.

An air assault infantry battalion looks exactly like an airborne battalion and has pretty much the same organization, right down to the barrel count on the rifles. Like their parachute brethren, the air assault grunts go with three rifle companies (A, B, and C) and an antiarmor company (D). In its five platoons of four gun carriers apiece, Company D relies on Humvees armed with a choice of TOW missile systems, Mk-19 automatic grenade launchers, or .50-caliber heavy machine guns. The headquarters outfit lists the same subelements found in the parachute infantry: company HQ, battalion HQ, scouts, 81mm mortars, communicators, mechanics, medics, and a catchall of supply and transport folks with Humvees.[63] Aside from an abundance of sling sets and PZ and LZ marking devices, it all mirrors the airborne lineup.

What makes heliborne troops different involves the refined version of thoughts introduced back in the ten days of air assault school. By their unique partnership with aviation, air assault infantry specializes in repetitive deep operations. To an enemy army, air assault battalions are not one-shot wonders but persistent threats. In order to keep fighting in this style over weeks and months, air assault formations build their tactics, supply, medical evacuation, and tempo around the speed and range of rotary-wing aircraft. These riflemen are either assaulting by helo or getting ready to assault by helo. But they always look to bring the combined aviation-infantry team into the battle, with all its range, speed, and fighting strength.

Using aviation takes extremely well schooled, practiced infantry. A check of the table of organization reveals that these grunts own exactly zero aircraft. Even in the 101st Airborne, with hundreds of helicopters, the fleet cannot scoop up all the troops at once. Thus, the same helos pick up about a brigade at a whack; the next night, it will be a different group of ground troops. To carry out brigade air assaults night after night, the infantry must use standardized procedures on PZs and LZs, well-understood loading and landing drills, and common methods.[64] There is no time to get intricate.

To gain proficiency to carry out these kind of evolutions at night, the infantry practices over and over, in the dark, and often with live

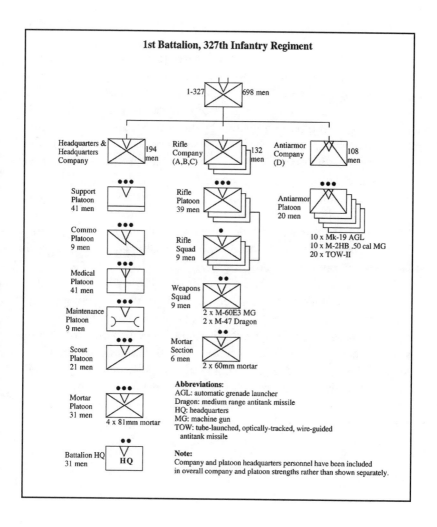

1st Battalion, 327th Infantry Regiment

1-327 / 698 men

Headquarters & Headquarters Company — 194 men

Rifle Company (A,B,C) — 132 men

Antiarmor Company (D) — 108 men

Support Platoon 41 men

Commo Platoon 9 men

Medical Platoon 41 men

Maintenance Platoon 9 men

Scout Platoon 21 men

Mortar Platoon 31 men — 4 x 81mm mortar

Battalion HQ 31 men — HQ

Rifle Platoon 39 men

Rifle Squad 9 men

Weapons Squad 9 men — 2 x M-60E3 MG, 2 x M-47 Dragon

Mortar Section 6 men — 2 x 60mm mortar

Antiarmor Platoon 20 men

10 x Mk-19 AGL
10 x M-2HB .50 cal MG
20 x TOW-II

Abbreviations:
AGL: automatic grenade launcher
Dragon: medium range antitank missile
HQ: headquarters
MG: machine gun
TOW: tube-launched, optically-tracked, wire-guided antitank missile

Note:
Company and platoon headquarters personnel have been included in overall company and platoon strengths rather than shown separately.

fire. Several standard templates exist, and the troops know them well. They can run variations off these themes with minimal fuss. In Desert Storm, 1-327th rehearsed the FOB Cobra takedown numerous times. Many run-throughs included only the key ground and air leaders. Three brought out the entire battalion. One involved all of 1st Brigade.[65] By the time of the actual operation, everybody knew exactly what to do, including "what if" excursions that taught the men how to react to unforeseen events, such as an Iraqi infantry battalion in the way.

This emphasis on developing and learning aviation-infantry standing operating procedures (SOPs) saves time under fire. Instead of going through a "now what?" episode of befuddlement, the men start acting right away. For a more lock-step opponent such as the Iraqis, it all rolls over them too quickly. The air assault training philosophy explains why officers such as Hancock, Best, and Russell rapidly worked their way through the challenge that met them. They had already done it many times in exercises.

Certain critics charge that a purpose-built air assault component makes little sense. After all, helicopters can pick up any foot soldiers. Why maintain nine air assault infantry battalions in the 101st Airborne, plus two identical units in the 2d Infantry Division in Korea? Can't anyone perform their function?

Here, we return to the root of the entire air assault idea. Yes, anyone can fly a helicopter, or a glider, for that matter. But not just anyone can be stuck inside the back part of a hurtling chunk of machinery, slung ninety-three miles into the void, and be expected to get out at the far end and go right at it with rifle and bayonet, determined to win the death ground. That takes chosen men, trained men, extraordinary men, and—just as important—aviators worthy of those confident young riflemen and machine gunners. Like lightning and thunder, hard fliers and hard grunts together bring down the storm.

Notes

The epigraph comes from John Kifner, "We Own This Piece, G.I. Proclaims," *New York Times* (25 February 1991), 1. Kifner accompanied the 1st Brigade, 101st Airborne, on their initial air assault. He quoted the command sergeant major of the 3d Battalion, 327th Infantry Regiment.

1. Lieutenant Colonel Frank R. Hancock, USA, *North to the Euphrates, Part One: The Taking of FOB Cobra* (Carlisle Barracks, Pa.: U.S. Army War College, 1993), 26; interview with Col. Frank R. Hancock, USA, Carlisle Barracks, Pa., 22 January 1998.

2. Major Robert K. Wright, Jr., USAR, 1st Lt. Cliff Lippard, USAR, and Rex Boggs, *Air Assault in the Gulf: An Interview with Major General J. H. Binford Peay III, Commanding General, 101st Airborne Division Air Assault* (Washington, D.C.: U.S. Army Center of Military History, 1996), 11, 29, 32. This edited interview transcript reflects a session held on 5 June 1991, within months of the Gulf War.

3. Colonel Thomas H. Taylor, USAR (Ret.), *Lightning in the Storm* (New York, N.Y.: Hippocrene Books, Inc., 1994), 264–65, 335.

4. Hancock, *North to the Euphrates, Part One*, 18.

5. Cornelius Ryan, *A Bridge Too Far* (New York, N.Y.: Popular Library, 1974), 599.

6. Karl von Clausewitz, *On War*, edited and translated by Michael Howard and Peter Paret (Princeton, N.J.: Princeton University Press, 1984), 117.

7. Captain Dominic J. Caraccilo, USA, *The Ready Brigade of the 82d Airborne Division in Desert Storm* (Jefferson, N.C.: McFarland & Company, Inc., Publishers, 1993), 150–51. Caraccilo commanded the headquarters company for the 82d's 2d Brigade, which served with the French 6th Light Armored Division on the 101st's western flank. See also Lt. Col. James J. Cooke, USAR, *100 Miles from Baghdad* (Westport, Conn.: Praeger Publishers, 1993), 98–99. Cooke, a college professor in civilian life, served as XVIII Airborne Corps liaison officer with the French division.

8. Michael R. Gordon and Lt. Gen. Bernard E. Trainor, USMC (Ret.), *The Generals' War* (Boston, Mass.: Little, Brown and Co., 1995), 284, 336.

9. Taylor, *Lightning in the Storm*, 241.

10. Major Kevin Smith, USA, and Burton W. Wright, III, ed., *United States Army Aviation During Operations Desert Shield and Desert Storm* (Fort Rucker, Ala.: U.S. Army Aviation Center and School, 1993), 131–32. Smith interviewed the Apache crews who flew the missions on 17 February 1991.

11. Taylor, *Lightning in the Storm*, 250–52; Smith and Wright, *United States Army Aviation During Operations Desert Shield and Desert Storm*, 153; Sgt. Richard Dennis Johnson, USA, *PSYOP: The Gulf Paper War* (Titusville, Fla.: self-published, 1992), 262. Sergeant Johnson's work offers excellent accounts from the 101st Airborne's psychological operations elements and enemy prisoner interrogation teams.

12. Smith and Wright, *United States Army Aviation During Operations Desert Shield and Desert Storm*, 142–43; 1st Lt. Clifford M. Lippard, USAR, *Command Report: 101st Airborne Division (Air Assault) for Operations Desert Shield and Desert Storm, 2 August 1990 through 1 May 1991* (Fort Campbell, Ky.: Headquarters, 101st Airborne Division [Air Assault], 1991), 39.

13. Wright, Lippard, and Boggs, *Air Assault in the Gulf*, 11, 28; U.S. Department of the Army, Headquarters, Third U.S. Army/Army Forces Central Command, *Desert Storm After Action Review* (King Khalid Military City, Saudi Arabia: HQ, Third U.S. Army, 12 March 1991), 3, 5, 7.

14. Lippard, *Command Report*, 41–43.

15. Johnson, *PSYOP*, 260. Johnson misidentifies the Iraqi unit as the 2d Battalion, 843d Infantry Brigade, which succumbed at FOB Cobra on 24 February 1991.

16. Sean D. Naylor, "Flight of Eagles," *Army Times* (22 July 1991), 12.

17. Lippard, *Command Report*, 43; Johnson, *PSYOP*, 264–72.

18. Taylor, *Lightning in the Storm*, 254; Wright, Lippard, and Boggs, *Air Assault in the Gulf*, 31. Taylor errs by placing Peay's meeting with the POWs on 17 February, at the time the border guards were taken. That is incorrect, because Peay himself refers to talking to the Iraqi infantry battalion commander captured by 1-187th Infantry on 20 February. Other 101st Airborne documents match Peay's timetable in this matter. Otherwise, Taylor's account is superb.

19. Hancock, *North to the Euphrates, Part One*, 24–25; Hancock interview. Hancock noted that his young captain and enlisted intelligence assistant figured out the situation and convinced him to do something about it.

20. Hancock interview; Hancock, *North to the Euphrates, Part One*, 25; Taylor, *Lightning in the Storm*, 292–94. Taylor's account credits the shift of LZ 1 to a report by the aviation brigade commander, Col. Tom Garrett, to Col. Tom Hill. That likely played a part in Hill's decision, but Hancock clearly remembers that the final choice involved a one-on-one encounter between the infantry battalion commander and his brigade commander. "They cleared the TOC [tactical operations center] for that one," Hancock said.

21. Lieutenant General Edward M. Flanagan, Jr., USA (Ret.), *Lightning* (Washington, D.C.: Brassey's Inc., 1994), 169–70; Hancock, *North to the Euphrates, Part One*, 28–29. On the large-scale air movement table prepared for the assault on Cobra, Hancock's elements originally expected to land at 0625.

22. Lippard, *Command Report*, 46; Capt. Rafael J. Garcia, Jr., *Paladin Zero Six* (Jefferson, N.C.: McFarland & Company, Inc., Publishers, 1994), 91. During the war with Iraq, Garcia commanded Company C, 1st Battalion, 101st Aviation Regiment, an Apache unit. He flew on the FOB Cobra air assault.

23. David C. Isby, *Weapons and Tactics of the Soviet Army* (New York, N.Y.: Jane's Publishing, Inc., 1988), 333, 419; Naylor, "Flight of Eagles," 14. For a superb look at the brigade's soldiers as they geared up for battle, see Col. Tom Hill's comments in Al Santoli, *Leading the Way* (New York, N.Y.: Ballantine Books, 1993), 330.

24. Santoli, *Leading the Way*, 332; Lippard, *Command Report*, 46.

25. Hancock, *North to the Euphrates, Part One*, 21–24, 27; Taylor, *Lightning in the Storm*, 246.

26. Santoli, *Leading the Way*, 332.

27. Flanagan, *Lightning*, 171; Garcia, *Paladin Zero Six*, 95; Wright, Lippard, and Boggs, *Air Assault in the Gulf*, 35. Some preliminary 101st Airborne accounts refer to the 1st Battalion, 82d Infantry Brigade, as the hostile unit, but this proved to be inaccurate. Nevertheless, it persists in some postwar versions of the FOB Cobra attack.

28. U.S. Department of the Army, *FM 90-4: Air Assault Operations* (Washington, D.C.: U.S. Government Printing Office, March 1987), 3-7–8, A-9.

29. Naylor, "Flight of Eagles," 14.

30. Hancock, *North to the Euphrates, Part One,* 30.

31. Ibid., 30–31; Flanagan, *Lightning,* 172–73. For a good photograph of the enemy position taken by the author, see Garcia, *Paladin Zero Six,* 97.

32. Hancock, *North to the Euphrates, Part One,* 32; Hancock interview.

33. U.S. Headquarters, 1st Brigade, 101st Airborne Division (Air Assault), *Tactical Command Post Daily Staff Journal* (FOB Cobra, Iraq: HQ, 1st Brigade, 101st Airborne Division [Air Assault], 24 February 1991), 3; Lippard, *Command Report,* 47; Wright, Lippard, and Boggs, *Air Assault in the Gulf,* 35–36. The other general on the scene, the 101st Airborne's assistant division commander of operations, was Brig. Gen. Hugh Shelton. He later rose to four stars and became chairman of the Joint Chiefs of Staff.

34. Hancock interview; Headquarters, 1st Brigade, 101st Airborne Division (Air Assault), *Tactical Command Post Daily Staff Journal,* 2. The 1st Brigade S-3, Maj. Ben Clawson, followed 1-327th's action and made certain the artillery battery moved into position to fire in support of the American attack.

35. Taylor, *Lightning in the Storm,* 309–10; Hancock interview.

36. Hancock, *North to the Euphrates, Part One,* 32–33; HQ, 1st Brigade, 101st Airborne Division (Air Assault), *Tactical Command Post Daily Staff Journal,* 2.

37. Hancock, *North to the Euphrates, Part One,* 33; Naylor, "Flight of Eagles," 14; Hancock interview.

38. Santoli, *Leading the Way,* 333.

39. Headquarters, 1st Brigade, 101st Airborne Division (Air Assault), *Tactical Command Post Daily Staff Journal,* 3. The 1st Brigade log records 1-327th's final maneuvers commencing at this hour, with surrenders reported at 1123 and again at 1142.

40. Hancock interview. Hancock states that his men did not have to open fire; the Iraqis quit as soon as the Cobra helicopter reengaged.

41. Taylor, *Lightning in the Storm*, 307–8; Hancock, *North to the Euphrates, Part One*, 34–35.

42. Hancock, *North to the Euphrates, Part One*, 34–35. Taylor, *Lightning in the Storm*, 307, identifies the Iraqi battalion commander as Lt. Col. Hassam Takriti, but that does not match 101st Airborne POW records, or the fact that other reserve infantry battalions had majors as commanders.

43. Flanagan, *Lightning*, 173; Hancock, *North to the Euphrates, Part One*, 36–37.

44. Naylor, "Flight of Eagles," 14.

45. Hancock, *North to the Euphrates, Part One*, 44.

46. For an account of the German coup at Eben Emael, see U.S. Department of the Army, Office of the Chief of Military History, *Airborne Operations: A German Appraisal* (Washington, D.C.: U.S. Government Printing Office, 1989), 11. For the British operation on the eve of D day, see Stephen Ambrose, *Pegasus Bridge*.

47. Clay Blair, *Ridgway's Paratroopers* (Garden City, N.Y.: The Dial Press, 1985), 51–54.

48. Ryan, *A Bridge Too Far*, 364–68, describes the only major American glider assault of the war, involving the 325th Infantry (82d Airborne) and the 327th Infantry (101st Airborne), into Holland on 18 September 1944. Losses were typical: twenty-two gliders from the 101st and sixty-nine from the 82d. For more on the promise and perils of World War II glidermen and paratroopers, see Col. Theodore L. Gatchel, USMC, "Hang Together or Hang Separately," *U.S. Naval Institute Proceedings* (November 1990), 58.

49. Captain Shelby L. Stanton, USA (Ret.), *Anatomy of a Division* (Novato, Calif.: Presidio Press, 1987), 9–11. Stanton offers an excellent summary of the rise of airmobile doctrine.

50. Ibid., 23–41; Michael Casey, Clark Dougan, Samuel Lipsman, Jack Sweetman, Stephen Weiss, and the editors of Boston Publishing Company, *The Vietnam Experience: Flags Into Battle* (Boston, Mass.: Boston Publishing Co., 1987), 157.

51. Patrick H. F. Allen, *Screaming Eagles* (London, U.K.: The Hamlyn Publishing Group, Ltd, 1990), 26–37, 140.

52. Flanagan, *Lightning*, 174.

53. U.S. Department of the Army, Headquarters, 101st Airborne

Division (Air Assault), *Air Assault Division and Brigade Operations Manual* (Fort Campbell, Ky.: HQ, 101st Airborne Division [Air Assault], 1 August 1988), 6-54–56, 6-64–67.

54. Ibid., 6-95–97.

55. Department of the Army, *FM 90-4: Air Assault Operations*, 3-28.

56. U.S. Department of the Army, Headquarters, 101st Airborne Division (Air Assault), *Gold Book: Tactics, Techniques and Procedures for the Brigade Air Assault (Draft)* (Fort Campbell, Ky.: HQ, 101st Airborne Division [Air Assault], 1 July 1993), 7, 42. For more on the BLU-82 Daisy Cutter, see Philip D. Chinnery, *Any Time, Any Place: A History of USAF Air Commando and Special Operations Forces* (Annapolis, Md.: U.S. Naval Institute Press, 1994), 256–57.

57. U.S. Department of the Army, Headquarters, 101st Airborne Division (Air Assault), *The Sabalauski Air Assault School Handbook* (Fort Campbell, Ky.: HQ, 101st Airborne Division [Air Assault], 1996), 1-4.

58. Wright, Lippard, and Boggs, *Air Assault in the Gulf*, 32.

59. U.S. Department of the Army, Headquarters, 101st Airborne Division (Air Assault), *The Army's Wings and Talons for Crisis Action* (Fort Campbell, Ky.: HQ, 101st Airborne Division [Air Assault], 1992), 33. Planning times for teardown/buildup (in hours) for air transport are UH-60A (3/4), AH-64A (3/3), CH-47D (18/24).

60. U.S. Department of the Army, Headquarters, 101st Airborne Division (Air Assault), *Desert Rendezvous II* (Fort Campbell, Ky., HQ, 101st Airborne Division [Air Assault], 1991), 7. The title comes from the division's code word for the ground war, 24–28 February 1991. An armored division uses about twice as much fuel as an air assault division. For actual Gulf War fuel consumption figures, see Rick Atkinson, *Crusade* (Boston, Mass.: Houghton Mifflin Co., 1993, 467–68, and Richard Jupa and Jim Dingeman, *Gulf Wars* (Cambria, Calif.: 3W Publications, 1991), 64.

61. In the Gulf War, U.S. Army helicopters used JP-4. Since that time, all ground vehicles and helos in the Army have converted to JP-8, a common fuel.

62. HQ, 101st Airborne Division, *Desert Rendezvous II*, 10. Had the war gone on another day, the division would have landed 1st Brigade on the road just north of Basra.

63. U.S. Department of the Army, *FM 101-10-1/1 Staff Officers' Field Manual: Organizational, Technical, and Logistical Data (Volume 1)* (Washington, D.C.: U.S. Government Printing Office, October 1987), 3-60–67, 3-151.

64. For examples of basic off-load drills taught to every air assault soldier, see Headquarters, 101st Airborne Division (Air Assault), *The Sabalauski Air Assault School Handbook*, 1-15, 1-17.

65. Hancock, *North to the Euphrates, Part One*, 24.

Chapter 3: Hell on Wheels

The great pursuit finally ran out on the third day. American Abrams tanks and Bradley infantry fighting vehicles at last hit a large number of Iraqi soldiers who refused to move or quit. Until then, it had been drive, drive, drive, with a little shooting to break the monotony. Here, northwest of Kuwait City, their backs to the waters of the Persian Gulf itself, the enemy chose to stand and fight.

For the Iraqis fleeing the Kuwaiti capital, the clock had passed the eleventh hour. If this batch of big tan M-1A1 Abrams tanks and their smaller M-2A2 Bradley consorts got across the road right here, at the Al Mutlaa Ridge, it was the ball game. Grabbing that key high ground, handily athwart the escape route from Kuwait City, doomed those enemy elements still trying to get out of the emirate. Having come this far, the U.S. 2d Marine Division intended to take Al Mutlaa Ridge, block the main highway, and seal the fate of those hostiles still to the south and east. No wonder the Iraqis turned to give battle.

The situation at noon on 26 February 1991 gave small comfort to the Iraqi forces trying to hold open their only remaining withdrawal route from Kuwait's capital city. To the far west, the U.S. XVIII Airborne Corps had footholds on the Euphrates River, having cut the highways leading from Kuwait to Baghdad. French light armor ran along the Coalition's distant flank, a hundred miles from Iraq's political center and its beleaguered maximum leader, Saddam Hussein. Worse, from the Iraqi perspective, the air assault brigades of the 101st Airborne stood one night's flight away from Baghdad, too. All they needed was the word to swing west and go. The Screaming Eagles already had the game plan ready.[1] Resistance out there had largely collapsed.

In the U.S. VIII Corps, massed armored formations carved up Iraq's Republican Guards and other tank outfits, smashing battalions and brigades to pieces. The border defenses parted like the Red Sea in front of Moses, so VII Corps ran riot, its mechanized formations wheeling east-northeast toward Basra and the Shatt-al-Arab, the headwaters of the Persian Gulf. When the Americans and their British comrades got there, the remnants of the Iraqi Army would be bagged and tagged, pocketed just like the German Sixth Army at Stalingrad in 1942–43.[2] And that would be the end.

Pushing up from the south, the U.S. Marine I Expeditionary Force shattered Iraq's lines in southern Kuwait, then roared north toward Kuwait City. If VII Corps wanted to close a big envelopment, the Marines steeled for a smaller arc. They hoped to trap the large number of Iraqis fleeing from Kuwait's capital and its environs. Arab forces on either Marine flank also rolled along in harness, but the major effort clearly fell to the aggressive, better-trained Americans. Now, on 26 February, converging U.S. Marine and Arab allied columns had long since run the enemy out of southern Kuwait and penetrated to the outskirts of Kuwait City.[3] Under the black pall of greasy smoke boiling up from burning, sabotaged oil well heads, the Marines advanced to finish the job.

The key role fell to the Marines' strongest armored organization, as one might expect in the endgame of a tremendous all-out mounted pursuit. Curiously, the Marines' most capable force consisted of U.S. Army soldiers—the 1st Brigade, 2d Armored Division, known as the Tiger Brigade. For the first time since World War I, a brigade of American soldiers served for a Marine division commander.[4] Good as the Marines were, they lacked the concentrated firepower of heavy armor. So Gen. H. Norman Schwarzkopf gave them some help.

Enter the Tiger Brigade. With its 118 M-1A1 Abrams main battle tanks and 72 M-2A2 Bradley fighting vehicles, this single outfit disposed more first-line armor than the two Marine divisions together.[5] More to the point, the Tigers brought a fighting skill and combative spirit to match those of their Marine colleagues. These soldiers

had something to prove, too. Their brigade represented the rump
of an organization slated for disbandment due to budget reductions.
Staff officers in Washington had weighed, measured, and cut dis-
passionately, and by early 1990 they recommended inactivating the
2d Armored Division at Fort Hood, Texas.[6] In the world of Pentagon
accountants and legislative liaison officers, it made sense. Armored
divisions eat a lot of money and manpower. Fort Hood still had the
1st Cavalry Division, enough to keep it open and appease the powerful Texas delegation in Congress. The 2d Armored had fewer battle streamers than infantry divisions that fought in Vietnam. So the
smart guys ran the numbers and pronounced the death sentence on
the 2d Armored Division.[7] The division had beaten the Germans in
World War II and held the line against the Russians in Europe for
decades, but they could not escape the end of the Cold War. Well,
peace can be hell.

A funny thing happened on the way to the boneyard, and because
it did, the Tiger Brigade went out like a cavalry regiment of old—
with guidons flying—following a great battle. When the Iraqis in-
vaded Kuwait, the U.S. Army activated Fort Hood's 1st Cavalry Division for duty in Saudi Arabia. But the 1st Cav had only two active
brigades; its third brigade, plus an equivalent slice of division support troops, belonged to the 155th Armored Brigade, Mississippi
Army National Guard. For a variety of good reasons, those happy warriors had not been called to federal service. Instead, the 1st Cavalry
took control of the 1st Brigade, 2d Armored Division.[8] And so the
Tigers headed off to war.

The 1st Cavalry Division served as Schwarzkopf's U.S. Central
Command theater reserve. From its ranks, he provided stiffening for
the undergunned Marines. The assignment went naturally to the self-
contained Tigers, still proudly wearing their 2d Armored insignia.
That triangle—gold for cavalry-armor at the apex, blue for infantry
and red for artillery at the base, with a black tank tread, a black cannon, and a red lightning bolt superimposed—rested on a gold strip
that announced in black capital letters: HELL ON WHEELS.
Whereas all other U.S. Army soldiers wore their unit patch on their
shoulder, a soldier in the 2d Armored wore that "pyramid of power"
on his left breast, over his fighting heart. The renowned patch and

famous motto, even how it must be worn, had been dictated by a former division commanding general, the great god of American tank warfare, George S. Patton himself. "If there was anything he wanted," recalled a Patton subordinate, "it was to make [them] tougher than the Marines and more spectacular than the Matterhorn. That triangle was the first step."[9] Now, with the Tigers leading those same Marines in the most spectacular armored campaign in history, Patton's vision had been achieved.

The Iraqis had the misfortune of getting in the way.

Colonel John Sylvester commanded the Tiger Brigade. By noon on 26 February, he and his men had been in action for almost forty-eight hours straight. This day, he knew that the war would be decided. His brigade would be there for the decisive stroke, taking Mutlaa Ridge to cork the bottle before the enemy got out.[10] The Marines wanted the Tiger Brigade for just this kind of mission. Sylvester and his soldiers stood ready to earn their pay, big time.

It had been a long road to get this far. For sixty hairy miles, scrapping and dodging the whole way, the Tiger Brigade had been living up to its motto, experiencing hell on wheels and occasionally causing it. The fun started on 24 February, day one of the ground war, when the brigade followed the 6th Marine Regiment through the breach in the Iraqi border minefields. That afternoon offered a horrific introduction to the ground phase of the Gulf War. Sylvester and his command group got up to the gap in the Iraqi earthworks and mines and directed traffic, just as senior officers are supposed to do. Under Iraqi artillery and mortar fire, it became interesting. The colonel later described the experience.

> It was tough because as you would go into one lane of the minefield, something would happen. Some vehicle would blow up in front of you. You had to back out of that lane, and go through another. Fortunately, they [the Iraqis] were not very good shots. They couldn't concentrate on where we were breaching and they had no ability to shift their fires. Of course, the first time they fired, a counterbattery went on them and knocked them out.[11]

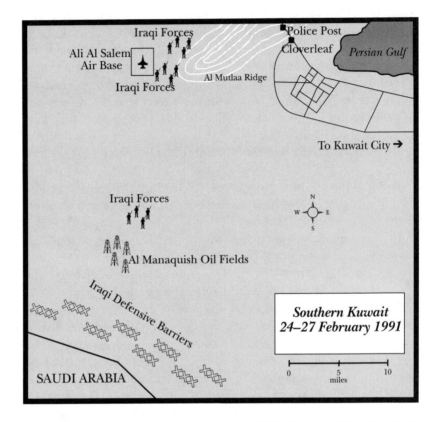

That counterbattery reference meant U.S. Army artillery. Guided by unerring AN/TPQ-36 Firefinder radars, Sylvester's gunners tracked the fall of Iraqi shells. Computers then plotted back up the ballistic rainbow, and American howitzers plastered the spots so indicated.

The Tigers passed through the lanes into Kuwait under ominous skies, shadowed by bubbling black clouds of oily smoke spilling from flaming, wrecked drill holes. Petro smog reduced the sun to a bloody red disk and imposed twilight in midafternoon, with the smell of brimstone strong in the desert air. Some nearby well heads gushed long, hot tongues of flame, Old Faithful in hell. The ground shook, flashes of artillery fire lit the churning bases of distant oil-smoke cloud banks, and wrecked Iraqi tanks and trucks smoldered near the openings in the border berms. Bodies heaved up by bombs and cannon fire lay like rag dolls on the ground. It was like something out of the Bible via Cecil B. DeMille. About the only thing missing might be ripping the veil in the temple from top to bottom; for all the Tigers knew, that could be happening, too.

The spectacle and the desultory enemy bombardment did not slow the passage. It went a lot faster than planned, even though it felt agonizingly slow to those in the middle of it. The brigade snaked through the various gaps, led by TF 3-41, then TF 1-67, and TF 3-67 behind, and finally the artillery. The vast procession, marred by starts and stops, looked for all the world like eight lanes of rush-hour traffic queued up to get through a highway tollgate.

But these were no idle commuters, no way. All vehicles crossed through in fighting order. Each four-company TF consisted of combined arms, tanks, and infantry, just as Patton had taught them decades before. That required swapping around some companies to get things properly set. The 3d Battalion (Mechanized), 41st Infantry Regiment, for example, had two of its own mech rifle companies, one tank company from 1-67th Armor, and another from 3-67th. The armor-based TFs had a single mechanized rifle company and three tank outfits. This made TF 3-41 balanced (two mech, two tank) and the others tank heavy (three tank, one mech), to use the common doctrinal lingo.[12] Given the uncertain situation, Sylvester led with his balanced TF, in case grunt work became necessary. When in doubt, tankers turn to men with rifles, even if they commute to the job site in rumbling Bradleys.

The three maneuver TFs clanked forward on tracks, as did the self-propelled artillery pieces. Untutored civilians seeing these tread-laying, slab-sided metal behemoths with gun tubes poking out would have called them tanks; indeed, many Gulf War reporters did so. But a closer look showed variations on the theme. The wide, angular, flat-topped giants with the long cannons were the famous Abrams main battle tanks, which weighed up to seventy tons fully loaded. Smaller (about thirty-three tons), chunkier, boxy things with slim silver-gray autocannons sticking out of hatbox-shaped turrets were Bradley infantry carriers, their rear compartments chock full of grunts. The thirty-two-ton kind with very long guns and tall turrets stuck on the

back of their wide hulls were M-109A3 self-propelled 155mm howitzers, armored artillery able to chuck a ninety-pound explosive
shell the size of a fat fire extinguisher out to fourteen miles.[13] Along
with these primary killers were others: armored ambulances, communications rigs, big tank retrievers capable of towing broken-down
M-1A1s, engineer squad carriers, air defense vehicles—dozens of
track-laying pilot fish streaming along in the wake of the big fighting sharks.

Behind these shooters and near shooters came the nonshooters,
the numerous but necessary legions of camp followers that kept the
war vehicles rolling. Even the most unenlightened viewers could not
mistake these for fighting machines. Endless columns of huge fuel
tanker trucks, ammunition carriers, mobile workshops, and all the
other hundreds and hundreds of wheeled vehicles puttered along,
snuffling through the openings in the enemy mine belts. The rows
of desert tan trucks stretched on and on. All of them, some eight
hundred in all, might have seemed superfluous, like strings of
garbage sucked along in the wake of a great ocean liner. But without them, John Sylvester's Tigers would be impotent within a day or
so.[14] These vehicles contained the hundreds of unsung technicians
and suppliers who stoked the furnaces and lubed the bearings that
made the Tigers into hell on wheels.

During the hours it took to move all of this, night descended,
made blacker still by the endless fonts of oil smoke. Thermal sights
fuzzed over, decoyed by the crackling, blazing drillheads. Passive
starlight scopes went blank, unable to gather in ambient light because none existed. One military policeman died when his Humvee
strayed off into the Stygian landscape and detonated a land mine.[15]
Word of that tragedy made a slow process even slower.

It took more than three hours to weave the brigade's fighting elements through the two Iraqi defensive belts opened by the 6th
Marines. That done, the Tigers halted for the night at 2100, compelled to wait for the night-blind Marines groping along on their
flanks. At least the pause let the vital fuel and ammo wagons catch
up.

Sylvester's brigade stopped some ten miles into Kuwait, way ahead
of the planned pace. The American soldiers had expected a bruis-

ing struggle to punch through thick, well-defended positions. Instead, the much-ballyhooed fourth largest army in the world barely fought at all, meekly ceding their paper-thin frontline berm and tossing a few odd mortar bombs in their wake as they skedaddled. Many surrendered, nearly eight thousand across the Marine frontage.[16] The majority of Iraqis simply ran away.

While thirsty Abrams tanks sucked up thousands of gallons of diesel to keep their big turbines purring, John Sylvester's units kept busy checking out the area. Wide-ranging U.S. patrols gathered in some two hundred bedraggled Iraqi prisoners. At the tip of the spear, starting around midnight, TF 3-41 scouts probed an extensive bunker complex a mile away. A small scrap with Iraqi foot troops also erupted in TF 3-67's area.[17] Meanwhile, the fuelers and cargo trucks kept coming. It took until after dawn to get the logistics trains through the minefields.

In the morning, marked by a gradual graying of the oily clouds hanging low overhead, the Tiger Brigade lurched onward through the fiery Al Manaqish oil fields, skirting pillars of flame that reached a hundred yards into the air. Task Force 3-41 fought until afternoon cleaning out the bunker system their scouts had bumped into the night before. The task force's tank main guns cracked out 120mm rounds, tearing apart four enemy tanks and several armored personnel carriers. American mechanized infantrymen dismounted to clean out the Iraqi holes, but the hostiles lacked the stomach to fight. A few bursts of 25mm chain gun from the U.S. Bradley fighting vehicles and the Iraqis quit. Most of an enemy battalion capitulated intact.[18] It took more effort to herd the hundreds of resultant prisoners than it did to take the position.

The Tiger Brigade's two armored TFs swung around the involved bunker fight, 3-67 to the west and 1-67 to the east. These tank-heavy formations caught Iraqi mobile reserves trying to pull back. Despite light rain and the consistent blanket of petroleum-flavored smudge that restricted vision to a few hundred yards, the American thermal tank sights worked superbly. The shooting started at almost two miles out. It was one-sided.

"I don't think they saw us comin'," said Sgt. Kevin Green, a tanker from Company A, 1-67th Armor. "Then, when we hit the first tanks, the other crews jumped off and ran."[19] Led by expert gunners such as Green, the Abrams crews devastated the Iraqis. Aimed by superb gunsights and even better men, 120mm depleted-uranium M-829A1 "silver bullets" punched through dozens of Iraqi T-55s and T-62s. Along with hundreds more prisoners of war, the Americans also inherited almost a brigade's worth of military hardware, most of it damaged more or less. It took hours to sort out this fight and clean up the mess after TF 3-41's bunker busting.

That mopping up—a public affairs officer euphemism if there ever was one—did it for 25 February. Once more, obeying Marine dictates, the Tigers laagered for the night.[20] In the morning, they would drive for Mutlaa Ridge, determined to choke off any Iraqi retreat from Kuwait City. Thus far, the war belonged mostly to Kevin Green and his skilled fellow tankers. The infantry had been along for the ride. But on 26 February, that would change.

Yes, riflemen were there, too. They were barely noticeable among all the combat vehicles, but they were there, patiently waiting for their hour. These soldiers did not hold the traditional 11B military occupational speciality seen in the rest of the U.S. Army's infantry force. Instead, this brand of infantry went by the identifier 11M— for mechanized—tied to the fact that they rode to battle in armored infantry fighting vehicles.[21] Their 11B counterparts went into action in various ways, most notably by parachute and helicopter. But in the end, in death ground, they all had to get out and fight on foot. At that level, 11B10s and 11M10s are all too equal, privates with rifles, grenades, and bayonets. The 2d Armored riflemen knew that fact quite well.

The life of an 11M is not a happy one. He rides for hours and hours—often for days—in the back of a dimly lit metal box with five or more of his closest friends crammed into a space about equal to the back end of an average American family's minivan. But this doesn't give the full story. After all, Joe and Jane Q. Public's children can see out big windows, enjoy cushy seats, and benefit from heat and air-conditioning as needed. Bradley guys get no such benefits.

The 11M private has a few tiny periscopes to look outside, each roughly the size of a mail slot and conveniently located over his shoulder. Maybe Harry Houdini could make the twists necessary to see through these thick, distorted vision blocks. But he did not have to wear a Kevlar helmet, chemical overgarment, gas mask, and fighting gear harness with ammo pouches and sloshing canteens, and wrestle with a loaded rifle while doing so.[22] As for heating, it exists on a Brad, with two options: red hot and broken. If you want air-conditioning, take up a different line of work.

Just to add to the fun, the mech rifleman sits on a seat built for sturdiness, not comfort, with his heavily laden comrades cheek to jowl, all sweating and rustling as the track lurches and shakes. Every square inch of the interior bristles with ammunition containers, radio cables, ration boxes, batteries of all varieties, oil cans, hand tools, gas mask filters, missile containers, camouflage netting, personal sleeping bags, spare parts, and extra bits and pieces of generic Army stuff. At mission start, it's all neatly lashed down with straps, Velcro strips, and tie-down cord, but as the hours go on, the Brad's interior proves the second law of thermodynamics: Entropy ensues. Items get used once and not put away, things break free on jolts and bumps, ammo gets shot but cans are saved, and things generally deteriorate. Riding in the middle of this swirling mass of wrappers, empty boxes, loose bolts, extra canteens, and wandering tools resembles taking a long trip inside a trash dumpster.

Only this dumpster buckets along at forty miles an hour across uneven ground, which has a tendency to mix up the contents pretty thoroughly. The suspension system does what it can, but forget about a smooth ride. The track pitches and shimmies, jumps up and plops down, and twists like a scalded fish when the driver gooses the controls. The men in the aft end hang on for dear life.

There are more distractions. The big turret with its 25mm chain gun, 7.62mm coaxial machine gun, and twin-tubed TOW missile launcher box squats in a huge, round tub in front of the dismount team's dismal enclosure.[23] That armament constantly spins and grinds away, imparting its own unique torque to the bouncing Bradley. When the autocannon fires, the entire vehicle rattles in time. Every so often, the two men in the turret holler down for more cannon shells, or 7.62mm bullets, or TOW missiles, or all of them at once. Then the riflemen jostle around in the bottom to unshackle these heavy items—the missile canisters alone are almost five feet long and eight inches across—and wrestle them into the rotating turret tub. The discarded empty tubes, cut wires, plastic fittings, cardboard spacers, wood slats, and heavy foil packaging get tossed into the stew churning around the precariously seated riflemen. Above it all, a soundtrack to bedlam, the turret motor whines and whirs. Its noise isn't so bad. You hardly hear it over the unending dull roar of the Brad's main diesel engine.

The paratrooper and heliborne riflemen endure similar torments, but for hours at most. For the 11M10 troops aboard a Bradley, it goes on and on. It takes hard men indeed to tolerate this torture, hell in a very small place. Even worse, you just know something awful is happening on the other side of the vehicle's armor. The smacks and pings on the hull, the yawing and dipping, the spurts of speed, and the steady drone of radio chatter on the internal speakers suggest a lot, not much of it good.

Over time, imagination fills in the blanks for what cannot be seen, heard, or felt of the war outside. The guys in back know about land mines and rocket-propelled grenades and tank sabot rounds that come screeching in without warning. Mounted, they cannot do a damn thing about any of these perils. The same stout armor that shields them from artillery shell fragments and small-arms fire will burn and crumple when hit by a big enough punch. But the idea of mechanized infantry is to go on mounted for as long as possible, paced by the tanks. An Abrams has better armor, and lots more of it, than a Bradley, and it has a much bigger gun. The Brad has just enough to get its grunts to the front.

Bradley infantryman Sgt. Thomas Patten of the Tiger Brigade spoke for many as he remembered the long ride through Kuwait: "You're ducks in a row, the whole task force. You'd sit there, you'd chew your gum, and you'd close your eyes and you'd think, 'well this Bradley could be blowing up any second now.'"[24] The whole experience tends to gnaw on you after a while.

The amazing thing is that in the middle of it all, without warning, you're expected to get out and fight. Nobody asks whether you're tired, bone rattled, pissed off, or confused. No, the entire back side is just dropped and out you go. When that ramp goes down in anger, you can be sure you have arrived in death ground. That is how mechanized infantrymen go to war.

The mech riflemen and tankers of TF 3-67 drew the main role in the Tiger Brigade's climactic attack on 26 February. Their goal was what Sylvester and his brigade wanted all along—where the Iraqi escape highway crossed Mutlaa Ridge. When taken, this high ground would seal off the enemy exodus from Kuwait City.

Seizing Mutlaa Ridge entailed grunt work. A look at the map sheet said as much. The ridge itself would surely be trenched and bunkered, suspicions enhanced by pilot reports and some fuzzy overhead photographs. Worse, the map showed that an unfinished Kuwaiti police complex dominated the highway heading north to Basra and Iraqi salvation. Tank gunnery alone promised only very cruel holes, and that might not be enough in this case. Somebody had to get out and secure the ridgeline, especially that well-sited police post.

Those somebodies came from Capt. Mike Kershaw's Team C, which provided the mechanized infantry for tank-heavy TF 3-67. Kershaw had two mech platoons, each with four Brads, plus a platoon of tanks. He had sent his 2d Platoon over to a tank company in return, a familiar enough task organization. So far, Team C had seen only minor actions. But today, they faced a big one. The young 11M10s knew it almost before Kershaw, having gotten the word via that jungle telegraph of rumors and possibilities that keeps junior soldiers informed. For TF 3-67, taking Mutlaa Ridge depended heavily on those few Bradley-borne riflemen.

Kershaw and his grunts worked for Lt. Col. Douglas L. Tystad, a tanker determined to drive hard to get astride Mutlaa Ridge.[25] Tystad's task force had about twelve miles to go, all opposed. They expected some real fighting, not the quick surrenders seen to date. Iraq had thrown in its last decent reserves to hold open the critical route home. The infantry had a key job at that police station.

For the big attack on 26 February, Kershaw received his orders at 0510, well before the sun slid up fat and red in the sooty skies. It took a few hours to sort out the details at battalion level; given the importance of this particular phase, it was time well spent. Everybody understood that once TF 3-67 launched, there would be no more time for plans and orders, only action.

Certain of Tystad's intent, Mike Kershaw returned to his company's position about 0900. The captain dropped the ramp on his command Bradley and called together his platoon leaders. The men gathered around their commander's map. Kershaw took a few minutes to issue an oral order. He did not have much to work with in terms of information or time.

Kershaw knew little of his final target, though luckily the company team commander's assigned Kuwaiti translator had been inside the police post several months earlier. The infantry captain hoped that this local guy had a good memory, because he represented all the intelligence that Team C was going to get. The Kuwaiti tried to explain the internal configuration of the double structure, no easy feat speaking in English and working without blueprints.

Based on this fractured account, Kershaw and his officers and senior NCOs got the picture, or as much of it as they could understand. The two rectangular three-story edifices seemed to follow the same institutional model as any school in America—a long, central hall on all three levels, a row of rooms down either side, and a stairwell at either end and one in the middle. All present understood: lots of rooms and probably lots of Iraqis in them.

To secure this double block and the ridge slope around it, Kershaw had two small infantry platoons, less than fifty dismounts total, counting himself and his radiomen. But he also had eight platoon Brads and four tanks, plus supporting artillery. If he used the whole company team together, tracks and dismounts, it ought to work out, as long as he kept it uncomplicated.[26] That was the trick, all right.

With all of this in mind, the young company commander designated the order of movement. The tanks would lead, followed by the two rifle platoons—1st, then 3d. Artillery fire from the direct support 155mm batteries would pummel the police compound as Team C approached. The tank platoon drew the task of shooting into the short southern end of both rectangular buildings, a pair of M-1A1s allotted to each structure. Their job was to pave the way, then face outward to knock out any Iraqi vehicles trying to relieve their brothers in the police post.

The 1st Platoon had to slide in south of the tanks and clean out the slope of Mutlaa Ridge, which featured "numerous enemy bunkers, vehicles, and surrendering enemy soldiers."[27] A good number of Iraqis might not be giving up this time, guaranteeing a hot afternoon for some of Kershaw's guys, including a dismounted hole-to-hole battle.

Lieutenant Dan Stempniak's 3d Platoon inherited the buildings, the real heart of the whole deal. The formal U.S. Army guidance for tackling enemy-held structures as substantial as these Kuwaiti police barracks suggested giving each to a separate platoon, or even a rifle company.[28] But with only two rifle platoons, and one of them already accounted for, Mike Kershaw could not afford that. Stempniak's bunch had to eat the whole enchilada. Training and supporting fires would make up for numbers.

When the attack started just past noon on 26 February 1991, Kershaw's company moved second in a column of four. A tank company team led, and the other two Abrams companies followed. Doug Tystad's men knew of one definite minefield to their front, and expected others. They also looked for (at last) a serious Iraqi defense.

Projected enemies included the Iraqi 5th Mechanized Division, 1st Mechanized Division, and 3d Armored Division, all veterans of the late January fight at Ras Al Khafji. Those mobile formations had been well and truly smashed during the ill-fated border incursion. Before the ground offensive kicked off, Marine intelligence analysts assessed the Iraqi 5th Mech at 40 percent strength, retaining only 32 tanks and 145 armored troop carriers, none the match of Tystad's Abrams and Bradley array. The enemy 1st Mech stood at 10 percent, with 13 tanks and a solitary armored personnel carrier—that was a precise estimate, all right. Iraq's 3d Armored Division had only 5 percent of its prewar combat power, 36 tanks and 23 infantry vehicles.[29] None of the Iraqi divisions could be properly identified. They had gotten utterly shattered and mixed up in the previous few days. Tystad's men expected to see parts of each.

They did not have to wait long. Within a few miles of their starting line, Tystad's first company banged into a defending Iraqi battalion. The lead company team leveled its 120mm guns and raced forward into the assault. These bad guys quickly gave up. Now TF 3-67 faced the usual prisoner square dance.

Tystad did not go in for that. Dismounting a few men to herd the
Iraqi quitters south, Tystad waved his main body forward.[30] Prisoners were no longer a novelty; everybody had seen plenty of them.
These Iraqis obviously had enough of the Gulf War. So Tystad did
not waste time on them. That's what all of those hundreds of follow-
on truck guys were for. Well, today some mechanics and clerks
could have a thrill and play prisoner guard. But TF 3-67 was moving
out. Tystad wanted Mutlaa Ridge. Without even altering formation,
the task force surged ahead. Still in second place in the big, open
column, Mike Kershaw and the others gunned their motors and
headed north to press the attack.

In the early afternoon, near the promised land of Mutlaa, TF 3-67
hit something more substantial along a low rise southeast of Ali Al
Salem Airfield. This high ground led to the Mutlaa Ridge–highway
juncture that beckoned the Americans forward. That important spot
was only three miles away. The Tigers were close.

But first, TF 3-67 had to sort out this problem. Dug-in, dismounted
Iraqi mechanized infantry with supporting T-55 tanks held a strongpoint, with a minefield right in Tystad's path. The Iraqis opened fire
as the Americans approached. Nobody was waving white flags in this
enemy outfit.

Based on map boundaries, the air base complex proper belonged
to the Arab allies to the west. This obstinate strongpoint, however,
protected the spot where Tystad's formation had to pivot to the east
to ascend Mutlaa Ridge. Waiting for the Egyptians to the west would
not work. So Tystad elected to assault, mines be damned.

Tystad's point tanks noticed that the enemy appeared to be facing east and that this Iraqi mine barrier might have been laid to
guard the south flank of a position intended to protect the airfield
from an attack off the coastline to the east.[31] Maybe this batch of
Iraqis had been planted to stop the great Iraqi bogeyman, a Marine
amphibious thrust. No matter that the Marines and their Tiger
friends had arrived from the south, not the east. It was just another
good opportunity for Task Force 3-67 to exploit.

Accelerating, Tystad's task force executed a hasty breaching drill,
the sort of evolution practiced time after time at the National Training Center in Fort Irwin, California, under the unforgiving guns of

the U.S. Army's homegrown version of a classical high Soviet-era motor rifle regiment. This time, the real enemy did not fight as well or shoot as true. But they weren't shooting blanks, either. So the Americans had to get it right.

They did. The two trailing tank companies came up on line and started engaging targets. Kershaw's Bradleys also opened up, the steady sharp *pop-pop-pop* of the 25mm chain guns barking across the open ground. Once the U.S. phalanx started shooting, the breachers moved up. Nobody waited for engineers, not in an armored battalion task force.

Instead, a few Abrams tanks headed north, each carrying odd ironworks on their slanted bows. A few had mine plows, triangular blades with thick metal teeth, capable of bulldozing up the Iraqi implements. Others pushed things that looked like agricultural disk harrows, rows of thick steel wheels hanging from a strong tubular frame. These rollers blew up mines by going right over them. It all happened fast, the plow and roller tanks shooting their onboard machine guns as they pushed forward.

Mines erupted harmlessly. Others were uprooted and shuffled aside by the snorting, furrowing U.S. tanks. Enemy tanks fired, their rounds high and wide. American gunnery proved much more effective. One, then two Iraqi vehicles brewed up into fireballs. Iraqi fire abated. Some enemy T-55 tanks and armored personnel carriers began moving to the northeast, toward Mutlaa Ridge itself and the golden escape road. Smoke from burning oil wells, blazing enemy tanks, diesel exhaust, and continuous explosions choked the air. It was hard to see.[32] The American gunners relied on their wonderful thermal sights. Without such technology, Iraqi vehicles blundered into their own mines, exploded, and began burning, adding to the thick gray-black clouds drifting over the field.

The obscuration confused the Iraqis, whose firing died away. As the plows and rollers crunched out of the mine belt, Company B of TF 3-67 moved out. The rest of Tystad's units followed. Glimpsing their quarry perhaps through rips in the prevalent smoke screen, a few Iraqis shot wildly as the Americans swung east. None hit.

The U.S. task force could not get bogged down here, not with the badniks on the run and Mutlaa Ridge dead ahead. In true cavalry

fashion, Col. John Sylvester brought up his next outfit—TF 3-41—
to finish off the strongpoint.[33] He let Tystad keep going.

The TF 3-67 commander did not need encouragement. His leading tank commanders in Company B saw the highway and counted
some eighteen Iraqi tanks charging north to safety, firing over their
back decks. To the north, enemy covering fire came from a pair of
unfinished three-story concrete and brick buildings that dominated
the roadway—the Al Mutlaa Police Post. To the south, enemy tanks
took up firing postures in the curves of a cloverleaf interchange. Add
a Stuckey's and a gas station and it would look like a stretch of the
interstate in Ohio or Indiana. Except that here, the sky loomed black
with petro-stinking soot, the road shoulders were littered with smoldering wreckage from earlier U.S. Marine air attacks, and the other
motorists wanted to kill you.

Company B's fourteen M-1A1s raced forward to block the road
soon to be known as the "Highway of Death." The first two U.S. tanks
fired on the move, keying on the northernmost hostiles. Two T-55s
sagged to a stop, finished. An Iraqi self-propelled 122mm howitzer
blew up. The other Iraqi armor stalled, their way barred. American
machine guns opened up, spraying a wave of bullets across the enemy hulls. Then the U.S. crews ceased firing, to see what would happen.

The stymied Iraqis did not disappoint. Hatches cracked open, one
after another, and heads poked up. Many began waving white cloths.
The Americans held on; they watched the opposing tankers climb
off their vehicles and form up into an unkempt parade, led by men
waving white fabric. In all, fifteen tank crews gave up; shocked and
jabbering, they shambled toward the Americans.

With Company B busy on the road, Tystad committed his follow-
on units. The Abrams tanks of Company D charged for the cloverleaf, knocking out a T-62 and another T-55 during their attack. They
established a southward-facing line of fire, thereby cutting the only
road left out of Kuwait City. During the next few hours, they potted
numerous other hostile vehicles. So far, so good—Doug Tystad had
almost done the job at the Al Mutlaa bottleneck.

Almost, but those twin enemy-held buildings still spat defiance
from the police station on the north stretch of Mutlaa Ridge. The

M-1A1 tanks' big 120mm sabot rounds didn't seem to bother the Iraqis inside. They held out. Tanks couldn't solve that one.

It was about 1545 on a bad afternoon. Colonel John Sylvester described the scene.

> I have never seen anything like it in my worst imagination . . . smoking pits with pieces of people, everywhere you looked. Bodies stacked up everywhere. Charred and melted vehicles. I'm not being melodramatic. It was a scene right out of Hell.
>
> Along the highway that was later called the Death Highway, there were a hell of a bunch of Iraqis still fighting. Especially the guys who holed up in a police post overlooking the highway. It was a multistory concrete cinder-block building [actually two identical buildings]. They had barricaded the windows and set up a bunch of bunkers up in the hillside. I guess somebody had told them to hold that road.[34]

Those two rectangular two-story buildings, the same unfinished Kuwaiti police station noted on the map, clearly controlled the Highway of Death. You could really see it out here on the ground. As long as the Iraqis held the facility, they had a foot in the door that the Americans wanted to shut. So Tystad had to take it out, just as he and Mike Kershaw had discussed at the battalion order session several hours and a lifetime ago, that very morning. For the grunts who had rocked, rolled, and waited in their metal cocoons, showtime had come.

Kershaw's strong voice came over Team C's radios: "This is it! Tanks center. First [platoon] right. Third [platoon] left. Dismount and assault through the objective."

Ahead, volleys of 155mm shells began to land around the police post. Team C fanned out smoothly, forming an assault line without slackening its tempo.

As his tracks slewed to the left in accord with Captain Kershaw's orders, Dan Stempniak saw his eventual target materialize out of the dirty air. A half mile or so ahead, the police compound waited, its windows glittering with gunfire. With its upper stories visible above the hump of the highway roadbed, the police buildings looked bigger than Stempniak expected, lots bigger. This was going to get interesting.

The book said to clear buildings from the top down, but that obviously would not happen here. Stempniak elected right then to try for a single entrance point, the center doors on the ground floor of the near building, which Mike Kershaw's Kuwaiti translator that morning had assured him led directly to a long, central hallway going left and right. That was where Stempniak wanted to feed in his rifle teams to start kicking in doors and cleaning out rooms. First of all, of course, the Americans had to cross the divided highway—probably under fire, and a lot of it. Come on, artillery.

The howitzer gunners would do their part; in fact, they already were doing it. To get Stempniak's dismounts safely across the lonely, open patch and into the bottom-floor hallway, the platoon's Brads needed to roll up firing their chain guns and coax weapons to push the Iraqis away from the windows. Then the 11M10s had to dismount and go in. Those grunts had better move like lightning, or several wouldn't have to worry about ever moving again.

Dan Stempniak's men already knew how to clear rooms. Lots of good training in that basic infantry battle drill gave them confidence as they moved up. Here, preparatory exercises really paid off.[35] The familiarity of that sequence calmed active minds and steadied nerves as the company team closed on its destination.

The artillery also helped. Even inside the Bradleys, with all the other howling sounds of engines racing, the men heard the big 155mm shells sighing overhead. Those who could see out the jiggling vision blocks watched fountains of sandy dirt springing up all around the buildings. It looked impressive. The Brads had gotten about halfway there when the howitzer barrage finished, having done nothing more than while away the time and keep the post's inhabitants ducking. Neither building took a direct hit, but the barrage quelled the opposing fireworks and let Stempniak's vehicles get in as tight as they were going to get. That would do.

To the immediate south, Team C's Abrams platoon stopped short a few hundred yards out and got to work. One of the U.S. tanks pumped three rounds into the end of one building, then it dusted

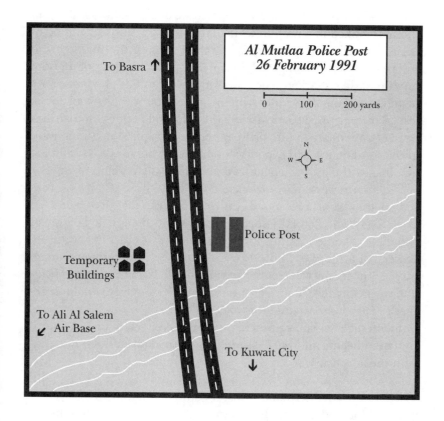

Al Mutlaa Police Post
26 February 1991

To Basra

Police Post

Temporary Buildings

To Ali Al Salem Air Base

To Kuwait City

the brickwork with coaxial 7.62mm machine-gun fire, chipping off flakes around the open doorway and presumably skipping slugs down the long hallway to do something useful. Its partner did likewise, pounding the other structure a few seconds later. An enemy rocket-propelled grenade (RPG) corkscrewed out, missing the tank and its three partners. The second tank fired again, punching a hole near the open doorway. No other RPGs came out.

Covered by the tanks, Dan Stempniak brought his platoon closer, just as in numerous training exercises. But this was real. Well, you fight like you train, they say. This platoon did. The young lieutenant gave the usual orders: "Come on line. Dismount left. Vehicles suppress buildings to our front."[36]

The 3d Platoon's four Brads crept closer, firing all the way. Around them, it looked like twilight with all of the grimy smoke hanging in the air. American Bradley gunners relied on their thermal sights to pierce the onerous, filthy veil. Bits of lightning tore the gloom; Iraqi muzzle flashes sparked from the windows. Bradley chain guns retorted, smashing the windows on the upper floors. In the back of the tracks, men gripped black M-16A2 rifles, locked plastic ammo drums onto M-249 squad automatic weapons, and fingered fragmentation grenades. The tracked carriers slowed, jockeying for the proper angle. Inside, the grunts exchanged glances; time to get to work.

The ramps went down. *Dismount! Go! Go! Go!*

Out they went, two squads on the ground with three hundred yards to go. The tip of the spear here at Al Mutlaa equaled eighteen riflemen, a lieutenant, his radioman, and his artillery forward observer. All around, obscured by dust and drifting, pungent smog, wandering enemy vehicles backed and filled; Iraqi troops ran hither and yon, a lot more than twenty-one. Nobody stopped to do the arithmetic. There was no time for that.

Stempniak was still getting his bearings when one Iraqi ran toward him brandishing an AK-47. The lieutenant had no choice but to deal with the adversary.

> He was an older man with a wild and dazed look in his eyes, and appeared as though he wanted to surrender. I halted him about five feet from C30 [Stempniak's Bradley], but he refused to lay down his weapon. Several tense moments passed, during which the muzzle of his weapon was repeatedly oriented in the vicinity of my chest. Just as I began to doubt his intentions to surrender, our eyes met, and he laid his weapon down.[37]

This challenge met, Stempniak turned to the assault.

He found his men deployed on line, Sgt. Donald Webb's 4th Squad to the north and SSgt. Eric Garza's 3d Squad to the south, both facing the highway embankment. Both elements were lying prone, taking sporadic Iraqi fire from the distant police post. This was everyone's first encounter with hostile bullets, and nobody wanted to get up and get going right away, a rather understandable response. It took Dan Stempniak a few minutes to get the men up and moving. Once he did, they kept on going, right across the highway, one squad shooting while the others moved. The platoon's Bradleys banged away, battering the Iraqi-held police buildings, guarding their dismounts. Once the ground soldiers crossed the highway, the Brads would be out of the fight, their lines of fire masked by U.S. riflemen. But for now, their powerful suppressive fire, and that alone, made movement possible across that lonely, open road.

Rushing ahead as their comrades and the Brads banged away, Eric Garza's men ran into four temporary structures, one of cinder blocks, the other three of light aluminum. Thinking fast, Garza tossed a fragmentation grenade into the cement building and had his riflemen check out the flimsy aluminum-shelled shelters, giving each a few well-aimed three-round bursts. Grenades in those glorified yard sheds might well have spat back hot fragments through the thin walls and shredded unwary throwers. No Iraqis opposed this effort.

The two squads continued across the highway, taking turns firing and moving. A blazing T-55 tank and a smoking 122mm self-propelled howitzer allowed for some protection for the squads as they rushed across the roadway. The bobbing, weaving Americans had to watch out for Iraqi ammunition randomly cooking off, crazy projectiles arcing out of the pyres as the stricken vehicles burned. Garza's 3d Squad got to the far side first.

On the ground floor of the western building, ten Iraqis showing a white flag huddled in the open doorway. Garza held his men's fire and motioned the hostiles forward. It might have been handy to speak Arabic at this point, but the Americans lacked that talent. So they whistled and waved and, most important, did not shoot. After a few minutes, the Iraqis came out, hands up. Garza passed them to Don Webb's trailing squad, and a four-man fire team herded them back across the bullet-swept highway.

As that happened, Dan Stempniak noticed that enemy shooting had slackened. This was a good time to go in. Stempniak, Eric Garza, and their 11Ms entered the first floor through the main entrance, all unscathed.

Swiftly, the two U.S. fire teams got inside the hazy, dark tunnel of a hallway. They crowded against the left wall and lined up in a half squat. Breathing hard, the men flipped down their night-vision goggles, just as in the drill. They couldn't see anybody in the hall intersection to their front, not yet, but they heard AK-47s hammering away upstairs. The lead American pulled out a hand grenade to roll down the hallway, but his lieutenant held him up. He sensed something, something close. Stempniak dropped onto his belly, crept to a corner, and peeked around to the left, down the unlit hallway.

It wasn't a pretty sight. An Iraqi with mangled legs inched along a few feet away, groaning, trailing blood in a long, slick smear. He was all that remained of this floor's defenders.

The lieutenant leaned back and waved forward two of his men. They hustled out, grabbed the wounded Iraqi,[38] and got him back outside, to Webb's guys, who added him to their charges and began first aid. Upstairs, the gunfire kept on going, shot after shot.

Floor one was now empty. Might as well start on the rest, thought Stempniak. He motioned his lead team up the central stairwell, determined to clean out the hard-core characters up top. Garza nodded and the squad went topside, using the noise of enemy shooting and explosions to muffle their footfalls. Even with the echoes and all the commotion outside, they could tell that the AK fire was coming from a room to the right. Garza decided to clear that end first.

The lead fire team moved forward carefully, right shoulders touching the smooth, cool, unfinished wall. They could not tell if anyone was in the first cubicle even though it had no door. The four riflemen lined up along the wall, as in training. While the back pair watched the empty hallway, just in case, the second man kept his rifle muzzle slanted down, ready to swing it up when he rushed in. In front of him, the first man prepared a grenade, yanking off the big pull ring and flipping away the little wire handle clip. (No, you never pull these with your teeth, not if you ever want to chew meat again.) Then the soldier inched his arm forward, wrist around the doorjamb, and let fly.

One thousand, two thousand, three—*ka-boom!*

Dust and debris blasted out of the opening and sprinkled the crouching riflemen. The lead twosome charged in, one breaking right, one left, each shooting a three-round burst. The bullets skittered off the hard cement floor and ricocheted around, bouncing off unyielding surfaces and almost coming back in their faces.[39] Both men flinched, surprised. Obviously, that technique worked better on dirt floors than on a flat, hard deck. Better pass the word to quit shooting arbitrarily. This time, there was nobody in there, but AK-47 magazines and spent casings littered the floor. It had all taken only a few seconds.

"Clear!" shouted the corporal.

Garza waved the next team into the room on the left. Again, the grenade blew and the men went in. The screams and lower sound of AK fire told all that the room had live occupants, or at least it used to have some.

"Clear!"

It took time to do it right. Garza slowly worked through the various rooms on the second floor of the west building. Some opponents surrendered; others did not. But Garza kept going, occasionally sending two-man teams down the center stairs to get more grenades or more magazines or to hand off cowed prisoners. Meanwhile, Stempniak and Webb began to look across to the eastern building, determined to get in there as soon as Garza took the third floor and stood by to support by fire.

The methodical *pop-pop-pop* of distant chain guns—they had their own prey now back at the highway—echoed off the pockmarked walls of the police post, punctuated by the thump of grenades and the quick, breathless chatter of rifle shots and SAW bursts. From inside, the Iraqis on the upper floor kept shooting back. One stray sniper round killed a TF 3-67 senior NCO at a nearby battalion tactical command post.[40]

The fight went on for hours, well into the night. The Americans knew of at least twelve enemy dead in the station; they had stood on the bodies. Out on the highway, TF 3-67 tank roadblocks nailed fleeing Iraqis from almost every opposing unit in the area. Prisoners kept trickling in. But at the Al Mutlaa Police Post, all that mattered was the next room.

Eric Garza got to the roof of the western building and took over prisoner and aid station security tasks from Don Webb's squad. Garza settled in his SAW gunners and prepared to shoot up the upper floors of the other building. Don Webb got ready to cross the small, open expanse. With Stempniak alongside, they waited to enter the second part of the police complex.

Just before Garza's teams opened fire, another fifteen Iraqis on the bottom level appeared in the main entrance; the white cloth they were waving was barely visible in the darkness. But the Americans saw the truce marker clearly in their night-vision goggles. Webb turned to his officer. Now what?

Dan Stempniak had his guys hold their fire. Once more, he and his radioman waved and shouted, trying to coax the wavering Iraqis to give up and cross over to the American-held building. After an agonizing delay, a few dashed across. The rest followed within a minute. Their more resilient fellows on the upper levels of the east structure snapped off several more shots, spurring the quitters on their way.

This interlude permitted Eric Garza and his men to redistribute ammunition and pick targets well. When it came time to dart across the death ground, Stempniak and Webb crossed easily, shielded by what the platoon leader later described as a "withering volume of fire."[41] The twelve Americans—Webb's riflemen and the lieutenant and his two partners—crouched alone in the unoccupied first floor. The sharp sting of cordite, gunpowder to the uninitiated, tickled their dulled noses. The staccato cracks of AK-47s still sounded over their heads. These Iraqis simply did not get the message. All of Webb's riflemen knew what that meant, all right: door to door, the terminal cleaning contract, grunt style.

Once again, the Americans crept up the chipped, cracked stairwell, bound for their room-clearing two-step, punctuated by the grenades and sharp reports of 5.56mm bullets. That commenced, just as before, just as in training. Some Iraqis went down fighting. Several more quit. Another hour or so crawled by.

Before midnight, right before Dan Stempniak and his tired men prepared to go up to the third floor, a white flag appeared in a window. By this time, Eric Garza's squad was on the ground level of the east building, helping out. His security element posted outside at the main entrance relayed the welcome news of the white flag to their tired counterparts upstairs. The timing could not have been better; the assaulting 11Ms had gone through almost all of their hand grenades. The physical effort of bursting into rooms and dragging out bodies had taken its toll, too.

Worked over by tanks, Bradleys, and now, for the last several hours, twenty-one determined American riflemen, the building's interior had become a slaughterhouse. The defenders had been literally torn apart by brutal American gunnery. "There was gore all over, literally pools of blood," recalled Maj. Robert Williams of TF 3-67. "Many were dismembered."[42] Their fate sealed, their war lost, the rest elected to save their skins.

With the Bradley gunners watching through thermal sights from back across the highway, and American dismounts standing by with weapons raised in the dark stairwell and outside, twenty-eight Iraqi soldiers filed slowly down the cracked, dirty stairs, their way lit by red-filtered flashlights. They emerged from the police station one by one, some stumbling, all with their hands up. The Iraqis wore distinctive, unusually crisp camouflage uniforms. Behind them, strewn through both buildings, were fifty-two dead comrades, more than twice the number of men who assaulted them. Aside from the unlucky sergeant killed nearby, the Americans suffered eight lightly injured.[43] Thanks to a handful of tough mechanized infantrymen, the road from Kuwait City belonged to the Tiger Brigade.

Colonel John Sylvester's Tigers demonstrated armored warfare at the doctoral level, administering a series of hard lessons to Iraqis on the receiving end. In doing so, the brigade clearly displayed the truth behind the 2d Armored Division's symbol, the pyramid of power. American armored units practice combined-arms warfare all the time. When U.S. Army leaders talk about armored forces—also called heavy forces—they mean the whole bunch, the entire Hell on Wheels conglomerate, not simply tanks.[44] That's why the patch has cavalry-armor gold, artillery red, and infantry blue. It represents the mounted warfare team.

That teamwork relies on cross-attachment.[45] The Tiger Brigade's lineup for Operation Desert Storm shows how this works. The 3d Battalion (Mechanized), 41st Infantry Regiment, formed the core of TF

3-41, but it also contributed a company to the brigade's two tank battalions, 1st and 3d of the 67th Armor. This explains why Mike Kershaw's infantrymen worked for Doug Tystad's tank headquarters. Without those 11M10s, TF 3-67 could never have grabbed the Al Mutlaa Police Post. But without his Abrams tanks, Mike Kershaw's riflemen might have paid a higher price for their success. Cross-attachment goes both ways. The armor battalions each gave a tank company to the 3d of the 41st, thereby turning all three of these outfits into tank–mechanized infantry task forces. Each TF then had the option of taking the process one more step, forming certain companies into company teams—such as Kershaw's Team C—by trading tank and mech infantry platoons. Whether the situation called for riflemen or tanks, all three battalion-sized organizations could deal with it.

In this manner, the Tiger Brigade headed north into Kuwait with combined-arms tank-infantry task forces. To facilitate this conscious mixing and matching, all heavy maneuver battalions in the U.S. Army in 1991 had four line companies each, which allowed for tank-heavy, mech-heavy, or balanced task forces, a lot of flexibility for America's mounted warriors.[46] Light forces make do with three rifle companies per battalion, but they rarely do these kinds of company-for-company swaps.

Not so the heavy contingent; they live with daily cross-attachment in combat and training. To make this easier, tank and mech battalions also employ virtually identical headquarters companies. The 3d of the 41st Infantry, for example, fielded the same six platoons in its headquarters company as the 3d of the 67th Armor, with essentially the same equipment. As long as the tank companies brought their unique repair parts, fuel trucks, and ammunition with them, and the Bradley units did the same, cross-attachment went smoothly.[47] It had been designed that way since World War II, and for good reason.

All armored units are considered largely interchangeable up to divisional level, and it is not unheard of for mech infantry officers to serve in tank units and vice versa. These forces all use doctrine created at the U.S. Army Armor Center at Fort Knox, Kentucky, although the Infantry Center at Fort Benning, Georgia, ensures that grunt interests get sufficient attention. This division of labor reflects the relative enthusiasm for the business.

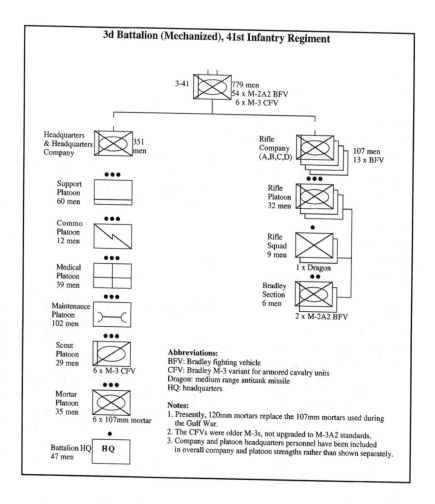

3d Battalion (Mechanized), 41st Infantry Regiment

3-41 — 779 men / 54 x M-2A2 BFV / 6 x M-3 CFV

Headquarters & Headquarters Company — 351 men

Support Platoon — 60 men

Commo Platoon — 12 men

Medical Platoon — 39 men

Maintenance Platoon — 102 men

Scout Platoon — 29 men — 6 x M-3 CFV

Mortar Platoon — 35 men — 6 x 107mm mortar

Battalion HQ — 47 men — HQ

Rifle Company (A,B,C,D) — 107 men / 13 x BFV

Rifle Platoon — 32 men

Rifle Squad — 9 men — 1 x Dragon

Bradley Section — 6 men — 2 x M-2A2 BFV

Abbreviations:
BFV: Bradley fighting vehicle
CFV: Bradley M-3 variant for armored cavalry units
Dragon: medium range antitank missile
HQ: headquarters

Notes:
1. Presently, 120mm mortars replace the 107mm mortars used during the Gulf War.
2. The CFVs were older M-3s, not upgraded to M-3A2 standards.
3. Company and platoon headquarters personnel have been included in overall company and platoon strengths rather than shown separately.

The Infantry Center has to crank out stuff for airborne, air assault, light, and Ranger units; these battalions outnumber the mech infantrymen three to two. So Benning naturally defers to Knox in these matters of mounted fighting. No less an authority than Gen. William E. DePuy, a brilliant infantry commander, once complained in the early 1970s that Fort Benning remained "in the hands of the light infantryman" afflicted with a "2½ mile an hour mentality." In those days, "they didn't do mech infantry well at all" at Benning.[48]

Thanks to men such as DePuy and the introduction of the Bradley fighting vehicle, things have improved since the lean years after Vietnam. The 11M10 riflemen and the individual and small-unit skill manuals from Fort Benning are good products indeed. But when it comes to the broader conduct of mounted warfare, the Armor Center calls the tune. It generates the basic combined-arms doctrine: *FM 71-1* for the company team, *FM 71-2* for the battalion task force, and *FM 71-3* for the heavy brigade. Not by accident does the gold of armored-cavalry stand on top of that power pyramid.

Colonel John Sylvester had plenty of doctrinal advice from those 71-series manuals and World War II battle experience to help him decide the proper proportion of tanks to infantry, and who leads. The more tanks, the faster you go and the harder you hit, especially against opposing mounted echelons. Tanks move out in open terrain when the opposition has broken and when the opponents have plenty of armor of their own. The best way to kill their tanks relies on our tanks. And when you get the enemy running, heavy U.S. armor can mow them down and over.

But sometimes, that roll over 'em approach won't work, and infantry must go ahead, mounted or at times walking—sometimes rushing, creeping, or crawling. The more infantry, the better to dig out entrenched badniks, clear towns, breach minefields, and generally grab contested turf. Infantry goes ahead in rough terrain, against fixed emplacements, and to pry out enemy antitank guns, missiles, and rocket launchers. With a brigade disposing more than a thousand vehicles, three-quarters of them on tires, not tracks, the right people had to be out front.[49] Otherwise, everybody pays for it when the wrong kind of hostiles open up on the long columns and bring an ugly halt to the bold armored thrust.

Present field manuals lead one to think that when tanks and mech troops are combined, they serve in an equal partnership. They do not. The nebulous verbiage in praise of combined arms in the formal doctrine underscores solid teamwork between Knox and Benning, with the Armor Center and the Infantry Center agreeing that the other is important. That answers DePuy's old concern. But it also masks a basic truth, one that DePuy argued strongly and correctly. Mechanized infantry exists for one purpose and one only—to speed the tanks forward.[50] On the mounted battlefield, infantry gets out and fights only as necessary. If they can, the men fight from their vehicles, slugging away to suppress enemy foot soldiers and keep the tanks rolling.

That explains the purpose of the M-2A2 Bradley fighting vehicle, a thirty-three-ton tracked armored troop carrier built to fight beside the M-1 Abrams series main battle tanks.[51] Earlier U.S. Army infantry carriers sported a .50-caliber heavy machine gun on an open pedestal and looked like shoeboxes on treads. They resembled a more robust species of truck, and got used that way, too. Only a neophyte would mistake an M-113 for a genuine tank. Not so the Bradley; it features an impressive turret complete with a 25mm Bushmaster autocannon, TOW antitank missile launchers, a coaxial light machine gun, and a wonderful thermal imaging sight—all served by a three-man crew, as is the light tank it resembled. True, a Bradley had room in the back for seven dismounts, but the more you considered this wonderful weapon, the more the 11M10s seemed like afterthoughts compared to those powerful turret weapons.[52] After all, dropping the rear ramp slab just slowed down the whole operation; if you could, why not send a bullet, not a man, in the good old American style?

Bradley sergeants and officers often jokingly claim the motto "death before dismount." But the jibe has teeth. The written descriptions of how a Bradley platoon fights reinforce the idea that you dismount only if you really, *really* have to. The stabilized 25mm cannon aims and fires nicely on the fly. It can do a job on any miscreants, not to mention bunkers, masonry structures, light vehicles, and even some tanks, all at a comfortably long range of more than a mile, and without anyone getting get out and running around in a lead hailstorm.[53]

What about the men in back? Even they had a mounted firing role in the original M-2 series vehicles. Early versions of the Brad actually included small M-16 rifle variants plugged in under the various vision blocks, designed to allow the riflemen inside to fire as they moved. Of course, that idea looked better on the drawing board than in real life. Somebody forgot about marksmanship. Uncontrolled streams of random bullets shot from swinging mounts as a track jounced and spun made nearby friendly crewmen nervous, especially neighboring Bradley and tank commanders with their heads out of the turrets. Wisely, the present generation of Brad does away with these accidents waiting to happen, except on the back ramp.[54] (Do not tailgate a Bradley.) The very thought of such firing port weapons surely strengthened the concept of death before dismount.

The present Bradley infantry platoon and squad manual, *FM 7-7J*, says as much: "The infantry remains mounted unless the enemy must be cleared from restrictive terrain, or unless forced to dismount by enemy resistance."[55] Those "unless" clauses explain why tankers need mech warriors, but the phrases do come second and sound kind of exceptional. If possible, the infantry should stay in the metal box and let the gunners do the killing.

When "unless" comes to pass, the book suggests a rather grudging, partial response. Most dismounted work involves privates, if anyone. In *FM 7-7J*, officers and sergeants are encouraged to stay in their turrets with the big radios, the good thermal sights, and the lethal autocannons and TOWs. In a particularly convoluted segment of the manual, the authors try to explain how the platoon leader decides to unplug and get out.

> If a dismount is executed in response to an unexpected, life-threatening situation where speed is essential, then only the squads dismount. The BFVs [Bradley fighting vehicles] immediately suppress and obscure the enemy while moving to covered dismount points. A quick estimate is made to determine if and when the platoon leader joins the dismount element.[56]

So let's get this straight. The book says that in an absolute crisis, in death ground, the privates and a few junior NCOs are dumped out, then the officers think about whether they *might* deign to join them in the firestorm? It's not exactly the old tradition of "follow me."

Fortunately, field manuals do not always carry much weight in the field. This should come as little surprise to Americans, a practical people notoriously impatient and cavalier with instructional literature. Not for nothing do most U.S. videocassette recorders blink "12:00" for years on end. Having learned from books such as *FM 7-7J* and trained otherwise, Dan Stempniak and Mike Kershaw did the right thing reflexively. They and their sergeants and corporals *led* their men into harm's way. When the ramps slammed down, the chain of command went out on the ground just as they should have, as do all decent infantry leaders.[57] But the written material surely makes you wonder.

Studying how the Army filled its Bradleys reinforces the strong impression that the fighting vehicles constituted a light escort keying on hostile infantry and lesser armored threats. It sure did not seem to be a battle taxi for grunts. In fact, in today's mech battalions, 11M10 grunts are in pretty short supply. Most Bradleys do not carry a full house. By design, the four Brads in a platoon have room for at least 28 foot troops. Instead, the Army chooses to authorize only 18, organized into two 9-man rifle squads.[58] That yields a maximum of only 54 riflemen per rifle company; the other 58 men in the outfit run the Bradleys. A full-strength mechanized infantry battalion totals 216 riflemen on paper, fewer dismounted trigger pullers in four line companies than a light infantry battalion has in two.

It's actually worse than that. Analysis of the Tiger Brigade shows why. Two task forces, TF 1-67 and TF 3-67, got by with 54 riflemen each. The erstwhile infantry task force, TF 3-41, had 108, a battalion-sized force with almost a thousand soldiers including attachments but less bayonet strength than an average light infantry rifle company.[59] And remember, that was before deducting any combat casualties, sentries, truck guards, relief drivers, and command post augmentees, not to mention sick, lame, lazy, or the like. Our 11Ms had better be good, because they are not many.

The Army's built-in lack of mechanized riflemen has garnered some high-level attention, as well it should. In an extremely pointed plea in *Infantry* magazine, house organ of the U.S. Army Infantry Center, commandant Maj. Gen. Carl F. Ernst strongly argued for filling Bradley platoons to three eleven-man squads, with a three-man track crew and eight dismounts each, bringing each platoon to twenty-four trigger pullers. A similar initiative in the 1st Brigade, 4th Infantry Division (Mechanized)—the U.S. Army Experimental Force—goes by the name 2 x 9 + 5. This program adds an extra five riflemen per platoon to the usual two nine-man squads.[60] In an army that has undergone steady reductions, these ideas will not be implemented without some pain. But the fact that they get discussed and tested demonstrates that the U.S. Army is well aware that its 11M10 tables of organization need a sharp upward revision.

Of course, it's one thing to authorize slots. It's another to fill them. In the Gulf War, the Tigers and their mech brothers enjoyed their assigned complements of 11M10 riflemen. Dan Stempniak had enough—just enough—men to cleanse the Al Mutlaa Police Post. To get Stempniak's eighteen riflemen required extraordinary measures across the force, including activation of the Individual Ready Reserve, stripping nondeploying mechanized battalions, and cannibalizing light infantry battalions, too.[61] In an eighteen-division Regular Army, that could be done. Today, it would not be as easy. Bradley battalions will probably fight with what they have.

What they have are shortages. Stateside and since the Gulf War, the pickings can get slim indeed. Battalions training at the Fort Irwin National Training Center routinely report plenty of Bradleys but low dismount strengths.[62] The Army's tactical manning guidelines lead commanders this way, because doctrine rightly encourages them to assign their strongest weapons first. When commanders get only some of what they need, the Brads get first dibs. Dismounts make do with the leftovers.

To add to this trend, the Infantry Center's decision to separate the enlisted force into 11M mech infantry and 11B light infantry (including airborne, air assault, and Ranger) has created an unfortunate side effect. Until the mid-1980s, NCOs routinely transferred from mech to light. The airborne guys brought in foot skills; the mounted folks taught combined-arms tank ops. Pre-Bradley M-113 mechanized units knew how to fight on the ground. In an undergunned, thinly protected M-113, trying to do it any other way got very risky very fast.

But those days are over. The force has divided. The 11Bs have gone to Ranger school and out on patrols and night infiltrations. The 11Ms opt for master gunner courses and live-fire battle run ranges. Although mech leaders acknowledge a need for dismounts with the "full skills and toughness of light infantry," that's one bunch of jobs too many for mechanized soldiers fully committed to learning the ins and outs of a complex, capable armored fighting vehicle.[63] The 11M specialty naturally puts a premium on the highly challenging

Bradley turret skills, running and gunning, not fighting on foot. Rank as an 11M is made by learning the hull and engine, then the turret. Only officers serve in both types of infantry; doing the ciphering reveals that about a third have to remain light no matter what. There just aren't enough mechanized infantry outfits for alternating mech and light assignments.

The 11B-11M enlisted separation and the latter's emphasis on the fighting vehicle, not the fighting men, leads to disturbing consequences if not checked by a determined chain of command. In some U.S. Army mech battalions, riflemen come from the newbies, the mechanically inept, and the unwanted.[64] Thus, the dismounted Bradley infantryman—already a minority in his own battalion—can become a disadvantaged minority at that.

So the soldiers getting the infantry forward outnumber the bona fide rifle troops, even in a mechanized battalion. That seems unprecedented, but not when considering the way cavalry regiments tangled with Plains Indians in the 1870s. Like Bradley infantry, frontier Regular Army cavalry rode to battle, and even tried to skirmish that way, but dismounted when serious shooting started. Somebody had to hold the horses, so one trooper in four did that while the other three potted away with trapdoor Springfield rifles. The mounts gave great mobility and speed, vital for closing with fleeting Indians. But it came at a cost in horse holders, fodder wagons, veterinary specialists, blacksmiths, saddlers, and the like.[65] Was it worth it? Ask the Indians.

Like the horses of old, the mechanized infantry's Bradleys give it cross-country mobility, with the advantage of the vehicle's own terrific firepower and its armored skin capable of repelling bullets and whizzing shell fragments. That's a hell of a horse. But as with the U.S. cavalry of the 1870s, speed, protection, and power levy a price, much higher than in the previous century. The horse holders now outnumber the foot shooters by three to one in a mech battalion. The Brads require their own vast stable of fully outfitted fixers and tinkerers, and trucks the size of moving vans are needed to carry fuel and ammunition—thousands of gallons of liquid, hundreds of tons of projectiles. Again, is it worth it? The Iraqis found out.

Still, we cannot draw too many conclusions from four days of heady pursuit against a pathetic foe. The Al Mutlaa firefight deserves attention to showcase mechanized infantry in action, but it was an exceptional encounter.[66] Most U.S. mech infantry did not engage in that kind of close combat, mainly due to Iraqi sloth and cowardice. But not all enemies succumb so willingly. Against harder foes, America's dwindling crop of foot riflemen, trapped in their Bradleys, may experience the bitter truth of death before dismount.

That did not happen in Mike Kershaw's Team C. Those men remembered why they came to the war. It was a long haul up to the Al Mutlaa Police Post, but riding around does not a war make. Training and leadership paid off. When the ramps went down, those mechanized riflemen hit the ground running. The tank may be the dominant player in armored combat, but in death ground, hard men must get out and fight.

Notes

The epigraph comes from U.S. Special Operations Command, *USSOCOM Pub 1: Special Operations in Peace and War* (MacDill Air Force Base, Fla.: U.S. Special Operations Command, 25 January 1996), C-1.

1. Colonel Thomas Taylor, USAR (Ret.), *Lightning in the Storm* (New York, N.Y.: Hippocrene Books, 1994), 264–65, 366. For the French role, see Lt. Col. James J. Cooke, USAR, *100 Miles from Baghdad: With the French in Desert Storm* (Westport, Conn.: Praeger Publishers, 1993), 101–2.

2. Tom Clancy and Gen. Frederick M. Franks, Jr., USA (Ret.), *Into the Storm* (New York, N.Y.: G. P. Putnam's Sons, 1997), 371, 372–75, 446.

3. Anthony H. Cordesman and Abraham R. Wagner, *The Lessons of Modern War*, 4 vols. (Boulder, Colo.: Westview Press, Inc., 1990, 1996), *Volume IV: The Gulf War* (1996), 630–33.

4. Russell F. Weigley, *History of the United States Army* (Bloomington, Ind.: Indiana University Press, 1984), 375, 393. The Marine Brigade served in the U.S. Army's 2d Infantry Division throughout World War I. The other brigade contained U.S. Army Regulars. Marine Major General John A. Lejeune took command of the 2d Division for a period in 1918.

5. Cordesman and Wagner, *Volume IV: The Gulf War*, 603.

6. J. Paul Scicchitano, "Eye of the Tiger," *Army Times* (10 June 1991), 12; Capt. Daniel Stempniak, USA, *The Battle of the Al Mutlaa Police Post, 26 February 1991* (Fort Benning, Ga.: unpublished manuscript, May 1994), 1, 3. Stempniak's forty-four-page manuscript tells the definitive story of the fight at the Al Mutlaa police station, with many superb incidental insights into mechanized infantry warfare.

7. The demise of the 2d Armored Division became quite confusing. Initial plans called for outright deactivation of the division at Fort Hood, Texas, and its forward brigade in northern Germany. In 1990, the Gulf War interrupted this process. After the war, deactivation commenced again. Then in 1991–92, U.S. Army leaders decided to move the 5th Infantry Division (Mechanized) from Fort Polk,

Louisiana, to Fort Hood. Briefly, it was reflagged as the 2d Armored Division. It has since been reflagged again as the 4th Infantry Division (Mechanized), along with all subordinate units except two: the 1st of the 67th and the 3d of the 67th Armor, now assigned to the 2d Brigade, 4th Infantry Division (Mechanized), at Fort Hood. The 2d Armored Division's colors have been formally retired.

8. Cordesman and Wagner, *Volume IV: The Gulf War,* 759–60. The 155th Armored Brigade finally went on active duty in November 1990. It proved unready for combat, and called into question the overall readiness of Army National Guard formations. Interestingly, the 3d Brigade, 2d Armored Division, stationed forward in northern Germany in accord with Cold War defense plans, also went to Desert Shield–Desert Storm. It served as the third brigade of the 1st Infantry Division (Mechanized). This was because of more post–Cold War cuts. The 1st Infantry Division's own forward-posted brigade in Germany had been drawn down too far to be resurrected. With two brigades of the 2d Armored Division in action, it amounted to a pretty fair showing for a division that supposedly wasn't needed anymore.

9. Major Dale E. Wilson, USA (Ret.), *Treat 'Em Rough: The Birth of American Armor, 1917–20* (Novato, Calif.: Presidio Press, 1990), 36; Lt. Col. Carlo d' Este, USA (Ret.), *Patton: A Genius for War* (New York, N.Y.: HarperCollins, Publishers, Inc., 1995), 215, 381, 403; Martin Blumenson, *The Patton Papers,* 2 vols. (Boston, Mass.: Houghton Mifflin Co., 1974), *Vol. II: 1940–1945* (1974), 20, 35, 40. The quote comes from 1st Lt. Will G. Robinson, who designed the armored force patch in accord with Patton's guidance in 1918. Robinson's comments referred to Patton's 1918 Tank Corps, but he applied the same philosophy, often in near-identical terms, when he led the 2d Armored Division in 1940–42.

10. Al Santoli, *Leading the Way* (New York, N.Y.: Ballantine Books, 1993), 335–36. Santoli interviewed Sylvester at some length.

11. Scicchitano, "Eye of the Tiger," 18.

12. U.S. Department of the Army, *FM 71-123: Tactics and Techniques for Combined Arms Heavy Forces—Armored Brigade, Battalion/Task Force, and Company/Team* (Washington, D.C.: U.S. Government Printing Office, 30 September 1992), 3-79–81, A-8.

13. Tom Clancy, *Armored Cav* (New York, N.Y.: Berkley Books, 1994), 60–71, 74–78, 109–13. With special rocket-assisted projectiles, that range extends out past eighteen miles.

14. U.S. Department of the Army, *FM 71-123: Tactics and Techniques for Combined Arms Heavy Forces—Armored Brigade, Battalion/Task Force, and Company/Team*, 8-1–3, A-8. This example of a typical brigade with two tank TFs and one mech TF, plus an artillery battalion and other usual attachments, totals 1,090 vehicles.

15. Ibid., 18.

16. Michael R. Gordon and Lt. Gen. Bernard E. Trainor, USMC (Ret.), *The Generals' War* (Boston, Mass.: Little, Brown and Co., 1995), 379–82. The Marines had far fewer night-vision devices than comparable U.S. Army outfits. Gordon and Trainor reported only 1,100 night-vision goggles for more than 85,000 Marines. It mattered little. Given the awful visibility caused by burning oil wells, these passive starlight scopes did not help at all.

17. Scicchitano, "Eye of the Tiger," 18; Stempniak, *The Battle of the Al Mutlaa Police Post, 26 February 1991*, 22.

18. Ibid.

19. Barry McWilliams, *This Ain't Hell . . . But You Can See It From Here!* (Novato, Calif.: Presidio Press, 1992), 148–49.

20. Cordesman and Wagner, *Volume IV: The Gulf War*, 616–17.

21. The other infantry military occupational specialties in the U.S. Army are 11C (mortarman) and 11H (TOW crewman).

22. U.S. Department of the Army, U.S. Army Infantry Center, *FC 7-21B: Bradley Infantry Fighting Vehicle Squad and Platoon Drills* (Fort Benning, Ga.: U.S. Army Infantry Center, May 1985), 1-10–12.

23. Clancy, *Armored Cav*, 75.

24. Scicchitano, "Eye of the Tiger," 18.

25. Colonel Richard M. Swain, USA (Ret.), *"Lucky War": Third Army in Desert Storm* (Fort Leavenworth, Kans.: U.S. Army Command and General Staff College Press, 1994), 265.

26. Telephone interview with Capt. Daniel Stempniak, USA, at Fort Polk, Louisiana, 1 February 1998; Stempniak, *The Battle of the Al Mutlaa Police Post, 26 February 1991*, 24–25.

27. Stempniak, *The Battle of the Al Mutlaa Police Post, 26 February 1991*, 28.

28. U.S. Department of the Army, *FM 90-10-1: An Infantryman's Guide to Combat in Built-up Areas* (Washington, D.C.: U.S. Government Printing Office, 12 May 1993), 3-9–11, F-1.

29. Cordesman and Wagner, *Volume IV: The Gulf War,* 605; Stempniak, *The Battle of the Al Mutlaa Police Post, 26 February 1991,* 22. Stempniak noted that his order from Capt. Mike Kershaw identified the 34th Brigade, Iraqi 3d Armored Division, as their main opposition on 26 February 1991. In reality, the Iraqis had become hopelessly intermingled by this point, with the enemy 34th Brigade only one of several broken units trying to hold on.

30. Lieutenant Colonel Dennis P. Mroczkowski, USMCR, *With the 2d Marine Division in Desert Shield and Desert Storm* (Washington, D.C.: Headquarters, U.S. Marine Corps, 1993), 64.

31. Ibid.; Scicchitano, "Eye of the Tiger," 18.

32. Santoli, *Leading the Way,* 336; Stempniak, *The Battle of the Al Mutlaa Police Post, 26 February 1991,* 27. In crossing the mine barrier, Kershaw's Team C actually went through an open bypass lane located by American reconnaissance.

33. Mroczkowski, *With the 2d Marine Division in Desert Shield and Desert Storm,* 64–65.

34. Santoli, *Leading the Way,* 338.

35. Stempniak interview; Stempniak, *The Battle of the Al Mutlaa Police Post, 26 February 1991,* 28–29, 35–37.

36. Stempniak, *The Battle of the Al Mutlaa Police Post, 26 February 1991,* 29.

37. Ibid., 30.

38. Ibid., 32–33; Stempniak interview.

39. Stempniak interview; Stempniak, *The Battle of the Al Mutlaa Police Post, 26 February 1991,* 33. For the room-clearing methods, see U.S. Army Infantry Center, *FC 7-21B: Bradley Infantry Fighting Vehicle Squad and Platoon Drills,* 3-111–112.

40. Stempniak, *The Battle of the Al Mutlaa Police Post, 26 February 1991,* 33–34; Mroczkowski, *With the 2d Marine Division in Desert Shield and Desert Storm,* 65; Jeffrey E. Phillips and Robyn M. Gregory, *America's First Team in the Gulf* (Dallas, Tex.: Taylor Publishing Co., 1992), 137.

41. Stempniak, *The Battle of the Al Mutlaa Police Post, 26 February 1991,* 33.

42. Scicchitano, "Eye of the Tiger," 61.

43. Ibid., 18, 61; Santoli, *Leading the Way,* 338; Stempniak, *The Battle of the Al Mutlaa Police Post, 26 February 1991,* 33–34. Sylvester thought that the defenders in the police station might have been "Republican Guard elite special forces," but this was never verified.

44. The U.S. Army Armor Center has fought a losing battle to get the mounted, mechanized forces designated as armored. Most U.S. Army doctrine refers to them as heavy elements, vice light units: airborne, air assault, and light infantry and their combined-arms associates. The term *heavy* has many perjorative overtones in terms of cross-continental mobility, not to mention the fitness of soldiers in the mounted arm. For those manuals over which the Armor Center holds sway, the term *heavy* is not used. See U.S. Department of the Army, *FM 71-3: The Armored and Mechanized Infantry Brigade* (Washington, D.C.: U.S. Government Printing Office, 8 January 1996), ii, C-2.

45. U.S. Department of the Army, *FM 7-20: The Infantry Battalion* (Washington, D.C.: U.S. Government Printing Office, 6 April 1992), 3-9; Department of the Army, *FM 71-3: The Armored and Mechanized Infantry Brigade,* 1-10.

46. This remains true in early 1998, but some plans exist to reduce tank and mechanized battalions back to three line companies each. Presumably, improved fighting vehicles will allow this economy measure, although the only known enhancements involve shared computer data link displays. Prior to the mid-1980s, heavy battalions had only three line companies. The big loss involves the capability to create balanced (two tank, two mech) battalion TFs.

47. U.S. Department of the Army, *FM 101-10-1/1 Staff Officers' Field Manual Organizational, Technical, and Logistical Data* (Washington, D.C.: U.S. Government Printing Office, October 1987), 1-46–47. In Department of the Army, *FM 71-123: Tactics and Techniques for Combined Arms Heavy Forces: Armored Brigade, Battalion/Task Force, and Company/Team,* 8-26–27, the authors state that "when a company is cross-attached, the CSS [combat service support] necessary to support it is also cross-attached." They describe this CSS as including an armored ambulance section, a maintenance team with spare parts and tools, one fuel truck per mech company and two or three per tank company, and ammunition trucks, two five-tons per mech company and two or three bigger trucks for tank units.

48. Major Paul H. Herbert, USA, *Leavenworth Papers #16: Deciding What Had to Be Done: General Williuam E. DePuy and the 1976 Edition of FM 100-5 Operations* (Fort Leavenworth, Kans.: Combat Studies Institute, July 1988), 41.

49. U.S. Department of the Army, *FM 71-123: Tactics and Techniques for Combined Arms Heavy Forces: Armored Brigade, Battalion/Task Force, and Company/Team,* 3-79–81, A-8.

50. This was frankly admitted in DePuy's brainchild, the 1976 edition of *FM 100-5: Operations,* the U.S. Army's fundamental doctrinal manual. See *U.S. Department of the Army, FM 100-5: Operations* (Washington, D.C.: U.S. Government Printing Office, 1 July 1976), 4-7–8 in particular. For the underlying logic, still intact in U.S. Army heavy-force doctrine, see Herbert, *Deciding What Has to Be Done,* 63–64, 88.

51. "Army Weaponry, Equipment, and New Technologies," *Army* (October 1997), 261. This article notes the weight of the M-2A2 Bradley as 66,000 pounds (33 tons), although some sources show it as 30 tons. The difference likely relates to how much fuel and ammunition has been counted in the weight.

52. For a typical example, see Maj. Todd R. Wendt, USA, "M-2A3/M-3A3: The Army Fighting Vehicle for the Next Century," *Infantry* (January–February 1997), 23–27. This excellent description of planned upgrades to the Bradley fighting vehicle goes on for five pages with several diagrams included. The dismounted riflemen that the Bradley exists to transport do not get mentioned—and this in *Infantry* magazine!

53. U.S. Department of the Army, *FM 7-20: The Infantry Battalion,* D-2–3. For the vulnerability of Iraqi T-55 and T-62 tanks to Bradley 25mm fires, see Cordesman and Wagner, *Volume IV: The Gulf War,* 696.

54. Clancy, *Armored Cav,* 75.

55. U.S. Department of the Army, *FM 7-7J: Mechanized Infantry Platoon and Squad (Bradley)* (Washington, D.C.: U.S. Government Printing Office, 7 May 1993), 2-81.

56. Ibid., A-5. The diagrams of who sits where could confuse a three-card-monte scam artist. The lieutenant rides in Brad #1, but his radioman rides in #2 (hoping it doesn't blow up or break down). The forward observer is with the officer, but his artillery radioman

rides in #4, with the platoon sergeant and the platoon medic. Getting this bunch together under fire upon dismounting would be quite a show. In reality, mech lieutenants cram their entire command group, especially the vital radiomen, into their own Bradley and live with the overcrowding.

57. Stempniak interview. To be fair, U.S. Department of the Army, *FM 7-7J: Mechanized Infantry Platoon and Squad (Bradley)*, A-5, does describe how the platoon leader can fight dismounted, including a detailed description of some applicable tactics and drills.

58. U.S. Department of the Army, *FM 7-7J: Mechanized Infantry Platoon and Squad (Bradley)*, A-1–5.

59. U.S. Department of the Army, *FM 101-10-1/1 Staff Officers' Field Manual Organizational, Technical, and Logistical Data*, 1-149. By table of organization, a Bradley-equipped mech battalion totals 779 men.

60. Major General Carl F. Ernst, "The Infantry Squad—How Much Is Enough?" *Infantry* (January–February 1997), 2. Ernst argues for three eleven-man squads in the light battalions, too, plus a weapons squad. He rightly observes that the Bradley replaces the machine-gun teams in the heavy infantry. For more on 2 x 9 + 5, see Gen. William W. Hartzog, USA, "TRADOC: Moving the Army Into the Future," *Army* (October 1997), 50, 52.

61. Swain, *"Lucky War,"* 163; Brig. Gen. Robert H. Scales, USA, director, *Certain Victory: The U.S. Army in the Gulf War* (Fort Leavenworth, Kans.: U.S. Army Command and General Staff College Press, 1994), 136; Capt. Thomas D. Dinackus, USA, *Operation Desert Storm: Allied Ground Forces Order of Battle* (Alexandria, Va.: self-published, 1996), 9–12, 7-2, 12-1–3. Light infantry battalions from the 10th Mountain Division (Light Infantry) and 25th Infantry Division (Light) sent a total of twenty-seven light infantry squads, a battalion equivalent. Nondeploying U.S. Army units in Europe shipped out twenty-seven Bradley platoon equivalents. Some of these filler dismounts proved unusual. Dan Stempniak received a combat engineer private as a rifleman, for example. See Stempniak, *The Battle of the Al Mutlaa Police Post, 26 February 1991*, 20–21.

62. Interview with Lt. Col. John Antal, USA, Carlisle Barracks, Pa., 27 January 1998. Antal noted that in the 1st Infantry Division (Mechanized) in 1992, battalions routinely borrowed dismounts from

other mech battalions to fill their Bradleys when en route to a rotation at the National Training Center (NTC) at Fort Irwin, California. The division commanding general put a stop to this practice, with the result that Bradleys averaged three or fewer riflemen on a 1992 NTC rotation. Current reports show that this has not improved. Most Bradley rifle platoons bring 50 percent or less of their authorized eighteen dismounts to the NTC. See Richard J. Newman, "Can Peacekeepers Make War?" in *U.S. News and World Report* (19 January 1998), 39–40, 43.

63. U.S. Army Infantry Center, *FC 7-21B: Bradley Infantry Fighting Vehicle Squad and Platoon Drills,* 1-9. For a good example of the excessive emphasis on the equipment over the riflemen, see U.S. Department of the Army, *TC 23-5: Bradley Fighting Vehicle Training Devices* (Washington, D.C.: U.S. Government Printing Office, 13 May 91). This manual runs more than a hundred pages without even mentioning the dismounted men the Bradley carries.

64. For examples of the contrast in emphasis between mounted and dismounted skill training, see Tom Carhart, *Iron Soldiers* (New York, N.Y.: Pocket Books, 1994), 36–38, 123. Carhart tells the story of the 1st Armored Division in the Gulf War.

65. Robert M. Utley, *Frontier Regulars: The United States Army and the Indian, 1866–1890* (New York, N.Y.: The Macmillan Publishing Company, Inc., 1973), 50–51.

66. Cordesman and Wagner, *The Lessons of Modern War, Volume IV: The Gulf War,* 699–700.

The M-60E3 machine gun is the basic heavy weapon of U.S. Army and Marine Corps rifle platoons. Nicknamed "the pig" in the Vietnam War for its voracious consumption of 7.62mm linked belts of ammunition, the M-60E3 is being phased out in favor of the newer M-240B. (U.S. Army)

Rifles ready, Marines train on clearing a stairwell in the abandoned town of Ras Al Khafji, Saudi Arabia, in late 1990. Note the standard "guns and eyeballs" weapon control postures. (U.S. Marine Corps)

Rigged for a jump, a staff sergeant of the 82d Airborne Division shows a typical airborne soldier's load. On his back is his main parachute, which is designed to open automatically as the jumper exits the aircraft. Below his hands is his reserve parachute, to be pulled open manually in the unusual event that the main does not open. Under his reserve rides his rucksack, loaded with ammunition, water, batteries, and other necessities. His M-16A2 rifle is stowed under his left arm in a weapons carrying case. (U.S. Army)

This picture of dawn training jump in Panama shows what it might have looked like as the 1st Brigade, 82d Airborne Division parachuted into Torrijos-Tocumen on 20 December 1989. The objects dangling beneath the paratroopers are rucksacks lowered to permit a cleaner landing. (U.S. Army)

A paratrooper sights his M-249 Squad Automatic Weapon (SAW) on likely targets during the 1989 Panama intervention. He has more ammunition on the ground near his right elbow. (U.S. Army)

During the Gulf War soldiers of the 101st Airborne Division (Air Assault) stage for their flight in Forward Operating Base Cobra on 24 February 1991. The weight of loads is evident. (U.S. Army)

A pair of UH-60A Blackhawk helicopters races across the desert floor during the Gulf War of 1991. In its various models and configurations, the Blackhawk is the workhorse of the U.S. Army and of American special operations forces. It forms the backbone of the 101st Airborne Division's air assault capabilities. (U.S. Army)

Weapons maintenance never ends. Flak vest on, an air assault rifleman of the 101st Airborne Division cleans his M-16A2. The pouch near his left ear contains a first aid dressing, and the sling across his chest suspends a gas mask, both common accessories for today's infantry. (U.S. Army)

This was Forward Operating Base Cobra on 24 Februrary 1991, as seen from a UH-60A Blackhawk helicopter. Rings of vehicles stretch across the flat desert floor. The inverted "v" symbol on each truck was a recognition marking to prevent casualties from friendly fire. (U.S Army)

This road leads to Al Mutlaa Ridge, barely visible in the upper right corner. Taken many days after the fighting in February 1991, the picture depicts U.S. Army Tiger Brigade M-1A1 Abrams tanks, Humvee light trucks, and some M-113 series armored personnel carriers. (U.S. Marine Corps)

The M-2A2 Bradley Fighting Vehicle is the basic weapon of U.S. Army mechanized infantrymen. Weighing from 27 to 33 tons in its varied models, the Bradley's turret carries a powerful 25mm Bushmaster light cannon and an antitank missile launcher box, all guided by a sophisticated, accurate thermal sighting system. (U.S. Army)

Inside the belly of the beast, two U.S. Army mechanized infantrymen lean against the rear ramp of a Bradley Fighting Vehicle. The soldier to the left wears a flak vest and carries his rifle, ready for dismounted action. The one to the right, likely a leader, wears a combat vehicle crewman helmet, allowing him to talk to the onboard crew. (U.S. Army)

Through the breach under cover of smoke, U.S. Army mechanized infantry-men train on crossing an obstacle belt during the Gulf War. Clearing defend-ed obstacles forms a major task for mounted riflemen. (U.S. Army)

An Iraqi tank burns after a direct hit by U.S. Army armored forces during the Gulf War, February 1991. (U.S. Army)

A pair of U.S. Air Force MH-53J Pave Low helicopters take off during the Gulf War in 1991. Equipped with air-to-air refuelling booms, superb navigation systems, and ample protective firepower, the Pave Lows played major roles in the war against Iraq and in the 1996 Liberia evacuation. (U.S. Special Operations Command)

This line of wrecked Iraqi armored vehicles marks the roadway north of Ras Al Khafji, Saudi Arabia, in February 1991. Along with the destroyed fighting vehicles can be seen a single unfortunate civilian automobile. (U.S. Air Force)

A Marine rifle squad trains in the streets of Ras Al Khafji, Saudi Arabia, in late 1990. Army mechanized soldiers faced similar structures and used like techniques to clear the Al Mutlaa Police Station on 27 February 1991. (U.S. Marine Corps)

Better safe than sorry, a pair of Marine riflemen clear a shack in Haiti. The lead Marine has his rifle barrel and eyes aligned, the classic "guns and eyeballs" technique taught in urban close-quarters combat drills. (U.S. Marine Corps)

A U.S. Marine Corps Light Armored Vehicle (LAV) waits on the runway in an unidentified foreign country. It carries the same 25mm Bushmaster automatic cannon used on the U.S. Army's Bradley Fighting Vehicle. Marine LAVs played major roles in the Panama intervention, the Gulf War, Somalia, Haiti, and various African operations. (U.S. Marine Corps)

Dismounting, mechanized infantrymen exit a Bradley Fighting Vehicle in a training drill on the outskirts of Mogadishu, Somalia, in November 1993. The entire rear of the vehicle drops to form a ramp. There is also a smaller hatch for individual exits if the crew wants to keep the ramp up. (U.S. Army)

Marines enter a suspected hostile hideout in Cap-Haitien, Haiti, in September 1994. The Marine on the stairs holding up his weapon has an M-16A2 5.56mm rifle with an M-203 40mm grenade launcher. (U.S. Marine Corps)

Speakers mounted, a U.S. Army psychological operations truck and its escorts carry the message of the day to the citizens of Mogadishu, Somalia in 1993. Seen at center left, dismounted riflemen accompany the trucks. The close contact with Somalis made it difficult to separate friend and foe. (U.S. Army)

Two paratroopers of the 3d Battalion, 325th Airborne Infantry Regiment demonstrate the view from their M-60E3 machinegun post in the U.S. embassy complex in Monrovia, Liberia, in 1996. Follow-on Marine forces fought several skirmishes from similar posts. (U.S. Army)

Two Marines watch for trouble from one of the security posts fronting the U.S. Embassy in Monrovia, Liberia, in April 1996. The closer Marine carries an M-249 SAW and has been using binoculars to look for rebel threats. (U.S. Marine Corps)

Special operators of Joint Task Force Assured Response direct rescued civilians from U.S. Air Force MH-53J Pave Low helicopters to a transfer point at Freetown, Sierra Leone, in April 1996. The noncombatants had been extracted from Monrovia, Liberia. In the lead, a U.S. Army Special Forces NCO acts as guide. Over his right shoulder, a U.S. Navy SEAL can be seen. (U.S. Special Operations Command)

The USS *Guam* (LPH-9) brought Marine riflemen and helicopters to Monrovia, Liberia, in April 1996. The deck is crowded with Marine CH-53E Sea Stallion heavy lift helicopters. On the bow, a company of infantry watches activities ashore. (U.S. Navy)

A U.S. Marine advance party team disembarks from a CH-46E Sea Knight (known among Marines as a "Frog") at the U.S. Embassy in Monrovia, Liberia, in April 1996. The tiny cement sports court offered the only landing zone for all flights in and out. (U.S. Marine Corps)

The future of infantry? Outfitted with the latest high-technology devices, this rifleman demonstrates several proposed improvements to the traditional dismounted soldier's ensemble. His helmet includes an integrated eyepiece data display over his right eye, a rifle with advanced night sight and laser aimer, and lightweight torso body armor. Under the bulging rucksack can be seen a black backpack with antennna, which sends out position signals and receives data inputs for transmission to the eyepiece. (U.S. Army)

Chapter 4: Direct Action

You men are Rangers and I know you won't let me down.
—Brig. Gen. Norman D. Cota

To bring the 75th Ranger Regiment into the Gulf War took a rocket scientist. In fact, it took several. The immediate batch of industrious cranks hailed from Iraq, but they built on the work of design teams from the Soviet Union. Those rocket engineers had long ago adapted technology developed by the granddaddy of them all, Wernher von Braun. That photogenic genius and his associates created Nazi Germany's A-4 ballistic missile, introduced to the world in 1944 as *Vergeltungswaffe-zwei*—Vengeance Weapon Two, the infamous V-2. Although von Braun and many of his colleagues later renounced Nazism, became stalwart U.S. citizens, and created the multistage rockets that propelled America's space program through its glory days of the 1960s, the German master rocketeer never quite shook his first creation. When Hollywood in 1959 released a motion picture about von Braun, studio publicists titled it *I Aim at the Stars*. Wags added, "And Sometimes Hit London."[1]

One of von Braun's many metal children, albeit descended through the disinherited Russian bastard branch of the family, found work along the same lines as the original V-2. Commencing within twenty-four hours of the start of the Coalition air offensive, Iraq began firing back with its own vengeance weapon, a forty-three-foot-long, single-stage finned tube with a pointed nose cone. The USSR called it the R-17E, the final letter referring to export, because this type had long since passed out of the Soviet Army inventory. The people of the world know it better by its common NATO nom de guerre, SS-1B Scud. That random code word, bestowed decades ago according to alliance practices—nicknames for Communist bloc sur-

161

face-to-surface missiles start with the letter *s*—soon became shorthand for distant death, Saddam Hussein's answer to Adolf Hitler's
V-2 terror weapon.

The Iraqis played right in tune with the old German sheet music.
Just as the Nazis mostly shot at their old British enemy in London
but also pounded Allied-held docks in Antwerp and the liberated city
of Paris, so the Iraqis followed suit. Baghdad's missileers preferred
to launch toward their Israeli nemesis in Tel Aviv. In addition, they
heaved Scuds at tiny Bahrain and at the ports of Al Jubail and
Dhahran in Saudi Arabia, and even lobbed several at the Saudi capital of Riyadh, just out of spite. These destinations appeared to be
the ones chosen. The Scuds had a tendency to go wide of the mark.
Their 1950s guidance hardware did not allow for fine tuning.

Additionally, Iraqi engineers modified the weapons somewhat to
increase range and allegedly tighten accuracy, but perhaps they did
not always consult the Russian owner's manual before going to it with
pliers, screwdriver, and hammer. Tinkering away, Iraqi technicians
stitched together super-Scuds, called in their various models Al-Hussein, Al-Abbas, and Al-Hijarah. Soviet production R-17Es carried full-
sized, 2,172-pound warheads. But Baghdad's Frankensteinian cut-
and-paste jobs gained range by trimming the punch down to as little
as 418 pounds of high explosives. All that diddling did nothing to
aid guidance, either. Iraq's flight test program might charitably be
characterized as haphazard: press the button and pray, good old
Arab *inshallah* (as Allah wills it) applied to ballistics. Indeed, Saddam
Hussein's rocket men tested their Al-Hussein variant by shooting five
into Iran in 1988. They tried out the new Al-Hijarah in combat in
1991.[2] To those on the receiving end, whether Iranians in 1988 or
Saudi Arabs and Israelis in 1991, they were just Scuds.

Not all left the ground. For those that lifted off, a percentage went
astray on the upward leg. But most continued on, arcing through
the top of the atmosphere, then tilting down for the wild ride to the
intended target. Whipping down through the thickening air, tiny
warheads still mated to empty fuel tanks, the red-hot, thin-skinned
tubes vibrated and twisted. A few tumbled end over end. Many shredded in flight. Others got smacked while still ten miles high, hit by
defending U.S. Army Patriot surface-to-air missiles. With chunks of

Scud screaming down hither and yon, it was hard to tell exactly where the things were supposed to have gone. Even when the Iraqi rockets worked as designed, the best they could do might be to impact within a few miles of their aim points. Anyway, only a fraction of the missile warheads actually came down and exploded, but a great many pieces of debris of substantial size rained down as well. It was like getting pelted with random metal junk, which now and then vaporized in small explosions.

Of course, had the Iraqis elected to fill the warhead with toxic chemicals rather than high explosives, close would have been just fine. Even a Patriot hit at altitude might have been bad news, serving to disperse a cloud of nerve gas or a packet of a horrific biological agent such as anthrax, ebola, or Q-fever, strains out of a late-night horror movie. Among Arabs and Americans on the ground, nobody could be sure which Scud might carry the death juice aboard. For the Israelis, it almost brought them off the sideline, an event almost guaranteed to sunder the Arab-American alliance and jerk the war against Iraq to a screaming halt—which amounted to the exact reason why Baghdad fired away at Israel. Saddam Hussein knew he could not win the shooting war. But there were other ways to hurt opponents. Hence, the Scuds flew.

For Gen. H. Norman Schwarzkopf and his U.S. Central Command subordinates, the enemy's Scud riposte did not come as a surprise. The big American general had planned for this eventuality. From the start, his waves of air missions included many hunting for Iraqi Scud launchers, both fixed and mobile. The news media salivated, running and rerunning footage of Israelis picking around smoking craters in Tel Aviv, and missile bodies streaking down through the night sky to blast Riyadh. Schwarzkopf tried to dismiss the Scud for what it was—a weapon of fear, and not even a good one. "Saying that Scuds are a danger to a nation is like saying that lightning is a danger to a nation," Schwarzkopf said with a snort. "I frankly would be more afraid of standing out in a lightning storm in southern Georgia than I would standing out in the streets of Riyadh when the Scuds are coming down."[3]

Facts bear out the American commander's belief that the Scud threat was greatly exaggerated. Despite ninety-one known Scud shots, U.S. casualties totaled twenty-eight dead and ninety-eight wounded, all suffered when a single missile sliced through the Patriot defensive umbrella and struck a barracks in Dhahran on 25 February. That definitely hurt, but it surely seemed the exception that proved the rule.

Although Tel Aviv and Haifa absorbed forty separate rocket strikes, revealed in alarming television news footage, a mere seventy-four apartments sustained serious property damage. Concussions, however, blew out thousands of windows. Only two Israeli citizens actually died from missile detonations or debris impact. One more suffered severe wounds, another nine received notable injuries, and 222 acknowledged superficial cuts and bruises, mainly from flying glass. None of these tragedies can be excused, but they cannot by any means be judged militarily significant.

But like Hitler's vengeance weaponry, Scuds existed to terrify civilians, not to weigh in the military balance of power. Terrify they did. In a telling count, a whopping 814 Israelis reported to authorities in utter distress. A few got trampled in the general confusion. About a quarter had needlessly injected atropine into their systems, thinking themselves under nerve agent barrage. The powerful chemical warfare antidote knocked people down, relaxed their muscles into jelly, and made them completely unable to function. More than half simply collapsed from nervous anxiety. In the most extreme cases, eleven Israelis died. Four suffered fatal heart attacks and seven suffocated in their general-issue gas masks, literally scared to death.[4]

Of course, the missiles frightened people into a lather largely thanks to endless gloom and doom blandishments from CNN and its electronic media running mates. Largely denied a traditional clash of arms by Iraqi martial passivity, the reporters seized on the only aggressive response from Saddam Hussein. That this reply appeared exotic, photogenic, and unprecedented added to the story. Fueled by reporting normally reserved for the end of life as we know it, Scud-o-mania ensued. It especially took hold in Israel, where politicians threatened to retaliate against Iraq in no uncertain terms. The bug also bit in America, where mothers and fathers feared for their children in uniform. The more Schwarzkopf and his people tried to downplay the issue, the more the journalists frothed.

But as often happens, a bitter kernel of truth lay beneath the frantic worrying. Although today we realize that no Iraqi Scud fired in 1991 carried a lethal chemical or biological surprise package, the picture at the time looked murky in the extreme. General Schwarzkopf himself might have been certain that the Scud threat was exaggerated. His intelligence experts were not. Their views have been encapsulated nicely by Schwarzkopf himself.

For two years, I had been guaranteed that they [Iraqi Scuds] did not have a chemical capability. The day the war started, their estimate shifted, and by one month later, it was that they probably did have a chemical warhead on a Scud missile, and nothing had changed out there in the way of occurrences or events. All they were doing is the bureaucracy there decided: "well, they may shoot a chemical missile, so we will cover our butts by saying they may have it." So we went to the "definitely do not," to "maybe," to "do have" in a period of two months.[5]

Despite the satellites and radar planes, the U-2s, the tracking networks, the code crackers, and all the other snoopers and sneakers, nobody really knew the deal. Maybe the Scuds carried poison. Who wanted to guess wrong? Many of the intelligence guys emulated Pontius Pilate, too uncertain to do anything else. They had raised the issue. Now the Coalition operators had to do something about it.

Staring into that same information vacuum, Israeli operators chafed to act. They believed in the maxim of better safe than sorry. The Israeli Defense Force readied their jets and prepared to insert commando teams to locate firing sites in western Iraq, and they made no secret of their intentions. By 19 January, only two days into the U.S.-led air campaign, the Israelis looked ready to intervene. That would paralyze the Saudis, the Egyptians, and the Syrians, plus all the minor Arab and Islamic actors, and right at the worst possible time. If so, Saddam Hussein might yet salvage his otherwise untenable military position.

United States president George Bush saw the looming disaster. He intervened personally. On his orders, America deployed Patriot defense missile batteries into Israel, the first U.S. units ever sent to fight on the soil of the Jewish state. Schwarzkopf also brought more batteries into Saudi Arabia to protect his own troops and their Arab allies. Together, these Patriot systems may have taken down a little more than half of all Scuds launched.[6] But they did nothing to stop the firings; after all, one Al-Hijarah load of anthrax would do the job.

So Bush injected an offensive component into the mix. He personally promised the Israeli prime minister, Yitzhak Shamir, "the darndest search-and-destroy effort that's ever been undertaken."[7] American airplanes had already been looking and bombing but not really finding and killing. Iraq kept right on lighting off Scuds. By 23 January, a week into the American-Coalition aerial campaign, Saddam Hussein's rocketeers had fired off thirty-three of the things. Despite many sorties, the American airplanes had not done anything to slow the pace.

To do that required better targeting, better reads on where the mobile launchers were scooting before shooting. The eyes in space and roving airplanes had tried and failed. So it came down to the usual answer—putting men into the rocky deserts of western Iraq, far from the rest of Schwarzkopf's assembling divisions. These soldiers would be on their own, beyond reinforcement, intentionally planted out in death ground. Not just anyone could be sent, so the American chain of command chose wisely. Orders went out and elite units responded, among others, the Rangers. On 7 February 1991, the Great Scud Hunt commenced.

The Rangers joined a war already in progress. Even as the United States formed its Scud-busting task force, an openly admitted Special Operations Command–Central Command (SOCCENT) of 7,705 soldiers, sailors, and airmen ran all the other special operations in theater. Under Col. Jesse L. Johnson of the U.S. Army, SOCCENT worked around the periphery of Schawrzkopf's main theater of operations, throughout occupied Kuwait and throughout east-central Iraq. The SOCCENT operators reconnoitered on the enemy side of the border, tried to recover downed pilots, spotted for aerial fires, assisted Arab Coalition brigades and battalions in working with the Americans, aided the Kuwaiti resistance, checked out potential landing beaches, ran deceptive missions, and conducted psychological warfare appeals by broadcast and leaflet.[8] The American military referred to SOCCENT as "white" SOF, because their efforts could be discussed in press releases and shared with other units. Discussions were subject to normal prudence about keeping ongoing and future missions under wraps.

The Scud hunters were "black" in that their activities went wholly unmentioned in press releases and normal military planning channels. Whereas Jesse Johnson's white SOF worked in, around, and among many conventional units, the black SOF went west into the Saudi desert almost as far as they could, to get near the Scuds and get away from prying eyes. They staged out of Ar Ar, a remote air base already in use by some SOCCENT units and by a few teams of the renowned British Special Air Service (SAS). The British had been going into Iraq since the air war kicked off. With only 150 men and their supporting rotary-wing aircraft limited in combat radius, the British seemed unable to quell Iraq's Scud offensive.[9] They welcomed the arrival of their American allies.

The Americans titled their contribution a JSOTF (Joint Special Operations Task Force) and called the entire affair by an apt name: Elusive Concept. It eventually totaled 1,049 special operators.[10] Like similar organizations developed in Grenada in 1983 and destined for hard service in Mogadishu in 1993, the mature Gulf War JSOTF included four building blocks: a command team, a special mission element, an aviation component, and a reinforced Ranger company. This allowed for a capable, flexible outfit able to get in and out of denied territory, where items such as Scuds liked to hide.[11] A JSOTF is the SOF equivalent of the conventional Marine expeditionary unit (MEU), another proven air-ground team. The exact size of each part of a JSOTF can be adjusted, or units such as SEAL teams can be added on if that makes sense. But, in general, a black JSOTF tended to resemble the bunch sent to get the Scuds in early 1991.

Major General Wayne A. Downing of the U.S. Army led the JSOTF. He normally commanded Joint Special Operations Command (JSOC), a standing headquarters designed to train and command precisely this brand of JSOTF. In 1979–80, when the United States had to rescue its hostage diplomats in Iran, the country tried to cobble together a headquarters under great time pressure. Things

came apart in the Iranian desert one tragic night, and thus was born
JSOC, which exists to run those kinds of operations when they become necessary.[12] With Scuds aflutter, they were necessary in January 1991. So Downing and his battle staff deployed to Ar Ar, bringing with them a state-of-the-art suite of communications and
intelligence downlinks.

Downing's principal ground arm consisted of a squadron (later
two) drawn from 1st Special Forces Operational Detachment—
Delta, the storied Delta force, the D-Boys, veterans of Iran, Grenada,
and Panama, with the purgatory of Mogadishu yet to come. These
handpicked, highly trained shooters normally expected to storm ter-
rorist-held buildings and airliners, but their marksmanship, clandestine movement, and surveillance skills suited them well to stalk
furtive Scuds. Ideally, the D-Boys could creep into the rocks and mark
targets with laser designators for loitering U.S. Air Force jets. In extreme cases, they could open fire themselves to botch an Iraqi
launch attempt.[13] One sniper bullet punched into the flank of a rising Scud could bring the flight to a quick end.

The Rangers provided a reaction force in case the Delta men got
into a jam. They joined the JSOTF on 14 February. Company B, 1st
Battalion, 75th Ranger Regiment, included an extra platoon drawn
from Company A, as well as some additional heavy-weapons teams,
all under Capt. Kurt Fuller. Major P. Kenneth Keen, the 1/75th S-3
(operations officer), commanded the entire Ranger contingent and
acted as liaison.[14] If the Rangers went into action, Ken Keen was there
to provide overall command while Kurt Fuller ran the ground battle. A major part of Keen's job related to coordinating aviation support from the JSOTF's own aircraft.

The JSOTF's private air force included a wide variety of Air Force
and Army SOF craft: USAF MH-53J Pave Low III helicopters, Army
MH-60L Blackhawks, MH-47E Chinooks, and various AH-6/MH-6
Little Birds, along with fixed-wing support from a family of C-130 variants, including AC-130H Spectre gunships.[15] Painted dull, nonre-
flective dark green, the Pave Lows and their Army counterparts account for many of the lunatic-fringe "black helicopter" sightings
commonly reported across the United States. Far from carrying
malevolent foreigners and dastardly government agents, the U.S.

black helicopters ferry the best of the country's SOF. They train in cities and towns around the country, buzzing deserted urban streets from Pittsburgh to St. Louis to San Diego, plus hundreds of sleeping hamlets, in an effort to be able to go deep into Indian country some awful night. Now that night had arrived, and with it the men of the USAF 1st Special Operations Wing, the Air Commandos, and the U.S. Army's 160th Special Operations Aviation Regiment (Airborne), the Night Stalkers. The Night Stalker motto said it all: "Death Waits in the Dark."[16] Thanks to these gifted, experienced fliers, death had wings, too.

Thus, the JSOTF came together, brains, teeth, and wings, a multi-taloned predator determined to kill Scuds. Steered by the eyes of Delta, Schwarzkopf's airmen shunted 1,460 combat sorties to aid in the Great Scud Hunt, with a thousand more trolling for possible launches or orbiting on standby for targets of opportunity. The D-Boys and their JSOTF air cover roamed western Iraq, claiming eleven confirmed missile kills while counting coup on nine of the wallowing transporter-erector-launcher (TEL) trucks. When caught emerging from underpasses and buildings, the TELs were easy enough to run down and wreck; the slow-moving, unmaneuverable behemoths were nicknamed "sperm whales" by the Soviets who invented them. Teams called in air-delivered Gator scatterable land mines to cut key roads and trails. Night Stalker MH-60Ls also strafed fiber-optic communications sites to degrade Iraqi communications out in the Scud belt.[17] The British SAS kept up the pressure, too.

Evidently, it worked. The tempo of Scud firings dwindled as Iraqis fled from the unwelcome attentions of SOF and their affiliated jets. After launching almost five Scuds a day at the war's outset—and those fired in volleys that threatened to overwhelm Patriot batteries—harried Iraqis struggled to get off a single missile or two once the SOF-warplane combination got untracked. Those few that did get fired showed evidence of hasty shooting, with even lousier accuracy than usual.[18] Israel stayed out of the war, and the Arab-American Coalition held together and trounced Saddam Hussein. By any measure, Elusive Concept accomplished its purpose.

Many postwar analysts, comfortably sifting through logs, photos, and old videotapes in air-conditioned offices, choose to find fault with the Great Scud Hunt. In dismissing SOF claims, they side with Doctor Eliot A. Cohen's otherwise exceptionally authoritative 1993 *Gulf War Air Power Survey.* Cohen and his panel of experts judged that "there is no indisputable proof of any TELs or MELs [mobile erector-launchers]—as opposed to high-fidelity decoys, trucks, or other objects with Scud-like signatures—having been destroyed by Coalition aircraft or special forces during Desert Storm."[19]

Well . . . maybe, as long as it's believed that every single one of those missile-carrier look-alike items on the videotapes was a carefully built phony and they were all orchestrated by an enemy that in every other situation displayed incredible military ineptitude. Post-combat, hands-on inventories by United Nations inspectors disclosed only nineteen TEL-MEL carriers remaining. Something must have happened to the other seventeen that existed before the 1990–91 Gulf War.[20] Based on their reduced level of activity, surviving Iraqi missile crews felt the heat and by and large left the kitchen.

That kind of indirect evidence does not cut it among hard-core bean counters. The Cohen group and others like it demanded absolutely certain data, definitive photos showing bona fide Scud wagons going *poof.* Given that it happened at night, in bad weather, in a desolate desert, and that the photographers were more concerned about staying alive than getting the perfect angle, the lack of quality pictures seems unremarkable. Only believers in some species of antiseptic push-button warfare would expect otherwise. So maybe trusting the debriefs from the D-Boys and the pilots, plus those grainy thermal and night-vision videotapes, isn't so dumb. After all, the SOF guys and fliers were there. Something slowed down the Iraqis. The truth surely lies somewhere in between, as it usually does.

The Rangers were in between, out there doing their bit to assist the Great Scud Hunt. They sallied forth only once, but the resultant mission produced a gem of a raid. Anyone who wonders what Rangers do for a living can learn a lot from Ranger Run I.

American special warfare people classify events such as Ranger Run I as direct action missions, defined as "short-duration strikes and other small-scale offensive actions by SOF to seize, destroy, capture, recover, or inflict damage on designated personnel or material in denied areas."[21] Direct action means taking a picked element into a critical target, doing the assigned deed, then getting out unscathed. Despite what Hollywood might lead Americans to think, it isn't easy in real life.

Direct action includes ambushes, assaulting to take key facilities, conducting standoff attacks by fire, guiding precision munitions, recovering U.S. prisoners or evaders, demolishing specific sites, knocking out hostile ships, emplacing mines at sea or on land, and clearing beaches for amphibious landings.[22] All of these demand special men to get them right. The Delta teams patrolling western Iraq certainly executed several categories of this taxonomy as they stalked Scuds.

By any measure, the toughest direct action task is clearly the raid. It sticks men smack into the maw of death, dangles them there for a bit, then endeavors to yank them back out before the jaws slam shut. The book says that any average rifle company can do it. That might be true, as long as all or part of several rifle units can be lost while workable techniques are being refined.[23] Those who survive will know the deal.

Long odds explain why raiding usually remains reserved for the elite of the elite. Good raids take a lot of focused training, much of it with live fire. Nobody knows that better than the Rangers. They work on it all the time.[24] Ranger companies serve in JSOTFs for two reasons: to provide a quick-reaction force for emergencies, and to raid.

To get in and out of death ground without the garage door slamming on your head, you must shock the enemy. Bigger forces generate shock action by overwhelming firepower to break hostile defenses and deep flanking maneuvers to pursue a befuddled foe. Exploiting such disruption defines classical armored warfare. Small forces, too, can stun an otherwise superior foe by coming in fast and hard and leaving just as swiftly. Raiders need superior combat power only once, when they hit the objective. By the time the bad guys react, the direct action team is long gone. That's the idea, the old in-and-out drill.

The trick involves getting there by surprise and not screwing around on the ground. Time favors the opposition. It's like trying to pull off an armed robbery. Getting balled up at the crime scene has few good outcomes for the crooks. If the enemy defenders are alert and well disposed, if some hostile commander guesses right and sets a trap, or if opposing reserves move with a purpose to pin down dawdling raiders, then all of the odds shift decisively. A small, lean assault team looks pretty undergunned and naked at that point. A raid gone wrong at worst equals the loss of the entire force, or a good chunk of it, and at best requires a pretty big outfit to arrive on the run to save the day.

To avoid that kind of fight, direct action missions demand not just good intelligence but great intelligence, the best of the best. A few SOF, no matter how well trained, cannot afford to have a major shoot-out in the target area, or en route to or from it. Additionally, the more the friendlies know about the objective, the better they can plan and rehearse, which speeds up activities in the beaten zone and permits a quicker egress. For SOF, especially Rangers contemplating a raid, intelligence must be detailed and accurate.[25] As British soldiers like to say, time spent on reconnaissance is seldom wasted. This goes double or triple for habitually outnumbered special operators.

Given the perils of discerning what's going on in Indian country, the intelligence laydown often dictates where and when any raid occurs. There may be a better objective, with a bigger potential payoff, but zipping off into the unknown or semiknown gets hairy. As much as it appeals to type-A Rangers and JSOTF leaders itching for action, "fire, ready, aim" is not a good policy for successful direct action. Smart SOF go where they know.

In Ranger Run I, the JSOTF went where they knew. Planners considered several possible targets, each related to the ongoing counter-Scud effort. The men attempted to find something worth raiding and not simply blow off the face of Iraq. Due to their persistent motion, the Scud TELs were obviously out; Delta and the Air Force held that portfolio. General Downing and his staff directed the Rangers to focus on fixed facilities, things that did not move around but provided communications related to Scud activities.

That guidance definitely tightened the Rangers' aim. It meant considering locations that needed to be erased yet seemed likely to yield useful tidbits of information, such as code books, software, enemy Scud firing plans, or even live prisoners. The British SAS had already done some of this same business, knocking out microwave towers and other communications buildings. In one strike, they nabbed an Iraqi officer laden with interesting maps and documents.[26] So it could be done, and it could prove worthwhile.

Ranger and JSOTF officers and NCOs looked at hitting certain Iraqi radar posts, cutting fiber-optic cables at key junctions, or taking out microwave towers. That last category promised a bonus in that the Iraqis had been using clandestine communications antennas along the Jordanian border to jam U.S., British, and other Coalition search and rescue and SOF radio frequencies.[27] Smashing a microwave radio relay tower and searching the affiliated buildings guaranteed a degradation of Scud communications. It might also frustrate the Iraqi jamming effort and perhaps even cough up documents or enemy soldiers who could shed light on these or other matters. It all fit together nicely. Thus, Ranger Run I went after a microwave mast and its compound, a remote position more than four miles from pro-Iraqi Jordan. The JSOTF set H hour for 2220 on 26 February 1991, as good a time as any to catch some enemy signalers dozing at their consoles. All good SOF work is night work. This was good SOF work, all right.

The mission went to the senior Ranger, Maj. Ken Keen, with Capt. Kurt Fuller as his ground commander and Maj. Joe Smith of the Night Stalkers as his aviation commander. With the ground war in progress, the Scud hunt running full blast, other missions in various stages of planning and rehearsal, and a need to keep aircraft and Rangers on standby for QRF contingencies, Downing allocated only a small force for the raid.[28] It would be enough.

Given only two MH-60L Blackhawks and a single USAF MH-53J Pave Low to carry their men, Keen and Fuller modified a standard Ranger platoon raid package to do the job. The Pave Low would carry Company B's 1st Platoon (forty-two Rangers), the main assault element. One Blackhawk was to ferry in a support (as in support-by-fire) element, a fifteen-man reinforced heavy weapons squad. That bird also doubled as an aerial command and control (C2) platform for Keen and Smith. The other MH-60L held fifteen more Rangers,

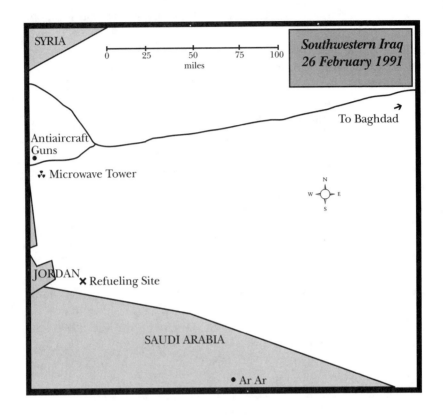

SYRIA

0   25   50   75   100
miles

**Southwestern Iraq
26 February 1991**

To Baghdad

Antiaircraft
Guns
•

✥ Microwave Tower

N
W —⬥— E
S

JORDAN
✖ Refueling Site

SAUDI ARABIA

• Ar Ar

split between a road security squad and Kurt Fuller's small headquarters team with their vital radios.

Along with his three assault birds, Joe Smith also brought four
AH-6G Little Birds, vastly uprated versions of the same egg-shaped
models used as scout ships in the Vietnam War. Although few Americans have seen actual Night Stalker AH-6Gs in flight, most have seen
similar Little Birds at work on the silver screen with the air cavalry armada in the movie *Apocalypse Now* and in the opening credits of the
television show *Magnum, P.I.*, among others. Well, Joe Smith's Little
Birds were not movie special effects but lethal realities, compact
chunks of raw firepower, hung with long black 7.62mm Gatling guns
and 70mm rockets and flown by the best pilots in the U.S. Army. The
Little Birds intended to suppress the objective—sort of the same way

a good lawnmower suppresses the grass—and flatten the steel slab gate just before the Rangers landed.[29]

Getting the force in took a few other moving parts. First, an MH-47E SOF Chinook had to fly forward and refuel the AH-6Gs before they crossed into Iraq. Little Birds have little fuel tanks. To fill them, a big twin-rotored Chinook had been packed with pillowy flexible bags brimming with kerosene-like aviation fuel. Appropriate hoses and pumps also went into the kit, along with a Ranger squad for local protection. The JSOTF selected an extremely isolated spot of unremarkable desert for the fill-up site in order to preclude Iraqi interference.

With all of this in the cargo compartment, the SOF Chinook became what the soldiers called a "Fat Cow," ready to suckle a litter of flying calves. On landing, the Ranger squad intended to hop out to secure the area. Then, the Fat Cow crewmen could unroll hoses and stand by to play gas station as the AH-6Gs flitted in.[30] Like the Rangers' platoon raid method, this was a standard SOF aviation task, well practiced by all the players.

For command and control, Joe Smith and Ken Keen prepared to use one of their MH-60Ls as a C2 helicopter. A conventional heliborne outfit, such as the 101st Airborne, usually resorted to a distinctive aircraft fitted with additional radios. Not so the 160th; all of its MH-60Ls had superb long-haul communications, including satellite transceivers. Taking advantage of the better range enjoyed by radios lifted above terrain blockages, the two majors could talk to the JSOTF, the Air Force, and all subordinates from a flying command post cum antenna. This good communications platform allowed them to orchestrate the entire raid. They anticipated landing their part of the raiding force, then moving with the other two lift helos to an aircraft ground laager site within a mile or so. While the Air Force Pave Low and the other Blackhawk settled down in the dust to wait, the C2 ship would orbit, providing good communications and a measure of security thanks to the onboard M-134 rotating-barrel 7.62mm miniguns. This technique cleared the objective area of choppers while the Rangers did their deeds and yet kept links back to the JSOTF.[31] It was the usual method, and Ken Keen and Joe Smith saw no reason to do otherwise.

Rather than invent some off-the-wall scheme, Keen and Smith followed long-used, well-understood standard operating procedures developed over many years of Ranger-160th missions. In the 160th, experienced aviators such as Joe Smith understood the rules: Keen was in charge, and the 160th owed the Rangers a ride in, cover on the objective, and a ride out. Once they touched down, the Rangers owned the objective and everything within a radius of almost six miles around the Iraqi post. Any shooting there required Ranger clearance. Smith and his Night Stalkers could hunt at will outside that magic circle.[32]

For his part, Ken Keen took his big circle and gave Kurt Fuller the actual objective area and its adjacent landing zones. Fuller took the stretch outside the enemy compound proper and left the innards to the assault platoon leader, 1st Lt. Joe Coale, the guy riding in the MH-53J Pave Low. At each level, the key leader freed the subordinate to do his job. Keen planned to control all the firepower, including Joe Smith's helos. Kurt Fuller would secure the raiding party's ground footprint and look outward, preventing Iraqi interference. Ranger rifle platoon leader Joe Coale had a single task—hit the microwave facility. The concept was simultaneously simple, elegant, and workable even if radios failed. Everybody knew his sandbox, and nobody crossed lines without asking, "Mother, may I?"[33] Obviously, as the overall commander, Major Keen had to keep it all straight, especially if things did go nuts. Hence, the C2 aircraft looked like a smart place to be.

Some uninformed observers criticize the whole C2 helo concept as an impersonal means of remote control, an unmanly shirking of bayonet-point leadership. There is merit in that argument, because the eye-in-the-sky approach definitely got out of hand in Vietnam.[34] Most of the time, but not always, it makes more sense to go in on the ground. In war, the commander must place himself where he can best influence the outcome. For a small force going deep, communications offer the single most important guarantee of keeping the thing on track, not to mention bringing in help if anything goes awry. Ken Keen could not have done that very well on the LZ, under fire, trusting in a short-range backpack radio. Up in the black firmament, with plenty of transmitters and receivers, he could keep it all together. It did not satisfy the ego, but it made tactical sense.

In a night mission such as this, it's difficult to sense much on the ground, even when wearing goggles. It's an endless, disjointed montage of jarring impressions: lots of flashes, running, tracers arcing up, explosions going off, strobe lights blinking, and bullets cracking. Nothing can actually be seen from the C2 bird, either. It all happens in the radio ether, in the theater of the mind. The sense of the battle comes from the radio messages, a virtual war playing out in the commander's imagination as he looks at his map and the Blackhawk radiates and sucks in transmissions, slowly turning and turning like the hinge of fate.

To allow all of that to go off, the force needed unimpeded entry and exit. Air Force F-15E Strike Eagles planned to bomb nearby enemy antiaircraft emplacements, killing some and distracting the rest as the Rangers flew in and out. Senior Air Force planner Brig. Gen. Buster C. Glosson argued that the F-15Es could just as easily topple the sturdy microwave tower without need for boots on the ground. But Downing and the JSOTF reminded all that Air Force Strike Eagles cannot search buildings or bring out prisoners. And although Glosson did not want to hear it, his superb F-15Es did not always hit their target, laser bombs notwithstanding.[35] To get this one for sure, Downing sent in his Rangers.

A JSOTF raid went by a timetable, known as an operation schedule, or opsched. Everything related to the raid, from the first assembly of men and aircraft to the final extraction, went on a long list, all in proper time sequence.[36] Entries included items such as Little Birds leaving the PZ, assault helos departing the PZ, Little Birds at the refueling site, crossing the Iraqi border, initiation of F-15E strikes, starting Little Bird gun runs, support-security elements down at the LZ, assault force landing at the LZ—all the way in and all the way out in careful detail. As each event happened, the executing leaders called in the appropriate line, and the guys in the C2 bird and other subordinate and superior headquarters checked it off. Little contingency branches, such as "helo #1 diverts to alternate LZ," or the like, could be built in at certain points. The opsched was written in planning, refined in rehearsals, then executed, a shot-by-shot screenplay for a raid. If the force stayed on the opsched, all was well. If not—well, like able actors and directors, the troops and commanders improvised.

To allow for short radio transmissions, each line had a specific number and a code word. The code words normally came from an agreed-upon list; thanks to SOP, training, and mission rehearsals, the terms themselves could contribute to following the action. For example, in the 1st Brigade, 101st Airborne Division, entries related to aviation used female first names; those related to ground units carried male names. Under fire and with spotty communications, hearing Susan would tell the listener that something related to helicopters was happening. That alone could trigger recollections from preliminary run-throughs.

One other opsched protocol also helped. On the list, soldiers referred to things that happened by number before they occurred and by code word after they occurred. A commander might have asked the status of "19" but have been told that "Mary" had begun, a cabalistic exchange of a few terse syllables that told all that, indeed, the AH-6G Little Birds had begun refueling at the Fat Cow. The opsched kept everyone on the same page of the hymnal. Other closely timed, difficult operations such as airborne drops and air assaults used this same technique. It was borrowed from the SOF world. It worked.

It served nicely for Ranger Run I, having been closely refined during multiple rehearsals. Many used live bullets and explosives. As they did with other potential targets, Keen's men had built outlines of the Iraqi enclosure and its buildings using wood and fabric, and even erected highly accurate mock-ups of the colossal steel microwave tower. Then, the men ran through the mission numerous times, day and night, practicing to get it right. They also tested reactions to things going wrong, from one helo down to all aircraft down. This reflected the usual Ranger-160th thoroughness in preparation. The process was not lengthy, because it drew on long-standing SOPs and firm personal relationships between flight crews and ground teams. As Joe Smith later stated, "This was not an unusual mission."[37] For these elite forces, it amounted to another night on the job, only this time the targets shot back.

Opscheds in hand, Ranger Run I began on schedule, about 2000 on 26 February 1991. Smith's aircraft took off on time, the C2 MH-

60L up first to track the unfolding raid. Next, the MH-47E Chinook Fat Cow and its Ranger squad headed out to the ground fuel site, followed by the quartet of laden AH-6Gs buzzing out to top off their tanks. Then the other Blackhawk, with Fuller and his security team aboard, joined up. Finally, the mighty MH-53J Pave Low fell into formation, bringing the feature player of the whole show, Joe Coale's assault platoon.

The small raiding party headed north into the badlands. It was almost two days into the Coalition's ground war. Far to the east, Iraqi armor and infantry divisions backpeddled and collapsed, rolled over by the American tank columns and their associates. But out here near Jordan, the hostiles struggled to pop off a few more Scuds at Israel. Maybe this time, the Iraqis had packed up some VX nerve gas or Q-fever.[38] To do that, the Iraqi rocket sections depended on targeting updates and firing clearances from Baghdad. Some of those commands might come via microwave, so the destination of Ranger Run I looked like a critical node.

Up in the command ship, with battle-ready Rangers shoved in tight around them, Maj. Ken Keen and Maj. Joe Smith kept book as the aircraft headed northward from Ar Ar. While Keen sat in back near the radio rack, Smith flew as copilot. The opsched held, with all the pieces moving exactly as practiced. The entry into hostile airspace happened without incident. For all aboard, it was a long, cramped ride. Some even dozed, nodding to the regular thrum of the helo engines. Might as well enjoy this segment; the hard part would start soon enough.

The opsched drew the formation toward that moment of truth, eating the minutes with practiced precision. Everything remained right on track. Shortly after 2200, things began to accelerate. On a high-powered radio set, Keen and Smith monitored Air Force flight controllers in an orbiting E-3C Sentry airborne radar plane.[39] The air bosses cleared a pair of F-15E Strike Eagles for their flak suppression strikes. That would start the shooting phase.

The Eagles headed in as the Little Birds clattered north from their refueling site, blacked out, making just less than a hundred miles an hour as their two-man crews scanned their rock-strewn, low-level routes through forward-looking infrared (FLIR) eyepieces. Through the thermals, the sparsely vegetated rock piles and desert floor looked like the bottom of the ocean, all shades of gray, indistinct, ephemeral, and ghostly. One almost expected to see the wreck of the *Titanic* loom up ahead. So as not to emulate the ill-fated liner, the Night Stalker aviators had to thread the needle in the sky, keeping below the Iraqi radar horizon while not merging with the ground relief in a terminal way.

Because the assault aircraft did not have to get fuel, they proceeded on their own separate route. Smith and his three assault craft merged in behind the Little Bird foursome at 2216, four minutes out. They arranged this aerial meeting by piloting skill and by clock and chart, not with any inertial gizmos or satellite positioners. Ken Keen kept listening, ticking off the lines on the opsched. The theater of the mind kicked into high gear. When the curtain went up on this show, Kurt Fuller and his Rangers would be center stage all the way.

Much faster than the low-flying helicopters, the two F-15E Strike Eagles sped to attack their designated antiaircraft position, a few miles northwest of the enemy communications tower. The Air Force pilots steered right to the target, talked in by the crew aboard the all-seeing Sentry radar plane. The warplanes roared out of the darkness, afterburners flaming, just out of enemy gun range. One flew ahead a mile or so, drawing fire. Its mate hung back, ready to plaster the Iraqi 57mm S-60 antiaircraft cannons as soon as they opened up.

The timing worked out perfectly. The USAF's finest appeared on the dot at 2216, right as Joe Smith's seven aircraft formed up for their final run to the objective. It correlated perfectly with the opsched and ensured an unmolested approach by the SOF aircraft. It suggested Hannibal Smith's signature line from the rollicking television adventure *The A-Team*: "I love it when a plan comes together."

Hapless to the end, the opposition followed its half of the script. Detecting the first F-15E bearing down on them, Iraqi air defenders started blazing away, pumping dozens of 57mm rounds. The sky lit up, man-made lightning showing the way to the objective. Enemy projectiles went all over, scratching the northwestern sky with fiery trails. Watching the flashes, some Rangers in their inbound helos thought it looked like the CNN videotapes from the first night of the air campaign.[40] It meant about as much, which is to say a cascade of sound and fury signifying nothing. But it sure made final aiming easy for the second American Strike Eagle crew.

At the Iraqi emplacement, the trailing U.S. jet rippled off six CBU-87 cluster bombs. These canisters shed their air shells and scattered out 202 bomblets apiece, each little chip off the lethal block fused to blow into more than 300 screaming hot fragments.[41] The Air Force crews reported their targets to be "suppressed," milspeak meaning incapable of shooting up the arriving Night Stalkers. Dodging bomblets and treating the wounded, not to mention being dead, can certainly prove distracting.

Taking advantage of the Strike Eagle attack, the Little Birds rolled in to do some suppressing of their own, zeroing in on the base of the massive microwave tower at 2218. For two minutes, the deadly bumblebees took turns plastering the rectangular walled compound. Each ship swept in, firing its Gatling-style 7.62mm minigun for about three seconds, then two 70mm rockets, a technique schooled to perfection on run after run at training ranges. Now the AH-6Gs blazed away in earnest, one after another, sounding like Paul Bunyan's chainsaw followed by two whacks of the hammer of doom: *rummmmmppp—boom, boom!*

They punched holes in the tower control building, blew out bits of roof, and smashed chunks off the cement walls. One Little Bird closed to within a hundred yards, right above the deck, and loosed two flaming bolts directly into the wide steel front gate. The rockets erupted in massive bursts, flinging the locked gate into the air. They also smashed a significant slab of the single-lane roadway leading into the fenced enclosure, not to mention showering the main building with hot fragments. Iraqi signalers and guards ran out of the compound as though their lives depended on it, as indeed they did.[42] Well, the opsched said "target suppressed" and, by God, it had been.

Wristwatches synchronized to global positioning satellite timers read 2220:00 as the last two Hydra-70 rockets erupted near the bottom of the hundred-yard microwave tower, its angular, oil-derrick-model latticework swaying with the concussion. All manner of debris and smoke slowly subsided back into the enclosed facility. That explained why the Americans wanted to land outside the enemy site. Those zinging chunks of red-hot metal and cement could cut a helo

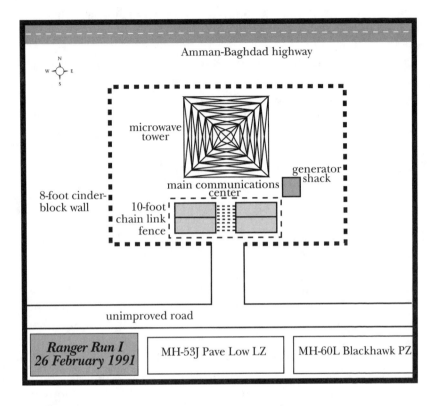

in half, much less a Ranger. Best stay outside that ring of pain, the leadership decided.

On a flat spot about a hundred yards from the southern face of the eight-foot cinder-block wall, two Blackhawks touched down. Although the Hawks each had their own M-134 miniguns for LZ suppression work, the Night Stalker door gunners held their fire. The Little Birds had more than done the job, and nobody wanted any ricochets bouncing off that cement wall or steel tower to tear up hovering aircraft.[43] So the miniguns on the MH-60Ls came in cold, saving their bullets for other prey.

In less than half a minute, thirty Rangers, night-vision goggles on, tumbled out exactly in the right place. Engines howling, dust clouds boiling, the MH-60Ls swung up and away, bound for the laager area.

The road-watch team moved into position on the only approach road, reporting no response from any Iraqis. Accompanied by Fuller and his small command group, the support team instantly aligned parallel to the southern edge of the cement barrier. A pair of Rangers moved up to an exposed spot on the edge of the fronting road. They took up a firing posture, with one man leveling a cut-down 84mm Carl Gustav rocket launcher at the ten-foot-high chain-link inner fence that surrounded the Iraqi main communications center.[44] The assistant loaded a single high-explosive rocket. His partner sighted on the hinge of the cyclone fence gate.

Just as the Air Force helicopter bearing Joe Coale's assault platoon swung down, the projectile spat out. Its tail a hard, bright flare, the round impacted smack on the hinge. The fence shivered an instant from the force of the blow, then the gate tore loose and spun crazily to the dirt. "A perfect (lucky) shot," the Ranger captain judged.[45] But luck was part of war, too. Fuller's Rangers took it and kept going.

Right on cue, the Pave Low floated earthward, its tail ramp already down. The USAF crews also did not fire their miniguns; they came in within fifty yards of the busted gate, and nobody wanted to eat a faceful of ricochets off the walls and roof of the main communications building. As the big Air Force chopper touched dirt, the Rangers poured out in precise order. It only took a few seconds. Then, its troops delivered, the hulking Pave Low roared up, smoothly arcing over to the helo holding area. The rehearsals and opsched indicated a twenty-six-minute ground time for the actual assault. So it would not be a long wait.

Joe Coale's platoon pushed into the communications site, taking advantage of the missing gate to enter the first building within ten seconds of exiting the Pave Low. Some covered their partners while fire teams searched the double building at the base of the tower. Another element checked out the small generator shed. One designated demolition team moved to the bottom of the microwave tower, its unlit pinnacle looming 270 feet above them, barely outlined against the night sky.

In the main building, lights were on but nobody was home. Fear of Coalition air had caused the Iraqis to paint over the windows, and fear of the F-15Es and Little Birds drove out the occupants before the Rangers descended on them. Signs of abject terror abounded. The Iraqis left behind warm pita bread, hot tea on the stove, disheveled bunk beds still dank with body heat, even shoes strewn on the floor. Only very scared men would run off into the stony desert without footwear.[46] The microwave system hummed away unattended.

In the generator shack, the Rangers found the same story. The motors ran, but the operators had flown the coop. The only people in the complex were U.S. Army Rangers. That explained the lack of return fire, which until now the Americans attributed to their own substantial efforts.

Fuller reported a dry hole, at least as far as enemy soldiers were concerned. In his C2 aircraft circling over the helicopter laager location, Ken Keen experienced some disappointment. This raid would bring back no talkative prisoners. But nobody had time to wring their hands. There was much to do, and the enemy might roll in unbidden at any moment. Premission intelligence credited the Iraqis with a mechanized company nearby, and who wanted to hang around to see if those people would show up?

So the opsched marched on, minus a resisting enemy. It figured. Why should Ranger Run I be any different than most of the rest of Desert Storm?

Teams carried out the same duties learned in their rehearsals. Designated Rangers grabbed armloads of documents and shoved them into backpacks brought along for the purpose. Other Rangers began placing thermite grenades on electrical connections and wrapping detonating cord around exposed coaxial cables. These nasty toys promised mayhem. Thermite grenades burn white hot when ignited, immolating anything nearby as thoroughly as if it was tied to a piece of the sun. Det cord looked like common clothesline, but it was filled with a thread of milk-white high explosives. A few turns could slice tempered steel like a knife cutting bread.

Along with placing carefully fused charges to disable the main and auxiliary generators, the Rangers found and prepared to blow the key junction box that tied the underground coaxial cables to the microwave switching lines. For this hardware, Coale's assault platoon used specially designed satchel charges—nylon bags packed with blocks of C-4 plastic explosive, plus M-18A1 Claymore mines, each guaranteed to spew seven hundred steel ball bearings all over the place.[47] No calls would be coming through here once this bag of tricks went off.

Other Rangers placed C-4 and det cord on all the obvious boxes and wires. When these blew, they would effectively tear the guts out of the place. As Kurt Fuller put it afterward, "Anything that looked important was destroyed."[48]

The gigantic microwave tower itself got special attention. Two JSOTF master breachers came along to supervise the placement of fifty-eight carefully shaped, double-primed metal-cutting charges. Twelve Rangers lugged in the hefty packages, ready for installation. A Ranger security element looked out as eight Rangers went to work, the JSOTF pair helping and watching. After shinnying up three of the huge metal stanchions, the demo men rigged the big metal microwave mast. They attached enough plastic explosives to knock a ten-foot chunk out of one leg, an eight-foot section out of another, and a six-foot piece from a third. If the dozens of explosive fixtures worked as designed, blasts would rip apart the three main struts in an asymmetric pattern. Gravity would push the thing over on its only remaining master beam, and the very weight of the huge ensemble should conspire to bring it down.[49] The Rangers and the JSOTF specialists unreeled time cords, then carefully set off measured ten-minute fuses, main and backup. With the duty done, the demo team leader announced the fateful words: "Fire in the hole!"

With that, the Americans ignited all other fuses and began to pull back. The fire teams and squads withdrew in sequence, just as they had practiced. The Rangers had been on the ground only twenty minutes. Setting all of the demolitions used up most of that time.

Ken Keen and Joe Smith, following the action from their perch in the circling C2 aircraft, had the lift ships in motion already. All extraction lifts came out of the original Blackhawk LZ, in case the tower fell down early; it was anticipated to flop right across those broken, gaping gateways. Fuller expected to get his assault element out, then follow with his protective screen.

Here the good Mr. Murphy intervened, in accord with his law—what can go wrong will go wrong. Somehow, the two Hawks got ahead of the USAF aircraft, placing Kurt Fuller in an awkward position. If he kept the birds there while he waited for the Pave Low, the Iraqis would gain a few more minutes to react, and those characters just might, ruining a fine night's effort. If Fuller loaded, he'd actually yank the security-support teams, himself included, before the assault platoon. But Coale had all his men at the LZ awaiting pickup, the MH-53J was en route, and the Iraqis remained absent. So Fuller passed the baton and climbed aboard. It wasn't classic Ranger SOP, but this time it answered the mail.[50]

Moments later, the Air Force pilots justified Fuller's faith. Their Pave Low descended on the LZ, wide blades whopping overhead, turbines bellowing, not in accord with the opsched but close enough. The Rangers came out in reverse order on the run, black goggles bouncing on their faces as they raced aboard the MH-53J. Once the platoon leader had again accounted for everyone, the Air Force craft raced its jet engines and shrugged aloft, its ramp closing as it wafted into the black sky. To the northwest, the previously suppressed Iraqi air defense post remained inactive, the dazed gunners evidently unwilling to risk another pasting.

Behind and below the aircraft at the deserted Iraqi complex, all grew silent. The shattered hinges of the front gate swung slowly in the darkness. It was 2246. The raid had taken only twenty-six minutes, from first boots down to last man out.

Five minutes later, the packets of explosives detonated. The men in the Little Birds watched a ripple of small bursts, including brilliant spurts of the thermite incendiaries, as cables parted, connector boxes shattered, and generators blew apart. With these pyrotechnics going full tilt, the grand finale erupted. The base of the mighty radio mast flowered into hot white stars, lots of simultanous bursts, some big, some smaller. The whole assembly shrugged up about two feet, as if to take off. Then, shedding pieces of torn steel, the heavy tower began a slow, sickening pirouette, a quarter-turn, half, three-quarters. There it stopped, hanging by a metal strut at a forty-five-degree angle, its internal latticework yanked like a bent hanger.[51] Good enough for Downing's JSOTF; no more messages to Scud units would go through this node.

Mission accomplished, the Rangers and their Night Stalker comrades flew out unmolested. Ken Keen marked off the opsched line after line, and he and his men came out of Iraq and back to Ar Ar. The small band of aircraft landed together in the wee hours of the morning. After a quick after-action "hotwash"—preliminary to a more thorough debriefing later—the Rangers and Night Stalkers cleaned their weapons, rested, and got ready to go again. The intelligence folks whisked away all the captured documents, the aircraft gun tapes, and the debriefing summaries; they were bound for thorough analyses.[52] It's not every night you penetrate deep into denied territory, shoot up the joint, blow things to smithereens, and get out to tell about it. The Rangers and their 160th aviator brothers knew they had done some fine government work, all right.

The Gulf War ended on 28 February 1991, before the Rangers mounted a second mission. But their direct action strike added to the Great Scud Hunt. After Ranger Run I, no more Scuds flew.[53] Electronically mute, hounded by air and ground, the Iraqi rocket regiments gave up two days early: effective suppression on a countrywide scale.

The end of hostilities left some Americans still out and about in western Iraq. With Rangers waiting as QRF, the JSOTF aircraft went out and collected their various D-Boy Scud hunters.[54] The pickups went smoothly, a successful end to a victorious war. For its part, the stubborn Iraqi microwave tower collapsed during the first week of March, outlasting Saddam Hussein's armed forces by several days.

What makes Rangers different? At first glance, a Ranger battalion looks like an upgunned light infantry battalion, with a headquarters unit and three rifle companies. Rangers share the same nine-man rifle squad as the rest of the U.S. Army infantry.[55] (And oh, what they and their more conventional brothers would not give for the Marines' strength of lucky thirteen.) Rangers do not have the Company D of armed Humvees that distinguishes airborne and air assault battalions. But they have other toys unique to Rangers alone.

Akin to the airborne and air assault troops, Ranger rifle platoons have weapons squads, but they have three machine guns apiece, each with a three-man crew. Other Army infantry get by with two men per gun, and hence often run short of ammunition.[56] The Rangers do not bother with the horrible old Dragon, a burden masquerading as an antitank missile that must be borne by most other U.S. Army rifle platoons.

Whereas other Army light infantry make do with a mortar section appended to the rifle company headquarters, Rangers retain the old weapons platoon, as do the Marines and as did the pre-1980s U.S. Army infantry. This platoon includes two 60mm mortars and a section of three 84mm M-3 Carl Gustav rocket launchers, much uprated versions of the venerable World War II bazooka designed in Sweden.[57] With a lieutenant and a platoon sergeant, this ensures that Ranger heavy-weapons teams get their full share of dedicated training time. The teams can be attached out to rifle platoons or, as in the Gulf War JSOTF, to other companies to add firepower.

In the battalion's headquarters company stay the usual subunits: the command group and staff, medics, communicators, and a small service support platoon. The Rangers field no scouts or mortars at battalion level, because these capabilities relate to sustained combat operations, not lightning direct action strikes.[58] Rangers rely on SOF intelligence sources to do their scouting. As for fire support, the Rangers have direct access to the 160th Night Stalkers and their USAF counterparts, among them the powerful AC-130 series Spectre gunships, not to mention F-15E Strike Eagles or whatever else they might need for a particular undertaking. To coordinate all of this firepower on tap, Rangers also keep U.S. Air Force forward air controllers, special operations aviation liaison officers, and artillery forward observers permanently attached.[59] Conventional units get similar attachments on a routine basis. So by and large, there is nothing remarkable here.

Yes, the Rangers do have some exotic weapons, courtesy of their affiliation with the larger SOF community. They get first call on new small arms and can buy special items as needed, such as the Bofors Carl Gustav recoilless rifle. Their radios are the best of new issue, including satellite sets at rifle company level, precious devices normally found at the divisional echelon in conventional units. Rangers get the latest field gear, such as the Gore-tex wet-cold ensemble, well before the rest of America's infantry force. Compared to other types of units, a Ranger company will have brand-new M-249 squad automatic weapon barrels, more refined night sights, better laser designators, lighter field gear, more ample weapons cleaning equipment, plenty of batteries, and all the useful extras that allow infantrymen to do their jobs.[60] It all helps.

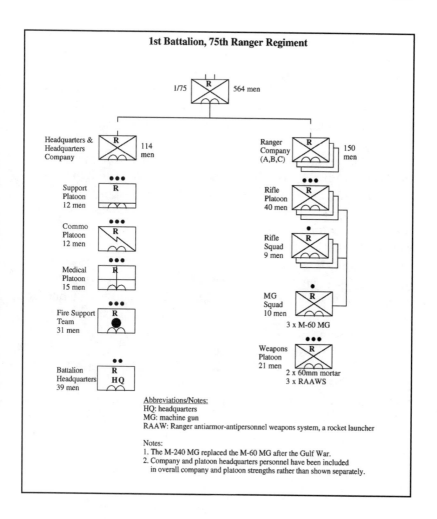

1st Battalion, 75th Ranger Regiment

1/75 — 564 men

Headquarters & Headquarters Company — 114 men

Support Platoon 12 men

Commo Platoon 12 men

Medical Platoon 15 men

Fire Support Team 31 men

Battalion Headquarters 39 men

Ranger Company (A,B,C) — 150 men

Rifle Platoon 40 men

Rifle Squad 9 men

MG Squad 10 men — 3 x M-60 MG

Weapons Platoon 21 men — 2 x 60mm mortar / 3 x RAAWS

Abbreviations/Notes:
HQ: headquarters
MG: machine gun
RAAW: Ranger antiarmor-antipersonnel weapons system, a rocket launcher

Notes:
1. The M-240 MG replaced the M-60 MG after the Gulf War.
2. Company and platoon headquarters personnel have been included in overall company and platoon strengths rather than shown separately.

Rangers have some vehicles, too, but not many. Over the years, Rangers have used motorcycles, modified jeeps, special-purpose Humvees, dune buggy variants, and off-road, all-terrain vehicles to increase ground mobility.[61] Though deliverable by parachute or helicopter and primarily foot mobile, the Rangers keep a changing stable of small transports and gun carriers to give them wheels as needed.

These weapons give Rangers many capabilities, but since the reactivation of the 1st and 2d Battalions in 1974 and the establishment of the 3d Battalion and the 75th Ranger Regiment in 1984, the force has focused on two primary roles.[62] Its battalions take airfields better than any other fighters in the American military, bar none. Ranger airfield takedowns paced the American interventions in Grenada (1983) and Panama (1989); the Rangers seized two airdromes (one a double set of runways) in the latter campaign. Had the 1994 Haiti forced entry operation gone off, Rangers would have had similar tasks in overwhelming the contingents trying to defend that small country.[63] Like their airborne comrades, the Rangers can fly off from their stateside posts and grab an airstrip overnight.

The Rangers' other role, working with JSOTFs, falls to separate Ranger rifle companies, usually beefed up a bit such as the one that Ken Keen and Curt Fuller took to Desert Storm. A Ranger company went with the Delta SOF to Grenada in 1983 and to Mogadishu, Somalia, ten years later.[64] As done with Major Keen, the 75th Ranger Regiment sends along a Ranger tactical command post team, headed by a field-grade officer, to assist in planning and run selected direct action operations. The actions of 1st Ranger Battalion's Company B in southwest Asia typify this kind of mission.

Lightly armed though they may be, the Rangers represent the heavy hitters of the SOF community, especially compared to Green Berets, SEALs, and Delta types. Those latter elements fight in small teams. The Rangers fight by regiment, battalions, or company, much like the conventional infantry they so closely resemble. In fact, Ranger officers and NCOs often refer to their organization as the finest light infantry in the world.[65] In theory, any solid rifle outfit can do what Rangers do. Some can, but not most, even in today's relatively elite American infantry force. What makes the 75th Ranger Regiment great does not involve unusual weapons, clever organization, or association with SOF. The strength of the regiment lies not in the caliber of its weaponry but in the caliber of its men.

Everyone in a Ranger outfit must be a volunteer several times over: for the U.S. Army, for the infantry or service with it (assigned signalers, medics, and the like), for airborne duty, and for the 75th Ranger Regiment. The Rangers set high standards for joining their regiment. Everyone must meet them. Older colonels and sergeants major get no free passes on the foot marching, running, pull-ups, compass courses, and other requirements.

Not every man has been through the U.S. Army's Ranger course, the fifty-six-day torture test built around small-unit patrolling in forest, mountain, and swamp. Most of the regiment's privates have yet to attend, because, with few exceptions, Ranger school enrolls fire team leaders and above. Almost all the officers and NCOs wear the highly coveted Ranger tab on their left shoulders; a chaplain, a cook, or some other specialist might not have earned the tab, but that is rare. Ranger school is the basic rite of passage to lead in the Ranger regiment.

The privates who join go through an abbreviated three-week version of Ranger school known as the Ranger Indoctrination Program, or RIP, a sobering name for a weeding-out that has at times claimed up to two-thirds of its aspirants. Like Ranger school, RIP stresses candidates through sleep deprivation and limited food and by pushing them on simulated patrols over hill and dale, often well past accustomed physical limits.[66] Those who make it join the regiment. Those who don't return to the Fort Benning personnel pool and are destined to join other infantry battalions.

The Ranger course or RIP may get men through the door, but the Ranger regiment is *not* Ranger school. In the school, it becomes hard to retain anything due to lack of sleep and food, and the tactics taught are rudimentary in the extreme. The Ranger regiment, however, teaches its men to become subject-matter experts on their weapons, their duty positions, and their roles in larger tasks. Ranger machine gunners, for example, display unparalleled skills in engaging targets day and night. Ranger squads can execute basic battle drills with speed and terrain savvy. And no unit raids as well as a Ranger rifle company or grabs an airport better than a Ranger battalion. Practice makes perfect, and these guys practice a lot, often with the first team: the 160th and their Air Force counterparts, the Navy SEALs, Delta, and the JSOC command group.

The regiment achieves these impressive training standards thanks to a generous annual budget and a massive practice ammunition account. The 1,868-man 75th Ranger Regiment routinely fires more live ammunition than some entire U.S. Army divisions, and the men participate in the most demanding joint exercises in the U.S. armed forces. Whereas most Army and Marine battalions must periodically furnish riflemen for post housekeeping and routine sentry duty, the Rangers stand apart from all that.[67] They can and do train as much as they want. In combat, the skill and teamwork really show.

Teamwork grows because the Rangers endeavor to grow their own leadership. Ranger sergeants generally start as Ranger privates. Senior NCOs spend much of their professional life in the regiment, broken by occasional tours in the 82d, the 101st, other light outfits, or the Ranger Training Brigade. Ranger captains start as Ranger lieutenants. Former company commanders return as majors or, as Ken Keen did, later take over battalions or even the regiment.[68] Outsiders with a Ranger tab may break into the fold at almost any level, and have done so, but they are the exception, not the rule. This wise recruitment and retention policy ensures that in this unit, most of the men know the deal without need for extensive retraining. The same SOPs carry over from year to year, adjusted by experience. It works superbly.

In essence, the Rangers short-circuit the typical U.S. Army individual replacement roundelay by creating a de facto regimental system, as the British Army has insisted upon for centuries. Men know one another, and leaders know their Rangers. The gains in cohesion make the training work, and they pay off in battle. Not surprisingly, those American units most like the Rangers, the 82d Airborne and the 101st Airborne, also get some of the same benefits from repeat assignments. The Marine Corps has enjoyed this circumstance for years. As American infantry ranks contract, more of this welcome development can be anticipated.

Rangers have fulfilled the charter given by Gen. Creighton Abrams in 1974 when he reactivated such battalion-sized organizations for the first time since World War II. In his initial comments, the pugnacious tanker, whom Patton once called the best armored commander in World War II, made it clear that he wanted solid professionals, not some jackleg *Dirty Dozen* knockoffs.

The battalion is to be an elite, light, and the most proficient infantry in the world. A battalion that can do things with its hands and weapons better than anyone. The battalion will contain no 'hoodlums and brigands,' and if the battalion is formed from such persons, it will be disbanded. Wherever the battalion goes, it must be apparent that it is the best.[69]

Abrams's customarily forthright directions still guide the regiment today.

The entire U.S. Army, especially its infantry battalions, has gained from the Ranger approach to warfare. Ranger training methods emphasize superb execution of the basics, and those techniques apply to all military instruction and exercises. Pursuant to the Abrams "no hoodlums" stricture, the Rangers enforce U.S. Army training and disciplinary standards fairly and impartially, a model for all units. Rangers are sharp in garrison and in battle. Best of all, these outstanding men go back and forth from the 75th Ranger Regiment to the conventional battalions, spreading the Ranger gospel.

The evident quality of this breed of infantry has energized the entire U.S. Army infantry community, showing it how to do business. Recognition of Ranger excellence, demonstrated in the 1983 Grenada intervention, underscored the Army's 1984–86 initiatives to remold America's general-purpose walking infantry into selected, hard-core light infantry battalions. These new-model light troops consciously emulated the Ranger framework.[70] As a side benefit, this Ranger–light troop ethos infused the airborne and air assault ranks as well.

The only real glitch happens in the mech world, where the Ranger Regiment's 11Bs cannot move into Bradley battalion 11M slots. That is too bad for both sides. The mech people could benefit from Ranger training techniques, rehearsal methods, and tactics. For their part, most Rangers do not know much about armored warfare, although officers occasionally come and go from Bradley units. But, in general, Ranger people don't do mech. This lapse in professional understanding played a part in decisions made in October 1993 in Mogadishu, where a JSOTF got into urban death ground without any armored protection. Ranger tabs are great, but bullets will not bounce off.

It's no wonder that the tough riflemen in the 75th Ranger Regiment sometimes think otherwise. They live up to their hype, and then some. Selected, trained, and led to excel in close combat, the Rangers provide an especially capable force in the American arsenal. Army Rangers today are the best foot infantry in the world, just like Creighton Abrams wanted them to be.

Every day and night, including Thanksgiving and Christmas, rain or shine, Rangers stand by, ready to launch out and do the country's bidding. They cannot predict the next call. (Who can?) But if Grenada, Panama, the Gulf War, Somalia, and Haiti tell us anything, they tell us that the call will come. It is why the 75th Ranger Regiment exists. Scant hours after that fateful ring of the telephone, the regiment or its constituent battalions and companies take to the air, bound for the worst places on Earth. When they get there, they will do the job or die trying. As the Ranger Creed concludes, "Readily will I display the intestinal fortitude required to fight on to the Ranger objective and complete the mission though I be the lone survivor."[71] That's the bottom line. In death ground, Rangers ensure that hard jobs get done.

Notes

The epigraph comes from Maj. John D. Lock, *To Fight with Intrepidity . . . The Complete History of the U.S. Army Rangers, 1622 to the Present* (West Point, N.Y.: unpublished manuscript, 1997), 143. Lock's book, the definitive history of the Rangers, will be published in 1998 by Pocket Books of New York, N.Y. Lock quotes Cota's words to the men of the 5th Ranger Battalion during the tough fighting at Omaha Beach on D day, 6 June 1944.

1. For more on von Braun, see Howard E. McCurdy, *Space and the American Imagination* (Washington, D.C.: Smithsonian Institution Press, 1997), 23, and Erik Bergaust, *Wernher von Braun* (Washington, D.C: National Space Institute, 1976), 368. A typical example of a barb directed at von Braun's role with the V-2 can be found in Norman Mailer, *Of a Fire on the Moon* (Boston, Mass.: Little, Brown and Co., 1969), 70. By the way, like many immigrants before and since, Wernher von Braun became a vociferous patriot and community servant. The civic center in Huntsville, Alabama, near the German-American's Marshall Space Flight Center and the U.S. Army Redstone Arsenal, proudly bears von Braun's name. The people of northern Alabama knew a good man when they met one.

2. Anthony H. Cordesman and Abraham R. Wagner, *The Lessons of Modern War*, 4 vols. (Boulder, Colo.: Westview Press, 1990–96), *Volume II: The Iran-Iraq War* (1990), 496–505, and *Volume IV: The Gulf War* (1996), 850–52, 854; David C. Isby, *Weapons and Tactics of the Soviet Army* (New York, N.Y.: Jane's Publishing Inc., 1988), 294–96; Eliot A. Cohen, director, *Gulf War Air Power Survey*, 5 vols. (Washington, D.C.: U.S. Government Printing Office, 1993), *Volume II: Effects and Effectiveness*, 317–19.

3. Rick Atkinson, *Crusade* (Boston, Mass.: Houghton Mifflin Co., 1993), 173–74.

4. Atkinson, *Crusade*, 416–21, 538. Cordesman and Wagner, *The Lessons of Modern War, Volume IV: The Gulf War*, 856–57. In a particularly cruel turn, the American dead and wounded mostly came from one small-town unit, Greensburg, Pennsylvania's U.S. Army Reserve 14th Quartermaster Detachment.

5. Michael R. Gordon and Lt. Gen. Bernard E. Trainor, USMC (Ret.), *The Generals' War* (Boston, Mass.: Little, Brown and Co., 1995), 522. Cordesman and Wagner, *The Lessons of Modern War, Volume IV: The Gulf War,* 858, state that after the war ended, U.N. weapons inspectors found thirty chemical warheads that could have been mated to Iraqi Scuds. The crude machining and small size suggested that they might not have worked all that well, but even a little nerve gas is not a happy prospect.

6. Cohen, *Gulf War Air Power Survey,* 118–19. Patriot batteries totaled seven in Israel (two Israeli, one Dutch, and four American) and twenty-one in Saudi Arabia (all U.S.). After some pretty inflated claims during the war, the U.S. Army now estimates that Patriots intercepted 40 percent (sixteen) of the forty Scuds bound for Israel and 70 percent (thirty-four) of the forty-eight rockets shot at Saudi Arabia. As discussed in Cordesman and Wagner, *The Lessons of Modern War, Volume IV: The Gulf War,* 874, the General Accounting Office can confirm only eight kills and credits fifteen as possible hits. Israeli experts think that one or two Patriots might have intercepted Scuds over Tel Aviv, but the real number may be zero.

7. Atkinson, *Crusade,* 144.

8. U.S. Senate Committee on Armed Services, *Operation Desert Shield/Desert Storm,* 102d Congress, 1st Session, 24 April 1991; 8–9 May 1991; 16 and 21 May 1991; 4, 12, and 20 June 1991, 375, 379, 393, 397.

9. Douglas C. Waller, *The Commandos* (New York, N.Y.: Simon & Schuster, 1994), 340–42. Waller offered some of the first open-source accounts of JSOTF operations, although now they are more widely discussed in many books and articles, including some U.S. government documents. For example, see Col. John M. Collins, USA (Ret.), *Special Operations Forces: An Assessment* (Washington, D.C.: National Defense University Press, 1994), 113. For more on the SAS role in Iraq, see Gen. Sir Peter de la Billiere, *Storm Command* (Dubai, U.A.E.: Motivate Publishing, 1992), 217–18; Cordesman and Wagner, *The Lessons of Modern War, Volume IV: The Gulf War,* 751.

10. U.S. Senate Committee on Armed Services, *Operation Desert Shield/Desert Storm,* 379, 397; U.S. Special Operations Command, *10th Anniversary History* (MacDill Air Force Base, Fla.: U.S. Special Operations Command History and Research Office, 16 April 1997), 40.

11. U.S. Special Operations Command, *Joint Special Operations Awareness Program Reference Manual* (Tampa, Fla.: Kapos Associates, Inc., 7 April 1994), A-9, A-13–19.

12. Collins, *Special Operations Forces,* 69–70.

13. Waller, *The Commandos,* 344–45; Atkinson, *Crusade,* 178–79. A detailed description of Delta Scud hunting can be found in Terry Griswold and D. M. Giangreco, *Delta* (Osceola, Wis.: Motorbooks, International, 1992), 106–23.

14. John W. Partin, *75th Rangers and 160th SOAR (A) Scud Hunters* (MacDill Air Force Base, Fla.: U.S. Special Operations Command History and Research Office, 9 December 1997), 4; Lance Q. Zedric and Michael F. Dilley, *Elite Warriors: 300 Years of America's Best Fighting Troops* (Ventura, Calif.: Pathfinder Publishing, 1996), 235; interview with Col. P. Kenneth Keen, USA, Carlisle Barracks, Pa., 3 February 1998. The interview with Colonel Keen was subject to normal strictures of U.S. Special Operations Command nondisclosure agreements.

15. Interview with Lt. Col. Joseph A. Smith, USA, Carlisle Barracks, Pa., 3 February 1998. The interview with Lieutenant Colonel Smith was subject to normal strictures of U.S. Special Operations Command nondisclosure agreements. The 160th Special Operations Aviation Regiment operated several variants of the MH-60 Blackhawk. According to Paul Jackson, editor in chief, *Jane's All the World's Aircraft 1996–97* (Alexandria, Va.: Jane's Information Group, Inc., 1996), 727, the 160th flew MH-60Ls in the Gulf War. The more advanced MH-60K entered the inventory in 1992, in time to serve in Somalia.

16. Griswold and Giangreco, *Delta,* 78–91; Waller, *The Commandos,* 172–73.

17. Cohen, *Gulf War Air Power Survey: Effects and Effectiveness,* 341; Partin, *75th Rangers and 160th SOAR (A) Scud Hunters,* 4; Cordesman and Wagner, *The Lessons of Modern War, Volume IV: The Gulf War,* 329–31, 861.

18. Cordesman and Wagner, *The Lessons of Modern War, Volume IV: The Gulf War,* 331–32.

19. Cohen, *Gulf War Air Power Survey: Effects and Effectiveness,* 340; Cordesman and Wagner, *The Lessons of Modern War, Volume IV: The Gulf War,* 862–65.

20. Cordesman and Wagner, *The Lessons of Modern War, Volume IV: The Gulf War*, 854, 858, 864.

21. U.S. Special Operations Command, *USSOCOM Pub 1: Special Operations in Peace and War* (MacDill Air Force Base, Fla.: U.S. Special Operations Command, 25 January 1996), 3-2.

22. U.S. Joint Staff, *Joint Pub 3-05: Doctrine for Joint Special Operations (Draft)* (Washington, D.C.: U.S. Government Printing Office, 1997), II-4–5.

23. U.S. Department of the Army, *FM 7-10: The Infantry Rifle Company* (Washington, D.C.: U.S. Government Printing Office, 14 December 1990), 6-22.

24. U.S. Special Operations Command, *Posture Statement 1996* (MacDill Air Force Base, Fla.: U.S. Special Operations Command, 1996), 34; Collins, *Special Operations Forces*, 55, 70; U.S. Special Operations Command, *Joint Special Operations Awareness Program Reference Manual*, A-14–17.

25. U.S. Joint Staff, *Joint Pub 3-05: Doctrine for Joint Special Operations (Draft)*, V-3.

26. de la Billiere, *Storm Command*, 220–21.

27. Ibid., 262; Partin, *75th Rangers and 160th SOAR (A) Scud Hunters*, 4-5; Keen interview; Smith interview.

28. Smith interview; Keen interview. The Rangers and their aviator comrades typically had one mission in planning, another in rehearsal, and a third ready to execute, a tough pace that kept all involved busy.

29. Jackson, *Jane's All the World's Aircraft 1996–97*, 667–68; Smith interview; Partin, *75th Rangers and 160th SOAR (A) Scud Hunters*, 5-6; Griswold and Giangreco, *Delta*, 86–87. U.S. Joint Staff, *Joint Pub 1-02: Department of Defense Dictionary of Military and Associated Terms* (Washington, D.C.: U.S. Government Printing Office, 1 December 1989), 355, defines suppression as "temporary or transient degradation of the performance of a weapons system, below the level needed to fulfill its mission objectives, by an opposing force."

30. Partin, *75th Rangers and 160th SOAR (A) Scud Hunters*, 5; Smith interview.

31. Smith interview; Keen interview; Griswold and Giangreco, *Delta*, 82–83.

32. Smith interview.

33. Keen interview.

34. Captain Shelby L. Stanton, USA (Ret.), *Anatomy of a Division* (Novato, Calif.: Presidio Press, 1987), 46. The dangers of micromanagement from overhead come through in Lt. Col. Kevin Corcoran, USA, *Maneuver Company Commanders and Their Battalion Commanders in Vietnam: No Shared Values* (Carlisle, Pa.: U.S. Army War College, 20 March 1989), 5-6.

35. Gordon and Trainor, *The Generals' War*, 258.

36. U.S. Headquarters, 101st Airborne Division (Air Assault), *Gold Book: Tactics, Techniques, and Procedures for the Brigade Air Assault (Draft)* (Fort Campbell, Ky.: HQ, 101st Airborne Division [Air Assault], 1 July 1997), 28, 29, 32.

37. Smith interview; Keen interview; Lt. Col. Kurt Fuller, USA, "E-Mail to Daniel P. Bolger, Subject: Ranger Run I," 10 February 1998. The e-mail with Lieutenant Colonel Fuller was subject to normal strictures of U.S. Special Operations Command nondisclosure agreements.

38. Cohen, *Gulf War Air Power Survey, Volume II: Effects and Effectiveness*, 337; Waller, *The Commandos*, 346.

39. The E-3C Sentry is also known as AWACS (airborne warning and control system). See Tom Clancy, *Fighter Wing* (New York, N.Y.: Berkley Books, 1995), 111–17.

40. Partin, *75th Rangers and 160th SOAR (A) Scud Hunters*, 6; Keen interview.

41. Cordesman and Wagner, *The Lessons of Modern Warfare, Volume IV: The Gulf War*, 453, 481; Fuller, "E-Mail to Daniel P. Bolger, Subject: Ranger Run I." Air Force postmission assessments credited this attack with destroying nine 57mm S-60 guns. Enemy casualties were not estimated.

42. Smith interview; Keen interview.

43. Fuller, "E-Mail to Daniel P. Bolger, Subject: Ranger Run I."

44. The M-3 Carl Gustav, built by Bofors of Sweden, is called the Ranger antiarmor antipersonnel weapon system (RAAWS) in Ranger service. See U.S. Special Operations Command, *Posture Statement 1996*, 56; Keen interview.

45. Fuller, "E-Mail to Daniel P. Bolger, Subject: Ranger Run I."

46. Ibid.

47. U.S. Department of the Army, *FM 7-8: Infantry Rifle Platoon and Squad* (Washington, D.C.: U.S. Government Printing Office, 22 April 1992), B-9.

48. Fuller, "E-Mail to Daniel P. Bolger, Subject: Ranger Run I."

49. Ibid.; Keen interview. The tower actually had an inner, load-bearing structure and an outer support superstructure. The Rangers sliced the main columns, which stood well inside the derricklike outer rigging.

50. Fuller, "E-Mail to Daniel P. Bolger, Subject: Ranger Run I."

51. Ideally, the Rangers would have stayed on the ground until the charges blew, in order to go back and finish the job if anything failed to explode. But the JSOTF commanding general directed them to double-fuse the packages and depart rather than remain too long so deep in enemy territory. The raid account draws heavily from Partin, *75th Rangers and 160th SOAR (A) Scud Hunters,* 5-6; Brig. Gen. Robert H. Scales, USA, director, *Certain Victory: The United States Army in the Gulf War* (Washington, D.C.: U.S. Government Printing Office, 1993), 186; Keen interview; Smith interview; Fuller, "E-Mail to Daniel P. Bolger, Subject: Ranger Run I."

52. Keen interview.

53. Fuller, "E-Mail to Daniel P. Bolger, Subject: Ranger Run I"; Cohen, *Gulf War Air Power Survey, Volume II: Effects and Effectiveness,* 337.

54. The JSOTF suffered seven dead in a helicopter crash on 21 February 1991. See Waller, *The Commandos,* 345–46.

55. Commander, U.S. Army John F. Kennedy Special Warfare Center and School, *Army Special Operations Forces Reference Data* (Fort Bragg, N.C.: U.S. Army John F. Kennedy Special Warfare Center and School, 8 February 1991), B-18–57.

56. U.S. Department of the Army, *FM 7-8: Infantry Rifle Platoon and Squad* (Washington, D.C.: U.S. Government Printing Office, 22 April 1992), A-1–3.

57. U.S. Department of the Army, *FM 7-10: The Infantry Rifle Company,* 1-8–10; U.S. Army John F. Kennedy Special Warfare Center and School, *Army Special Operations Forces Reference Data,* B-44–57.

58. Recent thinking in the 75th Ranger Regiment indicates that each battalion may soon consolidate its company 60mm mortar sec-

tions into a battalion-level mortar platoon. In addition to allowing the option of a six-tube 60mm platoon, Ranger mortarmen would also maintain and train on complete sets of 81mm, 120mm, and even obsolescent 107mm (the World War II–era 4.2-inch weapon). This would permit quite an expansion in current Ranger mortar combat power and allow leaders to select from a menu of mortar firepower appropriate to varied missions.

59. U.S. Army John F. Kennedy Special Warfare Center and School, *Army Special Operations Forces Reference Data*, B-20.

60. Ibid., B-37, B-57; Collins, *Special Operations Forces*, 34–35, 38–39, 128.

61. Collins, *Special Operations Forces*, 48; U.S. Army John F. Kennedy Special Warfare Center and School, *Army Special Operations Forces Reference Data*, B-52.

62. Joel Nadel with J. R. Wright, *Special Men and Special Missions* (London, U.K.: Greenhill Books, 1994), 121–22. Ranger battalions numbered 1–6 served in World War II, and separate companies fought in Korea and Vietnam.

63. U.S. Special Operations Command, *10th Anniversary History*, 1, 19, 50.

64. U.S. Special Operations Command, *Joint Special Operations Awareness Program Reference Manual*, A-9, A-14, A-16–17. On A-14, the *Manual* states: "at any one time, at least one of the three battalions is designated as a support asset for national level joint special operations [that is, JSOC]." For the Grenada case, see Daniel P. Bolger, *Americans at War, 1975–1986: An Era of Violent Peace* (Novato, Calif.: Presidio Press, 1988), 296. For Mogadishu, see Chapter 5 of the present book.

65. U.S. Special Operations Command, *Joint Special Operations Awareness Program Reference Manual*, A-9, A-13.

66. Zedric and Dilley, *Elite Warriors*, 235; Mark Lloyd, *Special Forces* (London, U.K.: Arms and Armour Press, 1995), 139–40; U.S. Government Accounting Office, *Army Ranger Training: Safety Improvements Need to Be Institutionalized* (Washington, D.C.: U.S. Government Printing Office, 2 January 1997), 2.

67. Collins, *Special Operations Forces*, 55; U.S. Special Operations Command, *Joint Special Operations Awareness Program Reference Man-*

ual, A-14. Purpose-built Ranger support elements back up each battalion, providing routine administration and service support to free the Rangers to train, deploy, and fight.

68. Now a colonel, Ken Keen offers a classic case. Having joined the Rangers as a captain, he served as a battalion S-3 and an executive officer in the 1st Battalion, which he later commanded. He is a strong candidate to assume command of the 75th Ranger Regiment. In another case, Col. William F. Kernan, now a lieutenant general, commanded a company in the Rangers, returned to take over 1st Battalion, and led the regiment into Panama in 1989.

69. Lock, *To Fight With Intrepidity . . . ,* 221. For Patton's thoughts on Abrams, see Brian M. Sobel, *The Fighting Pattons* (Westport, Conn.: Praeger, 1997), 176–77.

70. Scales, *Certain Victory,* 28–29; John L. Romjue, *The Army of Excellence: The Development of the 1980s Army* (Fort Monroe, Va.: U.S. Army Training and Doctrine Command, 1993), 53.

71. For the present version, see http://www.ranger.org/~ranger /creed.html.

Chapter 5: Brave Rifles

Soldiers learn to sense when a situation begins to go sour, when the options start to slip away and the enemy gains the upper hand. The soldiers can feel it going, like a bus sliding over a cliff at seventy miles an hour. At first, the driver thinks he's handling it, steering out of the crunchy gravel, still biting real pavement. "I've got it, I've got it," he hisses to himself, grinding gears, stomping brakes, accelerating, trying this, then that, one thing after another, hoping to urge the yawing contraption back from the brink. But then a front wheel slips out into the void, the other follows, and the long cabin lurches across the lip, suspended, teetering, teasing, before the front end tilts downward. And it's gone.

In a firefight, once matters go over the figurative edge, pulling things out depends on what else can be brought to the battle, and how fast. Military historians dignify this phenomenon by talking about culminating points in operations, or referring to the loss of "the initiative," but these remain ex post facto constructs imposed to explain how things went wrong. Grunts have their own term, characteristically laconic—losing it.

The special operators lost it in Mogadishu, Somalia, at precisely 1629 on Sunday, 3 October 1993, when the second U.S. helicopter went down.[1] Oh, they still maintained their discipline and fought well, exceedingly well. But when that second MH-60K Blackhawk smacked into the cluster of seedy, dusty sheds southeast of the hostile Bakara Market neighborhood, the options ran out. With two choppers down, a road relief column being flailed, and no reserves left, the special operations forces ran out of chips to toss on the table. The thin stick men of the Somali National Alliance (SNA), known as "skinnies" to the American special ops types, had called America's bluff and found Maj. Gen. William H. Garrison's elite Task Force Ranger holding a pair of fours.[2] Gleeful Somalis threw down a full house: hundreds of armed militiamen, rocket-propelled grenades—those damned RPGs—crowds of women and children pressing all around, and tin-roofed, ramshackle urban clutter to hide the entire hostile lot. To add to the frenzy, most of the locals chewed *khat,* a natural vegetable stimulant, organic Somali cocaine—as if these people needed any energizing. They flocked to the downed American helos like sharks drawn to blood.

It wasn't supposed to be like this, not at all. The men of TF Ranger had pulled off six prior raids without so much as a scratch, quickie in-and-out jobs, grabbing local Somali bigwigs to cut the insides out of warlord Muhammed Farah's key leadership circles. Oh, the Americans wanted Muhammed Farah, nicknamed "Aidid," one who tolerates no insult. But that guy had been on the run since early June. The Rangers and their Delta friends had not arrived until late August, and by then, given Aidid's two-and-a-half-month head start, it was the coyote chasing the roadrunner. The D-Boys certainly snatched a few Aidid cronies, small to medium birds. But that old roadrunner Aidid just beep-beeped and eluded them, always one step ahead of Garrison's Delta teams. Today, finally, the cartoon turned ugly, and the anvil dropped on poor coyote's head.

Garrison launched his TF Ranger to raid a building near the Olympic Hotel, in the heart of Aidid-held Indian country. The U.S. force included the usual JSOTF lineup: forty or so skilled counterterrorists of Squadron C, 1st Special Forces Operational Detachment-Delta; two platoons and a company command team from Company B, 3d Battalion of the 75th Ranger Regiment; and a fleet of eight MH-60K Blackhawk SOF assault helos, four MH-6 Little Birds to carry in Delta shooters, and four AH-6J Little Bird attack models to fly cover, all from the 160th Special Operations Aviation Regiment, the best combat helicopter aviators in the world. This bunch had been practicing since June for these kinds of missions, and the one on 3 October matched their well-oiled battle drills.

The scheme for that Sunday afternoon outing seemed like simplicity itself. Based on a solid sighting from intelligence and recon

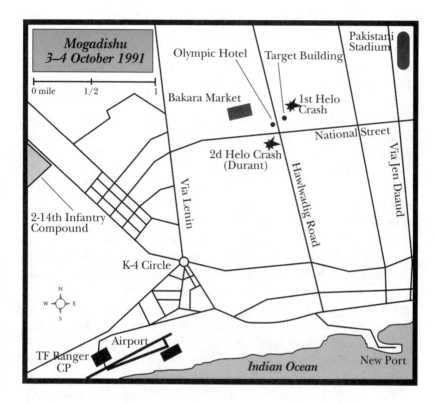

Mogadishu
3–4 October 1991

Olympic Hotel   Target Building   Pakistani Stadium

0 mile   1/2   1

Bakara Market   1st Helo Crash

National Street

2d Helo Crash (Durant)

Via Lenin

Hawlwadig Road

Via Jen Daaud

2-14th Infantry Compound

K-4 Circle

N
W — E
S

Airport

TF Ranger CP   Indian Ocean   New Port

teams scouting the battered city of Mogadishu, Garrison planned to
hit a gathering of Aidid lieutenants near the Olympic Hotel. Without any decent LZs in the twisted, crowded warren of sheds and cinder-block hovels, the raiders would slide down three-inch-thick,
spongy cords known as fast ropes. The Rangers drew their usual task,
forming the outward-facing security cordon. The D-Boys had to take
down the target building, busting doors and making the pickups.
Then, a twelve-vehicle convoy of armed, protected trucks would
move in and yank out the prisoners and the TF Ranger elements.
Above it all, the Little Birds and MH-60Ks would orbit in the bright
blue afternoon sky to suppress any troublemakers.

Of course, in retrospect, the entire concept displayed a streak of
incredible boldness bordering on arrogance. The Americans entered in broad daylight, on about two hours' notice. Although a con-

ventional chopper had been downed eight days before, blown out of the night sky by Somali RPG volleys, TF Ranger did not reconsider flying in by rotary-wing aircraft in the full light of day. What happened to other less-skilled units did not appear to apply to them. They were the best troops in the United States, with the best small arms, the best aircraft, the best communications, the best training, and, above all, the very best men. They could outfly and outfight whatever the Somalis sent after them. The badniks wouldn't dare to interfere. They had never reacted quickly enough in the past. Task Force Ranger was too fast for them.

Underestimating the foe can be terminal, especially when the hostiles are a warrior people who have spent the last two decades tangling with the Ethiopians, the Kenyans, and one another, not to mention the odd United Nations element. Once starving, they had all been fed, and now a good number in Mogadishu decided that these gringos had to go.[3] They relished a chance to go *mano-a-mano* with the vaunted TF Ranger, darlings of the American news media. (So much for operations security—this JSOTF's cover story had been compromised from the outset.) And the American SOF, in their impatience to strike swiftly, gave their opponents a perfect opening. Aidid subordinate Col. Ali Aden saw it clearly: "If you use a tactic twice, you should not use it a third time."[4] This was iteration number seven.

The Americans got down okay, starting at 1542. They snagged twenty-four shocked neighborhood militia leaders with minimal delay. Ranger-driven trucks appeared in accord with the hallowed operations schedule, the standard opsched for this well-templated evolution. Each line was ticked off, monitored by Garrison in his seaside airfield command post, as well as by a circling C2 helicopter. The D-Boys hustled their dazed charges into the waiting ground convoy. On the perimeter, there sure seemed to be a lot of firing on this particular warm Sunday. But no matter; TF Ranger was about ready to get out.

Then at 1610 the first chopper crashed, hit by RPGs. Okay, that had been foreseen—the SOF guys had that possibility covered. The on-scene commander diverted an orbiting MH-60K with a standby fifteen-man search and rescue element. Those SOF folks fast-roped down to secure the wreckage and await retrieval. The ground convoy could certainly get everyone out. It had been a setback, but manageable. The big bus was skirting the cliff, but it was still on the roadbed, going like hell.

But nineteen minutes later, a second Blackhawk took an RPG through the tail and fluttered down. That did it for the opsched. At that moment, Task Force Ranger entered uncharted badlands. The old bus headed for the edge.

From above, other U.S. helo crews saw packs of Somalis rush the wreckage of the second Blackhawk. The four crewmen, undoubtedly stunned and likely crippled, looked doomed. Without hesitation, TF Ranger's final reserve went in: two Delta snipers, MSgt. Gary I. Gordon and Sfc. Randall Shughart. Their calm, inspiring bravery in plunging down to the jaws of death earned them both the Medal of Honor.[5] The hopeless situation on the ground ensured that those awards would come posthumously.

Three of the Blackhawk's four-man crew died in the wreckage, killed by hordes of hopped-up Somalis. Thanks to the sacrifice and superb marksmanship of Gordon and Shughart, one injured pilot, CWO Michael Durant, survived to be taken captive. His unlucky crewmates got dragged through the yellow dirt of Mogadishu, a revolting scene run over and over by fascinated American news networks. At least those brave men had passed beyond caring about the degradation inflicted on their earthly remains.

For the ninety-nine SOF soldiers still alive and in contact near the original objective and the nearby carcass of the first dead helo, the news got worse and worse. Three more of the 160th's powerful Blackhawks went off station and limped back to base, smashed up so badly that they were out of the fight. The ground relief convoy got lost and shot to pieces. Unable to locate their encircled comrades, the riddled trucks pulled back toward the TF Ranger base at the airfield. Many aboard were wounded, including the commander, and they lost a five-ton truck in the tumult. The dead aboard included one of the two dozen Somali prisoners still traveling with the column. In TF Ranger's mounting struggle to survive, folks almost forgot that the Aidid faction leaders were the reason for the entire battle. The captives sure seemed like yesterday's news by this point. Tires flattened, cabs holed, ammunition gone, men bruised and bleeding, the

Ranger convoy crawled back to TF Ranger's oceanfront base camp around 1818.[6] They were out of the fight for now.

A sick, sorry, nameless feeling clawed at the guts of the ninety-nine Delta shooters and Rangers stuck out in death ground, the gnawing tendrils of long-stifled U.S. Army tribal memories, fine units ravaged: the 7th Cavalry at Little Big Horn in 1876, the Rangers at Cisterna in 1944, the 9th Infantry at the Chongchon River in 1950.[7] Those poor guys had been cut off, surrounded, and killed, parts of each command wiped out to the last man. Now TF Ranger's men found themselves likewise pocketed and pressed. It did not take calculus to figure out that there were more Somalis than the Rangers and D-Boys had bullets, and the big equalizers, the 160th Special Operations helos, were barely holding their own.[8] No aircraft could swoop down and beam them up, not from this maelstrom.

To get out—if they got out at all—the Rangers and Delta men had to break through on the ground. Burdened by all their dead and wounded, almost half the little force, that was not going to happen. With the sun sinking steadily toward the smoky horizon, more than one embattled member of TF Ranger wondered if the ragged perimeter would make it through the night. Not as if that promised anything, because the SOF men would run out of ammunition long before sunrise. In their haste to conduct the raid, the men had left behind vital night-vision goggles and sighting aids, extra ammunition, and canteens of badly needed water. They were supposed to be back at base by now. And around them, like flocks of deadly ghosts, the relentless Somalis fired and moved, fired and moved, inflicting the death of a thousand cuts on America's finest.

Yes, it had that whiff of doom, all right. Garrison and his people back at their seaside airfield command post knew it only too well. The good opsched, the game plan, was a memory. Hell, it wasn't even the same game; it was like going out to play basketball and discovering that your opponents had elected to confront you in rugby, with about twenty teams to your one. And you could not leave the arena until the bad guys got tired, if ever. If you lasted that long.

In a perfect world, the AC-130H Spectre gunships might have arrived overhead to hose down the aggressive Somalis with accurate streams of 40mm cannon rounds or even a few big 105mm blasts.

But the Spectres were gone, sent away to Djibouti weeks before. General Garrison had just known that his AH-6-series Little Birds and MH-60K armed Blackhawks had enough firepower to defeat ragtag Somali street fighters. Under normal circumstances, Garrison's estimate would have sounded reasonable. But this Sunday, the Somalis also deviated from their usual opsched; they chose to stand and fight, RPGs in hand.

Maybe an armored column of clanking Abrams tanks and Bradley fighting vehicles could have broken through to the imperiled Ranger platoons and Delta troop. But they were not in country. Commanders senior to Garrison requested a mechanized contingent, foreseeing exactly this kind of crisis. Unfortunately, Secretary of Defense Les Aspin ignored military advice and tabled the request.[9] So Garrison had no access to U.S. tanks or Brads.

Some of America's United Nations allies in Mogadishu used obsolescent armored vehicles, but Garrison's TF Ranger did not want to mess with foreigners. The U.N. soldiers might have loose lips around Somalis, not good for surprise direct action strikes. Besides, who could really trust the Italians, Pakistanis, or Malaysians in a demanding direct action mission? No, TF Ranger trusted the proven JSOTF team that had done so well in Panama and the Gulf War. Now that team had run flat out of tricks at the worst possible time.

The only hope to save TF Ranger rested on the skill and will of five hundred or so light infantrymen of the 2d Battalion, 14th Infantry Regiment, serving as the ground combat unit for the brigade quick reaction force that served to protect the service units of U.S. Forces Somalia. The prospect of relying on those 2-14th people made some of the men in TF Ranger shudder: conventional grunts, described acidly to a reporter as "poorly trained Regular Army schmoes, just a small step removed from utterly incompetent civilianhood."[10] Without more SOF, Spectres, or tanks, those light infantry "schmoes" represented TF Ranger's last good chance of living to see another dawn.

Had the men of TF Ranger bothered to learn more about Lt. Col. Bill David and his 2d Battalion of the 14th Infantry Regiment, they might have been more sure of their salvation. Far from being schmoes of any sort, David's Dragons knew urban warfare in Mogadishu, and they brought exactly the right set of talents to the fray. Moreover, they entered the contest with a collective desire to close with and kill whatever foeman got between them and their ultimate goal—saving TF Ranger. Seldom has the instrument so suited the hour.

Bill David and his chain of command focused on three core competencies: physical fitness, marksmanship, and small-unit tactics. There is no better distillation of the essence of light infantry. The Dragons consciously exceeded the usual U.S. Army standards in each of these crucial areas and sustained that high level of performance over time. That included their long deployment to Mogadishu. Despite daily operations, the 2d of the 14th kept training—hard.

Strong bodies and tough minds came first. "Light infantry operations are cruel to the human body" is Bill David's succinct summary. To endure and triumph when exhausted, thirsty, beaten up, and, yes, wounded, lightfighters must draw on reserves of strength and willpower not tapped by normal men and rarely used even by other soldiers. The Dragons created those reservoirs over time, using the direct, brutal, unforgiving means that always work. The Army requires a timed two-mile run from all soldiers, from clerks to Rangers. Most infantry battalions settle for running four miles in formation in thirty-two minutes, tough enough with more than five hundred men together, not all of them young. David's battalion went to eight-mile runs as the standard, and at that same pace of eight minutes per mile, sometimes faster. In the same way, whereas most higher headquarters mandate a twelve-mile speed march as the test of foot movement, the Dragons trained over a twenty-five-mile course, with all combat weapons and equipment. They had eight hours to finish it by unit, and although the first twenty miles or so could be knocked out based on youth and overall fitness, the last five called for real guts. The 2-14th commander rightly called this "the infantryman's marathon."[11] To get to these thresholds took daily sessions of weight training, running, and periodic marches, often in multiple exercise periods, such as football "two-a-day" practices. It all helped teach these young men to go past their aches and pains. In the light infantry, the men themselves move the unit forward in death ground.

No parachute, helicopter, or armored carrier does that. When it's time to go, go they must. And that takes effort over months to make it happen.

To move, light infantrymen must shoot to kill. They carry only so much ammunition. Most of their weaponry consists of shoulder arms. So every shot must count. David and his people knew this and trained accordingly, determined to become "masters of all facets of marksmanship." Most U.S. Army units settle for qualification, trusting in standardized ranges with small plastic silhouette targets at regular intervals. The Dragons went way beyond those basics. Every time a soldier in 2-14th fired his rifle, grenade launcher, or machine gun, he shot to kill. Because real opponents move and hide, the battalion built their own moving targets: aiming at bottles dangling from strings in the breeze, engaging bunker and window apertures to hit partially exposed targetry, and even resorting to old standbys such as can popping to keep skills sharp. Off the beach in Somalia, they floated bottles on the roving waves and banged away. And to try killing a thinking foe, they used the Army multiple integrated laser engagement system (MILES) projectors on their firearms and receivers on their helmets and load-bearing harnesses, playing laser tag in earnest. In doing this, the battalion used up more than its fair share of yearly training ammunition. That raised some eyebrows, but to their credit, David's superiors back at the 10th Mountain Division (Light Infantry) in Fort Drum, New York, scrounged the extra rounds.[12] The Dragons shot and shot, day and night. They could kill with single rounds. That came in handy in Somalia.

Strong, enduring men who could shoot had to get welded into fire teams, squads, and platoons. To do this, the 2d of the 14th created and ran difficult live-fire exercises, with most iterations at squad and platoon level. They emphasized movement to contact—hunting for the enemy—and night deliberate attacks, and they ran all possible variations. Often, the battalion brought in Cobra attack helos and supporting mortars and artillery, shaking the earth and teaching the men just how close they could get to this deadly stuff. Always, David insisted on realistic targetry and repetitive runs, each one a bit harder than the one before. Before deploying to Somalia and while there, the Dragons consistently spent time honing these battle skills in room-clearing and street combat conditions. "Close combat remains a fight won or lost at the squad level," David noted.[13] The Dragons trained to win.

Training mirrored combat. Combat resembled training. The Dragons arrived in Mogadishu on 29 July 1993. From that day onward, they kept up their strenuous training regimen while at the same time playing quick reaction force for the 4,000 American logistics troops and, at times, the other 24,000 U.N. soldiers. The battalion executed five major operations prior to 3 October and performed superbly on each. In these missions—two no-notice rollouts, two raids, and a deliberate attack—the battalion experienced two big firefights and a small one, killing or wounding 265 Somali gunmen for a cost of 6 Americans wounded in action. As one account of the Somalia intervention observed, by 3 October, "this unit had already seen more action than any other United Nations military group in Somalia" and "may have seen more close combat battle action than any other U.S. military battalion" since the war in Vietnam.[14] That included TF Ranger, at least until their fateful seventh raid.

Just as importantly, the battalion's riflemen learned from their firefights. Frederick the Great supposedly groused that if experience in war meant so much, a mule that he knew had been on enough campaigns to be a field marshal. In other words, simply getting shot at teaches soldiers nothing unless they learn from the occasion. The Dragons learned. They figured out how to fight in crowded, crumbling streets and dusty alleys, and they recycled that knowledge into their local training program. They also discovered the difference between hearing fire and really receiving fire and what it's like to see RPGs scream down the street. Best of all, their clashes convinced them as individuals and small units that they knew what to do under fire.[15] The battalion validated their precombat training in the ultimate test.

The afternoon of 3 October 1993 found the battalion ready, if not exactly sure of the task. During previous TF Ranger direct action strikes, General Garrison routinely assumed operational control (OPCON) of a reinforced rifle company, designated to back up the Delta-Ranger units in the event of an unforeseen situation. There had been very sketchy planning and discussion, and David's staff had a TF Ranger radio to listen in during the missions. But so far, that OPCON company had never been called.

This day, at the battalion base camp at the Mogadishu University complex, the men of Company C waited near their six sandbagged five-ton trucks. Nobody in 2-14th—not Bill David or Company C's commander, Capt. Mike Whetstone—got anything more than the usual requirement to stand by, ready to launch on a thirty-minute warning. Nothing new there; those TF Ranger folks always played it close to the vest.

While David's command post crew listened to the unfolding TF Ranger mission, the rest of the battalion carried on their normal routine. This particular seventy-two-hour period found Company C ready to go as needed, along with Bill David's tactical CP, the Humvee-borne tac team. The troops of Company A also stayed at the 2-14th base camp, but they had a more lax response time. They did weapons maintenance and physical training, having just come back from urban warfare training at an old Soviet military facility two miles north of Mogadishu. Company B was out there now, doing the same close-quarters battle live fires, drilling on cleaning out rooms. Few anticipated any excitement, even as they watched the TF Ranger helos cross the eastern horizon heading toward their target. At 1537, the SOF command cell checked with David to ensure that Whetstone's riflemen were standing by on thirty-minute recall.[16] They were.

When the first chopper went down at 1610, David told Mike Whetstone to have his soldiers mount up, just in case. The TF Ranger net crackled with reports: "We got a Blackhawk crashed in the city . . . 61, 61 down."[17] David knew that this would bring his guys into the fight. But Garrison and his CP staff did not give the order. So the 2-14th riflemen stood by. Company A remained at ease, interested but not yet drawn in. Company B kept on training at their remote site.

Ever hungry for "the word," grunts maintain a terrific informal information channel, so news got around quickly that TF Ranger's mission had gone south. Dragon soldiers near the battalion CP perked up. One of them, SSgt. Richard Roberts, remembered that "things were getting more and more active." Then, at 1629, came the fateful call.

Roger, we just lost another Blackhawk. We are taking a lot of RPG fire. We lost it south of the Olympic Hotel, south of National [Street]. We got another Hawk overhead. We need to ask the Kilo if they can respond and give them some help.[18]

The "Kilo" referred to Bill David, Mike Whetstone, and Company C. The formal order came on the heels of the initial report of the second aircraft's crash. But it was an afterthought. The first Dragon truck was already headed out the gate.

The company rolled with six five-tons, big six-wheeled trucks with sandbagged cargo beds open at the top and metal drop gates in the back. Two of these tall, belching diesel monsters carried each rifle platoon. Bill David's two tac CP Humvees followed after the lead platoon. Eight Humvees, every one mounting a potent 40mm Mk-19 automatic grenade launcher, provided armed escort. Because David's battalion made up the ground component of the U.S. QRF, he checked in with Col. Lawrence Casper, the 10th Mountain Division Aviation Brigade commander. Casper commanded the entire QRF—Task Force 2-25 Aviation, Cobras and Blackhawks, as well as 2-14th. The senior aviator had to understand that TF Ranger had just taken OPCON of Company C and Bill David's tac team.[19] Already well aware, Casper acknowledged the situation. He also warned David to take the twelve-and-a-half-mile urban bypass to the south, skirting the mobs of wild Aidid supporters blocking the much shorter direct route to the SOF base at the airport.

Going directly to the Olympic Hotel would not work. Oh, yes, in the movies, guys simply jump aboard and shriek out the gate bound for glory; but in real life, that's a quick ticket to the morgue. Left out of the TF Ranger planning for the raid, David did not even know exactly where the SOF guys had holed up or precisely where the two helos went down. Sure, anybody could see the columns of smoke mushrooming up out of the Bakara borough, but that would not cut it for locating men fighting to the death in an urban jungle. After all, the TF Ranger ground convoy got lost trying to move four blocks from the objective to the first crash site. Support from the Little Birds, agreed linkup signals, and a quick summary of fire control procedures would all ensure that the Dragons contributed to the solution, not the problem. And that meant getting down to the airfield and going head to head with Garrison and company, getting some kind of read on the situation. There'd already been enough hip shooting this grim afternoon.

After a fifty-four-minute ride, bone jarring as usual but blessedly free of gunfire, Company C pulled into the TF Ranger compound. Things did not look good. People were running here and there, not exactly scared but definitely involved, caught up—moving with a purpose, as the drill sergeants like to say. Medics were unloading wounded from a shot-up Humvee. At the nearby flight line, some battered Blackhawks definitely were not going anywhere soon. As Bill David headed for the TF Ranger CP, Mike Whetstone's Company C dismounted key leaders to await the word. No, this did not look good.

The radios in the joint operations center blared from speakers as David entered. A Ranger NCO there at about the same time heard a commander transmit from out there in the city: "Pay attention to what's going on and listen to my orders!" He judged that "it smelled like panic," probably a hasty conclusion, but it sure smelled like something bad.[20] For his part, David knew immediately that it was going to be a big fight.

With overall QRF commander Casper present and listening, Garrison motioned Bill David over to a big city map. He outlined the situation. Task Force Ranger had ninety-nine men in and around the four blocks between the Olympic Hotel and the first dead helo. They were holding their own and not in immediate danger—not yet, that is.

The TF Ranger ground convoy had gotten ripped up and confused trying to find the first downed MH-60K. It had been forced to turn back, carrying the twenty-three live Somali prisoners and one dead one, plus a large number of its own wounded. David could expect no help from them. Indeed, they might have to be added to the "to be rescued" list unless their luck turned. For the present, they were still on the way home, constituting another moving part on a bloody, sloppy chessboard.

Several blocks south of the Olympic lay Durant's chopper, with Shughart and Gordon on the ground for more than an hour. The

TF Ranger commander pointed at the street diagram and stabbed at the second helicopter's resting place. "Bill," said Garrison, "I need you to move here quickly and see what we have left."

"Roger, got it," said David.[21] What else could he say?

The planning did not last long. With night coming on, David wanted to try to find Durant's helicopter while he could still see well. He hoped that TF Ranger was pointing him in the right direction. As he, Mike Whetstone, 1st Sgt. Gary Doody, and the other Company C leaders gathered around the hood of David's Humvee, the battalion commander outlined a rudimentary plan. They would go northeast to the K-4 traffic circle, then due north on Via Lenin, then east on wide National Street, and south on Hawlwadig Road to get to the stricken bird. The route was about three miles. David wanted to stay mounted as long as possible.

Seven Ranger trucks, four Humvees and three five-tons, joined the column. Along with every able-bodied—or nearly so, some were injured—SOF guy at the airport, these additional crews included some men who had been at the objective area earlier and had escaped to bring out a few wounded Rangers. They got back before the two helos crashed and the locals got really restless. Grateful for the help but obviously uncertain about its polyglot nature, David and Whetstone organized the twenty-three vehicles as best they could. Things were pretty loose. Battle drill would have to make up for lack of information. The force sallied out at 1747.[22]

They made it to K-4 and not much past it. Ranger Sfc. Richard Lamb said, "We were taking fire almost from the time we left the gate." The trucks gunned their motors and kept going. Stay mounted . . . keep moving.

Just north of K-4, SNA militiamen opened up with withering fire, including those ubiquitous RPGs. One Ranger Humvee veered off the street, burning. Another shook as an RPG grazed the hard-topped cab. The Somalis had debris choking the Via Lenin, blocks and steel beams too big to breast with five-tons, let alone Humvees. The enemy held the high ground. Opposing gunmen opened up from the roof and the upper floors of an old milk factory, raining down bullets and more of those damn rockets.

Mike Whetstone described the scene.

It was a lot more than we expected. Tracers were flying every-where. We were hit by probably 200 to 300 rocket propelled grenade attacks and lots of small arms and machine-gun fire.[23]

The ferocity of the attack stunned even the battle-wise Dragons. This was a new degree of Somali resistance, although admittedly and thankfully the enemy did not aim their shots, preferring to spray AK-47 rounds all around, mostly high. American riflemen dis-mounted, squirreled into doorways and alley openings, and returned fire. In the growing evening gloom, red U.S. tracers knifed back into the milk factory. Fleeting shadows stumbled, but who could be sure?

To add to the confusion, the smoking, rattling, shattered TF Ranger ground convoy creaked out of the north, its string of limp-ing trucks coming along opposite David's attempted direction of at-tack. Despite flattened tires, cracked windscreens, and blackened RPG scars on most of the vehicles, they kept rolling, actually at a fairly decent clip. "They were traveling lickety-split, and it was clear they weren't going to stop," recalled the 2-14th commander.[24] The Amer-icans held their fire. The Somalis redoubled theirs.

After about ten minutes of trading bullets, the outcome near K-4 became certain. With Somalis firing down into the open-topped five-tons, his men out fighting in the streets, and two miles to go, David understood that this route was not going to work, not without some very big tanks and engineer dozers, plus a lot more U.S. firepower. Garrison agreed and, at 1821, reluctantly told Casper to order David to pull back.

Getting turned around took its toll. Dismounted riflemen covered the big trucks as they backed and spun in the filthy, garbage-strewn roadway. The Dragons fired carefully, picking their targets, just as on those many practice ranges. The U-turn took almost twenty minutes. In accord with the dictates of geometry and the frictions of war, the riflemen found their trucks on the opposite side of a very open street. To leave, the Dragons had to cross death ground, fast.

First Sergeant Doody moved with the rear guard squad, last out of the beaten zone, as befitted Company C's senior NCO. One fire team engaged. The other ran back to the idling trucks, sparks of bul-lets nipping at its heels. Then, Doody and the trail fire team moved.

Breaking into pairs, the six men bounded back. While one raced from rubble pile to doorway, the other snapped off rounds to cover his buddy's rush. In the middle of this, Sgt. John Carroll went down, his chest and shoulder smashed.

Doody darted out and grabbed the slumping sergeant. He braced Carroll on his side, then dragged him to the trucks. Somali warriors rained down bullets but somehow missed the pair.

The opposition had trouble making their bullets count, thanks to the bravery of men such as Pfc. Eugene Pamer, an M-60 machine gunner who provided murderous covering fire. A bullet penetrated Pamer's flak jacket in the back, but the gunner stayed prone and poured it on. The Somali militiamen shrank back.[25] Both Doody and Pamer won Silver Stars for gallantry.

Spurred by such efforts, the convoy broke free. Many of the 2-14th riflemen trotted back several blocks, turning to brace and fire at intervals. So protected, the convoy recrossed the bullet-torn K-4 circle. Then the soldiers clambered onto the slowly rolling, bullet-holed five-ton trucks. Green enemy tracers hurried them on their way.

While their beat-up vehicles rumbled slowly back to relative safety, American riflemen continued to dismount as needed to break ambushes. It took almost an hour of scrapping to get back to TF Ranger's airport base. The aborted effort cost three wounded Dragons and several Ranger casualties. To this must be added a few men of TF Ranger, doomed to die of wounds while the Americans regrouped for another push.

"We had a bit of a mess on our hands," said Bill David later. "It was pretty apparent to me that we were going to have to mount a completely different kind of effort if we were ever going to make it into the objective area."[26] Put bluntly, the Dragons had failed.

That might have done for a lesser unit than the 2d of the 14th. But all those eight-mile runs and twenty-five-mile marches, the hard training and uncompromising standards, combined to foster a burning determination to overcome adversity. Rather than folding under pressure, the battalion rose to meet it. The men in Company C desired a second crack. The other units wanted in on the kill, too. Though discouraged and rightly worried about the Americans trapped in a sea of hostile Somalis, Bill David trusted in the mettle of his men.

> Sometimes, close combat boils down to a test of willpower between adversaries. Because I had seen our soldiers' guts and determination in training, I was confident we would have the mental resilience to bounce back quickly from our unsuccessful effort. Moreover, I was confident our soldiers would have both the mental and physical staying power to see the task through to the end, even when the situation appeared grim. On both counts, the soldiers proved me right.[27]

As the bloodied truck column recoiled to the airfield, David ordered his other two companies to mount up and move from the university to the beachfront airfield. This was possible due to some great initiative back at the Dragon base camp. While David, Whetstone, Doody, and the rest fought it out north of the K-4 traffic circle, the rest of 2-14th had gathered for action. Captain Drew Meyerowich's Company A waited at their trucks, lined up to go on command. The battalion's third rifle unit, Company B, came back from its distant live-fire exercise, ready to do its part. It all happened without Bill David having to issue orders, because the subordinates understood their parts. They paid attention and acted without being told, the marks of a fine combat outfit.

The men still at the university finally received their call. Drew Meyerowich's Company A headed out first, followed by the battalion's scouts. Both units took the same long, roundabout bypass route as Company C and thus avoided skirmishes on the way. Meyerowich pulled into the airfield at around 2030.

The scene there had not improved over the few hours since Company C pulled in. To the north, a network of green and red tracers rose above the dark, jagged Mogadishu skyline. Beneath that sky show waited TF Ranger, having been cut off for hours in a bad place. The steady clatter of helicopters droned in the distance, and others roared away on the nearby flight line. Near a few low administration buildings, clusters of medics worked above prostrate forms.[28] This looked serious, worse than it sounded on the radio.

While his people made their way to the seaside airdrome, Bill David had to go back into the TF Ranger CP and face his QRF commander, Larry Casper, as well as a concerned General Garrison. Besides these familiar faces, David saw Brig. Gen. Greg Gile of the 10th Mountain Division and a new face, Maj. Gen. Thomas Montgomery, overall commander of all U.S. troops in Somalia and deputy commander of the entire U.N. contingent. Casper normally worked for Montgomery, but back at Fort Drum the aviation colonel answered to Gile, and in this crisis he was OPCON to Garrison. Garrison, however, reported directly to the overall theater commander at U.S. Central Command, as did Montgomery, both on separate channels. Montgomery also served a Turkish general under his U.N. role. If it sounds confusing, it was. For all the later slings and arrows hurled at the U.N., the Clinton administration, and others, let it be noted that this convolution arose strictly from decisions made or avoided within the ranks of America's professional soldiers. The Monday morning quarterbacks certainly wore themselves out berating the snarl.

For Lt. Col. Bill David, that armchair expertise meant nothing. He had a job to do, and these high-ranking commanders could help. In the small space of the CP building stood the main men from all three (sometimes four) of David's chains of command: Casper of the QRF, Garrison from TF Ranger, Gile from Fort Drum, and Montgomery, representing Casper's superior in country as well as the authority, such as it was, of the United Nations.[29] Well, at least the Dragon commander would not lack for supervision.

To their credit, the senior officers had concocted an innovative plan in pretty short order. Montgomery, an armor officer, realized that David's 2-14th needed some punch and protection to reach the embattled SOF. Aided by Gile, who just happened to be in Somalia on a long-scheduled visit to his 10th Mountain troops, Montgomery prevailed upon his fellow U.N. commanders for help. With TF Ranger's cover well and truly blown, and their very existence in question, niceties of security classifications and SOF secrecy went out the window. The Italians offered tanks and armored carriers, but they were too far away. The Pakistanis and Malaysians, however, based near the new port facility, stepped forward to answer Montgomery's call.

Gile told Bill David that he would be leading a relief column of his own Dragons, remaining Ranger elements, and these two U.N. components, four Paki tanks and thirty-two Malay armored infantry carriers. The battalion commander acknowledged and backed out of the lighted CP, anxious to get cracking. But in his mind, David knew that this was going to be a tough scheme to carry out.[30]

It took an hour to move the Dragons and their Ranger affiliates a mile or so up the waterfront to the new port base. There, on a large, ill-lit parking lot, waited rows of Malaysian wheeled armored cars, in regulation white U.N. paint schemes, and four big tanks, with plenty of oddly uniformed soldiers milling around. This sure promised some challenges.

David later described the next few hours as a "mess"; one of Montgomery's staffers said it looked like "a three-ring circus." The Americans could talk in English to the Paki and Malay officers, lingering legacies of the British Empire, but the crews—forget it. Lacking Pashto, Punjabi, Urdu, Chinese, and Malay speakers, getting the word to the Dragons' new teammates took time. It also took time to get the newly arrived Company A squared away and to rearm Company C after its shootout. Orders groups gathered on vehicle hoods, checking maps with red lens flashlights.

Although it took a while to get the word out, these minutes made a difference. Simply heading 'em up and moving 'em out risked a repetition of the earlier repulse near K-4. This one had to work. There could be no other. So David took enough time to get organized for a long fight, including getting the individual riflemen familiar with the picture. During the various conclaves and backbriefs, Drew Meyerowich of Company A gave out the best guidance thus far. He told his second-in-command "to hand out every bit of extra ammunition."[31] Everybody knew what that portended.

David kept his plan simple in the extreme. Cognizant that all of his forces had found the indirect bypass route open, he chose to approach the TF Ranger position from the northeast, looking to proceed out to National Street on some obscure side way. Paki officers knew a good, safe avenue, Via Jen Daaud, outside the influence of Aidid faction supporters. The Pakistani units used the street to run back and forth to their base camp, a sports stadium. David accepted the Pakistani recommendation. Aerial recon reported that road to be clear, at least compared to other choices.

Once the convoy got to National, they could then turn southwest on that wide thoroughfare, with a mile to go to reach their objective. Within blocks, they would enter Aidid territory. Upon getting to Hawlwadig Road, most of 2-14th would move the few blocks to the Olympic Hotel area. Another unit had to push south a similar distance to check out the wreckage of Mike Durant's chopper, as if anything could possibly still be alive down there. After linking up, David then wanted to extract back to the airfield to treat the wounded.

To deconflict aviation fire support, National Street and points north and west belonged to the Little Birds, whose precision fires had so far done much to keep TF Ranger alive. The QRF's TF 2-25th AH-1F Cobra gunships would handle matters up to that point. This allowed the 160th aircraft to focus on supporting their encircled brothers, and it allowed Larry Casper to make good use of the experienced Cobra crews of 2-25th Aviation.

The ground plan gave the main effort to Drew Meyerowich's Company A, fresher than Whetstone's outfit. Meyerowich received the difficult advance guard mission. With it came a platoon of four Pakistani M-48 tanks, old U.S.–manufactured models with 90mm main cannons. Those U.N. soldiers made all kinds of negative noises about leading the attack, but with David's help, the Paki officer agreed to cooperate, at least as far as National Street.[32] The Americans settled for that arrangement.

Meyerowich also got nine thirteen-ton Malaysian Condor armored personnel carriers, built by Thyssen-Henschel of Germany in the early 1980s, exactly the sort of handy light-armored vehicles that the U.S. Army contrived *not* to have in its inventory, let alone available that horrific night in Mogadishu.[33] The Condors offered nothing special, but they were there, and that meant everything. Looking like a windowless metal station wagon, the German-made fighting vehicle rode high on four fat rubber tires; it resembled a monster truck at an American county fair. For firepower, the Condor sported a 20mm cannon and a 7.62mm machine gun in a small turret. A Malay gunner and a driver completed the package. The Condor had three doors, one rear and one on each side, all restricted to one man at a time. Thin armor promised to deflect most small-arms rounds— maybe.[34] At least the short, squat smiling Malay crewmen seemed game enough.

Company A divided its men among the Condors and lined up. In the lead came the Paki tanks, then 2d Platoon on three carriers with Meyerowich's command Humvee, then 1st and 3d, each with its own three Condors. They would go all the way to the Olympic.

Behind them came the rest of the battalion, ninety-three vehicles strong. It included Mike Whetstone's Company C riding Malay Condors—destined for Durant's downed bird—the battalion antiarmor Humvee platoon, an attached antiarmor Humvee platoon from 1-87th Infantry, six armored Humvees from the Rangers, and fourteen Condors empty except for drivers and turret operators. That last bunch would pull out the ninety-nine men of TF Ranger still fighting for their lives around the Olympic Hotel and the scene of the first helo crash. Squeezed out by lack of space in the Condors, Company B had to stand by at the docks, waiting in reserve. David certainly preferred to bring them, but not in open trucks. That method had been tried and found wanting. So Company B remained behind, perhaps to insert at sunup by helicopter.

Along with the two lightfighter companies and the Humvees armed with Mk-19 automatic grenade launchers, the column included plenty of medical support and vehicles loaded with water, ammunition, and batteries for radios and night sights. Unlike TF Ranger, caught out long after dark, David's men brought their night-vision goggles and laser aiming devices. Every bit of this loading and checking took precious time, but it appeared sure to help out in the contested slums. As the *Ranger Handbook* says, "Don't forget nothing."[35] Making good use of their stint pierside, the Dragons followed that advice.

Nobody gave any pep talks or rah-rah speeches. Instead, the American grunts focused on the task at hand: Save the men of TF Ranger, all of them, dead and alive. None were to be left behind in Aidid's urban wasteland. "The company commander made sure we all understood that we would not come back without all American dead and wounded," remembered Company A's executive officer.[36]

The men nodded. They knew the deal. Without further discussion, Company A's leaders went to their trucks. It was time.

Out in the blackness—surrounded, thirsty, ammo running out, wounded still stacking up—TF Ranger waited for the Dragons. Deep in the twisted, dark warrens of the Bakara, Somali gunmen reloaded and set new ambushes. David's force moved out at 2320.

The Pakistani tankers knew their neighborhood. The armor bashed aside a flimsy barrier at one point and successfully got the column to National Street in only a half hour. The M-48s then pulled off, having done their part. David had made it most of the way to his prize, but the hard part came next.

The Americans and Malaysians drove on, slowly. In the armed Humvee cupolas, Mk-19 gunners swiveled back and forth, eyes peeled for action. In the back of the Condors, the riflemen could barely see through the bouncing view slits. They were cargo at this point. Most would have preferred to get out and fight on the ground, but they had their orders to stay aboard as long as they could, using the Condor's armor plate to get them through any enemy gunfire.

Shortly after midnight, as the two-mile-long snake of vehicles crossed onto Aidid turf, the Somali militiamen made their presence known. Lieutenant Charles P. Ferry saw it start.

> Suddenly, near the head of the column, red [mostly green, in fact] streams of enemy fire erupted from both sides of the street, and the familiar sound of incoming small arms fire and RPG fire broke the silence. Almost simultaneously, return fire was concentrated on several buildings and alleys. After two minutes or so, the firing died down and we continued to move. After moving several more blocks, the entire company came under fire. Small arms fire whizzed over my Humvee, and an RPG round exploded near the vehicle in front of me. Everyone in the column was firing into every building and alley that could be used as an enemy firing point.[37]

The Condor turret cannons pounded away, joining the bark of U.S. Mk-19s, which chugged egg-sized grenades into the structures.

American machine guns rattled in anger. Catching glimpses of Somalis moving through the shattered buildings on either flank, Ferry suggested to Meyerowich that Company A dismount to clear the route.

With three-quarters of a mile to go, this was a moment of truth. By nature, 11B10s want to fight on the ground. Their Condors shaking with impacts, the men wanted out. But Meyerowich kept his eye on the ball. Getting out here and now guaranteed nothing. This whole awful city featured nests of ambushers. The company could afford to dismount and deploy but once. Meyerowich wanted that to be near TF Ranger, where it mattered, not out here in the middle of Indian country. Company A pressed on, its turret and cupola weapons blazing away to both sides, the hulls vibrating from the incessant hail of Somali gunfire.

This tactic brought the Americans to Hawlwadig Road, where the company dismounted to move north to find the Rangers and D-Boys. They did it minus most of 2d Platoon, two of whose three Condors executed smart left turns and promptly drove out of sight, their incommunicado Malaysian crews oblivious to the shouts of the American riflemen aboard. Meyerowich wanted to go after them, but he knew that his mission lay with TF Ranger. He let them go. The mission comes first, an easy thing to say in a classroom and a hard rule to carry out when your guys need your help now to escape certain disaster.

The pair of misguided squad carriers had the ill luck to stumble into a major RPG den near Durant's empty, broken MH-60K. One rocket killed the lead Malay driver; another wrecked the trail Condor's motor. Lieutenant Mark Hollis and his men dismounted to duke it out on foot. The Malays stayed in their vehicles, determined to keep under armor. More RPGs smacked into the white hulls, showering ugly sparks. That damned peacekeeping paint design, whiter than bone with the big black letters *UN* centered on the side, must have made it easy for the enemy to draw a bead.

Finding no decent cover, the resourceful lightfighters made their own. Using a seven-pound prepared C-4 explosive charge, Hollis and his men blew their way into an adjacent courtyard. The rubble provided a fine barrier for their work. Hiding behind it, the Americans fired carefully, aiming at ghostly figures that shimmered when seen through the greenish eyepieces of the U.S. night-vision goggles. Several Somalis went down, taken out by the accurate American marksmen. Good enough, but the ammunition wouldn't last forever. Enemy fire continued to ping off the halted, smoking armored carriers. One wounded Malaysian, his face in shreds, crawled into the tiny twelve-man U.S. perimeter.

Hollis called for help. Busy with a major clash at the National/Hawlwadig intersection, Meyerowich did not answer. David did. Ignoring all radio protocols, Hollis gave a blunt situation summary: "We've got a bit of a s— sandwich down here, sir, and we're taking a huge bite."

"Roger, Terminator 26 [Hollis]," David replied calmly. "I understand your situation. Just keep doing what you're doing and we'll get some help your way as soon as we can."[38]

Whetstone's Company C was already en route. They had found nothing but a smashed airframe, already stripped, at the Durant crackup site. Now Mike Whetstone had some live folks to help. Over the next few hours, Whetstone's outfit fought its second major battle that night. In addition, TF 2-25 Aviation Cobras diverted to assist, their 20mm cannons hosing down several troublesome knots of enemy resistance. This punishing house-to-house struggle, with the Malaysian vehicles in support, eventually retrieved Hollis and his men. But this entire interlude cost the Dragons two killed and several wounded, the worst reverse suffered by the 2d of the 14th in its Somalia stint.[39]

Meanwhile, Company A advanced carefully toward TF Ranger. All Mk-19 and machine-gun fires north of National Street had to be cleared by Drew Meyerowich, for fear of hitting the Dragons or their Ranger and Delta counterparts. For more than an hour, the light infantry fought it out, room after room, shack after shack, with grenades and rifles. The lead squads kept looking for signs of the Rangers.

The stationary American SOF had been told to turn on small strobe lights with infrared filters, visible through 2-14th's AN/PVS-7B night-vision goggles. Sergeant Robert L. Jackson and his men moved slowly, picking their way along the sides of cinder-block buildings. They traded shots with fleeing Somalis and moved by fire teams, one crouching and running, the other shooting carefully to keep hostile heads down. Thanks to his night-vision headset, Jackson had a fine view of it all, the thin bullet tracer streaks clearly evident against the fuzzy green backdrop.

As the squad leader moved up to the bullet-chipped corner of a tin-roofed, single-story house, a rifleman motioned with his right hand. "Sergeant Jackson," the private whispered, "what are those blinking lights up front?"

The NCO looked where his man pointed. Sure enough, he saw the rhythmic pulsing of several small lights, man-made fireflies lighting the way to TF Ranger.[40]

Jackson's men announced themselves. "10th Mountain. Don't shoot!"

"Ranger! Ranger!" came the reply from the perimeter, where the tired SOF troopers had no night-vision sights.[41] Linkup had been achieved at 0150 on 4 October 1993.

Fighting continued all night and into the morning as the Dragons and TF Ranger loaded the wounded and the dead. Like the disciplined Regulars that they all were, the men of 2-14th and TF Ranger brought back every American, all the weapons, and every vehicle that could still move. They finally pulled out at about 0530 on 4 October 1993, just as the sun rose fat, hot, and red out of the placid Indian Ocean. The final extraction required close support from low-flying Cobra attack helos. Brass 20mm casings rained down as the Condors, armed Humvees, and a few five-tons gained speed moving northeast on National Street. Dismounted Dragons and Rangers surrounded the vehicle column and its precious wounded, clearing the front of certain buildings and laying down fire to cross disputed alley openings. After a few anxious minutes, the Cobras and foot teams got the job done.[42] The Somali scourging petered out as the column headed toward sanctuary at the Pakistani-held stadium, a destination chosen to avoid the risk of the long, dangerous daylight run back to the airfield. The convoy entered the sports arena at 0545, bloodied and exhausted but safe at last.

All in all, TF Ranger suffered eleven known dead, five missing and presumed killed, one captured, and sixty wounded, a horrendous casualty rate for a company-sized force. The Dragons lost two killed and twenty-four wounded. Malaysian Condor crews reported one dead and seven hurt. Somali chieftans later admitted to an incredible 1,126 losses, 312 of them fatal.[43] It had been a rough night, the largest close-combat clash involving Americans since the Vietnam War.

Afterward, General Garrison wrote: "The mission was a success. Targeted individuals were captured and extracted from the target."[44] In a precise sense, he was certainly correct. But it sure did not feel like winning. The American public expressed revulsion at the grisly film footage of half-clothed U.S. corpses being dragged through the dirt. Chasing a warlord was one thing, but not if it came to this. Worse, the wily Aidid remained at large, along with dozens of like-minded local strongmen. Mogadishu looked like a bottomless pit of woe, unfixable by any known military means short of mindless thermonuclear erasure. But sending in more ground troops? Forget about it.

No matter how you sliced it, the price in the 3 October raid far outweighed any legitimate gain, despite attempts to portray it as a military success. To recall the lament of ancient king Pyrrhus of Epirus, "One more such victory and I am lost."[45] Pyrrhus knew the real score. United States president William J. Clinton, horrified by the episode in Mogadishu and besieged by irate domestic opinion, ended TF Ranger operations. He also set a timetable for American withdrawal from Somalia, having had a bellyful of battling Somali chiefs and their pugnacious henchmen.

What honor accrued to the American special operators came from the way the Rangers, Delta, and the Night Stalkers held their own in death ground, in the finest traditions of those elite forces. Their conduct in action deserves the highest praise. As for the decisions and thinking that put them in that mortal predicament, the professional military, not to mention Congress, the news media, and academia, have filled many pages with detailed analyses of what went wrong and why, as if a few adjustments here or there might have fixed everything. But this misses an obvious consideration. Reverses, even serious ones, come with the package whenever a raid is conducted. By their very nature, direct action missions always walk a tightrope of risk, without much room for recovery when things go wrong. On 3 October, things went very wrong.

One thing did not go wrong—the 2d Battalion, 14th Infantry Regiment. Despite tremendous opposition, it persevered and got the job done. As the 10th Mountain Division commanding general wrote some time later, "Only a really extraordinary infantry battalion could have gotten the Rangers out that night."[46] Fortunately for all concerned, the Dragons proved to be just that kind of outstanding organization.

The 2d of the 14th Infantry's performance that terrible night in Mogadishu amounts to more than relieving the encircled men of TF Ranger, an impressive enough achievement. In the space of about eighteen hours, the battalion carried out numerous difficult tasks, many simultaneously, the majority more than once, generally under fire, and mostly at night: tactical motor march, passage of lines, tactical movement on foot and mounted, meeting engagement (banging into unexpected resistance), attack of a built-up area, infiltration (tactical foot maneuver toward the objective), breach of defended obstacles, defense of a built-up area, bypass of enemy forces, final assault (multiple examples), withdrawal under pressure, linkup, consolidation (getting unscrewed to hold an objective), reorganization (getting ready to move on after a fight), exfiltration (tactical foot maneuver away from the objective), employment of aviation fires, command and control, maintaining communications, running the command group in combat, performance of intelligence operations, evacuation and treatment of casualties, and provision of supplies under fire. By the U.S. Army's own reckoning, 2-14th carried out twenty-two of the sixty possible tasks for an infantry battalion.[47] That's well beyond any realistic estimate of what any infantry battalion can do. But the 2-14th did it.

Anyone who seriously suggested such a convoluted, stressful scenario in training may have been thought subject to delusions and sent for a mental health evaluation. Do not forget, either, that even this extensive doctrinal enumeration excludes such essential but unforecasted oddities as working with Pakistani tanks, directing Malaysian armored carriers, navigating at midnight through the ruins of a Third World capital, coordinating the fires of SOF helicopters, and, perhaps most important of all, discerning missions from clues and cryptic remarks over a crowded radio net and in a few painfully brief visits to a tumultuous SOF command post. The 2-14th soldiers did all that, too.

The Dragons executed all this with minimal casualties, even though they waded through the same storm of Somali fires that savaged the special operators. Equally impressive, they conducted their multiple missions without a single instance of friendlies shooting one another, hard enough in any city combat let alone in an unrehearsed night linkup intermixed with hostile warriors.[48] That reflected the battalion's unforgiving training regimen and sound understanding of the mean streets of Mogadishu.

It also showed the greatest strength of a fully trained light infantry battalion—adaptability. Limited to 560 men and few heavy weapons, lightfighters depend on skill, not firepower. Bill David's Dragons epitomize exactly what the U.S. Army leadership had in mind when it reinvented light infantry in the mid-1980s. Given a choice to invest in people or in things, in this case the Army chose to put its faith in highly trained riflemen, not technology. On one gruesome night on the east coast of Africa, that trust in men, not bullets, really paid off.

Light infantry used to mean guys who walked. Or, to be more exact, it referred to soldiers who trucked or helicoptered to the fray but always fought on foot. Although U.S. history cites specially skilled light troops as far back as the colonial era, they have not been a feature of American ground organization in this century. True, in Vietnam some battalions bore the title "light," but that meant less stuff, not any unique selection or training. Indeed, the infamous 1st Lt. William Calley, perpetrator of the My Lai massacre, served in the 1st Battalion (Light), 20th Infantry Regiment, a unit with less equipment and substantially less discipline than other U.S. forces in Vietnam.[49] In this sense, "light" implied nothing useful.

After the Vietnam War, the light organization disappeared altogether. The U.S. Army kept a certain amount of standard, or "leg," infantry but no designated light battalions. By the late 1970s, preoccupation with the Cold War in Europe led the Department of the Army to consider converting all but the airborne, air assault, and Ranger battalions to a mechanized configuration.[50] The Soviets had already done exactly that. Even the USSR's airborne units had tracks, cute little airdroppable critters with big, nasty guns. Walking infantry in the U.S. Army looked to be finished, doomed by the need to gear up for the Big One in the Fulda Gap.

Sanity prevailed. Senior infantry leaders pointed out an undeniable fact. Since 1945, dismounted American infantry has gone in harm's way time after time, from Korea (1950–53), to Lebanon (1958), to the Dominican Republic (1965–66), to Vietnam (1965–75), to Grenada (1983)—and rarely aboard armored fighting vehicles. Why? Well, infantry consists of people with hand weapons, easy to toss on a plane and ship out, and handy in the jungles, mountains, and urban rats' nests that mark the Third World. All those shiny mechanized arrays require lots of oversized aircraft, lots of cargo ships, lots of fuel, lots of spare parts, lots of helpful support troops, and lots of time, all things in short supply in international crises. So after almost taking the leap of faith to lock in a military structure suited for clashing with 1944 *Wehrmacht,* the Army backed off. It kept the walking infantry.

Still, something had to be done. Each of the leg battalions still had more than a hundred vehicles and trailers, leaders and men sent in by random personnel policies, and training as generic as it could be. Put them in death ground and they'd back away and call for artillery and air strikes, good enough in the draftee era but not by the 1980s, when dangerous expeditions to unhappy little countries demanded a lot more out of a lot fewer men. Ideally, those foot troops might have all converted to the air assault model, except the associated aviation would have broken the budget, even in those heady days of the Ronald Reagan adminstration and its big dollars for defense. As for making them paratroopers, why bother? The U.S. Air Force could not even lift the entire 82d Airborne in one shot, so adding more jumpers made no sense. Instead, the Army settled on deployable light infantry, "derivative of the Rangers," purposely built as "elite units" in terms of personnel selection and training.[51]

The battalions that resulted were incredibly lean, with three rifle companies and a headquarters unit. They had no antiarmor companies with armed Humvees but settled instead for a four-truck platoon in the headquarters company. Whereas airborne or air assault units had weapons squads, and Rangers and Marines had entire weapons platoons, the lightfighters sucked it up with less. Built to fight in bad weather, bad terrain, and at night, the light riflemen substituted technique for weight of shot and shell.[52] To become light implied more than shedding excess equipment. It also required changes to fighting style and to personnel selection and discipline. To make this concept work, lightfighters had to be both hard and smart.

Light infantry battalions went through grueling conversion and validation training in the mid-1980s. As much as possible, every NCO and officer attended Ranger school, although that course's natural attrition ensured that only about half of an average battalion's chain of command wore the coveted tab. (Even the 75th Ranger Regiment has to work to keep all its leaders qualified.) Whether or not they wore a Ranger tab, though, all battalion leaders went through difficult light infantry tactics courses, later expanded to include entire small units. These standardized lightfighter programs ran up to three weeks, followed by a brutal week-long exercise labeled "rites of passage."[53] Average men did not keep up. Most became better than they were. Some fell out. That's what elite means—chosen men.

During this transitional phase of 1985–90, many light infantry battalions also benefited from an innovative personnel system called COHORT (cohesion operational readiness and training). In COHORT, a company of 130 young men began basic infantry training together at Fort Benning, Georgia, and stayed together for three years, led by the same officers and sergeants from induction to discharge. At about the eighteen-month mark, the company went to Korea, Panama, or Berlin, to similar light infantry battalions. At the end of three years, the unit disbanded; its leaders, and the younger soldiers who elected to reeenlist, went elsewhere. In many cases, they formed the junior NCO cadre for the next such COHORT cycle.[54] These COHORT units learned lessons once, not over and over, and so achieved high levels of skill in soldiering, especially small-unit tactics. The 6th Infantry Division (Light) in Alaska, the 7th Infantry Division (Light) at Fort Ord, California, the 10th Mountain Division (Light Infantry) at Fort Drum, New York, and the 25th Infantry Division (Light) in Hawaii relied on this revolutionary means to create cohesive, well-trained infantry battalions.

Thanks to Ranger training, lightfighter schools, and COHORT, the light battalions became chosen troops, hard men indeed. These

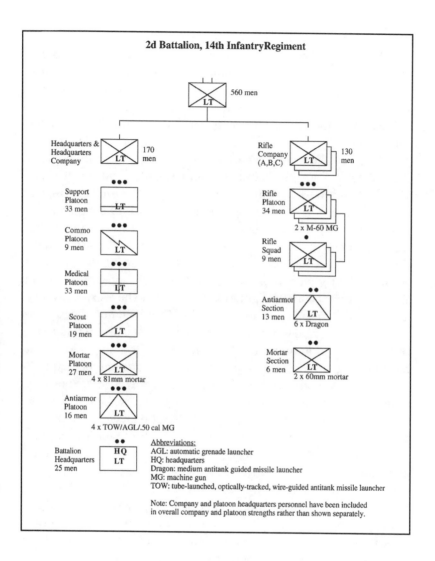

2d Battalion, 14th Infantry Regiment

560 men
LT

Headquarters & Headquarters Company — LT — 170 men

Rifle Company (A,B,C) — LT — 130 men

Support Platoon 33 men — LT

Rifle Platoon 34 men — LT
2 x M-60 MG

Commo Platoon 9 men — LT

Rifle Squad 9 men — LT

Medical Platoon 33 men — LT

Antiarmor Section 13 men — LT
6 x Dragon

Scout Platoon 19 men — LT

Mortar Platoon 27 men — LT
4 x 81mm mortar

Mortar Section 6 men — LT
2 x 60mm mortar

Antiarmor Platoon 16 men — LT
4 x TOW/AGL/.50 cal MG

Battalion Headquarters 25 men — HQ LT

Abbreviations:
AGL: automatic grenade launcher
HQ: headquarters
Dragon: medium antitank guided missile launcher
MG: machine gun
TOW: tube-launched, optically-tracked, wire-guided antitank missile launcher

Note: Company and platoon headquarters personnel have been included in overall company and platoon strengths rather than shown separately.

units could deploy, and fast, zipping out by air for contingencies in Honduras in 1988 and the Panama operation in 1989. But could they hang in there over time, or were they, as critics complained, "too light to fight"?[55]

The bloody nose taken by the 2-14th at the K-4 circle gave credence to this complaint. Men protected by (at best) a helmet and a flak vest have a tough time crossing heavily defended spaces. Even Bill David's battalion required reinforcement by an extra platoon of armed Humvees from another battalion, plus the sandbagged trucks with .50-caliber machine guns on cab-top ring mounts. That worked most of the time, but not at K-4, where the numerous Somalis had RPGs and the heights. An air assault or a parachute infantry battalion might call up its Company D, chock full of .50 calibers and Mk-19s; a mechanized unit certainly would turn to its Bradleys and their 25mm chain guns. But the light infantry had mostly hand weapons, and so had to pull back and reinvent themselves. Their selection and training inculcated the right degree of adaptability to out-think their foes, especially when the Dragons proved unable to outgun them. Hence, the battalion incorporated U.N. armor, a different route, and the cover of darkness to get the job done.

Given the right circumstances, as in Panama City, Mogadishu, or Port-au-Prince, Haiti, the light infantry proved to be every bit as good as advertised. True, it did not play in the Gulf War, but after all, the ground phase there lasted a hundred hours; the close action lasted only a tiny fraction thereof. Bill David's 2-14th fought in close combat longer than that in its several skirmishes and one big battle in Mogadishu. At night, in cities, in rough or heavily vegetated terrain, in quick-deployment situations, the light guys met the test.

And yet, there are troubling signs. The eighteen light infantry battalions no longer benefit from specialized lightfighter leader training. It was centralized at Fort Benning in the early 1990s, then discontinued due to fiscal concerns. Ranger school remains as good as ever, but it, too, has been limited by money concerns. Most light battalions now have only a third of their leaders wearing tabs, and not enough slots are available to train many more. Any remaining rites of passage occur at the unit level. Daily training and operations have long since overtaken that useful experience.

Even more disturbing, the wonderfully effective COHORT process died of neglect, shelved by Department of the Army personnel bureaucrats who charged that it cost too much. Somehow, the British, Australians, Canadians, and New Zealanders afford a regimental system on shoestring budgets. But for the much-better-funded United States Army, it became "too expensive."[56] Bill David's men might disagree, as did the taciturn British paratroopers who tabbed across the frozen tundra of the Falklands back in 1982. Unfortunately, the number crunchers won out over the grunts on this important issue.

Shorn of some specialized training and denied its COHORT personnel system, light infantry retains its elite status built on ingrained SOPs and solid leadership. For now, that may be enough. But over time, the training edge may erode. That edge allows light riflemen to adapt to friction and danger. Without those hard-won battle skills, they will become the sum of their limited tables of organization, a few men on foot with machine guns and nothing more.

In Mogadishu, though, the lightfighter ideal held true. Postbattle analysts bemoaned the lack of U.S. armor, a valid enough omission that probably led to many deaths. But remember, foreign armored personnel carriers did eventually intervene with decisive effect, thanks to the good officers of the 2d of the 14th. How might things have ended without the 2-14th's infantrymen? They were the real key to saving TF Ranger. Those dauntless 11B10s accomplished the impossible because, from Bill David on down, they did the unexpected and they knew the fundamentals.

Doing the unorthodox thing and doing it well usually pays off in battle. Mogadishu witnessed a paradox in that the special warfare units eventually displayed a rather predictable approach whereas a Regular Army infantry outfit did not. For a variety of reasons, many perfectly sensible, TF Ranger evolved a standard raiding template. Better marksmen by far than the Dragons, the D-Boys and Rangers unfortunately got stranded in a position that demanded every bit of that formidable shooting ability. Not so the members of the 2-14th; they came on foot, by truck, by Malay light armor, by helicopter, and in combinations thereof, a variety that clearly overwhelmed the Somali opposition.[57] They used night, supporting aviation fires, and urban terrain to close on their objectives and kill the enemy. Students of light infantry warfare would recognize in David's operations the nonlinear infiltration and exfiltration patterns characteristic of good light troops.

As for fundamentals, they don't get done much better than in the Dragon battalion. Shooting, moving, and communicating, carried out in great peril for hours on end, justified the battalion's extensive and strenuous precombat training. Lacking any high technology except night sights, the 2d of the 14th simply outfought its foes. Its mission record and casualty toll tell their own stories.

A hundred and forty-six years before Bill David led his Dragons into the bullet-swept, cratered streets of Mogadishu, a few hundred U.S. Regulars stormed a defended urban stronghold. The commanding general's tribute to those fighting men applies equally well to the efforts of the 2d Battalion, 14th Infantry Regiment, on 3–4 October 1993: "Brave rifles, veterans, you have been baptized in fire and blood and have come out steel."[58] To come out steel—this is why the United States has light infantry, brave rifles indeed.

Notes

The epigraph comes from the motion picture *Pork Chop Hill* (Hollywood, Calif.: Melville Productions, 1959). James Webb wrote the screenplay based on the book by Brig. Gen. S. L. A. Marshall, USAR (Ret.), *Pork Chop Hill* (Nashville, Tenn.: The Battery Press, 1986 reissue). George Shibata played Lieutenant Ohashi. Gregory Peck portrayed Lieutenant Clemons. The movie and book tell the story of Company K, 3d Battalion, 31st Infantry Regiment, in the fight for the title hill in 1953.

1. Mark Bowden, "Chapter 24: Disarray in Command, and Trapped" in *Blackhawk Down*, at www.phillynews.com/packages/somalia, 9 December 1997, 3-4. This superb inside account is due to be published as a book in 1998.

2. This term referred to the characteristic tall, thin people of the Samaal ethnic group that lives in Somalia. It also refers to a similarly described and named enemy race in Robert A. Heinlein, *Starship Troopers* (New York, N.Y.: Ace Books, 1987), 12–15. Slang names for the Bakara neighborhood included Bosnia (after the war-torn European state) and the Black Sea, supposedly after a local restaurant but also in reference to the throng of dark-skinned Somalis that crowded around U.S. soldiers that fateful 3 October 1993.

3. For a good overall summary of the ill-fated U.S. expedition to Somalia, see Daniel P. Bolger, *Savage Peace: Americans at War in the 1990s* (Novato, Calif.: Presidio Press, 1995), 266–338.

4. Rick Atkinson, "The Raid That Went Awry," *Washington Post* (30 January 1994), 1. Atkinson's reporting on this mission offered the first complete story.

5. Major John. D. Lock, "Chapter 23: Somalia: The Creed in Action" in *To Fight With Intrepidity . . . The Complete History of the U.S. Army Rangers, 1622 to the Present* (West Point, N.Y.: unpublished manuscript, 1997), 21–22. This book will be published in 1998 by Pocket Books of New York, N.Y.

6. Mark Bowden, "Chapter 15: Ambush After Ambush: Fighting Just to Stay Alive" in *Blackhawk Down*, at www.phillynews.com/packages/somalia, 30 November 1997, 1-6.

7. Accounts of these American defeats abound. In each case, the enemy wiped out a large portion of the U.S. Army units engaged. For Little Big Horn, see Robert M. Utley, *Frontier Regulars: The United States Army and the Indian, 1866–1890* (New York, N.Y.: The Macmillan Publishing Co., Inc., 1973), 264–69. Remember, despite the romance of the 7th Cavalry's "Last Stand," seven of twelve cavalry companies (what today we call cavalry troops) were not wiped out. For the debacle at Cisterna, see Dr. Michael J. King, *Leavenworth Papers No. 11: Rangers, Selected Combat Operations in World War II* (Fort Leavenworth, Kans.: Combat Studies Institute, June 1985), 29–41. The Rangers lost 761 of the 767 infiltrators who crossed the line of departure, trapped and eliminated by German armored and infantry units. To learn more about the 9th Infantry Regiment's purgatory on the Chongchon River in Korea, see Lt. Col. Roy E. Appleman, AUS (Ret.), *Disaster in Korea* (College Station, Tex.: Texas A&M University Press, 1989), 214–30.

8. Kent DeLong and Steven Tuckey, *Mogadishu: Heroism and Tragedy* (Westport, Conn.: Praeger Publishers, 1994), 90. In supporting TF Ranger, Little Birds burned up 50,000 rounds of 7.62mm Gatling gun ammunition and 63 aerial rockets.

9. Secretary of Defense Les Aspin, "Memorandum for Correspondents No. 302-M" (Washington, D.C.: U.S. Department of Defense, 7 October 1993). This inaction eventually cost Aspin his job.

10. Mark Bowden, "Chapter 26: At Rescue, Relief Tinged with Sorrow" in *Blackhawk Down*, at www.phillynews.com/packages/somalia, 11 December 1997, 2.

11. Lieutenant Colonel William C. David, USA, *Developing a Supercharged Battalion* (Fort Drum, N.Y.: Headquarters, 10th Mountain Division [Light Infantry], 1 June 1995), 13–18.

12. Ibid., 28–35.

13. Ibid, 28, 39–47; Capt. Charles P. Ferry, USA, "Mogadishu, October 1993: A Company XO's Notes on Lessons Learned," *Infantry* (November–December 1994), 32–33. As a lieutenant, Ferry served as second-in-command of Company A.

14. DeLong and Tuckey, *Mogadishu*, 45; David, *Developing a Supercharged Battalion*, 3–4. The DeLong and Tuckey book offers the best view of the battle from the 2d of the 14th's perspective. Read along-

side Atkinson's insightful articles and Bowden's extremely detailed TF Ranger story—it begins to give a clear idea of this bruising engagement.

15. Ferry, "Mogadishu, October 1993: A Company XO's Notes on Lessons Learned," 33; Lt. Col. William C. David, USA, *Infantry Pre-Command Course 6-94 Videoteleconference, Fort Drum, N.Y., to Ft. Benning, Ga.* (Fort Benning, Ga.: U.S. Army Infantry School, 4 March 1994).

16. Captain Charles P. Ferry, USA, "Mogadishu, October 1993: Personal Account of a Rifle Company XO," *Infantry* (September–October 1994), 24. This is a companion piece to the November–December 1994 *Infantry* article that analyzed the fighting for broader lessons.

17. Mark Bowden, "Radio Transmission Audio Clips" in *Blackhawk Down,* at www.phillynews.com/packages/somalia, 10 December 1997, 1.

18. Ibid.; Sfc. Elroy Garcia, USA, "We Did Right That Night," *Soldiers* (February 1994), 18–19.

19. Brigadier General Greg Gile, assistant division commander of the 10th Mountain Division, was also in Mogadishu on a visit, having just installed Casper as the aviation brigade commander in a brief ceremony a few days earlier. Gile played an important role in getting the 10 Mountain QRF integrated with the evolving TF Ranger operation on 3 October 1993.

20. Mark Bowden, "Chapter 2: Dazed, Blood-Spattered, and Frantic" in *Blackhawk Down,* at www.phillynews.com/packages/somalia, 17 November 1997, 2; Mark Bowden, "Chapter 10: At the Base, Bravery and Hesitation" in *Blackhawk Down,* at www.phillynews.com/packages/somalia, 25 November 1997, 1.

21. Delong and Tuckey, *Mogadishu,* 47.

22. Ibid., 47–48; Rick Atkinson, "Deliverance From Warlord's Fury," *Washington Post* (7 October 1993), A1.

23. Ibid., A1; Garcia, "We Did Right That Night," 18–19; Sean D. Naylor and Steve Vogel, "A Smooth-Starting Raid Ends in Catastrophe," *Army Times* (18 October 1993), 8.

24. DeLong and Tuckey, *Mogadishu,* 47; Mark Bowden, "Chapter 16: Furious Attacks on a Second Convoy" in *Blackhawk Down,* at www.phillynews.com/packages/somalia, 1 December 1997, 3.

25. Colonel Lawrence E. Casper, USA, "Quick Reaction Force: Summary of Combat Operations on 3 October 1993" (Washington, D.C.: U.S. Army Staff, October 1993), 1-2; DeLong and Tuckey, *Mogadishu*, 50–51.

26. DeLong and Tuckey, *Mogadishu*, 48.

27. David, *Developing a Supercharged Battalion*, 26.

28. Ferry, "Mogadishu, October 1993: Personal Account of a Rifle Company XO," 26.

29. Colonel Kenneth Allard, USA, *Somalia Operations: Lessons Learned* (Fort McNair, Washington, D.C.: National Defense University Press, 1995), 27, 57–58, 60. Allard characterizes the various parallel command chains as "highly unusual," burdened by TF Ranger's separate reporting channel, an "additional complicating factor." Furthermore, Allard states, "*the greatest obstacles to unity of command during UNOSOM II* [United Nations Operations in Somalia II] *were imposed by the United States on itself* [emphasis in original]."

30. DeLong and Tuckey, *Mogadishu*, 51, 63.

31. Ibid., 61–65; Ferry, "Mogadishu, October 1993: Personal Account of a Rifle Company XO," 26; David, *Infantry Pre-Command Course 6-94 Videoteleconference;* Atkinson, "Deliverance from a Warlord's Fury," A1; Naylor and Vogel, "A Smooth-Starting Raid Ends in Catastrophe," 8.

32. Mark Bowden, "Chapter 25: Confusion as Rescue Convoy Rolls Out" in *Blackhawk Down*, at www.phillynews.com/packages/somalia, 10 December 1997, 2-3.

33. To assist in their rear area operations, the U.S. Army's military police have ordered ninety-five Condor-like vehicles, with delivery of four prototypes commencing in February 1997. To date, none of these military police vehicles has been adapted for infantry use. See Scott R. Gourley, "XM-1117 Armored Security Vehicle," *Army* (February 1998), 60–61. The U.S. Marines do have their LAV series in wide use, and it could have been made available in 1993. Marine LAV units played major roles in earlier periods of the Somalia intervention, as well as in Panama (1989), the Gulf War (1990–91), Haiti (1994), and other small engagements.

34. Christopher F. Foss, ed., *Jane's Armour and Artillery 1990–91* (Alexandria, Va.: Jane's Information Group, Inc., 1991), 348–49.

35. U.S. Department of the Army, *SH 21-76 Ranger Handbook* (Fort Benning, Ga.: U.S. Army Infantry School, March 1987), I. This famous aphorism supposedly comes from Maj. Robert Rogers's "standing orders" for Rangers written in 1759. In fact, it comes from Kenneth Roberts's 1936 novel, *Northwest Passage*. Rogers's actual orders were written in more formal terms. For details, see Lock, *To Fight With Intrepidity...*, A-3.

36. Atkinson, "Delivered from a Warlord's Fury," A1; Naylor and Vogel, "A Smooth-Starting Raid Ends in Catastrophe," 8; Ferry, "Mogadishu, October 1993: Personal Account of a Rifle Company XO," 26–27.

37. Ferry, "Mogadishu, October 1993: Personal Account of a Rifle Company XO," 27. Soviet-made ammunition, as for AK-47s, uses green tracers. American tracers are red. Some Somalis had U.S. weapons and ammunition.

38. DeLong and Tuckey, *Mogadishu,* 69.

39. Ibid., 68–71; Bowden, "Chapter 25: Confusion as Rescue Convoy Rolls Out" in *Blackhawk Down,* 3-5.

40. George Boehman, "Soldier Braves Somali Fire for 'My Guys,'" *Washington Times* (8 October 1993), 1.

41. DeLong and Tuckey, *Mogadishu,* 77; Bowden, "Chapter 26: At Rescue, Relief Tinged with Sorrow" in *Blackhawk Down,* 2; Ferry, "Mogadishu, October 1993: Personal Account of a Rifle Company XO," 29.

42. DeLong and Tuckey, *Mogadishu,* 93–97.

43. David, *Developing a Supercharged Battalion,* 4; DeLong and Tuckey, *Mogadishu,* 77–80, 93–97; Bolger, *Savage Peace,* 326–27.

44. Mark Bowden, "Full Text Document" in *Blackhawk Down,* at www.phillynews.com/packages/somalia, 14 December 1997, 1-2. Bowden reproduces a handwritten note to President William J. Clinton, which Garrison gave to Representative William P. Murtha (D., Pa.) when the congressman visited Mogadishu after the raid.

45. R. Ernest Dupuy and Col. Trevor N. Dupuy, USA (Ret.), *The Encyclopaedia of Military History from 1500 B.C. to the Present, Second Revised Edition* (New York, N.Y.: Harper & Row, Publishers, 1986), 59. King Pyrrhus said these famous words after defeating the Romans at the battle of Heraclea in 280 B.C.

46. David, *Developing a Supercharged Battalion,* 1. The words came from Maj. Gen. David C. Meade.

47. U.S. Department of the Army, *Mission Training Plan for the Infantry Battalion* (Washington, D.C.: U.S. Government Printing Office, 27 December 1988), 4-21, 5-4–6. The example training exercise allocates twenty-seven hours to carry out nine tasks.

48. Mark Bowden, "E-Mail from Col. Bill David, USA" in "Round 12 of Q&A," in *Blackhawk Down,* www.phillynews.com/packages/somalia, 22 December 1997, 6.

49. Samuel Lipsman, series ed., *The Vietnam Experience,* 25 vols. (Boston, Mass.: Boston Publishing Co., 1981–88); Michael Casey, Clark Dougan, Denis Kennedy, Shelby Stanton, et al., *Volume 20: The Army at War* (1987).

50. Russell F. Weigley, *History of the United States Army* (Bloomington, Ind.: Indiana University Press, 1984), 574–75.

51. John L. Romjue, *The Army of Excellence: The Development of the 1980s Army* (Fort Monroe, Va.: U.S. Army Training and Doctrine Command, 1993), 53.

52. U.S. Department of the Army, *FM 7-72: Light Infantry Battalion* (Washington, D.C.: U.S. Government Printing Office, 16 March 1987), i.

53. Romjue, *The Army of Excellence,* 62.

54. Weigley, *History of the United States Army,* 588–89. The COHORT experiment also extended to some mechanized units and, indeed, other combat arms. But it was most heavily used in the 1980s light infantry program.

55. For a fine summary of the light force debate, see Romjue, *The Army of Excellence,* 113–21.

56. One outspoken proponent of COHORT was Lt. Gen. John M. Keane, who commanded a brigade of the 10th Mountain made up of such soldiers. For his views on the close relationship between cohesion and training, see Tom Clancy, *Airborne* (New York, N.Y.: Berkley Books, 1997), 35.

57. Ferry, "Mogadishu, October 1993: Personal Account of a Rifle Company XO," 31. The battalion used helicopters to extract from the Pakistani stadium on 4 October 1993.

58. The quotation from Gen. Winfield Scott referred to the 3d Cavalry Regiment, which fought dismounted to seize the National Palace of Mexico City on 14 September 1847. Cavalryman Gen. George S. Patton used the same words to praise Third Army in January 1945, following its epic campaign in the Ardennes. Quoted in Maj. Gen. H. Essame, British Army (Ret.), *Patton: A Study in Command* (New York, N.Y.: Charles Scribner's Sons, 1974), 231.

Chapter 6: Africa Corps

Dial 911—we are the world's emergency phone call.
—Pfc. Michael Rosenberger, USMC

The only things in Liberia worse than the fighting were the cease-fires. It was expected that people would get blown away during the long, bloody months of active fighting. That was always a given, to the tune of 150,000 dead (some whispered 300,000) over six and a half years of civil war. Death came only too easily in Liberia. Just as in Somalia, killing sometimes became an end in itself. By August 1995, the factions du jour, led by Charles Taylor and his former ally Roosevelt Johnson, had long since finished off madman Samuel K. Doe. Now these brutal inheritors and their armed retainers squared off to dispute control of Liberia's battered capital, Monrovia.[1] Nobody expected the truce to last. The optimists gave peace a chance. Pessimists stocked up on ammunition.

For a few months, words replaced bullets as Taylor and Johnson joined a self-appointed six-man ruling council. As with previous cease-fires, the half million inhabitants of Monrovia relaxed their guard a little. Innocents, women and children, came out of their hovels. They emerged into the blasted streets and tried to restart an approximation of normal life. Markets reopened. Schools resumed classes. Maybe this time would be different.

It wasn't. In late March 1996, Taylor and Johnson argued, openly splitting the ruling council. Taylor and his followers tried to arrest Johnson, who escaped to rally his own well-armed associates, representing the Krahn ethnic group. That started the fun, sparking a running gun battle near the capitol building that soon spread throughout Monrovia. Gleeful teenage gunmen and ragtag soldiers of all varieties grabbed their autorifles, swigged their liquor, and took to the streets.[2] Technically, the cease-fire was still in effect. This would have been news to the dead.

So it went in Monrovia, starting on 5 April 1996. Dull explosions thumped and rumbled. Bullets flew. Shells shattered cement-block buildings; their crumpled facades slid into the twisted, narrow streets. Within hours, rubble and corpses dotted deserted boulevards. Dried blood smeared walls and stained sidewalks. The sting of spent gunpowder and the drifting smoke of a hundred fires hung in the thick, humid air, a miasma of suffering hanging like a pall over the seaside city. The U.S. Embassy at Mamba Point stood just west of the smoldering Greystone slum-cum-refugee camp. That put it smack in the path of this growing storm. The Americans began to feel the backlash as Liberia's long civil war reignited.

On foot and from the back of speeding pickup trucks, rampaging factional fighters intermittently sprayed the low walls surrounding the U.S. legation buildings. Machine-gun rounds stitched the roofs of various buildings. Rocket-propelled grenades sailed overhead, launched by youths eager to see the streaking things hit walls and explode. Some of this incoming fire seemed accidental. Some did not.

Along the six-acre American facility's long, urban perimeter, Sgt. Luis Sanchez and four other young Marine security guards held the line, assisted by a few dozen contracted Liberian sentries. Later, Sanchez tried to describe his thinking as the trouble grew worse: "We had to take things very, very seriously. For a while, things got a little scary."[3] *Scary*—a good word, and the unarmed embassy staff felt it more than a little.

An escalation to more scary, indeed to terminally scary, seemed like a mere matter of time. Fighting grew in intensity and scale. As long as opponents were killing one another, with careless cross fire and stray rounds in abundance, the situation was bad enough. It only got worse. Lightly armed Nigerian peacekeeping troops of the Economic Community of West African States Cease-Fire Monitoring Group (ECOMOG) might have intervened. Instead, fearing certain and significant casualties, they stood aside, well out of the line of fire, hoping for somebody else to keep the peace. United Nations observers objected to the rampaging war parties and, for their troubles,

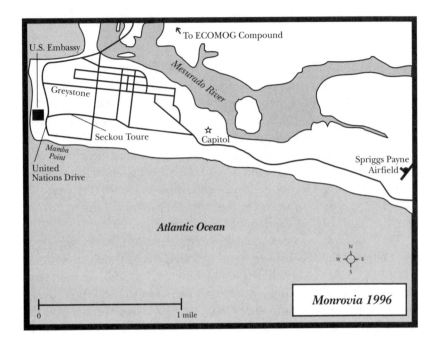

Monrovia 1996

watched their offices stripped by rifle-toting looters as besotted crowds roared their approval.[4] After two days of this, by 7 April, foreign aid workers and diplomats knew what came next on the menu of mayhem.

The U.S. Embassy staff knew, too. Sooner or later, a certain number of jokers would elect to take a few cracks at the Americans. Some of the hostiles wanted American blood. Some wanted American loot. Some just wanted to fire up the Yankee compound for the hell of it. With more than two hundred people crowding into the embassy grounds, including more than a hundred from other countries, Ambassador William B. Milam called for help, military reinforcements, in no uncertain terms.[5] If a chance remained to save the people trapped at the embassy, let alone hold the facility at all, American forces needed to act soon.

The heavily armed gangs looked certain to overrun the U.S. Embassy within a day or so, within a few dozen hours—in fact, whenever they felt like it. Both Taylor and Roosevelt backers had their reasons. When they came, these numerous, bold rebels would quickly finish off the handful of Marines and Liberian rent-a-cops. The sequel promised to be equally quick and ugly. Militias seemed sure to slaughter the other Americans, plus all the other foreigners unlucky enough or stupid enough to overstay their welcome in this charnel house known as Monrovia.

It might be said that intemperate U.S. policies preordained these unfortunate circumstances, which would be correct. But none of the beleaguered American diplomatic staff, or their outgunned defenders, had the stomach for that sort of esoteric debate. The key question now revolved around basic survival, life or death. The Apaches were swarming at the gates. Where was the cavalry?

Actually, to be precise, where was the infantry? These encircled Americans didn't need frontier horsemen. And, of course, a cruise missile or a smart bomb couldn't be used. For better or worse, these Americans needed rifle-bearing reinforcements, then rescue. With a stout outfit employed, the Americans could certainly hold the embassy. That meant sending men, not bullets. Two of those few American infantry battalions, following some initial teams of bold special operators, were about to get an unexpected trip to the worst place in the world.

The U.S. station in Monrovia had been to this party twice before, in 1990–91 and again in 1992. In the first case, a small contingent of Marines kept the rebels at bay while helicopters and Air Force transport planes flew into Liberia and extracted their endangered fellow citizens and a good number of Third World nationals, a classic noncombatant evacuation operation (NEO). The 1992 version was an Air Force show run through Freetown in neighboring Sierra Leone, Africa.[6] Both of these featured "permissive" environments, the U.S. Department of Defense way of saying that the locals did not interfere too much. This time, the situation rated as "nonpermissive," the prevailing euphemism for landing inside a raging civil war, absolute death ground.[7] This time, speed counted.

Ideally, running an NEO in coastal Liberia neatly matched the capabilities of a Navy-Marine amphibious readiness group. The Marines and their Navy "gator" comrades routinely trained for this type of mission. The usual landing force consists of a Marine expedition unit (special operations capable), an MEU (SOC). Built around a Marine infantry battalion with a few tanks, engineers, and other key attachments, the MEU also included a capable helicopter squadron and a service support group with fifteen days' worth of supplies, plus a colonel and a staff with adequate communications to run operations across hostile shores. Best of all, an MEU (SOC) trained to execute NEOs, along with twenty-one other likely amphibious warfare tasks. They knew their business.[8] Unfortunately, the nearest MEU (SOC) floated in the Adriatic Sea, backing up U.S. troops ashore in Bosnia. Good as they were, 22d MEU remained a week or more away by sea.

It was the perfect answer but too late. Screwing around increased the chance that by the time American troops got there, they would find a smoking hole at Mamba Point, plus a rack of dead bodies to boot. Someone had to go now.

That led to the next best answer, and it came in piecemeal, hustled out of Europe. On the big maps in the Pentagon, the country of Liberia fell under the purview of U.S. European Command (USEUCOM). Long accustomed to waiting for World War III in the Fulda Gap, the operations officers at USEUCOM headquarters in Stuttgart, Germany, did, of course, realize that the Cold War was history. Quite sensibly and predictably, following the Gulf War excursion and its lingering aftermath, the USEUCOM crowd and their NATO allies transferred their attentions to the bleeding wound of Bosnia. By spring 1996, the American 1st Armored Division was on the ground, up to its turret rings in Serbs, Croats, and Muslims, none of them happy. Bosnia was the main event. The folks in Stuttgart looked at violent Africa as the geographic, economic, and military subbasement of their sprawling theater. They were only too glad to have pawned off the eastern third, horrible Somalia and its equally awful neighbors, on the U.S. Central Command.

More than four decades of staring down the Soviet bear had made USEUCOM powerful enough, even in its reduced state seven years after the Berlin Wall came down. The command controlled the U.S. Navy's Sixth Fleet, the Seventh Army, and three numbered Air Forces: the Third, Sixteenth, and Seventeenth. If some miscreant launched a panzer onslaught or a massive bomber raid, USEUCOM guaranteed a powerful riposte. That said, the theater's forces were (surprise) woefully shy of infantry. Aside from the 22d MEU sailing south as fast as its inelegant gray amphibs could churn water, and its half-dozen mechanized battalions committed to Bosnia or stripped to assist in that endeavor, USEUCOM found the cupboard pretty bare. To deal with the horror show in Monrovia, European Command turned to the special operations forces of Special Operations Command, Europe (SOCEUR), plus the theater's single airborne battalion, the 3/325th Airborne Battalion Combat Team (3/325 ABCT, the Blue Falcons), in Vicenza, Italy.[9]

Even that slim force wasn't all there. Working for Brig. Gen. Michael A. Canavan of SOCEUR, the Blue Falcons had one reinforced rifle company in Croatia that was recovering the remains of Secretary of Commerce Ron Brown and the thirty-four others killed when the airplane in which they were passengers slammed into a mountain. Another 3/325th company waited in Hungary, standing by as a QRF if anything blew in Bosnia. This left available the rump of the 3/325 ABCT, Lt. Col. Mike Scaparotti commanding, with his twenty-five-man tactical command post and Company C, reinforced with additional crew-served weapons. The solitary company-plus joined SOCEUR elements: a small command group; a SEAL platoon; two companies or so of Green Berets from 1st Battalion, 10th Special Forces Group (Airborne); and a clutch of five SOF helicopters (only four of them actually proved flightworthy). It wasn't much, but it had one big virtue. It could go now.

Canavan organized for the Liberia mission on the fly. He learned of the Monrovia NEO on the runway on 7 April, after returning from the discouraging search of the plane crash in the Croatian mountains. After a flight to Stuttgart for some sketchy planning at USEUCOM headquarters, the general took off again within hours, flying toward Sierra Leone. Napoleon Bonaparte once observed that "the strength of an army, like the momentum in mechanics, is estimated by the weight multiplied by the velocity."[10] Bringing his small SOCEUR teams in one by one but very quickly, Canavan substituted speed for numbers.

Launched south beginning on 7 April, Canavan's Joint Task Force Assured Response (JTF-AR) closely resembled the Gulf War's black

JSOTF and Somalia's ill-fated Task Force Ranger. In this case, SEALs and Green Beret A teams replaced the Delta shooters, Air Force special ops helos substituted for the typical TF 160 birds, and Scaparotti's Company C stood in for the usual Ranger company. A pair of powerful AC-130H Spectres went along to fly cover. Thanks to numerous missions in Bosnia, the Blue Falcon riflemen knew their SOCEUR counterparts well. Hastily assembled, JTF-AR hit the ground in Monrovia less than forty-eight hours after being told to go.[11] It got there in time.

Factional fighting throughout the capital escalated even as Canavan's JTF-AR postured for action. As in the 1992 iteration, an Air Force airlift terminal element, supplemented by SOCEUR staffers and State Department experts, set up a "safe haven" reception base in Dakar, Senegal. Another, larger SOCEUR team established a transfer site, an intermediate staging base at the international airport in Freetown, Sierra Leone. Evacuees would leave embattled Monrovia via SOF helo, switch to U.S. Air Force MC-130H Combat Talon and C-130E Hercules transports in Freetown, then head to Dakar to await final movement back to the United States. The SOF helos, transports, and Spectre gunships could park at ISB Freetown. Mike Scaparotti's Blue Falcon paratroopers assembled there, too, to stand by as an overall QRF, ready to join the fight if things really went crazy after the first waves of special operators went in. Like the rest of the JTF gathering at the ISB, the 3/325 men would launch as necessary to get in and out of the wild Liberian capital. Of course, that was the challenge, wasn't it?

Getting in went quickly enough for the first element. Skimming in over the sea from ISB Freetown, the lead MH-53J Pave Low flared up over the seventy-five-foot seaside cliff and plopped down. It was about 1600 on the warm afternoon of 9 April. Somehow, the big SOF helicopter squeezed into the embassy's basketball court, its single main rotor whacking away at overhanging tree branches. Things looked bad. The racket of firing, wriggling tracer trails, and drifting smoke filled the eastern horizon over Monrovia, right up to the wall of the U.S. compound.

Upon landing, the JTF-AR liaison team disembarked, looking to find the ambassador and his key staff. Simultaneously, a dozen-man

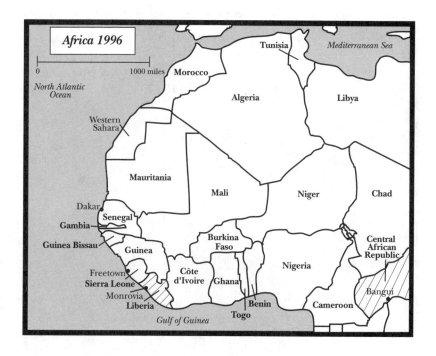

Africa 1996

0   1000 miles   Morocco

North Atlantic
Ocean

Tunisia   Mediterranean Sea

Algeria   Libya

Western
Sahara

Mauritania

Mali   Niger   Chad

Dakar
Gambia   Senegal

Guinea Bissau   Guinea

Burkina
Faso

Freetown   Côte
Sierra Leone   d'Ivoire Ghana

Monrovia
Liberia

Nigeria

Central
African
Republic

Bangui

Benin   Cameroon

Togo

Gulf of Guinea

SEAL platoon got out, heavily armed and bearing a full load of ammunition. Three guarded the tiny LZ, cutting away offending tree
limbs and beginning to marshal a crowd of cowed civilians anxious
to leave. Meanwhile, the other nine SEALs moved tactically to the
embassy's eastern boundary, overlooking United Nations Drive and
the burning, rowdy Greystone camp.

The SEALs attracted heavy but ineffective fire. Their leader, Lt.
Comdr. Steve Grzeszczak, reported Liberian teens "shooting RPGs
all over the place." Sweating in the heat and humidity, the SEALs
skillfully took up security positions without returning shots, though
Grzeszczak said the Americans stopped now and then for some "concrete belly dancing."[12] Working with Sergeant Sanchez and his four
other Marine guards, the small SEAL detachment fanned out to

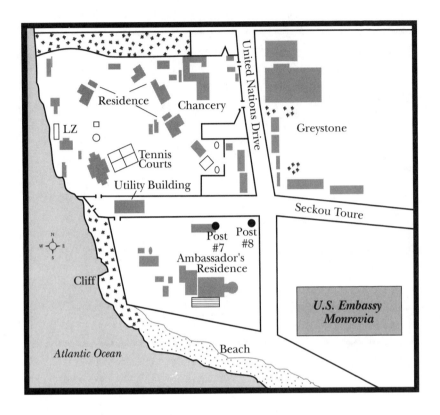

cover by fire all the major approaches into the six-acre embassy complex.

Behind this thinnest of thin screens, the Air Force Pave Low helicopter took off with twenty-six evacuees, outbound on a ninety-
minute run to ISB Freetown. It finally returned in darkness, at 2010.
Its passengers included Canavan himself, six more SEALs, plus the
lead team from 1/10th Special Forces (SF). The MH-53J left laden
with departing citizens, twenty-five to be exact. Two more similar
flights took place before daybreak.

Over that long first night, the SEALs and the newly arrived SF men
kept watch. By the next morning, more arriving Green Berets allowed a better division of labor. A mix of Army Special Forces officers and NCOs, totaling forty-three, took the northern half of the

complex, around the chancery building. The thirty-four SEALs handled the south, around Milam's ambassadorial residence, which just happened to be the old British Embassy compound.[13] Outside, the Krahn and their Liberian enemies continued to fight, with more than a few shots whizzing into and over the embassy grounds.

The fun started soon enough on 10 April, just as all knew it would. The succession of big, wallowing American SOF aircraft attracted militia attention. After the first few sorties, two successive inbound MH-53Js watched volleys of RPGs whooshing skyward. Three rockets came way too close to the first chopper; the second swerved to avoid an RPG that passed within a hundred meters. Both flights waved off. With rueful memories of the helo scourging in Mogadishu in 1993, General Canavan elected to switch to night flights to minimize exposure. Though armed, armored, and rigged with every sophisticated, high-technology navigation device known to man, the Pave Low birds were just too big and slow to play dodge with Liberian RPG rounds. Losing an SOF bird crammed with civilians would unhinge everything.

Restricted largely to night flights for several days, the evacuation process ground slowly along. Endangered U.S. citizens and selected foreigners departed from the embassy's single-ship LZ. By 20 April, 2,126 evacuees, including more than 436 Americans, had escaped the fighting. Each inbound chopper also brought in food and water for those waiting to leave, the JTF-AR troops, and the isolated embassy staff. All this took ninety-eight helicopter sorties, one at a time, night after night.[14] So far, so good; yet, holding on by the fingernails and sneaking out by night hardly produced a feeling of security. Ambassador Milam didn't want to pull out, to relive Saigon '75. But, absent more infantry and more backup warpower, he had to think about it. Monrovia burned on.

By day, SEALs and Green Berets watched the sniper fire, street clashes, and looting in the Mamba Point neighborhood. By night, the embassy's beefed-up guard force witnessed Liberia's capital gushing flames and tracers. Both the Johnson and Taylor people claimed that they were not targeting the U.S. Embassy. But as always, as in Cap-Haitien, Mogadishu, and all the other garden spots, incidents kept occurring. Bullets and rocket-propelled grenades kept on peppering the compound. Liberian gang leaders shrugged off the situation as the fortunes of war. To the young American men getting shot at, it sure looked intentional.

On 11 April, three youths scaled the embassy wall near the ambassador's residence. A female security guard tried to stop them, but they pushed her aside and slapped away her weapon. Intent on looting, the trio did not get far. Marine security guards led by Sgt. Luis Sanchez and a SEAL reaction team responded to the incursion. The SEALs aggressively charged the interlopers. The Liberians dropped their stolen goods, raised their hands, and ran like hell. Alarmed by the penetration, which might have been a disaster had the looters nabbed Ambassador Milam, Canavan ordered a beefed-up SF presence in the residential segment of the U.S. compound. He also brought forward a rifle platoon from Company C, 3/325 ABCT. They had waited for days to respond to just these kinds of emergencies.[15] Now they had their chance.

Nobody died in this episode, but all hands read the implications. Too much wall, too few sentinels; the bad guys were finding the weak spots. The next hostile intruders might be more heavily armed and less easily cowed. As Sanchez said, "It made for some long nights."[16] Even with ample numbers of fine night-vision goggles and hand-held thermal sights, the paratroopers and SEALs could see only a dozen yards at best into the ravaged line of white structures that marked the lip of the Greystone ghetto, just across pocked, debris-strewn United Nations Drive. Ten blocks away, a block away, right behind that collapsed wall or inside a smoking car wreck—who really knew? Nobody wanted to find out.

As the helicopters made their slow transits out to sea toward Freetown and back, Johnson and Taylor backers kept battling for control of the once-impressive Mamba Point neighborhood. More false alarms, more stray rounds, more near misses, and more hits on and in the U.S. compound marked every passing day. It was like watching a raging forest fire creep closer and closer to a campsite. The wind wasn't shifting favorably, either.

One day, a SEAL sniper watched a Liberian male calmly shoulder an RPG launcher, leveled for what looked like a shot right into the chancery building. But the SEAL held his fire; something felt wrong.

Sure enough, the local militiaman looked away and commenced to raise a sandwich with his other hand. The SEAL relaxed his trigger finger.[17] Almost every American with a firearm remembered similar, if less dramatic, confrontations. It was a game of inches.

The tumult in the streets did more than pin down and endanger the people at the embassy. Diplomatic staffers reported dozens of other Americans holed up across tortured Monrovia, cut off by the continued gun battling. The JTF-AR command post and the ambassador's staff kept tabs by telephone on these pockets of Americans as well as other worried foreigners. On 11 April, two MH-53Js extracted some U.S. contractors from a building near Spriggs Payne Airfield. The next day, another two-shipper clattered north to the ECOMOG barracks on Bushrod Island, where Blue Falcon riflemen guarded the LZ as hundreds queued up for flights to safety.[18] Both of these quick diversions went off successfully.

Several other times, preemptive extractions or even hostage rescue efforts began, only to be called off as all involved elected to wait for gaps in the chaotic violence. To be honest, with only a few rather vulnerable helicopters, about 140 SOF troops (including headquarters personnel), and a single airborne rifle company to hold the embassy compound—no guarantees there, either—sending numerous pickup teams into the Monrovia maelstrom sounded too risky. With insufficient boots on the ground to do much else, JTF-AR stayed put and waited.

Daily, everyone in Liberia, no doubt including all enemies present and potential, tracked the movements of 22d MEU as it sailed toward West Africa. The U.S. presence in Liberia amounted to a small, unpleasantly tenuous six-acre footprint, with too many frightened civilians trying to get out through the eye of that particular needle. One helicopter crash on the tiny legation LZ, one good Liberian rush at the walls, some hooliganism that resulted in dead American civilians stuck in outlying residences, and the thin ranks of the JTF-AR would pay up on their bluff to date. They had no margin for friction, nothing else to throw into the pot when the opposition upped the ante. Staked to the embassy complex, Canavan's SOCEUR JTF bore an unpleasant likeness to a tethered goat—mean enough, but a rather small beast nevertheless.

On 20 April, all that changed. The MEU arrived in town, their great gray naval fleet visible offshore. Prominent among the four vessels, the destroyer USS *Connolly* (DD-979) showed off her pair of 5-inch (127mm) naval cannons, one fore, one aft.[19] Not surprisingly, both the Johnson and Taylor factions suddenly decided "jaw, jaw" to be better than "war, war" and declared a cease-fire. Of course, as the Marines soon learned, the only things in Liberia worse than the fighting were the cease-fires.

Colonel Melvin W. Forbush brought the 22d MEU (SOC) into Monrovia ready to fight. Like all Marine expeditionary units, this one brought its own secure base in the form of three big amphibious warships, each carrying key pieces of Forbush's command. From the naval flagship USS *Guam* (LPH-9—landing platform helicopter, a small aircraft carrier), the MEU's aviation element staged ashore as necessary to bring Marines into Monrovia, evacuate more citizens, and resupply the U.S. community. It was a guaranteed air bridge from sea to beach. About a third of the MEU's ground punch, the same 2d Battalion, 2d Marine Regiment, that secured Cap-Haitien in 1994, also lived aboard *Guam*. With its well deck full of landing craft and its wide, single-spot helo deck, USS *Portland* (LSD-37—landing ship dock) carried another third of 2/2 Marines. Finally, with a two-aircraft helipad, a small hanger, and another big well deck, USS *Trenton* (LPD-14—landing platform dock) held the bulk of Marine Service Support Group 22, the MEU's logisticians, complete with fifteen days' worth of beans, bullets, fuel, and spare parts. The *Trenton* also bore some of the MEU's attachments: SEALs, the force recon platoon, and amtracs.[20] The destroyer *Connolly*, bristling with firepower, rounded out the flotilla.

Something was missing. Namely, one of the newer ships in the Navy's amphib stable, USS *Tortuga* (LSD-46, an updated version of USS *Portland*), experienced what sailors call a "casualty" in her boiler system. She put in to Haifa, Israel, for repairs. As a result, Company E and about a third of 2/2 Marines marked time on the eastern coast of the Mediterranean, out of the fight.[21] Forbush and 22d MEU pressed on without them.

At dawn on 20 April, rattling old CH-46E Sea Knights, the familiar, ancient Frogs, began landing one by one at the embassy's little basketball court LZ. Along with Colonel Forbush's MEU headquarters team and a battalion-level team led by the 2/2 commander, Lt. Col. W. E. Gaskin, the Frogs deposited Capt. Eric Mellinger and Company F with about a hundred more Marines from Weapons Company, including the 81mm mortar platoon and the heavy-weapons platoon. Handover with the SOCEUR contingent commenced right away. Forbush and his men had the ball by 1400 local.

Mellinger's rifle squads fanned out to replace Army paratroopers around the embassy perimeter. The mortarmen took over the evacuation control center from the Army Special Forces teams, assisted by Navy medical corpsmen and others from the service support group. Finally, huge CH-53E Super Sea Stallions, navalized brothers of the special operators' MH-53J Pave Lows, delivered six souped-up black dune buggies to the heavy-weapons platoon. Coming in by sling ropes, dangling beneath the roaring heavy-lifters, the half-dozen fast attack vehicles (FAVs) gave the Marines mobile firepower. A pair had M-2HB .50-caliber machine guns, two more sported TOW missile tubes, and the others held Mk-19 automatic grenade launchers. If the badniks came over the walls now, the Marine FAVs guaranteed immediate fire to stop them dead in all senses of the word. By sunset, some 276 Marines and attached sailors secured the U.S. compound at Mamba Point.[22] In the face of this doubling of American capability in town, the factional cease-fire held. Nobody wanted to try these guys—yet.

The MEU's arrival fundamentally altered the situation in Monrovia. With three times the riflemen of Company C, 3/325th, a quartet of CH-53Es and a dozen old CH-46E helicopters, plus AH-1W Sea Cobra attack birds, artillery, mortars, and the like, 22d MEU had the gunnery to blow apart any Johnson or Taylor gangsters itching for a fight. Moreover, those amphibious ships allowed Mel Forbush the luxury of a safe staging base. Instead of an embattled islet in a sea of pain, the American embassy became an advanced position, a fulcrum to pivot even more combat strength into Monrovia as needed. Ambassador Milam and his staff relaxed, and all talk of bugging out vanished. Instead, as Captain Mellinger noted, "The embassy staff seemed overjoyed that the Marines are now here. There's a tradition with Marines being at embassies."[23] The old cliche held up. The Marines had landed, and the situation was well in hand.

While the SOCEUR men quickly pulled out, bound for more adventures in the former Yugoslavia and elsewhere in mainland Europe, 2/2 Marines settled in. The Liberian militias opened formal negotiations, and the U.S. assistant secretary of state for African affairs, George Moose, announced plans to come to Monrovia to serve as an intermediary beginning on 30 April.

And why not? After all, here was one black African state with unquestionable links to the United States. Tracing back to its founding in 1847 by emancipated American blacks, Liberia consciously modeled itself on the United States. This explained Liberia's capital that commemorated James Monroe, the widespread use of common American surnames, the prevalence of Christianity, the American-style flag, and the legal and political traditions borrowed from the United States. When President Abraham Lincoln occasionally talked about sending freed slaves "back to Africa," he meant to Liberia, the first free African republic.[24]

Until the 1980 ascendancy of that lunatic Samuel K. Doe, the country avoided the usual pattern of dictatorial rule that plagued its fellow West African countries. But beginning with Charles Taylor's uprising on Christmas 1989, Liberia made up for all those quiet years in an orgy of blood and fire. The sputtering civil war pitted the tiny American-descended elite against indigenous ethnic groups. Longtime American political and economic interests, personified by the diplomats and businessmen who pursued them, naturally ended up in the cross fire. Hence, the NEOs of 1990–91, 1992, and 1996 all formed part of a pattern. In stages, unwillingly, the United States was abandoning its ugly, violence-ridden West African offspring.

The MEU's presence stopped that trend, at least for the moment. Things in Monrovia settled back to as near calm as they ever were. Militiamen slung their arms; some even left them behind. The looting subsided. The shooting dwindled. Smoke cleared. And, once again, the city's inhabitants came out of hiding. Life picked up where it had left off two weeks before. Many desperately prayed that, this time, the peace would last. These prayers, too, were destined to go unheeded.

Easing tensions slowed the NEO to a trickle. Many U.S. expatriates decided to stay the course. The same families whose distant homes once conjured images of hostage dramas and bedeviled Ambassador Milam's staff now told the U.S. mission they intended to stay put. Only 49 more Americans departed, along with 260 more third-country nationals.[25] The rest stood pat.

With the streets calm and the NEO mostly over, a lesser breed of fighting man might have let down his guard. But Marines knew better, especially the 0311s, those who held the specialty "rifleman." Nobody in Liberia relaxed, not yet. Bitter experiences in Beirut in 1982–84, Monrovia in 1990–91, Mogadishu in 1991 and again in 1992–94, and Cap-Haitien in 1994 conjured powerful memories. These Third World cities featured ambushers and horrors by the gross. The opponents came when you slacked off. So the Marines learned not to slack off—ever. They wouldn't be safe until they got back to Camp Lejeune.

Local patrols, battle drills, and emplacement improvement went on day and night. To keep the edge, Companies F and G swapped out on 27 April, the beginning of a weekly rotation between guarding the legation buildings and standing by as a sea-launched QRF. "Things are mostly quiet now," mused Colonel Forbush on 26 April. "But you never know for sure with this type of thing . . ."[26] In the dark, dank back alleys of Monrovia, somebody did know. On 30 April, they acted.

Nobody ever figured out exactly for whom the eight toughs worked, though the Krahns eventually took the blame. As usual, the toughs wore no uniforms. (Who did anymore?) They might have been Johnson fighters. They may have been freelancers. It mattered little.

Shortly after 0830 local time on another warm tropical morning, the Liberians decided to shoot up a sandbagged perimeter post not far from the ambassador's home. Their first fusillade nicked an American sniper, Cpl. Jason S. Farrand, tumbling him out of his perch overlooking the Marines' Post #7, at the northeast corner of the ambassador's residence section. Marines on and around Post #7 chambered rounds and watched for further Liberian action. The enemy formed out on Seckou Toure Street. Evidently, somebody wanted a showdown this morning.

Meanwhile, comrades brought sniper Farrand to a nearby medical site, where Navy corpsmen debated about whether to send him to the clean, well-staffed wards onboard the USS *Guam*. But Farrand wanted none of that. Before the amazed aidmen could restrain him, the corporal grabbed his bloody shirt and snaked out of the aid station. "I knew something was going to happen," he said, "and I couldn't live with myself if something happened to my team and I wasn't there."[27]

Something was happening, all right. Corporal William A. Gardner and his fire team at rooftop Post #7 watched Liberians moving in a wedge, directly toward the Marine position. The hostiles "flagged" their rifles, Marine-speak for pointing the muzzles at the Americans. It was like a scene from a western movie, the Earps strolling down the street, guns drawn and ready, high noon come three hours early in Monrovia.

The Liberian point man calmly raised his shoulder arm and shot. *Crack!* The round missed Gardner and a Marine SAW gunner by six inches and smacked into the plywood that held up his post's sandbagged roof. The Marines all ducked, but that did it.

"Open up! Fire! Fire!" commanded Gardner, shooting his own M-16A2.

Marine rifles barked their slow cadence of aimed fire, that same lethal rhythm that bowled over Cap-Haitien's finest in short order. The fire team's SAW gunner ripped off two hundred 5.56mm bullets. The big 7.62mm M-60E3 machine gun, the ugly old "pig" of Vietnam fame, spat a belt of quarter-inch-long slugs into the street. Every fifth bullet was a tracer. These hit the pavement and spun upward at crazy angles, red sparks arcing into the morning sky. Then, the Marines paused, eyes wide.

Four Liberians lay broken on the hot pavement, finished. Two more stumbled and moaned, winged and out of the fight. Leaving their dead comrades, the other two enemies fled.

One of the "dead" showed plenty of life. He rolled prone and took up a firing stance, clipping off another round at Post #7. Gardner ordered the M-60 gunner to fire again. The pig hammered through another belt, flipping the Liberian over with multiple impacts. That ended it. The Marines watched wraithlike figures emerge from the shadows, strip the bodies of weapons and shoes, then scuttle away. Later, dogs crept out to feed on the corpses.[28] None of it was pretty.

An hour later, more Liberians appeared at the next Marine post, #8. Marine sentries counted forty to fifty people across United Nations Drive, apparently conducting a house-to-house battle with some rival group. Tracers and ricochets cascaded upward and outward. Once again, for no apparent reason, the hostiles wheeled on the Marines. They fired first, high and outside as ever.

The Marine fire team responded instantly, its methodical mix of M-16A2 and SAW shots knocking down more Liberian gunmen. Most of the enemy scattered, panicked. But a few kept blazing away, undeterred.

Enter Cpl. Jason Farrand, patched up and back in the fight. Restored to his high window, the Marine sniper finished this dozen-man foray decisively. With a long black .50-caliber Barrett M-82A1A sniper rifle in hand, the master marksman coolly took aim. *Blam!* One Liberian autorifleman pitched over, his leg ripped from its socket by the merciless slug. *Blam!* Another hostile fell back, his chest blown apart.[29] Those two big shots ended it, both for that incursion and the entire day.

Farrand found it hard to recall exactly what happened that day. "It's like I wasn't even there," he recounted much later. "My body was doing what the Corps taught me. After the last shot, I was amazed at what had happened."[30]

As inhuman and awful as this sounds—and make no mistake, it is—the Barrett sniper rifle is certainly kin to the F-117A Nighthawk stealth jet. Those technophiles advocating fleets of slick, racing black stealth fighters plinking two-thousand-pound bombs right down the old chimney had better remember what happens at the receiving end. It's all the same: evisceration, sucking chest wounds, torn-off limbs, death in technicolor, screams and all. And unlike the soaring stealth jockey, a poor Marine sniper such as Jason Farrand has to live with the faces. Because day or night, a sniper sees his quarry. Thanks to a superb ten-power Unertl scope, a Marine shooter doesn't miss a bit of it. It's very personal.

The Marine encounters coincided with U.S. envoy Moose's entry into Monrovia. Evidently, nobody wanted to talk quite yet. Although the troublemakers studiously avoided the fields of fire around the U.S. Embassy, they worked out on one another. The fighting kept Moose contained in the chancery building on Mamba Point. But with most Americans gone and the embassy well defended, the assistant secretary could afford to let the gun battles sputter out on their own. By nightfall, they did.[31]

The Marines' good shooting created an effect similar to the aftermath of the bloody confrontation in Cap-Haitien in September 1994. Once more, local parties decided to quit challenging the Americans. In fact, both the Johnson and Taylor factions eventually came to the peace table in Accra, Ghana. Roosevelt Johnson of the Krahns rode there in one of 22d MEU's helicopters.[32] Although there were other sparks of mayhem, Monrovia's latest round of civil war ended with a few bangs and a whimper. As Col. Mel Forbush expressed it, "We're finally getting back to as close to 'Monrovia-normal' as we can."[33]

As tensions ebbed in Monrovia, a relief Navy-Marine team, cobbled together from forces just returned from their own six-month MEU float, boarded USS *Ponce* (LPD-15, sister ship of the *Trenton*) and headed toward a late June 1996 changeover date. Meanwhile, with the appropriate chunk of 22d MEU embarked, USS *Trenton* broke station and headed off toward the Mediterranean Sea on 9 May, to join the rehabilitated USS *Tortuga* and various Spanish units for Exercise Matador 96.[34] It was like the sideshow performer with many plates spinning: *Guam* and *Portland* and their Marines cruising off Monrovia, the embassy security team ashore, a NEO transit site in Freetown, the safe haven in Dakar, and, now, a NATO exercise. You had to feel for Mel Forbush and his people. Somewhere, some staff geniuses thought Monrovia wasn't enough to keep 22d MEU busy. So while the USS *Ponce* prepared to sail, the plates on the sticks spun on.

A plate fell off on 19 May 1996, when the Central African Republic imploded. The local excuse for an army mutinied over pay complaints, and the disgruntled soldiery turned on the helpless populace. United States Ambassador Mosina H. Jordan called for help.

Staff experts in USEUCOM looked at the giant mapboards, saw that
Colonel Forbush and 22d MEU were in the neighborhood, relatively
speaking, and so ordered the Navy-Marine team to get cracking and
send succor to Bangui, Central African Republic.

Well, this was interesting. The Marines and their gator brothers
were "nearby" in the same way that New Orleans is nearby San Francisco—two thousand miles away.[35] But with everyone else tied down
in and around Bosnia, and nobody closer, the European Command
brain trust had few options. Marines knew NEOs. Let them pull off
another.

Led by Maj. Norman J. Robison and a few staff types, a Marine rifle platoon moved by helicopter to Freetown, Sierra Leone. There,
the thirty-five-man detachment boarded a Marine KC-130R Hercules
transport and flew east, toward Bangui. Simultaneously, a small
Navy-Marine detachment moved to Yaoundé, Cameroon, to establish a safe haven. When Robison and his men landed on 21 May,
frightened U.S. citizens left on the same Hercules that brought in
the reinforcements. Over several days, some five hundred Americans
and other endangered foreigners left for Cameroon courtesy of Marine transport planes.

Norm Robison and his platoon of Marine grunts found that rebel
soldiers often took shelter at the base of the embassy walls in Bangui. Opposing units refused to take the bait, fearful of provoking the
well-armed Marines. "Everyone knows there is no pointing weapons
towards the embassy. There has been no problem with that here,"
Robison stated.[36] A second Marine platoon arrived soon after, serving to underscore American intentions to protect its diplomatic staff
and their installation. Though odd rounds continued to fly, some
into the embassy grounds, none of the insurgents or their government foes chose to test the patience of the Marine 0311s protecting
the U.S. legation.

Moving with customary alacrity into a former African colony, an
aggressive French paratrooper task force also deployed into Bangui.
Patrolling in strength and more than willing to shoot recalcitrants,
the tough French paras soon restored order throughout Bangui.
French diplomats compelled both sides to the bargaining table.[37]
Cowed by the will of France's *Force Action Rapide* and a few U.S.

Marines, the military rebellion in the Central African Republic slowly subsided.

By 20 June 1996, USS *Portland* and its Marines departed what the Navy had begun to call "Mamba Station," the waters off Monrovia. A week later, USS *Guam* followed, with Col. Melvin Forbush and the remnant of 22d MEU embarked. Following its rapid crossing of the Atlantic Ocean, helo carrier USS *Ponce* began slowly turning ovals off Mamba Point, and Special-Purpose Marine Air-Ground Task Force (SPMAGTF) Liberia took over. For a few weeks, they, too, spread Marines and sailors across Senegal, Sierra Leone, Liberia, Cameroon, and the Central African Republic, finishing up business at the NEO sites and embassies. This pickup team came home in August 1996, mission accomplished.[38] Thanks to 22d MEU's work, especially in convincing locals to stay well back from Uncle Sam's real estate, the follow-on force enjoyed a relatively uneventful time of it.

It had been quite a float for 22d MEU, demonstrating the tremendous flexibility and reach of elite Marine infantry. No other brand of U.S. infantry could have carried out the simultaneous Monrovia-Bangui NEO and embassy security missions. As Col. Mel Forbush told an interviewer, "Doing two [NEOs] doesn't even come up in training. Who would ever think of something like this happening at the same time?"[39] That was a question for America's enemies to ponder. In West Africa in 1996, a small number of Marines made it look easy. In doing so, they wrote another page in their glorious tradition of arms and earned a new-old nickname: the Africa Corps.

What makes Marine infantry special? Asking the question that way misses the most fundamental point about the United States Marine Corps. In the Marines, everyone—sergeant, mechanic, cannoneer, supply man, clerk, aviator, cook—is a rifleman first. The entire corps, all 170,000 or so on the active rolls, plus the reserves, are all infantry. All speak the language of the rifle and bayonet, of muddy boots and long, hot marches. It's never us and them, only us. That is the secret of the Corps.

If Army infantry amounts to a stern monastic order standing apart, on the edge of the wider secular soldier world, Marine infantry more resembles the central totem worshiped by the entire tribe. Marines have specialized, as have all modern military organizations. And despite the all-too-real rigors of boot camp, annual rifle qualification, and high physical standards, a Marine aircraft crew chief or radio repairman wouldn't make a good 0311 on a squad assault. But those Marine technical types know that they serve the humble grunt, the man who will look his enemy in the eye within close to belly-ripping range. Moreover, all Marines think of themselves as grunts at heart, just a bit out of practice at the moment.[40] That connection creates a great strength throughout the Corps.

It explains why Marine commanders routinely, even casually, combine widely disparate kinds of capabilities into small units. Marines send out pretty small teams for pretty big jobs. Think of Lt. Virgil Palumbo and his squad in Cap-Haitien, Cpl. William Gardner and his fire team in Monrovia, or Maj. Norm Robison and his platoon in Bangui. Marines send junior officers and NCOs out from their line rifle companies and expect results. They get them, too.

Even a single Marine has on call the firepower of the air wing, the Navy, and all of the United States. Or at least he thinks he does. A Marine acts accordingly. He is expected to take charge, to improvise, to adapt, to overcome. A Marine gets by with ancient aircraft (the ratty CH-46E Frog, for example), hand-me-down weapons (such as the old M-60 tanks used in the Gulf War), and whatever else he can bum off the Army or cajole out of the Navy. Marines get the job done regardless, because they are Marines. They make a virtue of necessity. The men, not the gear, make the difference. Now and again, the Marines want to send men, not bullets.

This leads to a self-assurance that sometimes comes across as disregard for detailed staff-college quality planning and short shrift for high-level supervision. Senior Army officers in particular sometimes find the Marines amateurish, cavalier, and overly trusting in just wading in and letting the junior leaders sort it out. In the extreme, a few soldiers have looked at the Corps as some weird, inferior, ersatz ground war establishment, a bad knockoff of the real thing. "A small, bitched-up army talking Navy lingo," opined Army Brig. Gen. Frank Armstrong in one of the most brutal interservice assessments.[41] That was going too far. But deep down, many Army professionals tended to wonder about the Marines. Grab a defended beach? Definitely.

Seize a hill? Sure, if you don't mind paying a little. But take charge of a really big land operation? Not if we can help it.

Anyone who has watched an amphibious landing unfold would be careful with that kind of thinking. The Marines actually have a lot in common with their elite Army infantry brothers, if not with all the various Army headquarters and service echelons. True, Marine orders do tend to be, well . . . brief. But so do those of the airborne, the air assault, the lightfighters, and the Rangers, and for the same good reason: Hard, realistic training teaches soldiers how to fight by *doing*, over and over, so they need not keep writing about it, regurgitating basics every time. More enlightened soldiers consider that goodness. A three-inch-thick order, a big CP, and lots of meetings do not victory make. The Marines consciously reject all that. And why not? Despite the occasional Tarawa or Beirut, it works.

A Corps infused with a rifleman ethos has few barriers to intraservice cooperation. The Army talks a great deal about combined arms and does it down to about battalion level, often with great wailing and gnashing of teeth. Marines do it all the way down to the individual Marine. Soldiers have defined military occupational specialties and guard their prerogatives like union shop stewards. Finance clerks don't do machine guns. Mechanics skip foot marches to fix trucks. Intell analysts work in air-conditioned trailers; they don't patrol. Marines, though, are just Marines. They all consider themselves trigger pullers. They even like it, as might be expected of an elite body.

Much as all Marines claim to be riflemen, only a minority truly do it full time. There are twenty-four battalions of designated Marine infantry, the men whom Mother Corps places in harm's way to destroy America's foes. All Marine infantry battalions are identical in structure. Superficially, they look a lot like Army battalions, with lettered line companies and the usual rack of headquarters, heavy weapons, and attachments. But digging a little deeper reveals that the Marines organize for combined-arms warfare in a most serious way. They are infantry battalions designed for and by fellow grunts.

Consider the 2d Battalion, 2d Marine Regiment, masters of Cap-Haitien, harrowers of Monrovia and Bangui. The structure relentlessly follows a three-one-one pattern: three maneuver elements, a small headquarters, and, above platoon level, a heavy-weapons element.[42] This begins right at the bottom. Three four-man fire teams and a squad leader (corporal or sergeant), all 0311s, make up a rifle squad. In close combat, thirteen is a lucky number. Two Marine squads (twenty-six men) equal three nine-man Army squads (twenty-seven men). That advantage means a lot when casualties stack up, as they tend to do at knife range, especially inside buildings. Marine squads are built to take and inflict punishment.

Three of these squads, plus a miniscule platoon headquarters (lieutenant, platoon sergeant, platoon guide, and radioman, with a Navy medic usually attached from battalion level), make a rifle platoon. Three rifle platoons and a headquarters with a captain, first sergeant, and so forth make a company. But here the Marines innovate. They add a weapons platoon with three 60mm mortars, six M-60E3 light machine guns, and six Mk-153 shoulder-launched multipurpose assault weapons (SMAWs), a modernized bazooka originally fielded in Israel as the B-300.[43] As an additional duty, the weapons platoon commander (all Marine officers in leadership roles are titled commanders, from platoon up) serves as his company's supporting arms coordinator.[44] This unique Marine concept translates as "Mr. Firepower." If a Marine outfit wants air support, naval gunfire, artillery, mortars, tank shots, or any other form of death by projectile not already owned by the requesting unit, the supporting arms coordinator ensures it gets there.

Along with the supporting arms coordinator, the Marines have another unique position in the rifle company headquarters. Reflecting the Corps' commitment to individual battle skills, especially marksmanship, each company employs a gunnery sergeant, the famous Marine "gunny" of film and literature. The gunnery sergeant plans and supervises all individual, NCO, and small-unit training in the company, with a special emphasis on shooting skills. He might be thought of as the company's S-3 (operations and training coordinator) but with genuine supervisory responsibility. In action, he is the man who spurs squads and platoons, which places him in the front of firefights and explains the prominence of these men in many U.S. Marine combat vignettes. Having a gunnery sergeant frees the first sergeant to focus on administrative and logistical matters and

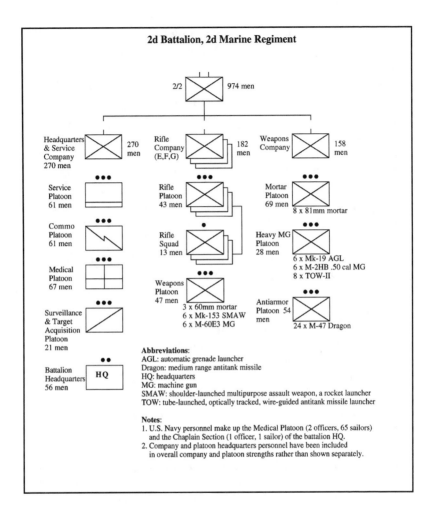

2d Battalion, 2d Marine Regiment

2/2 — 974 men

Headquarters & Service Company 270 men — 270 men

Rifle Company (E,F,G) — 182 men

Weapons Company — 158 men

Service Platoon 61 men

Rifle Platoon 43 men

Mortar Platoon 69 men — 8 x 81mm mortar

Commo Platoon 61 men

Rifle Squad 13 men

Heavy MG Platoon 28 men — 6 x Mk-19 AGL / 6 x M-2HB .50 cal MG / 8 x TOW-II

Medical Platoon 67 men

Surveillance & Target Acquisition Platoon 21 men

Weapons Platoon 47 men — 3 x 60mm mortar / 6 x Mk-153 SMAW / 6 x M-60E3 MG

Antiarmor Platoon 54 men — 24 x M-47 Dragon

Battalion Headquarters 56 men — HQ

Abbreviations:
AGL: automatic grenade launcher
Dragon: medium range antitank missile
HQ: headquarters
MG: machine gun
SMAW: shoulder-launched multipurpose assault weapon, a rocket launcher
TOW: tube-launched, optically tracked, wire-guided antitank missile launcher

Notes:
1. U.S. Navy personnel make up the Medical Platoon (2 officers, 65 sailors) and the Chaplain Section (1 officer, 1 sailor) of the battalion HQ.
2. Company and platoon headquarters personnel have been included in overall company and platoon strengths rather than shown separately.

provides some badly needed senior NCO depth in the small-company headquarters.[45] As with the thirteen-man squad, the gunnery sergeant represents another smart concession to the importance of quality Marine training and the realities of small-unit combat. There can't be too much decent training, and of course there can't be too many seasoned hands when the bullets start flying.

Three rifle companies, a headquarters company (with the scout-snipers such as Cpl. Jason Farrand in its surveillance and target acquisition platoon), and a weapons company make up a Marine infantry battalion. The weapons company amounts to the company weapons platoon writ large. The mortars become 81mm models, eight in all. The company's sextet of machine guns translates into the battalion heavy-weapons platoon, with eight TOWs, six .50-caliber machine guns, and six Mk-19 automatic grenade launchers, all on Humvee mounts. Six of these weapons, in any combination, may be placed on the battalion's FAV dune buggies, as happened in Monrovia. Finally, the small Mk-153s give way to an antiarmor platoon that carries twenty-four antiquated Dragon missile systems, overweight and underranged and packing a weak warhead, as unimpressive in Marine service as in Army ranks. Again, as in the rifle company, the weapons commander coordinates all supporting arms for the battalion. The Army leaves this to staff guys. The Marines give it to commanders. Guess which system is more responsive?

All those supporting arms and all that other attached capability comes into play when 2/2 Marines organizes as a battalion landing team (BLT), the equivalent of an Army battalion TF. As mentioned, the Marines tend to actually give a lot of units to their lower-level commanders. A typical BLT includes its own artillery battery (six towed 155mm howitzers), a recon platoon (more scouts, in addition to the battalion's organic platoon), a seven-vehicle armored recon platoon of eight-wheeled, light armored vehicles, a platoon of four tanks (M-1A1 Abrams models), an amtrac platoon (fifteen AAV-7A1 tracked, armored ship-to-shore amphibians), an engineer platoon (with earthmovers), and a shore fire control party to make all the shells and bombs hit their targets.[46] It is the most powerful general purpose battalion-sized force fielded by the United States.

When the BLT joins a MEU, it reaches full capability for long-range, forced-entry operations. (The Navy-Marines often prefer to call it "forcible entry," but that sounds like a house burglary.[47]) The MEU is a brigade-scale formation. Run by a colonel, it can command several more reinforcing battalions and coordinate extensive air and surface supporting firepower. A MEU includes ground (a BLT), air (a composite helo squadron), and logistics units, each at about battalion strength. With a typical mixture of twelve shaky old CH-46Es and four stout CH-53E heavy haulers, MEU aviation can pick up a rifle company in a single lift escorted by AH-1W Super SeaCobra attack helicopters. Sometimes, AV-8B Harrier II jump jets or even F/A-18D Hornet fighter-bombers come along. The service support group can sustain the MEU ashore for fifteen days in all supplies and up to thirty in some. In addition, the MEU brings in its own force recon detachment of deep-penetration scouts and can draw on the amphibious group's embarked SEALs, too.

Three aspects of Marine infantry organization deserve special comment. First, the Marines stress reconnaissance and speed. A BLT has its own scout-sniper platoon, an attached foot recon platoon, and a LAV recon platoon. In addition, the MEU has its own force recon element and access to the amphibious group's SEALs. This allows for plenty of dedicated lookers to pull along the grunts, who organize for speedy exploitation of whatever the recon guides them toward. One rifle company usually air assaults aboard the Frogs, drawn in by one of the recon teams. Another rifle company typically mounts in the amtracs for surface beach assault and/or inland mech operations, led by the LAVs. The third company may infiltrate by ground, follow in on a second helo lift, or wade ashore from World War II–style landing craft. Again, a scout force shows the way. This pattern of "recon pull" and quick air-surface maneuver underpins all basic Marine tactics.[48] To the opposition, the Marines seem to come in from all directions at once, quickly and well focused. This is how a small force imposes its will on a big one. The Marines train for it.

These tactics make sense, given the second significant characteristic of Marine Corps organization. Marines embrace their traditional role in brushfire conflicts, the realm of small, elite, infantry-based forces. To fight and win small wars, NEOs and the like, doesn't take much, but what there is must be willing to walk on death ground and be tough, fast, and, above all, self-sufficient far from home. The rifle companies and other warriors of the BLT give toughness, boots on the ground. The helicopters ensure speed and range. The service support group provides sustenance. It's a lethal, well-balanced team, and all deployed Marine contingents, from brigade-scale MEUs to divisional Marine expeditionary brigades (MEBs) to colossal Corps Marine expeditionary forces (MEFs), reflect this same mix of grunts, aviation, and logistics.[49] Though the Marines have regiments and divisions suitably structured for World War III, the Corps leadership doesn't expend its main effort there. That's a backup, just in case the Army needs help. Instead, the Marines put their stock in small, deployable expeditionary forces. That evolutionary line can be traced back to the Old Corps, to ship's landing parties, from the halls of Montezuma to the shores of Tripoli,[50] not to mention Haiti, Nicaragua, Somalia, and Liberia.

Contrast this to the Army approach. Despite a long record of minor conflicts, the Army optimizes for the Big One. It made a lot of sense in the Cold War, and it still makes sense along the Korean demilitarized zone (DMZ) or in a southwest Asian confrontation. When soldiers think of war, they don't think of battling Somali warlords or yanking nervous diplomats from a bullet-scarred consulate. No, they hearken back to the good old days, the Great War in 1944–45: George Patton, Omar Bradley, and the boys toe to toe with the *Wehrmacht*.[51] The Gulf War matched the preferred style, Panama less so, Somalia and Liberia not at all.

The Army organizes for battle accordingly. Send soldiers in by divisions, as in the Gulf War, and the battalions show up hale and hearty, ready to hook and jab: cogs in the great green machine. By long practice and written doctrine, U.S. Army infantry battalions depend on all kinds of help from their brigades and divisions, plus ample nondivisional troops. With only so much aviation, engineer, artillery, and other support to go around, Army generals earn their pay by shifting this stuff around to weight the main effort.[52] In a big-unit campaign, that's smart use of limited resources.

It's counterproductive for minor operations, however, even though these kind of operations keep happening all the time. There is only so much helpful stuff to attach. If one battalion is deploying alone, can the division afford to ship it off with a lot of helicopters, artillery, or engineers? They might be considered lost forever (effectively) in some distant corner of the world, unavailable when the bell rings for Armageddon, round two, against North Korea or Iraq. This explains why there can be no Army MEUs. Tied to large-scale war plans, no division would part with that much critical combat power on a standing basis.

In trying to preserve its competency for fighting major wars, the Army necessarily goes through major gyrations to prepare, configure, and dispatch battalion and brigade task forces for contingency missions. Ever conscious of the major theater war missions, the Army cuts corners and slices the salami pretty fine. Everything comes with strings attached, if it comes at all. The Army looks at these brushfire clashes as annoyances, distractions, even "operations other than war"—a short-lived term from the early 1990s.[53] For Army units such as Bill David's 2-14th Infantry in Mogadishu, it gets painfully ad hoc, a deviation from the norm. For the Marines, sending self-contained landing parties to minor conflicts constitutes business as usual.

The Marines' final major organizational characteristic flows from this emphasis on deploying for minor actions. Small wars are infantry wars. Marines know that only too well. Lacking branch parochialism and committed to self-sufficiency in small-scale combat, Marines willingly subordinate dissimilar units to infantry commanders. Unlike the Army system, in which attachments come from higher-level outfits that may take them back as priorities shift—Division giveth and Division taketh away; blessed be the name of Division—there is no diddling about with direct support or operational control agreements. A BLT commander afloat owns his tanks, his artillery, his engineers, his amtracs, and all the rest. The MEU commander owns the helicopters. It allows for rapid orders and fast action.

It amounts to infantry heaven, the gospel according to Saint Grunt. The Corps talks about itself as "America's 911 force," seemingly omnipresent and omnipotent, at least in small wars. No airborne Ranger thinks any less of himself, to be sure, but that's not to say that the Marine line goes uncritiqued. Great War National Guard artilleryman and eventual president Harry S. Truman once bitterly griped that the "Marines have a propaganda machine equal to Stalin's."[54] Sometimes, that seems true. But we must get beyond the public relations and chest thumping. What can Corps infantry truly do? And where does it fall short?

To learn what Marine riflemen can do, ask them. A MEU earns its special operations capable (SOC) sobriquet by demonstrated, evaluated proficiency in twenty-two key tasks.[55] These are no secret.

Like Babe Ruth, the Marine MEU (SOC) does not hesitate to point to the fence and dare badniks to stop it. Here are the shots they call.

Amphibious Assault

This most basic Marine task actually had to be added to the list in the early 1990s. It undergirds almost all the other missions, but it does bear distinct consideration. Although the bulk of MEU operations start with an amphibious landing by helicopter and watercraft, few feature an outright assault. Even so, the amphibious assault remains the ultimate expression of why we have a Marine Corps. None of America's foes wants to be on the receiving end of one of these.

Backed up by its gator Navy brethren, destroyer and cruiser gunfire, and repeated air strikes, a MEU can storm a defended shore. With only a BLT to send ashore, hitting the enemy "where they ain't" is much preferred. The Corps earned its reputation in gory beach attacks such as Tarawa and Iwo Jima, but nobody wants to try that kind of thing if they can help it. So MEUs look for holes in enemy defenses and plunge through.

A balanced MEU team bristling with sharpshooting Marine 0311s and all their other friends, from tanks to howitzers and helicopters, can make a difference tearing around loose in the enemy secondary, inland from a hostile coast. Marines executed two critical amphibious assaults to pace the 1983 Grenada intervention, then did another a little more than a week later to help mop up resistance on an off-shore islet. The second of the three landings involved a cross-island night mission executed on minimal notice. The men of BLT 2/8 Marines conducted a chopper move and a major beach assault. This maneuver broke the will of defending Cubans and their Grenadan allies. Despite a decent showing against Army Rangers and paratroopers the day before, the opponents never recovered from the shock of waking up to find Marine ground pounders and a few tanks closing on their capital from the "wrong" direction.[56] That's the way it is designed to work, fast and decisive.

Amphibious Raid

The raid amounts to an amphibious assault with a planned withdrawal. It's the same profile as the Ranger strike on the Iraqi mi-

crowave tower in February 1991 or Delta's actions in Mogadishu—
the old in-out. Whether by air, amtrac, or both, the MEU practices
the raid to destroy fixed targets, wipe out enemy units, or pick up
prisoners or other intelligence. Striking from the sea, Marines can
be there and gone before the enemy can react. All of the enemy's
coastal assets are at risk, and thanks to modern helicopters, *coastal*
really means hundreds of miles inland. Most of the world's population centers and affiliated military targets lie comfortably within
range of MEU raids.

Pure raids are often practiced but seldom executed. Perhaps the
most classic of all MEU raids never occurred, despite extensive
preparation, reconnaissance, and rehearsal. On 25 February 1991,
as the ground phase of Desert Storm rolled through its second day,
Marines and sailors expected to attack Faylakah Island, off the coast
of Kuwait, in an operation called Desert Slash. A 2,500-man Iraqi
brigade would have been eviscerated, its command posts and supply dumps ravaged. It might have been quite an event, but circumstances ruled against the daring stroke. With both the cruiser USS
Princeton (CG-59) and the helo carrier USS *Tripoli* (LPH-10) having
already been damaged by sea mines, the overall ground attack ex-
ceeding all expectations, and qualms over how the Iraqis might gar-
ner political points by portraying the planned Marine withdrawal after their raid as some kind of "retreat," Desert Slash no longer made
sense. General H. Norman Schwarzkopf converted it to a mere feint
using helicopters.[57]

Though Desert Slash never happened, other similar operations
have gone off. The basic raid format allows for many variations.
There are NEO versions, as in the daring Mogadishu extraction of
January 1991. The 1995 rescue of Air Force pilot Capt. Scott O'Grady
from Bosnia also relied on a modification of the standard raid
model.[58] With a small but potent force, the MEU has a default setting that appears to be the raid. The Marines ratchet up or down
from there.

Limited Objective Attack–Deception Raid

Launched to divert enemy attention from the main event, this
kind of MEU operation generates a huge sound and light show. If

done well, it looks real but exposes only a few Marines or sailors to danger. Some variations merely show an aircraft or landing craft movement toward the enemy coast, as in the false approach to Faylakah Island during the Gulf War. In other cases, men go ashore shooting and killing, raising enough hell to make the enemy buy the story. Done well, a limited objective attack–deception raid causes the opposition to overreact, opening the way for other U.S. forces to deliver the finishing blow.

Along with the Marine helicopter feint toward Faylakah Island, the Gulf War featured an even better example of this kind of stuff. At 0100 on 24 February 1991, an eighth-mile stretch of the Kuwait surf line erupted in spurts of smoke and flame, with explosions going off at odd intervals for a half hour thereafter. In the intermittent flashes of light, shocked Iraqi beach defenders clearly saw lines of marker buoys bobbing on the dark sea, harbingers of inbound Marine amtracs. Panicked Iraqi generals repositioned two divisions to meet the threatened invasion. Of course, it never came. Fifteen SEALs did all of that in a classic limited objective attack.[59] Using their own means and a bit more manpower, the MEU (SOC) can do likewise.

Airfield Seizure
Taking an airfield opens up a whole range of good possibilities for our guys and greatly complicates the life of the enemies. With an airport in hand, the MEU can bring in follow-on forces and pull out endangered civilians. Marines know how to take airdromes by heliborne or beach assault and have done so time after time, in Grenada, Somalia, and Haiti, to name a few.

Noncombatant Evacuation Operation
The pugnacious Sir Winston S. Churchill once growled that "the exertion which a nation is prepared to make to protect its individual representatives or citizens from outrage is one of the truest measures of its greatness as an organized state."[60] By Churchill's standard, the United States is very great indeed. Of all the tasks in the MEU (SOC) kit bag, NEO is the one most likely to get yanked out. The Marines know it.

So does the Department of State. In response to ambassadors caught in bad places, the roll call of Marine NEOs since 1989 reads like a guide to all the world's hellholes: Liberia (1990–91), Somalia (1991), Somalia (1992–94), Haiti (1994), Somalia (1995), Liberia (1996), Central African Republic (1996), Albania (1997), Zaire-Congo (1997), and Sierra Leone (1997).[61] With an average of three MEUs afloat at any one time, it's easy enough to do the math. If the Marines deploy with an amphibious readiness group, they're likely to get a chance to go somewhere nasty to save their fellow Americans, plus as many others as they can. And there will be shooting.

Well prepared for this most typical of MEU tasks, Marines have saved a lot of Americans over the last few years. The future promises no letup. There are always plenty of potential NEO customers, all too many wandering around in actual or potential horrific situations throughout the unhappy Third World. More than 11 million Americans leave the homeland yearly for business and pleasure. Two million others live abroad. An additional half million are in uniform or government service work in foreign countries.[62] When the roof caves in, all of them look for American fighting men to come and save them. They look for Marines. Rarely have they been disappointed.

Security Operations

Sometimes, the Corps draws a more extended stint than a simple NEO (as if a NEO is ever simple). Ambassadors want to keep Old Glory on the pole, so they have been known to ask for help guarding the legation compound. This is what happened in Monrovia and Bangui in 1996, along with the NEOs.

Let's face it, Marines can secure most anything. Because MEUs are handy, they often get told to secure facilities or key terrain, sometimes even hostile urban neighborhoods. Occasionally, as in Haiti or Liberia, they get plopped into the middle of horrendous civil strife. Here, men of Mother Corps keep in mind the awful specter of what happened in Beirut, Lebanon, in 1983. That time, the 0311 riflemen got it wrong, dead wrong.

Told to secure the U.S. sector, the doomed grunts of BLT 1/8 took a little too passive a role in war-torn Lebanon. The Americans played evenhanded peacekeeper roles; ate bullets, shells, and rockets; took casualties; and generally hung around, not patrolling, not digging in, and rarely shooting back. In a city such as Beirut, that encouraged the bad guys to act. Act they did. On 23 October 1983, a terrorist truck driver drove into the overcrowded BLT barracks, killing 239 unlucky Americans.[63] The tragedy still reverberates throughout the Marine Corps, a warning to every future BLT.

The lesson was clear enough. When told to secure an area, Marines do not screw around. This explains why in both Cap-Haitien and Monrovia, although other U.S. forces held their fire, young Marine leaders did not hesitate to shoot.[64] They remembered Beirut. No MEU (SOC) will countenance a repeat performance.

Military Operations in Urban Terrain (MOUT)

Marines expect to fight in cities, a reasonable assumption given recent history. It's actually hard to think of any recent combat that did not happen in and around a populated, built-up area. Even the great desert clash of Desert Storm saw considerable action in Kuwait City, Khafji, and other smaller towns. People live in communities. Enemy forces fight there. Our guys must do likewise.

Accordingly, a large part of a MEU's training focuses on actions in built-up areas. The Marines devote considerable energy to understanding the terrain of cities and towns, and it is a focal point during intensified predeployment training. Along with using their own simulated urban centers, such as Camp Lejeune's large, exquisitely realistic "Combat Town," MEU infantry and their associates train in actual U.S. cities. Marines have trained in New Orleans, San Francisco, and Mobile, Alabama, among others.[65]

The Corps' interest in city fighting mirrors similar efforts in the SOF and among Army infantry. The special operators work routinely in both actual and simulated built-up areas; they pioneered carrying out training in largely abandoned high-rises, subways, and parking garages while U.S. cities slept. Conventional Army training centers also feature excellent urban warfare blocks, and soldiers wrestle with the same issues as their Marine brothers. Few battalions knew more about house-to-house fighting than Bill David's 2-14th Infantry, and it came in handy in dreadful Mogadishu.[66] Still, most Army unit exercises do not stress war in the streets to the degree seen in a MEU train-up. Soldiers could learn a lot from the Marines in this important kind of warfare.

Seizure-Destruction of Offshore Platform Facilities

This task combines aspects of a raid and specialized demolition operations. Offshore oil rigs, floating docks, and the like have become more prevalent over the years. Marines understand this, and they train to destroy or grab them as necessary. Against certain enemies, and with the right backup, this can be an important measure.

This mission profile has been employed only once in anger but with dramatic results. During the Iran-Iraq war, Iranian sailors challenged the U.S. fleet in the Persian Gulf. On 18 April 1988, men of Contingency Marine Air-Ground Task Force 2-88 seized and wrecked the Saasan oil platform, devastating a base used by Iranian naval forces for mining and hit-and-run attacks. Stung by the loss of its base, the Iranian Navy came out to fight. By nightfall, sure-shooting U.S. Navy warships and carrier-based jets had sunk or damaged almost every noteworthy surface combatant in the hostile fleet.[67] The Marine attack certainly accomplished its purpose and then some. This is precisely why MEUs retain this important capability.

Maritime Inspection–Maritime Assault

In the earliest days of the Corps, Marines formed boarding parties to seize enemy and suspect ships. This has been an important task in support of U.S. naval battle groups enforcing blockades in the Persian Gulf and the Adriatic Sea, keeping Iraqis and the Bosnian Serbs isolated from seaborne arms shipments. A MEU (SOC) can contribute trained boarding elements to go on ships and search for contraband. Even a few combat-ready Marines make an impression that a gaggle of armed sailors do not.[68] Most merchant vessel skippers submit without any resistance, not exactly willing but not desiring either to find out what a 5.56mm bullet feels like.

Sometimes, things get more exciting. Ships may have to be taken by force, as when Company D, 1/4 Marines, took back the SS *Mayaguez* in 1975 off the coast of Cambodia. A similar situation evolved in 1985, when terrorists took over the Italian cruise ship *Achille Lauro;* they fled before SEALs and Delta shooters could storm the ship.[69] Marines also train for this kind of situation, although in most cases JSOC and their counterterrorists would handle this type of crisis. A MEU (SOC) would certainly support, though, if in the area.

Reinforcement Operations

The MEU (SOC) can reinforce any unit already ashore, American or allied. This happened in Monrovia, with the Marines relieving the SOCEUR forces. With a battalion of infantry, a squadron of rotary-wing aircraft, and fifteen days' worth of supplies, plus all kinds of handy attachments, the MEU can almost always provide something needed ashore by almost any force. To expedite this process, Marine liaison teams often fly ahead of the amphibs to begin arrangements for reinforcement. This is what happened in Liberia on 18 April 1996, forty-eight hours before the actual transfer of responsibility for the embassy from SOCEUR to 22d MEU.[70]

Show of Force Operations

Almost all MEU (SOC) deployments feature this kind of posturing. The amphibious squadron has the ability to loiter offshore for months, which often sends a message to those considering mayhem against U.S. interests. Essentially, cruising off the beach reminds enemies of the other twenty-one things the MEU can do to enforce U.S. policy. Before and after its African excursion, 22d MEU (SOC) was carrying out this typical task off the Dalmatian coast of the former Yugoslavia.

Humanitarian Relief Operations

This has been a post–Cold War addition to the MEU (SOC) repertoire. Often, the amphibs turn out to be the closest U.S. military contingent when famine, flood, or pestilence spurs the president to order action. Most Marine landings in the Third World require some degree of humanitarian aid, regardless of the assigned mission. With shipboard hospitals and some earmarked relief supplies embarked, not to mention a definite capacity to impose and keep order, Marines participate in many of these operations.

One of the largest, Operation Sea Angel in Bangladesh, occurred in the wake of the Gulf War in 1991. Homeward-bound Marine expeditionary battalions diverted into this poor, overpopulated country to succor coastal villages smashed by a huge typhoon. Other distinctly humanitarian missions include support to the Kurds in northern Iraq in 1991 and the initial phases of the 1992–94 Somalia intervention. In all these cases, the Marines need to remember that they are not safe at home and to keep their powder dry. Fighting sometimes comes in the wake of humanitarian assistance.[71] When it does, the BLT riflemen must be ready.

Civic Action Operations

Even when the four horsemen of the Apocalypse have not ridden hard on the locals, Marines come to win hearts and minds. Medical teams give shots and tend aches and pains. Engineers and troop labor complete minor engineering projects such as well digging and road repairs. School restoration is always popular. Marines on exercises or on security patrols interact with the people. They train to do so.

Civic action is a time-honored approach for Mother Corps, inculcated over years of experience around the world. Some credit the Marine Combined Action Platoon program in Vietnam as one of the few successes of that entire unsuccessful interlude.[72] Despite Army pressures, notably from overall commander Gen. William C. Westmoreland, Marines stuck with their approach in Vietnam. They still stick with it. Working closely among the common folk accords with the best advice of Mao Tse-Tung, a man with a pretty good track record in people's wars, better than that of William C. Westmoreland, to be sure.

As with Mao, this is not all due to idealism. In fact, it's practical. Civil wars are, at root, struggles to control the populace. When Marines show up in the midst of this kind of fracas, they must gain popular support, and with it the intelligence so crucial to ferreting out and destroying whatever local crops of insurgents oppose the American presence. Tossed into "Banana Wars" in Latin America for years on end, Old Corps veterans understood this lesson well. As the venerable *Small Wars Manual* put it: "In small wars, tolerance, sympathy, and kindness should be the keynote of our relationship with the mass of the population."[73] The people respond in kind, effectively isolating and fingering rebel bands for the Marine grunts to handle as necessary. Civic action works.

Mobile Training Team (MTT)
All the skills afloat in a MEU (SOC) allow for effective teaching in a wide range of military and military-related techniques. Usually done with military counterparts but occasionally extended to police or paramilitary outfits, too, MTTs build expertise in allied and neutral countries. This is a supporting measure on many MEU (SOC) floats. Therefore, the Marines deploy with the necessary training aids, lesson plans, and language abilities needed to carry out this kind of instruction.

Specialized Demolition Operations
Like MTTs, specialized demolition forms a subset of other MEU (SOC) operations. Although accompanying SEALs, force recon teams, and combat engineers have most of the expert knowledge, all Marines learn how to employ standard-issue and expedient explosives to blow down doors, demolish bridges and piers, and crater roads and runways. Demolition elements played a key part in the 1988 raid on Iran's Saasan offshore oil rig.

Initial Terminal Guidance (ITG)
Another supporting task, ITG is the Marine name for what Army airborne and air assault troops know as pathfinder operations. Normally carried out by the MEU's ample array of recon detachments, these preliminary insertions mark beaches, landing zones, and airstrips for eventual landings. Along with other reconnaissance and surveillance activities, a thorough ITG effort ensures that amphibious assaults, raids, and NEOs go where they are supposed to go, no easy feat in odd, blasted foreign cities that rarely match old colonial map grids.

Some outside analysts see this ITG business as a holdover from the era before contemporary global positioning system (GPS) satellite downlinks. In theory, all Marines and sailors should get a detailed readout on their hand-held or wrist-mounted GPS receiver and thus know exactly where they stand and where they're going. That's all fine, except that the famous satellite constellation isn't perfect, resulting in errors of up to three hundred meters, not to mention outright blank spots.[74] Worse, without a real-time set of detailed, annotated photographs, knowing an exact position doesn't help avoid that new high-rise on the helo flight path, or reveal that the targeted beach eroded away in last year's hurricane. The opposing force won't bother to report in, either. Until the day when those kinds of friction and fog disappear, the Marines will continue to demand and execute sound ITG.

Fire Support Control

As their country's 911 force, Marines actively take on roles that require the United States to send in men, not bullets. But that said, the MEU always keeps a good number of mighty bullets ready, just in case. Firepower allows a relatively small BLT, backed up by the MEU and whatever else Uncle Sam can muster, to defeat significant larger forces. With its designated supporting arms coordinators in key posts, the Marine-Navy team prides itself in delivering massive, timely, accurate air and surface fires in support of littoral fights. Had the situation demanded it, the destroyer USS *Connolly* and the 22d MEU's brace of Marine SeaCobra attack choppers would have made its presence felt in Monrovia.

Tactical Recovery of Aircraft, Equipment, and Personnel (TRAP)

This ancillary function amounts to the Marine battle drill for combat search and rescue of downed fliers. One platoon in the BLT and a designated helo team stand by to execute TRAP during all Navy-Marine air operations over hostile territory. Marines do not leave their comrades behind. When a Marine or a Navy bird goes down, or when directed in response to any American or allied airman in distress, the TRAP team launches.

A Marine TRAP force from 24th MEU (SOC) carried out the famous Scott O'Grady pickup in Bosnia in 1995. Indicative that the TRAP iteration comes from a well-schooled playbook, the BLT 3/8 Marines turned to their battalion mortar platoon to provide the ground security component. Thanks to lots of exacting rehearsals, both before and during their deployment to the Mediterranean Sea, the mortarmen knew what to do and did it.[75] This TRAP capability cements the bond among Marine aviators and grunts. Marine airmen fly the closest close air support known. Marine riflemen come when their aviators go down. It's a partnership forged in blood.

Clandestine Recovery Operations

Sometimes, for political reasons, Marine expeditionary units must get in and out without being noticed. In this case, the MEU will conduct a variation of the TRAP profile, with emphasis on stealth. A limited objective attack or a deception raid may be part of this, to distract hostile attention from the secretive pickup of people or equipment in denied territory. If a MEU (SOC) has done this task in earnest, it has yet to be discussed in public. But the tactic remains in the bag of tricks. Some day, it will get used, even if not openly acknowledged.

Clandestine Reconnaissance and Surveillance-Counterintelligence

All that reconnaissance capacity in a MEU allows for a good look at whatever needs to be seen. Afloat, Marines can insert small teams to watch roads, ports, and airfields. Even with reliable satellite imagery and all kinds of databases, nothing beats seeing for yourself. The various brands of MEU scouts practice doing that without getting caught.

Looking is only one of their talents. When equipped with laser designators, these careful teams can spot for smart bombs. A few hidden Marine force recon men can spit invisible laser light at some hostile installation, then watch distant fighter-bombers blow down buildings one by one with unerring precision. Those inside the targeted structures never even sense death coming.

When ashore, reconnaissance continues, with an added twist. As with all good infantry in a strange place, Marines routinely patrol for information. But there is more. All that civic action stuff includes counterintelligence teams, to hear the rumors in the market and make assessments. Having relearned hard lessons in Lebanon in 1982–84, the Corps keeps its eyes and ears open. It has paid off in numerous dicey situations.

Signal Intelligence Electronic Warfare Operations

In a technical variation of the Marine passion for reconnaissance, the Marines employ various electronic collectors to listen to potential and actual foes. Every float sees some of this. Because today's commercial telecommunications can be encrypted, not to mention routinely coded military traffic, this is not an easy undertaking. The MEU (SOC) feeds to, and draws on, national-level intelligence services to supplement its own systems. It all contributes to awareness of local conditions.

The Marines do a good job of getting this information to the rifle squads. Thanks to directed monitoring of local civilian radio stations, the 0311 types on the embassy perimeter heard about the Liberian Krahn faction's unwillingness to repeat the firefights of 30 April 1996.[76] This gave an important hint of enemy intentions, and it allowed squad leaders to make some key adjustments and avoid more bloodshed through miscalculation. It offers a good example of how listening in can help.

In-extremis Hostage Rescue

This one created a lot of queasiness in the JSOC-Delta end of the galaxy. The full-time counterterrorist shooters questioned whether a bunch of Marines, no matter how good, could truly take down a building, an airplane, or a ship full of intermixed hostiles and hostages. After all, the British Special Air Service, the Israeli experts, and Delta operators find those to be daunting challenges. They select personnel carefully and train constantly to respond to those same contingencies. But to turn over a hostage rescue to a bunch of Marines? That looked like certain failure, a cure worse than the disease.

Maybe the able Delta ninjas need to brush up on their Latin. Those first two words, *in extremis*, mean "under extreme situations." In street language, that says "only if we must." If time has run out, if JSOC has gotten tied down elsewhere, the United States will send in the Marines. To date, this has not happened. But it will. And it just might work. The Marines think so, at least.

This, then, represents the MEU (SOC) menu, twenty-two tasks practiced to perfection. They can be used in various combinations or singly, as circumstances dictate. The SOC tactics are drawn from an evolving playbook heavily flavored by day-to-day experience in actually completing these missions, many of them multiple times and often with real rounds coming the other way. Headquarters, Marine Corps, spells out the standard: "A primary goal for all MEUs is certification as SOC prior to deployment."[77] And that doesn't just happen.

To earn its SOC title, a MEU trains together. Over a six-month period prior to sailing into harm's way, Marines and amphib sailors carry out a series of increasingly difficult, realistic live-fire and force-on-force exercises, culminating in a large-scale special operations capable exercise (SOCEX). Real State Department civilians, role-playing locals, skilled Marines acting as opposing-force units, and merciless observers add to the quality of the simulations. Some are carried out in actual U.S. cities. Botched tasks are rerun until everybody gets the picture. No corners are cut.

In all this, the Marines do not neglect live-fire shooting of all weapons, including air strikes and artillery. Clearing rooms gets a lot of attention. So do all kinds of demolitions. Special emphasis goes to individual marksmanship, of course.[78] Would you expect any less from the Marine Corps?

At the end of all this preparatory work, the Corps has another MEU (SOC) ready to go.[79] Three MEUs sail the world's oceans on any given day, ready to carry out one or several of their twenty-two specialties or try whatever else comes up. Admitting that, we come to the only significant drawback of these superbly packaged, well-skilled Navy-Marine combat teams.

There aren't enough of them.

This is compounded by the same sea transport that gives them their wonderful array of supplies, helicopters, and amtracs. Landing ships carry a lot, but they move at about twenty-five miles an hour at best. Crises spring up much faster. This explains why SOCEUR and some other SOF and Army units have begun to work on NEOs, too. The three Marine contingents afloat are often way out of position when the 911 call comes in.

Because speeding up ships seems unlikely in the next decade or so, maybe the answer requires more MEUs on the water. Unfortunately, it's not possible to send out more. True, Mother Corps has twenty-four infantry battalions on hand. Ground force professionals say that it takes three battalions to keep one deployed, allowing for one in a six-month train-up, one on duty, and the third in a six-month postfloat period.[80] That should allow for a maximum of eight MEUs, with the other third of the grunts either getting ready or retraining afterward. But remember, MEUs are more than 0311s.

The real crimps on MEU numbers come from the other partners. The U.S. Navy has only twelve amphibious groups, and Marine aviation can furnish but a dozen helicopter squadrons suitable to serve in the MEU stable.[81] Using the same three to one ratio, the maximum number of deployed MEUs becomes four. But that's one too many in real life.

The actual MEU count becomes three in practice. This is because, almost always, an equivalent fourth force has also been dispatched, a scratch team lacking any dedicated six-month MEU (SOC) train-up.[82] These special-purpose MAGTFs also have infantry, aviation, service support, and gator fleet ships, sometimes more than a standard MEU but usually less. Examples include SPMAGTF Carib in Haiti in 1994 and SPMAGTF Liberia in summer 1996. Although not run through the grueling SOC mill, these forces can and have executed some of the missions drawn from the twenty-two-task playbook. Trying one of the harder ones, the raid or the in-extremis hostage rescue, though, might not turn out so well for a SPMAGTF.

Today, the Marines are out there, steaming along or on the ground, ready to respond. Like the rest of America's infantry force, the Marines do not lack for dirty work. But given the trend, in not too many years all that dirty work may lack for Marines.

Notes

The epigraph is from David Browne Wood, *A Sense of Values* (Kansas City, Mo.: Andrews and McMeel, 1994), 21.

1. Cindy Shiner, "U.S. Marines Kill 3 Rebels in Monrovia," *Washington Post*, 1 May 1996, A22.

2. Gil High, "Liberia Evacuation, *Soldiers* (July 1996), 4; John W. Partin and Capt. Rob Rhoden, USAFR, *Operation Assured Response: SOCEUR's NEO in Liberia April 1996* (MacDill AFB, Fla.: United States Special Operations Command History and Research Office, September 1997), 1-2. For an overall description of Monrovia, still fairly accurate, see U.S. Department of State, *Liberia Post Report* (Washington, D.C.: U.S. Government Printing Office, March 1988), 1, 9.

3. Jon R. Anderson, "In Liberia, U.S. Dials 1-800-Marines," *Navy Times* (6 May 1996), 4.

4. High, "Liberia Evacuation," 4. For a description of ECOMOG, see U.S. Director of Intelligence, Central Intelligence Agency, *Worldwide Peackeeping Operations, 1993* (Springfield, Va.: National Technical Information Service, May 1993), entry 30.

5. President William J. Clinton, *Communication from the President of the United States to the Hon. Newt Gingrich, Speaker of the House of Representatives: Status Report on Liberia* (Washington, D.C.: The White House, 11 April 1996), 1.

6. Lieutenant Colonel T. W. Parker, USMC, "Operation SHARP EDGE," U.S. Naval Institute Proceedings (May 1991); U.S. Department of Defense, "Defense Almanac," *Defense 96* (September 1996), 41–42.

7. For a discussion of permissive versus nonpermissive NEOs, see Lt. Col. H. T. Hayden, USMC, and Lt. Col. D. R. Blankenship, USMC (Ret.), "Marine Expeditionary Unit (Special Operations Capable) (MEU [SOC])" in Lt. Col. H. T. Hayden, USMC, ed., *Shadow War* (Vista, Calif.: Pacific Aero Press, 1992), 35.

8. Ibid., 34–36; Tom Clancy, *Marine* (New York, N.Y.: Berkley Books, 1996), 240–45.

9. Clinton to Gingrich, *Status Report on Liberia,* 11 April 1996; Gen. Henry H. Shelton, USA, "When SOF Were Needed, They Were There," *Special Warfare* (December 1996), 41.

10. Napoleon Bonaparte, "Military Maxims of Napoleon" in Brig. Gen. Thomas R. Phillips, USA, *Roots of Strategy: The Five Greatest Military Classics of All Time* (Harrisburg, Pa.: Stackpole Books, 1985), 410.

11. Partin and Rhoden, *Operation Assured Response,* 6–14; interview with Lt. Col. Michael Scaparotti, USA, Carlisle Barracks, Pa., 16 October 1997; Lt. Col. Richard D. Hooker, USA, E-Mail to author, "Re: Assured Response," 14 October 1997. Lieutenant Colonel Mike Scaparotti commanded 3/325th ABCT. Major Rich Hooker served as the S-3 for the Southern European Task Force, the higher headquarters for 3/325th Infantry during Operation Assured Response, the Liberia mission. It should be noted that JTF-AR's air component eventually included MH-47E SOF Chinook helicopters of the 160th Special Operations Aviation Regiment.

12. Partin and Rhoden, *Operation Assured Response,* 20, 35.

13. Ibid., 15, 21–23, 27.

14. Ibid., 34, 36–42, 45–46; William Matthews, "Troops Aid in Liberia Crisis," *Army Times* (22 April 1996), 11; President William J. Clinton, *Communication from the President of the United States to the Hon. Newt Gingrich, Speaker of the House of Representatives: Status Report on Liberia* (Washington, D.C.: The White House, 20 May 1996), 1; Shelton, "When SOF Were Needed, They Were There," 41. Four Army SOF MH-47E Chinook helicopters of 3d Battalion, 160th Special Operations Aviation Regiment (Airborne), joined the USAF MH-53J Pave Lows on 12–19 April 1996.

15. Partin and Rhoden, *Operation Assured Response,* 24.

16. Anderson, "In Liberia, U.S. Dials 1-800-Marines," 4; Matthews, "Troops Aid in Liberia Crisis," 11.

17. Shelton, "When SOF Were Needed, They Were There," 41.

18. Partin and Rhoden, *Operation Assured Response,* 40–43; Scaparotti interview.

19. Anderson, "In Liberia, U.S. Dials 1-800-Marines," 4. For details on the Spruance-class destroyer USS *Connolly,* see Ray Bonds, ed., *The U.S. War Machine* (New York, N.Y.: Salamander Books, 1983), 138.

20. "Operation ASSURED RESPONSE: Liberia," *Marine Corps Gazette* (June 1996), 3. For ship characteristics, see Clancy, *Marine,* 156–57, 175–78, 182–83; Bonds, *The U.S. War Machine,* 146–48.

21. "Operation ASSURED RESPONSE: Liberia," 3.

22. Partin and Rhoden, *Operation Assured Response*, 46; Sgt. R. A. Smith, USMC, SSgt. Phil Mehringer, USMC, and Sgt. David J. Ferrier, USMC, "In Liberia, 'Assured Response' Came from Marine Rifles," *Leatherneck* (July 1996), 11. Both Smith and Mehringer served in Liberia with 22d MEU.

23. Smith et al., "In Liberia, 'Assured Response' Came from Marine Rifles," 11.

24. U.S. Department of State, *Liberia Post Report*, 1; Bruce Catton, *The Coming Fury* (New York, N.Y.: Washington Square Press, 1967), 86.

25. U.S. Department of the Navy, *The Navy/Marine Team: Posture Statement 1997* (Washington, D.C.: U.S. Government Printing Office, 1997), 31.

26. Anderson, "In Liberia, U.S. Dials 1-800-Marines," 4.

27. Lance Corporal Jason Angel, USMC, "Marine Exhibits Courage Under Fire," Marine Corps News Release (3 October 1997), 2–3; Maj. James Antal, USMC, *Interview of Sgt. William A. Gardner* (Camp Lejeune, N.C.: Marine Corps Oral History Program, 15 August 1996), 31–33. Gardner was a corporal at the time of the firefight.

28. Antal, *Interview of Sgt. William A. Gardner*, 14–18, 21.

29. Clinton to Gingrich, *Status Report on Liberia*, 20 May 1996, 1; Jon R. Anderson, "Marines Show Metal in African Conflicts," *Navy Times* (17 June 1996), 12; Smith et al., "In Liberia, 'Assured Response' Came from Marine Rifles," 10; Angel, "Marine Exhibits Courage under Fire," 3. For an excellent description of the Barrett sniper rifle, see Clancy, *Marine*, 77.

30. Angel, "Marine Exhibits Courage Under Fire," 3. Corporal Farrand won a Bronze Star for Valor for his actions on 30 April 1996.

31. Associated Press, "Marines Kill 3 Liberians in an Attack Near U.S. Embassy," *New York Times* (1 May 1996), A3.

32. Reuters, "Marines at U.S. Embassy Again Fire on Gunmen," *New York Times* (7 May 1996), A6.

33. Jon R. Anderson, "Covering the Gap," *Navy Times* (24 June 1996), 14.

34. Major John T. Germain, USMC, "Monrovia Revisited," *Marine Corps Gazette* (February 1997), 51; Anderson, "Marines Show Metal in African Conflicts," 13. Major John Germain served as combat cargo officer on the 22d MEU's Liberia operation.

35. Ibid.; President William J. Clinton, *Communication from the President of the United States to the Hon. Newt Gingrich, Speaker of the House of Representatives: Status Report on Activities in Bangui, Central African Republic* (Washington, D.C.: The White House, 23 May 1996), 1.

36. Sergeant Craig W. Larson, USMC, "From 'Assured' to 'Quick' Response: 22d MEU Evacuates Americans from the Central African Republic," *Leatherneck* (July 1996), 13; Anderson, "Marines Show Metal in African Conflicts," 13.

37. "22d MEU (SOC) Responds to the Call," *Marine Corps Gazette* (July 1996), 6.

38. Germain, "Monrovia Revisited," 51; Navy News Service, "Home from Liberia," *Leatherneck* (November 1996), 33.

39. Anderson, "Marines Show Metal in African Conflicts," 13.

40. For the source of this belief system, see Thomas E. Ricks, *Making the Corps* (New York, N.Y.: Scribner's, 1997), especially 132–49.

41. Colonel Robert Debs Heinl, USMC (Ret.), *Soldiers of the Sea* (Baltimore, Md.: Nautical and Aviation Publishing Co. of America, 1991), 516. General Armstrong made this quip in jest in 1949, before an Army-Navy athletic contest. Unfortunately, it ended up in the *Saturday Evening Post* and infuriated many Marines, who did not see the joke. Reporter Hanson W. Baldwin softened "bitched up" to "fouled up," at least. Almost all standard Corps histories refer to this cutting remark. Some negative U.S. Army attitudes about the Marines have persisted through World War II, Korea, Vietnam, and the Gulf War. For recent examples from the 1990–91 war against Iraq, see Michael R. Gordon and Lt. Gen. Bernard E. Trainor, USMC (Ret.), *The Generals' War* (Boston, Mass.: Little, Brown and Co., 1995), 70–74, 177–79. In fairness to all, these differences in service perspectives rarely extend to the fighting level. There, Marines and soldiers cooperate willingly.

42. All organizational data following comes from U.S. Department of the Navy, Headquarters Marine Corps, *Fleet Marine Force Organization* (Washington, D.C.: U.S. Government Printing Office, 2 March 1992), 4-6–11.

43. Clancy, *Marine*, 102–3.

44. U.S. Department of the Navy, Headquarters, Marine Corps, *FM 2-7 Fire Support in Marine Air-Ground Task Force Operations* (Wash-

ington, D.C.: U.S. Government Printing Office, 26 September 1991), 1-5–6, 4-7. Doctrinally, the battalion's weapons company comman- der runs the fire support coordination center (FSCC), and a sup- porting arms coordination center (SACC) exists only at MEU level. But practically, the weapons platoon commander does the same at company level, and all echelons refer to employing "supporting arms" to mean nonorganic firepower. Marines define supporting arms as close air support, naval gunfire, artillery, and mortars.

45. U. S. director, Marine Corps Institute, *Marine Battle Skills Training Handbook, Book I: Priviate to Gunnery Sergeant, General Mili- tary Subjects* (Washington, D.C.: U.S. Government Printing Office, January 1993), iii–xii. The U.S. Army recognizes the value of the gunnery sergeant and has experimented with similar concepts. In some Bradley companies, a master gunner fulfills much the same role as the Marine gunnery sergeant. But to date, this concept has not been widely implemented. Most master gunners work at the bat- talion level, and company master gunners are also platoon sergeants. There is no equivalent at all in nonmechanized rifle companies. By the way, the U.S. Marine term *gunner* refers not to a gunnery sergeant ("gunny") but to a warrant officer commissioned from the ranks and assigned to a fighting outfit.

46. Clancy, *Marine,* 220–22.

47. Tom Clancy, *Airborne* (New York, N.Y.: Berkley Books, 1997), xv, quotes Gen. Gary E. Luck, USA (Ret.), former JSOC and XVIII Airborne Corps commanding general, in favor of "forced entry." Navy-Marine literature generally goes with "forcible entry."

48. For one example among many, see U.S. Department of the Navy, Marine Corps Institute, *MCI 7401 Tactical Fundamentals* (Wash- ington, D.C.: Marine Corps Institute Press, 1989), 10, 12, 62–63.

49. Lately, the U.S. Marine Corps has begun to refer to the Ma- rine Expeditionary Brigade (MEB) as the Marine Expeditionary Force (Forward) (MEF-F).

50. The words of the Marines' hymn can be found in Chuck Law- less, *The Marine Book* (New York, N.Y.: Thames and Hudson, 1988), 177. The reference to the "halls of Montezuma" refers to service in the Mexican War of 1846–48. The phrase "shores of Tripoli" recalls the 1800–1805 war against the Barbary pirates in North Africa.

51. Carl Builder, *The Masks of War* (Baltimore, Md.: Johns Hopkins University Press, 1989), 132.

52. For a good description of this Army approach, see U.S. Department of the Army, *FM 71-100 Division Operations,* final approved draft (Fort Leavenworth, Kans.: Command and General Staff College, 15 November 1988), 1-1, 1-29–30, 2-1.

53. U.S. Department of the Army, *FM 100-5: Operations* (Washington, D.C.: U.S. Government Printing Office, 1993), 13-2–3. The phrase *operation other than war* (OOTW) has been replaced by the generic phrase *stability operations* in more recent doctrine.

54. Heinl, *Soldiers of the Sea,* 546–47. Truman wrote this caustic remark to Representative Gordon L. McDonough of California in 1950. The president publicly apologized to Marine commandant Gen. Clifton B. Cates. As with General Armstrong's dismissal of the Corps as "bitched-up," almost all Marine histories address this flap.

55. Agustino von Hassell, *Strike Force: U.S. Marine Corps Special Operations* (Charlottesville, Va.: Howell Press, 1991), 123–25; U.S. Department of the Navy, Headquarters Marine Corps, *Marine Corps Capabilities Plan, Volume I* (Washington, D.C.: U.S. Government Printing Office, 26 June 1992), 18; Wood, *A Sense of Values,* 61–62; Hayden and Blankenship, "Marine Expeditionary Unit (Special Operations Capable) (MEU [SOC])," 34–36; Clancy, *Marine,* 240–45. Although all sources agree on the MEU (SOC) concept, there are variations on the number of missions that make up the list. The Marine Corps Capabilities Plan lists ten, all of which can be found on the other lists. Hayden and von Hassell agree on the same eighteen tasks. Tom Clancy describes nineteen, four not described elsewhere, and three combining tasks listed separately in other references. Just to muddy the water, Wood mentions twenty-two tasks but does not include a tabulation. To ensure that all tasks are covered, I have added the unique tasks discussed only in Clancy to the eighteen described by von Hassell and Hayden. This totals twenty-two. Clearly, the exact MEU (SOC) task list evolves over time.

56. Lieutenant Colonel Michael J. Byron, USMC, "Fury from the Sea," *U.S. Naval Institute Proceedings* (May 1984), 127–29. On Grenada on 25–26 October 1983, U.S. Army troops fixed the bulk of the hostiles facing south. The 24th MEU (BLT 2/8 Marines) then landed

to the north, behind the enemy main body and their capital city. Mass surrenders followed.

57. Rick Atkinson, *Crusade* (Boston, Mass.: Houghton Mifflin Company, 1993), 240, 321–30, 405; Gordon and Trainor, *The Generals' War*, 388, 485.

58. For the most complete story of the evacuation of the U.S. Embassy in Mogadishu, see Adam B. Siegel, *Eastern Exit: The Noncombatant Evacuation Operation (NEO) from Mogadishu, Somalia in January 1991* (Alexandria, Va.: Center for Naval Analyses, October 1991). A good short summary of the O'Grady rescue is found in Clancy, *Marine*, 208–9.

59. Orr Kelly, *Brave Men, Dark Waters* (Novato, Calif.: Presidio Press, 1992), 241–43.

60. Churchill is quoted in Viktoria M. Lopatkiewicz, "Sending in the Marines . . . and Trained Civilians," *State Magazine* (September–October 1997), 17–18.

61. U.S. Department of Defense, "Defense Almanac," *Defense 96*, 41–42.

62. United Nations, *1989 Demographic Yearbook* (New York, N.Y.: United Nations Press, 1991), 521; Don Mace and Eric Yoder, *Federal Employees Almanac 1993* (Reston, Va.: Federal Employee News Service, 1993), 332; U.S. Department of Commerce, *Statistical Abstract of the United States* (Washington, D.C.: U.S. Government Printing Office, 1993), 357, 839.

63. U.S. Department of Defense, Commission on the Beirut International Airport Terrorist Act, October 23, 1983, *Report of the Department of Defense Commission on the Beirut International Airport Terrorist Act, October 23, 1983* (Washington, D.C.: U.S. Government Printing Office, 1984), 99, 106. A total of 241 died, which included 218 Marines, 18 sailors, 3 soldiers, a French paratrooper, and a Lebanese civilian. There were also 112 wounded, 80 of them seriously.

64. Marines on a security mission also shot first and asked questions later on 12 April 1988, at the Arraijan Tank Farm in Panama. See Lt. Gen. Edward M. Flanagan, USA (Ret.), *The Battle for Panama* (McLean, Va.: Brassey's [U.S.], Inc., 1993), 18–19. Postincident analysis credited the Marines with killing one or two and wounding two or three, some of them possibly Cuban special forces. In a more

recent incident, when a shepherd shot at a Marine counternarcotics surveillance post on the Texas-Mexican border, Cpl. Clemente Bañuelos and his fire team returned fire, killing the local. See William Branigin, "Questions on Military Role Fighting Drugs Ricochet from a Deadly Shot," *Washington Post* (22 June 1997), A3.

65. Wood, *A Sense of Values*, 58; Clancy, *Marine*, 248; von Hassell, *Strike Force*, 51.

66. Lieutenant Colonel William C. David, USA, *Developing a Supercharged Battalion* (Fort Drum, N.Y.: Headquarters, 10th Mountain Division, 1 June 1995), 35–36.

67. Anthony H. Cordesman and Abraham R. Wagner, *The Lessons of Modern War, Volume II: The Iran-Iraq War* (Boulder, Colo.: Westview Press, 1990), 377.

68. Tony Cappacio, "SEALs Await Call to Spot Bosnia Targets, Board Ships," *Defense Week* (12 October 1993), 1; Comdr. Massimo A. Annati, Italian Navy, "Stand By, We Are Boarding," *U.S. Naval Institute Proceedings* (March 1994), 55.

69. Captain Walter J. Wood, USMC, "Mayday for the *Mayaguez:* The Company Commander," *U.S. Naval Institute Proceedings* (November 1976), 100–101; Scott C. Truver, "Maritime Terrorism, 1985," *U.S. Naval Institute Proceedings* (May 1986), 166–67.

70. Partin and Rhoden, *Operation Assured Response*, 46.

71. John F. Morton, "The U.S. Navy in Review," *U.S. Naval Institute Proceedings* (May 1993), 125; Col. James L. Jones, USMC, "Operation Provide Comfort: Humanitarian and Security Assistance in Northern Iraq," *Marine Corps Gazette* (November 1991), 99; Lt. Col. T. A. Richards, USMC, "Marines in Somalia: 1992," *U.S. Naval Institute Proceedings* (May 1993), 133.

72. Lieutenant Colonel Andrew J. Krepinevich, USA, *The Army and Vietnam* (Baltimore, Md.: Johns Hopkins University Press, 1986), 172–77.

73. U.S. Department of the Navy, Headquarters, Marine Corps, *Small Wars Manual* (Washington, D.C.: U.S. Government Printing Office, 1940), 32.

74. Coverage in many Third World areas is particularly spotty. For one division's experience with GPS in the Gulf War, see Thomas Taylor, *Lightning in the Storm* (New York, N.Y.: Hippocrene Books, 1994),

273–75, 297. For other, similar accounts of GPS problems, see Carsten Stroud, *Iron Bravo* (New York, N.Y.: Bantam Books, 1995), 261, and Capt. Dominic J. Caraccilo, USA, *The Ready Brigade of the 82d Airborne in Desert Storm* (Jefferson, N.C.: McFarland and Company, Inc., Publishers, 1993), 157–58.

75. Clancy, *Marine*, 208–9, 237–39.

76. Antal, *Interview of Sgt. William A. Gardner*, 22–23.

77. Headquarters, Marine Corps, *Marine Corps Capabilities Plan, Volume I*, 17–18.

78. Lopatkiewicz, "Sending in the Marines . . . and Trained Civilians," 17–18; Clancy, *Marine*, 248–49; Wood, *A Sense of Values*, 70–78. Lopatkiewicz describes her experience as a State Department role player in a mock NEO. Clancy offers an excellent overview of 26th MEU's preparation for a 1995–96 float. Wood describes a 24th MEU urban warfare training event at Camp Lejeune's Combat Town. All accounts stress the integration of civilians (real and role players) and the emphasis on city fighting. Clancy and Wood also address live-fire portions.

79. The standing MEU headquarters are 11th, 13th, and 15th affiliated with I Marine Expeditionary Force (I MEF) at Camp Pendleton, Calif.; the 22d, 24th, and 26th tied to II MEF at Camp Lejeune, N.C.; and the 31st from III MEF on Okinawa. Only three are at sea under normal circumstances; the others are in various stages of preparation or recovery.

80. U.S. Department of the Army, *United States Army Posture Statement FY 98: Soldiers Are Our Credentials* (Washington, D.C.: U.S. Government Printing Office, February 1997), 42.

81. U.S. Chairman of the Joint Chiefs of Staff, *National Military Strategy of the United States of America* (Washington, D.C.: U.S. Government Printing Office, 1997), 23.

82. Headquarters, Marine Corps, *Marine Corps Capabilities Plan, Volume I*, 11.

Epilogue: The Last Riflemen

They have yet to make a jet fighter-bomber with a bayonet stud.
—Col. Walter B. Clark, Infantry, U.S. Army

The Iraqis started the battle by surrendering.

Just before last light on 29 January 1991, U.S. Marines manning Outpost 8 (OP-8) watched three bedraggled privates trudge slowly down the coast road, hands up. One waved the obligatory white flag. The trio stopped to check in, well aware of the protocol for quitting. The Iraqis definitely knew that drill. When an Arabic speaker in OP-8 queried the three, the men announced that they had come south because their officers had fled north, spooked by the Coalition's massive bombing effort.[1] The Marines briefly held the Iraqis at the two-story cement customs post commandered from the Saudis for border surveillance, then packed them into a desert-tan Humvee for transport to the rear. There, the three reluctant warriors joined their several fellows in a Saudi Arabian prisoner compound.

With any other opponent, that kind of episode might have seemed strange, but not with these people. A steady trickle of line crossers conditioned the border outposts to this kind of behavior. Iraqis began giving up almost as soon as the Americans reached the border back in late summer 1990. Now, with the bombing in its twelfth day and no letup in sight, the number of quitters skyrocketed. This latest encounter amounted to more of the same.

The enemy soldiers stepped out from the nearest known Iraqi troop concentrations, a screen of small teams occupying camouflaged bunkers strung along the international boundary. Previous defections originated farther north, among the main belts of dug-in Iraqi infantry formations. A few even came from the mobile armored brigades backing up those defenses. An inventory of the Coalition

296

POW cages nicely reflected the array opposite the Americans and their Arab associates, with the closer outfits more heavily represented. The Iraqi defensive laydown was leaking men from the bottom, more every day that the rain of bombs continued. This most recent Iraqi threesome entered Coalition lines, such as they were, through what would have been called no-man's-land in World War I. Out west, such deserters usually met vigilant United States Marines patrolling along the international boundary aboard their speedy light-armored vehicles. But the LAVs did not run in this lonely stretch. Here along the Persian Gulf, the main Coalition defensive positions lay almost thirty miles to the south of the Kuwaiti border. In this area, empty desert—no-man's-land—had to be crossed.

Of course, as in World War I, the evocative term did not match reality. As the Iraqis knew well, there were Americans in places such as OP-8—not many, but the sort who promised results out of proportion to their numbers. From north to south these included Army Special Forces and Navy SEALs across the border in occupied Kuwait; Marines of the 1st Surveillance, Reconnaissance, and Intelligence Group (1st SRIG) holding OP-7 and OP-8 on the international boundary; various SEAL-SF forward operations cells in and around the abandoned coastal town of Ras Al Khafji; and a smattering of Saudi-Qatari elements to provide early warning and show Arab flags. Then there was a yawning gap of open desert, backstopped by the only significant ground contingent, 3d Marine Regiment's Task Force Taro.[2] In American military terminology, this region allowed for economy of force, a secondary effort to free up troops for more vital commitments elsewhere.

It all made good tactical sense. The Coalition had plenty of work to do well to the west. No American commanders wanted—or expected—a major fracas here on the coast. So a buffer zone in this locale served to absorb whatever the Iraqis might have in mind, so far mostly surrendering, plus a few odd artillery harassing rounds. This diddling hurt nothing. After all, Saudi Arabia had plenty of desert to spare.

This unimportant stretch, unlikely to be struck, made a good parking lot for the suspect brigades of America's Arab allies. On the big

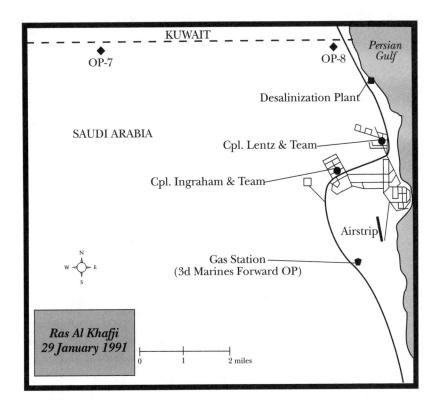

KUWAIT

OP-7

OP-8

Persian Gulf

Desalinization Plant

SAUDI ARABIA

Cpl. Lentz & Team

Cpl. Ingraham & Team

Airstrip

N
W — E
S

Gas Station
(3d Marines Forward OP)

*Ras Al Khafji
29 January 1991*

0   1   2 miles

charts at U.S. Central Command, the area around empty Khafji belonged to Joint Forces Command—East, an impressive name for a
rather unimpressive collection of unblooded Saudi Arabian and Gulf
Arab units. Nobody seriously expected these people to fight.[3] Thus,
in reality, the Khafji neighborhood belonged to less than a hundred
elite Americans. Their main job was to contain any Iraqi effort without disturbing or drawing in other American ground units. Although all hoped that the Arabs would do their part, any serious
shooting to be done here depended upon Americans staying at their
posts and bringing down the thunder of allied airpower from the
night skies.

The Americans began yet another typical evening by delivering a
dose of that fire from above. At about 2000, Marine air–naval gun-

fire spotters attached to 1st SRIG detected some Iraqi artillery moving into a shooting configuration just across the border. Captain Douglas Kleinsmith and his men called in an air strike. Marine A-6E Intruder jets responded, racing into enemy airspace to knock out the Iraqi howitzers. The horizon lit up with bomb bursts. Secondary explosions rumbled across the dark desert for ten minutes thereafter. The pilots claimed to have knocked out at least two 152mm pieces.[4] Nobody at OP-8 thought much of the engagement. That sort of thing happened a lot up there. Kleinsmith and his crew had done it before and fully expected to do it again.

About an hour went by with nothing else from the Iraqis. Then, peering through night-vision scopes, the Americans saw something new. It got everyone's attention.

Emerging out of the darkness, a long file of enemy tanks rumbled south on the coast road. Nobody had seen this kind of display in previous scraps. What did it mean?

The Americans scanned carefully, trying to divine the enemy's intentions. The Iraqi armor showed as shadowy blobs in the greenish viewers of the starlight scopes and as white-hot—or black-hot, depending on the setting selected—geometric forms in the thermal devices. Based on previous training and experience, the Marines agreed that the lead hostiles looked like T-55s, old Russian-made tanks sporting 100mm main guns, plus the requisite suite of machine guns.

In a minute, they convinced one another of what they saw: more folks ready to throw in the towel, and in a big way. The Iraqi T-55 tanks motoring along the coastal highway had their turrets facing backward, a time-honored signal of surrender. Flat-topped, low Chinese-model Type-63 armored infantry carriers followed behind the first several tanks. It looked like a mass capitulation.[5] Maybe those three privates who had surrendered earlier had the picture. Perhaps the Iraqi leadership really had skipped town, and now the lower ranks were voting with their feet—or treads, to be precise.

The Marines held their fire. No one wanted to cause an unfortunate incident. Some Americans began to call in reports, alerting the 3d Marines to expect a lot of prisoners. The enemy armor continued to roll, closing steadily on the silent American-held outpost.

A flare went up from the lead tank, then another: red, then green. Uh-oh, that did not look quite right. Kleinsmith and his men exchanged glances. Something definitely felt wrong about this.

Yellow stars blossomed suddenly over the coast road as unseen Iraqi artillery batteries popped open parachute flares to light the way for their comrades. Illuminated by the pale saffron glow aloft, the enemy T-55s spun their turrets. Big 100mm cannons barked, and machine guns began to stutter. This was no surrender, not at all. These guys were attacking.

Looking west, Kleinsmith and his men saw more flares floating above OP-7. The radios crackled with contact reports. Well to the west, the Marines in their LAVs described additional major firefights with Iraqi armor. Calls for air support and artillery fire came from all stations.

Dozens of Iraqi armored vehicles closed on the little border station of OP-8. The enemy fired indiscriminately, rounds pinging off the outpost's cement walls. Four men of SEAL Team One, who shared the OP with Kleinsmith's Marine observers, moved outside to the roadbed to get a closer look at the foe. They got that in spades.

Pharmacist Mate 3d Class Joe Baxter and his teammates huddled in the roadside ditch. Baxter held a loaded 40mm grenade launcher, and his partners carried throwaway AT-4 antitank rockets. All four took aim at likely targets.

They could have done some damage, and they knew it. Baxter later wrote that "tracers as big as beer bottles were zipping right over our heads, but we knew they [the Iraqis] couldn't see our camouflaged bodies. If we fired back, it was sure to bring a hail of devastating fire directly into us."[6] With the Marines in the tower to consider, and with the certain knowledge that their show of resistance would likely be futile, the Navy special operators stayed concealed and let these angels of death pass by.

Save for the unfocused Iraqi shooting, the column ignored the SEALs and the little OP. When it looked as though the enemy column had passed, Kleinsmith and his men, including Baxter's quartet, piled into their Humvees. Wisely ignoring the coastal highway; the Marines bounced out into the desert, heading south for Khafji.

Kleinsmith and his partners wanted to get to a designated linkup point at the town's water tower. Little did they realize that the Iraqi armored force had the exact same destination.

Five miles to the west, the neighbors out at OP-7 also prepared to pull back, but not before calling in night-capable Marine AH-1W Sea-Cobra attack choppers. The U.S. spotters counted some twenty-five enemy vehicles in their vicinity, all streaming south toward Khafji. They hunkered down in their little concrete border fort and guided in the Marine helos.

Four SeaCobras flew out to support OP-7, led by Maj. Michael Steele. They roared in less than fifty feet off the black desert floor, passing over OP-7, looking for targets. Their voices calm and busi-nesslike—amazingly so, given their isolation and peril—Marine ob-servers pointed the arriving helicopters in the right direction.

About a mile north of Khafji, Steele and his wingmen found their quarry. Six squat Type 63s waited, engines running, crewmen milling around, utterly unsuspecting. The little cupola hatches with their long black 12.7mm heavy machine guns stood unmanned. The Ma-rine fliers tilted forward and opened up.

Steele's 5-inch Zuni rocket gutted one of the troop carriers, tear-ing it open in a bright flash. The other vehicles scattered, three flee-ing south, two circling their stricken comrade. The Iraqis fired back, not with particular skill but with enthusiasm. More U.S. rockets and 20mm chain guns answered. Steele thought his men nailed another Type 63 before the SeaCobras broke off.[7] It seemed a small stroke, but it underscored an important characteristic of the battle. Each little U.S. team felt obliged to call in some firepower. A self-propelled gun lost here, an armored troop transport lost there, and over the hours the toll mounted. The Iraqis began to suffer the first of a thou-sand cuts, courtesy of rampaging American airmen above and a handful of stoic men on the ground.

That certainly happened when the enemy armor banged into the next major clot of Americans. A mile or so down the coast, OP-8's first warnings alerted the mixed bag of twenty-odd SEALs, Green Berets, and Marines working at the desalinization plant. While some of the special operators frantically scooped up cryptological gear, se-cret documents, and maps showing cross-border missions involving the Kuwaiti resistance, others moved outside to confront the enemy armored thrust. It arrived within minutes, as advertised.

As they had done at the border OPs, the T-55s pushed on, oblivious to the dark figures moving around the periphery of the desalinization plant. Finally, one of the trailing mounted infantry elements took some interest in one group of Americans.

As a few flat-topped Type-63 personnel carriers raced by, one Iraqi in his little cupola sighted Marines and SEALs at the roadside. Without even asking his driver to slow down, the enemy gunner casually sprayed machine-gun bullets at the Americans lying prone about fifty yards away. The wild burst dug up sand and dirt to no effect. One Marine fired back with an M-203 40mm grenade launcher, but he missed, too. The Iraqi armor pressed on, ignoring the U.S. teams.

The SEALs made the Iraqis pay for their cavalier attitude. Using superb SOF radios and hand-held compact laser designators (CLDs) to mark targets, these Navy special warfare men called in some night-rigged A-10A Warthogs. As the Marines, Army SF teams, and other SEALs packed quickly to move south, the SEALs guided in a relay of Air Force jets. This violent sequence nicely covered the American extraction back to Khafji, to that same water tower assembly point sought by Doug Kleinsmith. A SEAL summarized it bluntly: "The A-10s just ate them up."[8]

The various Americans filtered into their predesignated assembly point near the Khafji water tower. The senior man, Lt. Col. Richard M. Barry of the 1st SRIG, knew that he might not have much time to get organized. He sent Capt. Jon Fleming and another Marine officer to the top of the eight-story structure to try to find the approaching Iraqis. Fleming and his buddy reached the upper deck and looked north.

It looked bad indeed. More than ten Iraqi T-55 tanks, with at least as many Type 63s right on their tails, had reached the northern edge of town. The enemy vehicles randomly shot up each building as they approached. Green tracers skipped off rooftops and careened off walls and paved streets. In between these bright sparks hung four or more unseen slugs. Fleming knew that staying on the exposed tower, not to mention in Khafji, probably meant death. He reported as much to Barry.

Rick Barry faced a hard decision. He had not accounted for all his men, let alone the SEALs and the Green Berets. The Arab allies, of course, had long since headed south at maximum speed. If Barry had time to burrow into the woodwork, he might well have stayed in Khafji to direct air strikes and artillery fires. But caught like this, on the run, with a bunch of enemy tanks nipping at their heels pretty much ruled out remaining in town. If Barry left now, he could call in one more air attack and save about thirty Americans for sure. The rest, the ones not here, knew how to get back on their own. They had rehearsed the withdrawal scheme in the past. If any of them expected to make it till morning, Barry could not wait. He chose the lesser of two evils and pulled the plug.

Called back suddenly, Fleming and his associate pounded back down the metal stairs. The first few Marine light trucks had already started south, with the Iraqi tanks crossing the causeway just north of the water tower. With no time to spare, Fleming and his fellow Marine leapt into a waiting Humvee[9] and sped off. A parting air strike call marked their departure.

Behind them, under the bombs on inbound U.S. aircraft, Barry and Fleming and their men left the advanced guard of Iraq's 5th Mechanized Infantry Division. The enemy held Khafji.

But holding a place and keeping a place are two different things. Yes, the Iraqis had about a brigade's worth of tanks and infantry carriers in a Saudi Arabian town. But unknown to Saddam Hussein's exultant warriors, they had company.

Some of that company did its duty far from Ras Al Khafji. American stay-behinds worked in the black world of clandestine cross-border operations. These SEALs and Green Berets aided Kuwait's resistance and did double duty calling in air strikes, along with teams sent in expressly to mark targets for American warplanes. These small elements ensured that the Iraqi forces trying to reinforce Khafji never got there. Their superb spotting gutted most of the Iraqi 5th Mechanized Division's follow-on echelon, along with the enemy's 1st Mechanized and 3d Armored Divisions. Intensified bombing and strafing in southeastern Iraq ravaged all three enemy formations. Some accounts also credited overhead radar imaging from specially outfitted aircraft, roaming drones with recon cameras, and other such useful gadgets.[10] But men on the ground, skilled SOF types, did all the heavy lifting. Their consistent reporting and targeting calls allowed the Coalition air armada to cut off the Iraqis that made it to Khafji.

In the town itself, two Marine recon teams remained in hiding. Inserted by Col. John H. Admire, commander of the 3d Marine Regiment, the pair of six-man elements went to Khafji before the Iraqi attack. They had been sent in to provide early warning for the main body of Marines defending to the south, a normal precaution in a security zone. More such scouts would be found closer to the major Marine battle positions. But out here in SOF and Arab land, two teams seemed like a reasonable investment.

The two recon outfits divided the little built-up area, coordinating their coverage before the Iraqis attacked. Corporal Lawrence Lentz's group had been in the empty village about six days, holed up in an unfinished two-floor building in the northeast corner of Khafji. Corporal Charles Ingraham and his five men came in on 28 January. They chose a four-story edifice in the southern half of town, overlooking the main street. Both young team leaders could have gotten out with Barry's Marines, the SEALs, and the rest. "I'm leaving it up to you," the 3d Marines' recon commander stated by radio as the Iraqi tanks clanked into town. Lentz did not hesitate. "We'll stay," he said.[11]

That gutsy decision doomed the Iraqi conquerors of Khafji. A more able infantry outfit would have searched the buildings on 30 January to clear out U.S. holdouts such as Lentz and Ingraham. But the Iraqis did not bother. They paid for their incompetence.

The two teams remained undetected for about a day and a half. They alternated calling for jets, armed helos, and artillery, peppering the Iraqi tanks and armored vehicles parked haphazardly in and among the ghost town's buildings. To the enemy, it must have appeared as though the Americans had precision strike systems, because missiles and bombs and shells screaming in from distant sites always looked to be on the mark. Iraqi leaders credited satellites, infrared snoopers, and similar high technology, not considering that the source of their torment hid in their midst.

Charles Ingraham had the only close call, about noon on 30 January. A squad of Iraqi riflemen entered the lobby on the ground floor. The Americans could see the green domed metal helmet tops clustered near the doorway and hear the lilting Arabic phrases. Its engine growling, a Type-63 personnel carrier waited in the street. The bad guys were looking for food, loot, or both as they wandered around the first floor. Their clomping boots echoed in the empty rooms.

Ingraham and his men coolly turned to their best weapons, their radios. "I called in artillery and close air support," Ingraham wrote later. "On one of the artillery missions, my assistant team leader got hit by shrapnel." The Marines brought the rounds in danger close, gunner parlance for right on top of the Americans. It worked. The Iraqis scuttled out, some howling, others tearing off across the street. Some fell to the bursting shells and bombs. A few made it into the nearby troop transport, which gunned its motor and drove off.[12] Ingraham and company could breathe again.

Larry Lentz also kept Marine artillerymen and U.S. aviators busy. One mission wrecked one of Iraq's prized Brazilian-model Astros II multiple rocket launcher. Another hammered an enemy ten-man foot patrol, tossing these unfortunates off the long causeway that connected the north part of town to the south.[13] Like Ingraham, Lentz put an orange VS-17 identification panel on his rooftop observation post. American pilots could easily pick out the two friendly buildings. Everything else became fair game.

While Ingraham and Lentz killed Iraqis, the Coalition prepared a counterattack. Marine colonel John Admire wanted to do it with his own superb 3d Marines, led by the LAVs, American tanks, and Marine riflemen of TF Taro. But this area belonged to Joint Forces Command-East, the Saudis and their Gulf Arab friends. If the Americans went ahead and retook Ras Al Khafji, that promised long-term repercussions in the fragile American-Arab alliance, the key to the whole polyglot anti-Iraq Coalition. It was high time to let the Saudi military earn its pay. Trusting in his two young corporals to do their part, Admire chose to let the Saudis carry the ball, "one of the most difficult decisions" he ever made.[14] To their credit, the Saudi commanders pledged to attack as soon as possible to rescue the two plucky Marine recon teams, not to mention ejecting the noxious Iraqis from the kingdom's holy soil.

After their fashion, the Saudi Arabian National Guard's King Abdul Azziz Brigade went into battle. It rumbled forward about 1700 on 30 January, its thirty or so V-150 armored wheeled scout cars led by twenty-two Qatari tanks. The brigade got as far as the gas station two miles south of town, where it met the advanced parties of the 3d Battalion, 3d Marines. They halted there for several hours to coordinate supporting fires, to be provided by the Americans through the good offices of attached American Marine observer teams and U.S. Army advisers of both conventional and SF flavors.

Sometime around 2300, with supporting fires still pretty well balled up as the Americans attempted to discern the somewhat confused Saudi plan, the attack started anyway. Saudi V-150 armored wheeled cars blithely outran the Qatari AMX-30 French-built tanks. They almost left behind several American liaison teams, among them the vital air and artillery spotters. The 3d Marines' watch center warned Lentz and Ingraham to take cover, good advice under the circumstances.

Without much evident organization, the whole blob of attacking vehicles rammed into Khafji. Larry Lentz and his men watched the Saudis blazing away, a vigorous fusillade matched and exceeded by the Iraqis. The lattice of red and green tracers reminded some Americans of a poorly run two-way night firing range, lots of noise generated and ammunition expended but few hits. Like most soldiers new to battle, both sides shot high and outside, inflicting casualties more due to volume than accuracy. By 0320, the Saudis pulled back to the edge of town, ready to pick up the fight after daybreak.[15] The Iraqis kept Khafji.

Although forced to stay at altitude by the wild crisscrossing web of tracers, American airpower kept up the pressure, steered by Lentz and Ingraham and their indefatigable partners. Artillery missions also continued, but the American airpower truly made its presence felt. The fliers had a field day, pounding the Iraqis in Khafji and all of their follow-on echelons strung back across the border. "It's almost like you flipped on the light in the kitchen late at night and the cockroaches started scurrying, and we're killing them," commented one Marine aviator.[16] Indeed they were.

The Iraqis finally achieved some measure of revenge early on 31 January, when a big, unmaneuverable AC-130H Spectre gunship stayed aloft too long after sunrise. During the night, two other Spectres tore up an eight-vehicle Iraqi column caught on the highway north of Khafji. Arriving just before dawn, this third ship started doing especially good work. The 105mm cannon, 40mm light cannon, and 20mm Gatling guns ripped up Iraqi vehicles stalled along the coastal road. Ground observers, likely SEALs near OP-8, tried to vector the Spectre toward a suspected enemy rocket launcher. The sun came up while the gunship hunted the elusive target. They should have turned for home, too vulnerable in daylight, but this Spectre crew wanted that rocket launcher, and so it kept flying. For a while, they got away with it.

Normally, riches could come to those who banked on Iraqi passivity and ineptitude. But this time, the bad guys proved able enough. An enemy shoulder-fired missile smacked into the AC-130H's left wing at 0623. The hit ignited fuel, and the plane shuddered. With a slow, ugly shrug, the big converted transport rolled over and plunged into the Persian Gulf. All fourteen aboard died.[17] It hurt, all right, but it did not stop the pressure from American air.

The Saudis resumed their attack about two hours after the Spectre went down. In daytime, the Saudi National Guardsmen and their Qatari allies managed to come to close quarters with the Iraqis. Tank fire and machine-gun rounds chewed up buildings, though the inexperienced Saudi infantry proved understandably reluctant to dismount. They suffered for that hesitation. Sixteen died when two thin-skinned V-150s exploded, one peeled open by a T-55's 100mm cannon, the other ripped apart by a volley of rocket-propelled grenades, those same ever-present RPGs fated to wreck the hopes of TF Ranger on a future long afternoon in Mogadishu. The roiling, inexpert urban scrum resembled a finish fight between the Keystone Kops and the Marx brothers, but nobody was playing it for laughs, least of all the poor soldiers getting killed as they learned and relearned the basics of street fighting.

Having seen enough of Saudi combat skill the night before, Ingraham elected not to wait for rescue by the allies. Instead, the corporal took advantage of the tumultuous tank battle. Around midmorning, he and his five men grabbed an orange VS-17 panel, the better to ward off overeager Saudi V-150 gunners. Weapons in hand, the Marines headed south on foot, weaving through the smoky, bullet-pocked streets. Ingraham's account downplays the team's skillful movement through the chaos.

> We escaped, linked up, extracted when the Saudis and their V-150s were just on the outskirts of the city. Either an Iraqi tank or APC [armored personnel carrier] was burning on the side of the building when we hit the street. The smoke and secondary explosions from it helped to cover our egress. We were very, very, very lucky throughout the whole ordeal.[18]

Charles Ingraham brought in all his men and caught a ride back with the Saudis. A few hours later, Larry Lentz also left. Lentz and his men had to shoot an Iraqi sniper on their way out, but M-16A2 rifle fire and two M-72A2 light antitank weapon 66mm rockets resolved that annoyance. Lentz actually drove out in his team's overloaded Humvee, battered, holed, and with tires shredded flat. About 1300, they finally met fellow Americans at the gas station south of town held by the 3d Marines.[19] Lentz, too, got all his men out without injury.

The Saudis and Qataris fought all day and into the next day, too, and finally took Khafji. Their effort earned some genuine respect from the Americans. At some cost, the Saudis had kept their word, and they had learned something about modern war.[20] But all involved knew who really won the clash at the border town.

American firepower, especially its air component, reigned supreme. Almost every American team in the Khafji fight brought in strikes, including those that displaced to the south. The stay-behinds outdid themselves. Guided by skilled SOF and Marine observers, men such as Larry Lentz and Charles Ingraham kept up the hammering day and night. The Iraqis cracked under the beating, and in a politically useful gesture, Saudis and Qataris gained credit for the denouement.

Postwar analysis reflected more than a thousand air sorties engaged in and around Khafji from 29 January through 1 February 1991. Marine Corps AV-8B Harrier II jump jets flew more missions than at any time except during the later ground campaign. Air Force A-10A Warthogs flew a staggering 293 sorties on 30 January alone, a performance not exceeded even in the ground phase of Desert Storm. Intelligence bean counters later assessed the total damage to be 377 tanks, 233 armored personnel carriers, and 397 artillery pieces. This essentially finished off the three Iraqi divisions staged for the Khafji incursion.[21] Although pilot claims must be taken with a grain of salt, even in this age of spy satellites and bombsight video-tapes, American warbirds certainly inflicted terrific carnage in the border battle.

To paraphrase the end of *King Kong*, it looked as though the air-planes got them. That in fact amounted to the verdict on the entire Gulf War. Most military pundits and defense experts sniffed a revo-lution in military affairs.[22] It looked, smelled, and sounded like that American holy grail, war without infantry and, hence, without casu-alties. All of that would have been news to Larry Lentz and Charles Ingraham, among others. But lacking doctorates in security studies, they were not consulted.

They should have been consulted, along with all the other Army 11B10s and Marine 0311s who knew better. Instead, many senior de-fense leaders, both in and out of uniform, seized on Khafji as the shape of things to come. Faced with an avowed requirement to stop a conventional invasion of an allied state in the Persian Gulf or Ko-rea, they found the events of 29 January to 1 February 1991 mighty appealing: a few Americans with good radios and stout hearts, lots of nifty satellites and loitering radar planes, a huge covey of jets, a mountain of ordnance, some of it brilliantly precise, and . . . *wham!* Scratch three hostile heavy divisions. We even let the junior Coali-tion partners police up the mess, good for the morale of all.

This is not some casual musing, either. The United States has be-gun to reshape its forces to re-create Khafji on a theater scale, should Iraq, Iran, or North Korea come calling.[23] Given that only the 82d Airborne and 101st Airborne ready brigades, the Rangers, a Ma-rine expeditionary unit, and assorted SOF can reach any war zone in days, how can a big enemy armored offensive be stopped quickly? The answer seems obvious. Consider this recent statement by Gulf

War air commander Gen. Charles A. Horner: "Because it demonstrated what airpower can do to an attacking armored force in a halt
phase scenario, I believe Khafji, though largely overlooked, was the
single most important land battle of Desert Storm."[24]

Once you do the big Khafji, the bad guys grind to a halt. Then,
as Air Force Maj. Gen. Charles D. Link suggests, "the ground war becomes an option rather than an inevitability."[25] It's sort of like the
world's most awesome artillery preparation, so good and so precise
that it just breaks the bad guys' will and leaves them blubbering in
their shattered, fuel-starved vehicles. Well, maybe. . . .

That all works, provided the enemy agrees to serve as a tethered
goat and not fight back all that much, and that the terrain and
weather make it easy to find the bad guys. The Iraqis surely proved
inordinately cooperative. Not all foes or climes so neatly match that
intriguing version of today's American way of war.

We have heard this siren song before, during the original revolution in military affairs, the Soviet Army's name for the changes in warfare caused by the introduction of nuclear weaponry. The nukes
meant no more infantry, no more mess and fuss, death from above.
So we heard back in 1945, after Hiroshima and Nagasaki burned. Instead, the United States inherited two big, dirty Asian wars that swal-
lowed riflemen like Moloch, not to mention a plethora of lesser interventions, evacuations, incidents, and accidents that also demanded
men with hand weapons, grenades, and bayonets. And then, just to
be fair, along with their own share of minor actions, the Soviets stumbled into a gut-shooting horror show in Afghanistan that contributed
mightily to the ultimate demise of the USSR. The great hydrogen
bombs have yet to be used in anger. Some revolution, huh?

Now the snake-oil salesmen are at the door again, this time hawk-
ing precision strike, victory through airpower. In our lust to get
"more bang for the buck"—in former Secretary of Defense "Engine"
Charlie Wilson's crass but oh so accurate phrasing—we can hardly
wait to buy another round. Nobody wants to pay for any infantry. Let
the airplanes do it.

But there is a flaw in this seductive line. Even at Khafji, the bombs
killed effectively because a few men, several very young indeed, had
the moral fiber to stand their ground and guide them in. Larry Lentz

did his grim work as personally as if using a rifle, albeit a big one. Few though they were, America's infantry was in and around Khafji and, even more important, nearby in numbers sufficient to pull the situation out of the hopper if everything went completely to hell. What will happen in a future war when, with only the wonderful warplanes, we bomb and bomb and the enemy does not crack?

Then the United States may learn that there can be worse things than dead riflemen—and we will have plenty of them, too. The United States went there before, in summer 1950 in Korea.[26] Sad to say, the country seems to be headed in the same direction again.

In a noble, worthy attempt to limit losses in some future war, the United States has chosen to trim the strength of those most likely to suffer, the infantry.[27] We will send bullets, not men. It may make us feel good, but when push comes to shove, somebody will have to go toe to toe with the North Koreans, the Chinese, the Russians, or the sub-Saharan African militiamen. The Iraqis or some other ill-trained rabble may fold without much of a fight, but others have not and will not. Task Force Ranger learned that lesson again in Mogadishu.

Infantrymen do not lack for employment, even as the United States tries to substitute other means for young men with rifles. America's ninety-one Regular infantry battalions stay busy, in Haiti, Bosnia, the Korean DMZ, Saudi Arabia, Kuwait, and Panama, plus afloat in amphibious shipping or on strip alert at Fort Bragg, Fort Campbell, and so on. Of course, during and in between all this, they must constantly train for battle. The skills that impelled the 2d of the 14th Infantry through the dark, deadly backstreets of Mogadishu take work to acquire and more work to keep. This effort sometimes obscures what has happened to the force as a whole. Only American enemies can draw comfort from these sobering developments.

One can argue historical realities and talk military common sense, but the trends do not lie. American infantry diminishes in number almost on an annual basis. Current recruitment data doesn't show that downward slide turning around.[28] Raising new battalions seems to be out of the question, though European brigades want some light-fighters to round out their Bradley-borne ranks. At this point, most Army infantrymen would gladly settle for the robust thirteen-man rifle squad that characterizes their Marine Corps brothers.[29] They will not get it under any known plans.

What infantry the United States disposes has been stretched tight, all right. Both stateside airborne divisions and both Marine divisions get by without a battalion or two, deployed to peace operations for the Army or afloat with a MEU for the Marines. The mechanized and armored divisions often have a battalion TF training in Kuwait and doing their bit to keep Iraq at bay. Rarely are all the infantry units of a division on the same post at the same time, even in the vaunted 82d Airborne. There's simply too much demand and too little supply.

Defense analysts do not let these conditions ruffle them. After all, with America's fine air and sea transports, the far-flung battalions can be quickly recalled for a major war. The air barons will hold back the hostiles while the legions assemble. Hell, they might just wrap the thing up before the groundlings show up. That sounds good, and it better be. The United States has not sent many riflemen to hold a line in the dirt until the cavalry gets there.

In the current priority confrontation, the ongoing conflict with Iraq, America's forward-deployed ground forces consist of a single airborne or air assault infantry battalion: two rifle companies, and a small headquarters guarding key facilities. True, Army mechanized and tank TFs often serve in Kuwait under the Intrinsic Action series of maneuvers. In the same vein, MEUs routinely sail into the Persian Gulf to conduct mock landings.[30] But by any count, at most three battalions of Americans guard this contested frontier. It seems pretty damn lean on the ground for an unfinished war.

Consider the ground forces earmarked to defend the Republic of Korea, where an uneasy armistice has persisted since 1953. Many Americans might find it odd that the only Army division in Korea fields only four infantry battalions, 10 percent of their ranks rounded out with specially chosen South Korean soldiers.[31] This dearth of Yankee infantry seems surprising in a land of switchback ridges and steep hills, not to mention an implacable enemy with hundreds of thousands of riflemen and almost fifty years of causing cross-border trouble. It's not as though everything went swimmingly in 1950–53 for the United States, either.

Worse, the American backup forces for a Korean flareup also lack rifle punch. The 3d Marine Division on Okinawa has only three battalions borrowed from the 1st Marine Division, plus a string on three more in far-off Hawaii. Also based in distant Hawaii, the Army's 25th Infantry Division (Light) has nine battalions of grunts, but three of those live at Fort Lewis, Washington.[32] It's a shell game in a certain sense. United States military leaders place enormous faith in our sensors and firepower, and the redoubtable South Koreans, to even the odds. American riflemen had better be good, because they will be seriously outnumbered.

Acknowledging that there will be fewer of them, what kind of infantrymen will the United States have in the twenty-first century? The tendencies here are most interesting. They are tied directly to technology. As the average rifleman said en route to Korea in 1950, it's largely "have-a-no."

The slick publication *Joint Vision 2010* touts the future of America's armed forces. The booklet overflows with precision strike, widgets and gadgets, eyes in space, and brilliant munitions shooting down the chimney. A few guys with rifles are shown in the color pictures, but the fine print reveals that the infantry has not been invited to the party. Well, maybe a few spotters or victory verifiers, as at Khafji—that might be acceptable.[33] But anyone trying to discern a role for airborne, air assault, Ranger, mechanized, light, or Marine outfits might well die of eyestrain looking for it. It's just not there.

The Army has tried to do something. Trees have been killed and electrons rearranged attempting to gussy up a rifleman to run around on the future mega-Khafji battlefield. Known variously as Soldier Integrated Protective Environmental System, Land Warrior, and Soldier Enhancement Program, and colloquially as the "Starship Trooper" rig (with apologies to Robert A. Heinlein), endeavors to equip our lad for twenty-first-century warfare have been carried out by Army and industry scientists and engineers. The results are a cyborg, a half-man, half-machine swathed in nightscopes, laser range finders, "heads-up" eyepiece position displays, chemical protective overclothes, body armor, and a mouth-mike radio. This fellow is crowned with a helmet bearing various sensors; he carries a firearm roughly the size and shape of a small unmounted sump pump. On his back hangs a unit about the size of a lawn-mower engine; it is intended to broadcast his location, verified by GPS satellite. This guy could see at night, shoot around corners, and survive in a cloud of nerve gas with his protective mask on.[34] Of course, wearing gear equal to his body weight—and we have yet to add ammo, water, and all the stuff that already equals his body weight—this new model grunt might not be able to take more than two or three steps before keeling over like an upended cockroach, limbs wigwagging weakly.

The expense, complication, and impracticality of this approach require no further discussion. Pieces of it will likely find their way into the ranks, like the immensely useful AN/PAQ-4C night "death dot" aiming laser that allows a soldier wearing night-vision goggles to hit targets precisely in the dark, or the dinky hand-held GPS to burp up verified map coordinates. But the money simply isn't there for tens of thousands of these bulky ensembles for the riflemen and their close-combat friends. The United States does not invest in its rifle troops. The fact that the average L. L. Bean shopper can buy far lighter, tougher, drier, and warmer camping gear than anything issued to the average soldier or Marine says a lot about service priorities.[35] Planes, ships, tanks, and missiles sell. They deliver a really big bang for a big buck, sending bullets, not men. Canteens and ammo pouches for foot soldiers . . . well, take a number. Make do. Learn to get by. Trust in the air forces.

With no Starship Trooper fighting suit on the horizon, America's infantry must use what it will get. Current procurement plans tell us much about the shape of the future infantry arm. In most cases, we have already seen the foreseeable future. It's here today. Not much new has been forecasted.

The airborne and Ranger infantry have their next ride to the battlefield in the form of C-17 Globemaster III jet transports replacing the venerable C-141B Starlifters. The C-17s have shown some teething problems with formation drops, and not all the bugs have been worked out. For shorter legs, upgraded C-130s (the C-130J is the latest) will continue to serve.[36] They offer proven capability. For the next few decades, the country can drop a full brigade's worth of paratroopers or Rangers, or lesser amounts of each in various packages.

In the air assault arena, the Blackhawk, Chinook, and Apache will be around for some time to come, with various advanced models of each likely at some point. Special operations aviation will also enhance its current stable, of interest for Ranger air assaults. A new light scout, the RAH-66 Comanche, might replace the OH-58D Kiowa Warrior, but funding for this new bird has all but dried up. The Army has approval to buy a paltry eight craft, for service around 2006.[37] After that, who knows?

The mechanized infantry can expect no follow-on to the M-2 Bradley series, at least not in the next decade. That only makes sense, because there is no replacement programmed for the Bradley's running partner, the M-1 Abrams series main battle tank. The Bradleys are magnificent machines, the best in the world in their class. How well they do long after the warranties expire remains to be seen. More time on maintenance looks certain.

Additional time messing with the vehicle means less time spent on dismounted fighting skills. When a Bradley unit runs short of men, the dismount slots go unfilled first.[38] As a result, the older tracks keep running, but only one or two overloaded men get out when the ramp goes down. The result is odd—an infantry unit with hardly any infantry. Or put another way, you get a bunch of weak tanks.

In addition, continued reliance on the heavy, outsized Bradley fighting vehicle limits rapid deployment, which means going by air. It would take several runs by America's entire C-5A/B and C-17 airlifter fleets to get a brigade of thirty-three-ton Bradleys and seventy-ton Abrams tanks into battle. Even then, the tanks would lack much of their backup service support, so it might be a pretty short war. All Army light armor programs have died stillborn. Army efforts to buy the Marine LAV and the lightweight XM-8 Buford armored gun system went by the boards. So although the U.S. Marines, allies, and enemies have deployable light armor to support their infantry, the U.S. Army does not.[39] American soldiers stuck in a remote airhead will have to wait for the Bradleys to dribble in.

The light infantry should continue to do some heliborne operations, a little truck work, and a lot of walking. Nothing much has been proposed to help them, other than continued tinkering with the present generation of firearms. The only notable additions will be the unwieldy Javelin antitank guided missile to replace the hideous old Dragon, and the exchange of Vietnam War–vintage M-60E3 machine guns for new M-240B weapons. Better night sights and laser aiming designators will be provided, too.[40] But these constitute small potatoes indeed and will go to all U.S. grunts, not just the designated light infantry. Well, lightfighters never had much to begin with, so they expect nothing special. Such minimal expectations will be met.

Having suffered at the short end of the stick for years, the Marines finally benefit from two long-overdue upgrades. In the air, they trade in their decrepit CH-46E Frogs for tilt-rotor MV-22 Osprey aircraft. Special operations aviation will also get some of these wonder craft, which fly like a plane but have rotating wings and props to land like a chopper. On the ground, the old amphibious assault vehicles give way to a new model, faster, better armored, and more heavily armed.[41] Both improvements will greatly increase the range and warpower of a MEU.

These modest improvements in basic capabilities mask the real evolution in American infantry, the one that Khafji clearly suggests. Larry Lentz, Charles Ingraham, and their recon Marines showed the way. United States infantry will be following Robert Heinlein's *Starship Troopers,* not in terms of the gizmos and toys but in the model he presents of tough, uncompromising training for a selected band of warriors. As Heinlein wrote, "There are no dangerous weapons; there are only dangerous men."[42] Though fewer than ever, U.S. infantrymen will become more and more dangerous, largely through emphasis on human factors.

Over the next few decades, America's few remaining specialized, elite infantry battalions will take the last steps and merge with their SOF brethren. Infantry appears on the road to become what we now call special operators.[43] Special operators are, after all, already highly skilled infantry.

You can see the pattern developing. Already, all forms of American infantry recruit volunteers, then subject them to distinctive training. Once they arrive in units, they receive additional specialized training for their type of infantry: helicopter assaults, amphibious raids, parachute drops, and so forth. This represents an enormous investment in every man. Unfortunately, because the infantry uses the same routine recruitment as the finance corps or the truck mechanics, many volunteers do not complete the initial series of training courses.[44] This is why SOF units assess potential recruits before taking them into training. Only the ones strong enough and smart enough to make it get permission to start.[45] The introduction of preinduction assessment seems like a logical and fairly cost-effective step for American infantry. It can be expected in the twenty-first century. At present, Army SOF choose most of their men from other infantry formations. Some go back after their SOF tours end. Not surprisingly, this cross-fertilization is having an effect. Indeed, this has always been one of the secondary purposes for the 75th Ranger Regiment. There will be more of it.

Today's infantry mission profiles increasingly mirror what used to be considered the purview of special operations. Examples include 2-14th's role as the TF Ranger quick reaction force in Mogadishu; the 3-325th's service with Special Operations Command, Europe, in Liberia as QRF; and the entire MEU (SOC) range of tasks. Both SOCEUR and its Pacific counterpart draw on Army airborne battalion task forces and MEUs to back up their intervention efforts, a role previously reserved for the Ranger regiment. It could be convincingly argued that Operation Just Cause in Panama in 1989 amounted to a large-scale integration of SOF and infantry. That one-night coup de main offers the prototype for organizing smaller-scale contingencies along the lines of the 1994 Haiti undertaking.

Many common small-unit, detailed techniques and methods permeate both conventional and unconventional forces. This explains matters such as 2-14th Infantry's use of SOF close-quarters battle drills in Somalia and the stay-behind tactics used by Marine recon teams at Khafji. The bleed-over has become strong.

With this in mind, the Army and Marine Corps have taken measures to accommodate these developments. Conventional-SOF exercises and deployments have become typical, with SF playing in largely conventional exercises and infantry joining SOF training. In one example from 1992, the 1st Brigade, 101st Airborne Division (Air Assault), joined the 75th Ranger Regiment, the Army Green Berets, the 160th Special Operations Aviation Regiment, the Navy

SEALs, and USAF MC-130H Combat Talons and AC-130H Spectre gunships for Joint Readiness Exercise Kopek Trade, conducted at Fort Chaffee, Arkansas.[46] Marines carry out similar joint training, integrating their own "special operations capable" MEUs with Army SOF and always with SEALs. This allows operations such as the 1996 Assured Response evolution in Liberia. All involved know one anothers' strengths and weaknesses.

The Marines have gone one step beyond, as befits the inventors of the MEU (SOC). Under a program known as Sea Dragon, Marines have drawn on the experience at Khafji and coupled it to their own unbreakable tie to Marine air. This experiment posits that "rather than a shooter, the infantryman becomes a spotter."[47] It breaks the MEU's infantry battalion into four-man fire teams, each with a long-range radio, a laser marker–range finder, and nightscopes, plus enough small arms for self-defense. These "infestation teams" spread out, go to ground, and emulate Lentz and Ingraham at Khafji. In essence, the Sea Dragon initiative converts Marines into more SEALs, hidden behind hostile lines, shaking down the thunder. Of course, like the underlying faith in distant punishment by firepower, Sea Dragon presumes an enemy susceptible to such a cascade of munitions, however accurate.

Granting that Sea Dragon represents an extreme—and perhaps the ultimate—form of future infantry, the present integration into special operations exemplifies today's most typical infantry role. Around the world, American grunts carrying live bullets may most often be found working the crowd in places such as Bosnia or Haiti, acting as a QRF in some African country by standing behind uncertain United Nations units, helping to evacuate endangered American citizens, or reinforcing true SOF units in action. Only in Korea, and there only in small numbers, does the United States deploy rifle troops to hold and take death ground. Everyone else has gone into the SOF business, it appears.

This tendency has spelled out the likely fates of America's six brands of infantry. Those who can eventually play in a Khafji–Sea Dragon scenario or work as quick reaction forces for SOF adventures all have a future. In the contemporary climate, the others do not.

Accordingly, the Marines and Rangers have bright futures indeed. The former bring a well-balanced middleweight air-ground force to bear far from home, tied in with a well-proven naval team. The latter specialize in intercontinental forced entry and direct action raids. Both live on the periphery of the SOF universe. Officially, the Marines remain outside and the Rangers stand inside, although just barely, as they organize, arm, and man like other light infantry, and their personnel alternate Ranger tours with time in the conventional Army.[48] These two types of infantry will certainly survive in their present form.

A few more Marine infantry battalions may be trimmed if budgets continue to decline. The U.S. Navy expects to maintain enough amphibious shipping to carry about half of the present infantry battalions configured as MEUs, a total of twelve. And even if the ships became available (they won't), the Corps itself has only enough aviation and supporting arms to create MEUs or MEU equivalents from about half its present infantry strength, including allowances for train-up and recovery cycles.[49] The expenses affiliated with the new MV-22 will likely make the aviation arm even smaller.

For the Army, the air assault battalions represent the most capable breed of infantry. Excepting the mechanized ground actions during Desert Storm, all Army and Marine infantry combat in the last three decades has relied on helicopters, often to a great extent. Indeed, since 1945, with the exception of parts of a hundred-hour campaign in southwest Asia, aviation has largely replaced armor in the traditional light cavalry duties of screening and reconnaissance. Now the Apache and Blackhawk, not to mention the Marine MV-22 Osprey, promise deep, powerful shock action on a brigade scale, the old heavy cavalry role. This marriage of aviators and riflemen pretty much supplants the old tank-infantry team, with consequent increases in intercontinental deployability, speed, and battlefield range.

That kind of fighting forms the raison d'être for air assault infantry, and these men do it better than anyone else. With integrated Army aviation, heliborne troops can fight in major wars, including beating back hostile armored threats using Apaches, TOWs, mines, and skilled riflemen. They also do well in smaller engagements, thanks to their relatively large contingent of riflemen. The 101st Airborne's Gulf War commander, Maj. Gen. J. H. Binford Peay III, explained it thusly: "We really are a kind of 'medium' division. We're a multipurpose division that can do both—fight low and high intensity."[50] In short, air assault units offer the nearest Army equivalent to the Marines, substituting better attack helos for the Marines' small amount of attached armored power. With money tight, a unit able to do several things makes government accountants happy. The air assault infantry meets that test better than any other kind of Army rifle unit.

Airborne infantry also has a future, although here the crystal ball is not as clear. Certainly, the two regional battalions (1-508th in Europe and 1-501st in the Pacific) nicely accord with threats, missions, and available airlift. How long the United States continues to bankroll the 82d Airborne Division as a nine-battalion structure remains to be seen. The U.S. Air Force does not have the long-range aircraft to drop the entire division, let alone the thousands of additional XVIII Airborne Corps support troops also on jump status. In fact, the USAF has signed up only for dropping a single full brigade, although task organization can be adjusted to supplement bigger jets with smaller C-130s to squeeze out more paratroopers, as in the planned 1994 invasion of Haiti.[51] Still, there is nothing like an airborne brigade on the way when you need it, as in the Dominican Republic in 1965, Israel in 1973, Grenada in 1983, Panama in 1989, Saudi Arabia in 1990, or Haiti in 1994. The 82d has probably prevented more small wars than any other U.S. Army unit. For that reason alone, it's worth keeping in its present guise.

If the money men descend on Fort Bragg, it might be useful to remind them that the airborne infantry organizes almost identically to heliborne troops. With some light armor or more aviation, paratroopers too might become a multipurpose middleweight arm. These men train to fight at night, in small groups, and using maximum initiative, ideas that translate well in most situations, especially a Sea Dragon "infestation" approach. They also have the right stuff to serve as QRFs for peace operations.

Unfortunately, the parachute infantry seem unlikely to get the light armor they need to assist their armed Humvees. A battalion of

M-551 Sheridans used to be part of the airborne troop list, but it went off the books in 1997. The proposed XM-8 Buford light tank might have nicely scratched that itch, but it fell to the green-eyeshade crowd.[52] Paratroopers have been told to shoulder their hefty Javelins and wait for the eventual arrival of follow-on heavy forces. But that presumes there will be any of those left to show up.

If the Army's twenty-four mechanized infantry battalions were wildlife, they would be listed as endangered species. They do one thing—expedite the advance of the tanks—and they do it superbly. This narrow portfolio, in addition to complete reliance on the most expensive piece of hardware in the infantry—the powerful Bradley fighting vehicle—means that when the tanks become expendable, so does the mech infantry. Mechanized battalions may linger in the half-life of the National Guard for a while, but these formations seem destined for deactivation. And that's too bad. They may not be required as much as they were once thought to be, but they are badly needed to stiffen the increasingly SOF-like U.S. infantry. Just ask the survivors of TF Ranger, veterans of Mogadishu.

That said, the Army's skilled 11M10s have the misfortune to be yoked to a corpse, the U.S. Army's heavy armored force. Proficient and well armed, manned by professionals, the self-described "combat arm of decision" excels at waging yesterday's war. Armor's time has passed. By its own measure, American armor has contributed exactly four days of honest work in the last five decades. The whole wing of the Army has the whiff of the old horse cavalry, held behind the lines throughout the Great War, waiting to charge. The horsemen were still waiting in 1939 when the panzers passed by. Today, the helicopters have flown past, working every day while tankers practice to refight the Big One against the Soviets. This is not just an idle jibe. Right now, American mechanized formations train daily at Fort Irwin, California, against a Soviet-model motor rifle regiment known as Krasnovians (based on the Russian word for red).[53] Never mind that the real Soviets quit and went home. It's only a matter of time before our expensive tanks do likewise, taking their mech infantry brothers with them.

Today, most of America's armored order of battle sits in the continental United States, dependent on ships to drag them across oceans into action. Saddam Hussein let that happen. In doing so, he afforded America's tankers their first real armored clash since 1945. After seeing the one-sided outcome, other American enemies will probably not be so kind.

Armor and mechanized troops since 1945 have definitely contributed. Although they hardly meet the fondest wishes of Fort Knox's Armor School, tanks and mechanized units have filled an important role: helping the infantry, just as in 1918. Tanks and mech men did that well in Korea, Vietnam, Grenada, Panama, and Haiti, to name a few. A couple of tanks and infantry fighting vehicles in Mogadishu in October 1993 might have made all the difference in the world. Old Pakistani tanks and obsolescent Malaysian personnel carriers certainly demonstrated that sometimes there's nothing quite as handy as a big, rolling fortress. But like the heavy cavalrymen of the early twentieth century, most U.S. Army armor leaders refuse to embrace this secondary status. They long for the slashing, long thrusts of all-out armored pursuit, a dream that the United States has evidently chosen not to afford.

Wedded to the massive seventy-ton M-1A2 Abrams and the equally clunky thirty-three-ton M-2A2 Bradley, unwilling to shift to lighter LAV types of frames, Army tankers have about weighed themselves out of the fight. True, the United States has hedged against armor's intercontinental immobility by emplacing prepositioned stocks in Kuwait, Europe (Cold War leftovers), and afloat (one brigade) and buying fast cargo ships to bring over stateside battalions. Even if the equipment yards and transport ships survive enemy attention, at best this combination delivers two mechanized divisions in thirty days and five in seventy-five days, a little late against any determined foe and actually not much better than the near-run American deployment to the Korean War in 1950.[54] Trying to work around the overweight armored corps is like a Hollywood director using mirrors, body doubles, close-up shots, and lens filters to shoot around an obese star. At the end of all the gimmickry, the actor remains too fat.

In the only major American mechanized deployment since the Gulf War, the world witnessed the 1st Armored Division's ponderous movement into Bosnia. The division pushed south deliberately by road, rail, and river barge, a phase lasting weeks. Despite three years of planning and numerous rehearsals, the columns stalled at the flood-swollen Sava River, marking time while engineers struggled to bridge the turbulent waterway. Rapid deployment it was not. By contrast, the 3-325th Airborne Battalion Combat Team quickly moved by air from Italy to Tuzla and awaited linkup with the tanks. That took a while.

Once in country, the U.S. armored division elected to strip out most of its tanks and heavier equipment, which simply choked roads and sucked fuel. All of those vehicles full of soldiers did not do any more toward controlling villages and patrolling towns in peace operations than police driving along in cars truly prevent urban crime. To dominate its sector of Bosnia, the 1st Armored had to get out on the ground. That meant grunts, not metal monsters.[55] Most of the riflemen in Europe eventually deployed to Bosnia to supplement infantry-poor armored contingents. Now everybody did good government work, and the truce held: great accomplishments to be sure. But it all resembled hammering a screw.

Even the Army leadership that originally sent the relatively nearby Germany-based armored brigades had second thoughts. By autumn 1997, the Army replaced the armored division with much more nimble forces, built around the armed Humvees of the 2d Armored Cavalry Regiment (Light), some mechanized infantry, a few tanks, and some lightfighters from the 10th Mountain Division.[56] The final outcome remains to be seen, but one thing is certain. The heavy force was too damn heavy for this one.

Like the horse cavalry, which to this day retains a certain military utility, the mechanized arm also has a niche, even in the evolving SOF-style American infantry component. In another round against Iraq or North Korea, the United States will want seventy-ton Abrams tanks and thirty-three-ton Bradleys full of mech infantry. Those threats alone justify a prudent commitment to some kind of armor. Additionally, small, dedicated tank-mech elements can greatly assist the Rangers, the airborne, and even the air assault infantry in their missions, especially meeting the persistent QRF requirements in the contested streets of cities such as Port-au-Prince, Mogadishu, and Monrovia. When available, even a few heavy gun bearers can make a big difference.

To meet this critical tasking, the 3d Infantry Division (Mechanized) in the XVIII Airborne Corps maintains an understrength rapid reaction company on alert status at all times. This bobtail company team consists of four Abrams tanks, four Bradleys, and some supporting trucks, all prepared to go out aboard gigantic C-5B Galaxy airlifters on eighteen hours' notice.[57] Such a capability definitely helps, but it compels the early-deploying units to grab and hold a runway capable of receiving the massive Galaxies—no sure thing in the Third World, even without opposition. This baby step in the right direction reflects the heavy community's sole concession to the importance of projecting power rapidly by air. No other measures appear on the horizon.

With that in mind, the grim fate of armor and mech battalions becomes all too clear. Surely the absence of any serious work toward developing a replacement for either the Abrams or the Bradley tells its own story. In its recent report, the independent National Defense Panel under Phillip A. Odeen strongly cautioned against any more investment in developing heavy armored forces, mainly because they move to the arena so slowly that the game will likely end before they get there. Odeen's position looks to be in consonance with Department of Defense thinking regarding all present and projected funding for the armored corps.[58] Barring a significant change of heart at the highest levels, American soldiers are driving the last main battle tanks and the last heavy infantry fighting vehicles they will ever receive. Whatever comes next, it will be lighter. Or it may be nothing. Settling for the latter will be a mistake measured in blood.

Speaking of lighter—as the Bible says, from those with little, what little they have will be taken. If the mechanized infantry looks vulnerable to reductions, how much more so are the underarmed U.S. Army lightfighters, who depend solely on skill in dismounted tactics as their specialty? Yet thanks to the pioneering effort of the light leaders, those same battle skills have permeated the air assault and airborne communities, and those units have the firepower and mobility to do something with them. The paratroopers and heliborne riflemen turn out to be just as deployable, and they are capable of forced entry, too. The light battalions cannot do much more than join smaller wars or handle peacekeeping, and because those have become growth areas in the American military, the Army has kept its light rifle units. But two divisions' worth out of ten probably amounts to too many. Any light infantry battalions that survive the fiscal ax will likely convert to the air assault configuration.

Thus, we see the outlines of tomorrow's 55,000- to 70,000-man rifle force: three Ranger battalions, the Marines (twenty-four battalions but perhaps with as few as eighteen), nine to eleven airborne battalions, nine to eighteen air assault battalions, and at most ten mechanized battalions. It ranges from forty-nine to sixty-six battalions, plus some 4,000 to 6,000 close-combat SOF types. And that, folks, is the best case. It could be worse.

The most serious peril in this increasingly elite, decreasingly numerous American infantry equation involves the one factor we can never control: the enemy. Our potential foes do not have big air forces or decent navies. But they definitely have sizable armies. Many states employ able infantry in large numbers, backed by lots of artillery, tanks, and the like. They do not have to worry about transoceanic deployment or sending bullets instead of men. They just have to concern themselves with winning, and the blood debt for victory may not be an issue.

Against this, the United States poses firepower technology steered by a few good men on the ground. That can become a dicey business. Special operations promise big payoffs for small investments, but these raids and reconnoiterings hinge greatly on stealth, surprise, and speed. When caught *in flagrante delicto*, special warriors can go down hard. Historically, about half of direct action missions fail.[59] Perhaps new technology will improve that .500 batting average. But with no larger body of ground-gaining soldiery to remedy botched attempts, the United States cannot afford many strikeouts. And there will be strikeouts. Look at Mogadishu.

Numbers offer the only hedge when the hostiles do not crack under bombardment, the direct action raid miscarries, or the SOF-model stay-behinds get overrun. With the bad guys belt to belt, somebody will have to take and hold ground. Airplanes cannot do that. Shells and bombs cannot do that. Only grunts can do that. And the fewer men we have, the less we can do that.

For those enamored of the Khafji example, consider a cautionary tale. During the war in Southeast Asia, the United States sent its best special operators into Laos and Cambodia as part of the innocuously titled Military Assistance Command Vietnam—Studies and Observations Group (MACV-SOG). Acting as tiny infestation teams, the most select men in the American military crossed the borders and brought down the thunder. For the cost of 300 superb Americans, MACV-SOG inflicted 45,000 North Vietnamese deaths, the highest kill ratio in a war characterized by body counting. Additionally, MACV-SOG destroyed thousands of tons of enemy supplies, wrecked stretches of the Ho Chi Minh Trail, and provided priceless early warning for conventional U.S. units.[60] Of course, the Vietnamese Communists won the war anyway.

You see, unlike the Iraqis but much like Muhammed Farah's Somali supporters, the North Vietnamese did not fear death ground. They did not buckle under bombs or rockets, although the United States rained these down in horrendous amounts. In the words of Maj. Gen. Robert H. Scales Jr., who served as an artillery observer at Hamburger Hill in 1969: "Every day I watched as aircraft dropped hundreds of bombs on top of that hill, and every night the North Vietnamese cooking fires would come on."[61] That's the real danger of not enough infantry, no matter how good and no matter what the firepower on tap. Against a lot of solid enemy armies, it's necessary to go forth into death ground at bayonet point and kill the other guy, face to face. It is the ultimate sanction of dangerous men.

There will be more wars. That can be counted on. Nobody can be certain where or when, but the record over the years points to fighting, with Americans in the fray. For the little wars, or even some of the big ones, the small band of SOF-style infantry may well suffice. High-quality, well-disciplined troops have always shattered those less skilled, often far out of proportion to the numbers engaged. To the credit of the sergeants and officers who made them so, the best riflemen in U.S. history, bar none, will be sent forth. They will fight.

But will they win? That depends on the opposition, on how much pounding they can take. If it comes down to house-to-house or hole-to-hole combat against a determined enemy—such as the Germans in both world wars, the Japanese in the Pacific, the North Koreans and Chinese of 1950–53, or the North Vietnamese—the economies and disproportionate trust in special warfare tricks and tactics will merely stave off the inevitable as units are ground down to powder in a wasting attrition struggle. American leaders say that such wars will not be waged; but, last checked, the enemy side votes in that, too, often at inconvenient times and places.

Worse, if the opposing army proves aggressive, they use their numerical preponderance, trading quantity to erode quality. If the enemy can absorb losses, they may surge forward and overwhelm our small outfits. America's remaining riflemen may someday die in place, facing forward, as did their equally able Regular Army and Marine Corps forefathers at Bataan, waiting for the regiments that will never come to save them.

At least in 1942, the United States had reinforcements whom they chose not to send. Today, absent months of mobilization and wholesale overhaul of reserves, the United States continues to trust in airpower and magical technology, then hopes for the best. It may work, but history offers no particular cause for optimism. Regardless of all the endless hype about smart bombs and a deluge of fire, somehow, someday, it will all come down to the raw and the primal, as it always does. On that day of reckoning, a few men must get up and go forward, a thin green line of soldiers and Marines advancing through death ground—America's last riflemen.

Notes

The epigraph comes from Col. Walter B. Clark, USA (Ret.), interview of 22 December 1997, by telephone from his home in Charleston, S.C. Colonel Clark epitomizes the professional infantry commander. As a lieutenant in Korea in 1952, he won the Silver Star in hand-to-hand combat with Chinese troops. He also served in the Second Korean Conflict (1966–69) and in the Vietnam War.

1. Rick Atkinson, *Crusade* (Boston, Mass.: Houghton Mifflin Company, 1993), 202.

2. Colonel Charles J. Quilter II, USMCR, *With the I Marine Expeditionary Force in Desert Shield and Desert Storm* (Washington, D.C.: U.S. Government Printing Office, 1993), 60.

3. For these sentiments, see Atkinson, *Crusade*, 205–6, and Michael R. Gordon and Lt. Gen. Bernard E. Trainor, USMC (Ret.), *The Generals' War* (Boston, Mass.: Little, Brown and Co., 1995), 285–86.

4. Lieutenant Colonel Charles H. Cureton, USMCR, *With the 1st Marine Division in Desert Shield and Desert Storm* (Washington, D.C.: U.S. Government Printing Office, 1993), 43.

5. Greg Walker, *At the Hurricane's Eye* (New York, N.Y.: Ivy Books, 1994), 180; Guy Gugliotta, "Iraqi Ground Troops Battle with Tenacity," *Washington Post* (4 February 1991), A13. Both Walker and Gugliotta interviewed participants. For details on the Chinese-designed Type 63, also known as the North China Industries Corporation model YW 531, see Christopher F. Foss, ed., *Jane's Armour and Artillery 1995* (Alexandria, Va.: Jane's Information Group, Inc., 1995), 286–87.

6. Orr Kelly, *Never Fight Fair* (New York, N.Y.: Pocket Books, 1995), 346–47. Joe Baxter is a pseudonym used to protect the SEAL's identity.

7. Philip Shenon, "Copter Pilot, After Battle, No Longer Sees Quick War," *New York Times* (3 February 1991), 15; Atkinson, *Crusade*, 202.

8. Orr Kelly, *Brave Men, Dark Waters* (Novato, Calif.: Presidio Press, 1992), 235–36; Atkinson, *Crusade*, 202–3; Kevin Dockery, *SEALs in Action* (New York: Avon Books, 1991), 291; Walker, *At the Hurricane's Eye*, 180–81. In Gordon and Trainor, *The Generals' War*, 291, the au-

thors charge that the U.S. SOF "abandoned their cryptographic material for encoding radio messages and other classified items."

9. Atkinson, *Crusade*, 203; Quilter, *With the I Marine Expeditionary Force in Desert Shield and Desert Storm*, 60.

10. U.S. Department of Defense, *Final Report to Congress: Conduct of the Persian Gulf War* (Washington, D.C.: U.S. Government Printing Office, April 1992), 131; Walker, *At the Hurricane's Eye*, 230, 239.

11. Atkinson, *Crusade*, 204; Gordon and Trainor, *The Generals' War*, 291; Cureton, *With the 1st Marine Division in Desert Shield and Desert Storm*, 43–44. These three sources together tell the full story of the two teams in Al Khafji. Atkinson talked to Lentz. Gordon and Trainor spoke with Ingraham. Cureton provides the view from the 3d Marine Regiment.

12. Caryle Murphy and Guy Gugliotta, "Saudi Town Reclaimed; Trapped Marines Freed," *Washington Post* (1 February 1991), 1; Gordon and Trainor, *The Generals' War*, 294. Murphy and Gugliotta interviewed the Marines who stayed in Al Khafji.

13. Atkinson, *Crusade*, 209.

14. Brigadier General John H. Admire, USMC, "The 3d Marines in Desert Storm," *Marine Corps Gazette* (September 1991), 68.

15. Lieutenant Colonel Martin N. Stanton, USA, "The Saudi Arabian National Guard Motorized Brigades," *Armor* (March–April 1996), 8–9; Atkinson, *Crusade*, 209; Trainor and Gordon, *The Generals' War*, 296; Cureton, *With the 1st Marine Division in Desert Shield and Desert Storm*, 44–45.

16. Atkinson, *Crusade*, 210.

17. Ibid.; Philip D. Chinnery, *Any Time, Any Place: Fifty Years of USAF Air Commando and Special Operations Forces, 1944–1994* (Annapolis, Md.: Naval Institute Press, 1994), 255–56; Walker, *At the Hurricane's Eye*, 230.

18. Gordon and Trainor, *The Generals' War*, 299. Ingraham's account appears to come from a postbattle letter to his father.

19. Atkinson, *Crusade*, 211; Cureton, *With the 1st Marine Division in Desert Shield and Desert Storm*, 45.

20. Stanton, "The Saudi Arabian National Guard Motorized Brigades," 10–11; Admire, "The 3d Marines in Desert Storm," 68–69.

21. Elliot A. Cohen, director, *Gulf War Air Power Survey*, 5 vols.

(Washington, D.C.: U.S. Government Printing Office, 1993), *Volume II: Effects and Effectiveness,* 237–40; Lt. Col. Theodore N. Herman, USMC (Ret.), "Harriers in the Breach," *U.S. Naval Institute Proceedings* (February 1996), 46–47.

22. U.S. Department of Defense, *Report of the Quadrennial Defense Review* (Washington, D.C.: U.S. Government Printing Office, May 1997), iv, 14, 39. Interestingly, the phrase "revolution in military affairs" was lifted, without attribution, from a Soviet book titled *Scientific-Technical Progress and the Revolution in Military Affairs,* translated and published in 1973 by the U.S. Air Force. Written in the 1960s, the Soviet original referred to the changes wrought by nuclear weaponry. This phrase reflects one of the American military's many direct borrowings of Soviet-era military jargon. Others include operational art (conduct of military campaigns, linking overall strategy and battlefield tactics) and weapons of mass destruction (nuclear, chemical, and biological arms). One of the more noteworthy nods to Soviet military prowess involved the code name for the Gulf War's offensive segment. In naming Operation Desert Storm, U.S. planners intentionally drew from the equally decisive and one-sided 1945 Soviet blitzkrieg of Japanese-held Manchuria, August Storm. The Soviet Union may be dead, but its military thought lives on in the professional discourse of its former foes.

23. Department of Defense, *Quadrennial Defense Review,* 3.

24. Quoted in James Kitfield, "To Halt an Enemy," *Air Force* (January 1998), 65. See also Rebecca Grant, "The Epic Little Battle of Khafji," *Air Force* (February 1998), 28–34.

25. Kitfield, "To Halt an Enemy," 65.

26. The classic version of this argument can be found in T. R. Fehrenbach, *This Kind of War* (New York, N.Y.: Macmillan Company, 1963), especially 426–43.

27. James F. Dunnigan, *How to Make War* (New York, N.Y.: William Morrow and Company, Inc., 1988), 25–26, 97.

28. Rowan Scarborough, "Army's Readiness Said to Be at Risk," *Washington Times National Weekly Edition* (4 January 1998), 1, 22; Rowan Scarborough, "Pentagon Blames Recruiting for Army Infantry Shortages," *Washington Times National Weekly Edition* (4 January 1998), 23. During 1997, Senate Budget Committee investigators looked at Army mechanized units training at the Fort Irwin,

California, National Training Center and found them to be missing up to 50 percent of assigned riflemen. They noted that light, airborne, and air assault battalions exercising at the Joint Readiness Training Center at Fort Polk, Louisiana, lacked up to 25 percent of their infantry numbers. The secretary of defense's office on 23 December 1997 agreed that these numbers were accurate and blamed them on recruiting problems. As spokesman Kenneth Bacon put it, "The Army has met its recruitment goals in the main, globally, but there are some specialties where there were shortfalls. One was infantry."

29. One senior U.S. Army infantry general made a strong public recommendation to increase the rifle squad from nine to eleven men for all kinds of infantry. See Maj. Gen. Carl F. Ernst, USA, "The Infantry Squad—How Much Is Enough?" *Infantry* (January–February 1997), 2. To date, there has been no indication that there will be action to implement the Ernst proposal.

30. U.S. Department of the Army, *Posture Statement FY 98* (Washington, D.C.: U.S. Government Printing Office, February 1997), 2, 6–7.

31. For the latest from Korea, see www.2id.korea.army. mil on the World Wide Web.

32. See the Appendix for the exact roll of current infantry battalions as of 1 January 1998.

33. U.S. Department of Defense, *Joint Vision 2010* (Washington, D.C.: U.S. Government Printing Office, 1996), 20. Significantly, the chart on that page concerning dominant maneuver includes every firing and sensing platform in the armed forces, plus a few still on the drawing board. The only soldiers pictured are those sitting in command posts watching computer screens. And that's in the segment about going head to head with the enemy. The only reference to close combat in the pamphlet comes on page 28, but it applies only to "some military operations" and includes air and sea close combat. Presumably the writers mean aerial dogfights, but at sea the meaning seems obscure. Perhaps they envision boarding actions.

34. U.S. Department of the Army, *Weapons Systems: United States Army 1997* (Washington, D.C.: U.S. Government Printing Office, 1997), 79. For the "Starship Trooper" nickname, see Tom Clancy, *Airborne* (New York, N.Y.: Berkley Books, 1997), 302.

35. To be fair, the widespread introduction of Gore-tex gear has greatly improved life in the field. Unfortunately, due to its expense, only parts of the force have this great weather-resistant outerwear. The rest get by with items little changed from those issued in the Korean War.

36. Clancy, *Airborne*, 173, 191–93.

37. "Army Weaponry, Equipment, and New Technologies," *Army* (October 1997), 289.

38. Scarborough, "Army's Readiness Said to Be at Risk," 22.

39. The U.S. Army's military police companies may soon receive a four-man armored car for their duties. This vehicle shows promise for adaptation, and although the miltary police only have 4 prototypes at present, with contracts for 95, some planners see a need for 1,740. See Scott R. Gourley, "XM-1117 Armored Security Vehicle," *Army* (February 1998).

40. Department of the Army, *Weapons Systems: United States Army 1997*, 201, 223.

41. Tom Clancy, *Marine* (New York, N.Y.: Berkley Books, 1996), 124–25, 145–48.

42. Robert A. Heinlein, *Starship Troopers* (New York, N.Y.: Ace Books, 1987), 61.

43. One of the most thoughtful arguments along these lines can be found in Col. Rod Paschall, USA (Ret.), *LIC 2010* (McLean, Va.: Brassey's [U.S.], Inc., 1990), 81–86, in particular. Colonel Paschall commanded 1st Special Forces Operational Detachment-Delta (Delta Force) from 1980 to 1982.

44. The Army routinely reports a loss of between 30 and 40 percent of all inductees during their first term of enlistment. So do the Marines. See Thomas E. Ricks, *Making the Corps* (New York, N.Y.: Scribner's, 1997), 239.

45. Paschall, *LIC 2010*, 84–86. For the protypical program, see Terry Griswold and D. M. Giangreco, *Delta* (Osceola, Wis.: Motorbooks, International, 1992), 41–47. The SEALs, Army Special Forces, and Rangers have similar programs, tailored to their unique needs.

46. At the time of the exercise in February 1992, Fort Chaffee served as the Joint Readiness Training Center, the Army's premier force-on-force light unit maneuver area.

47. Captain Michael R. Lwin, USA, and Capt. Mark R. Lwin, USMC, "The Future of Land Power," *U.S. Naval Institute Proceedings* (September 1997), 83. See also Brian Nichiporuk and Carl H. Builder, *Information Technologies and the Future of Land Warfare* (Santa Monica, Calif.: RAND, 1995), 64–66, which refers to "soldiers as sensors," not shooters.

48. On the Marines, see Headquarters, Marine Corps, *Send in the Marines: The Art of MAGTF Operations* (Washington, D.C.: HQ, Marine Corps, 1997), 2. For the Rangers, see U.S. Special Operations Command, *1996 Posture Statement* (MacDill Air Force Base, Fla.: U.S. Special Operations Command, 1996), 34.

49. U.S. Department of Defense, National Military Strategy (Washington, D.C.: U.S. Government Printing Office, 1997), 23. The Department of Defense, *Quadrennial Defense Review*, 46, lists the current purchase goal of 360 MV-22 Ospreys, a reduction from the 425 presumed to be necessary to replace the CH-46E Sea Knights (Frogs) in the twelve active and three reserve medium-helo squadrons. The active medium squadrons form the air component for MEUs.

50. Major Robert K. Wright, Jr., USAR, 1st Lt. Cliff Lippard, USAR, and Rex Boggs, *Air Assault in the Gulf: An Interview with Major General J. H. Binford Peay III, Commanding General, 101st Airborne Division (Air Assault)* (Washington, D.C.: U.S. Army Center of Military History, 5 June 1996), 30.

51. Clancy, *Airborne*, 216–19.

52. The only remaining Army light-armor initiative is the Future Scout and Cavalry System Team, which may be nothing but a heavier Humvee. It presently exists only as an office at Fort Knox, Kentucky, headed by a major. Directorate of Force Development, "Development Mission: Getting the Best 'Stuff' for Mounted Force Soldiers," *Armor* (November–December 1997), 15.

53. General Gordon R. Sullivan, USA, "Flexibility Sets the Pace at Combat Training Centers," *Army* (July 1993), 31–33.

54. U.S. Department of the Army, *Posture Statement FY98*, 14–15. By 15 September 1950, eighty-three days into the war, the United States had five Army divisions and one Marine division in combat. Four of the Army divisions came from occupation duty in nearby Japan, an option no longer available.

55. For a good view of patrolling in Bosnia, see Dennis Steele, "The 2d ACR in Bosnia," *Army* (February 1998), 38–44.

56. Ibid.; Gen. Eric K. Shinseki, USA, "America's Soldiers: Our Ambassadors for Democracy," *Army* (October 1997), 68, 70; "2d Armored Cavalry Regiment: Back from Haiti, Then on to Bosnia, the Army's Light ACR Remains 'Always Ready,'" *Armor* (November–December 1997), 23–24.

57. Clancy, *Airborne*, 215.

58. "NDP Takes Aim at 'Two War' Strategy," *Air Force* (January 1998), 14.

59. For an excellent summary of the success rate for SOF direct-action missions, see Benjamin F. Schemmer, *The Raid* (New York, N.Y.: Harper and Row, 1976), 41, 237–38, 266.

60. For the best one-volume unclassified history of this unique organization, see Maj. John L. Plaster, USA (Ret.), *SOG* (New York, N.Y.: Simon and Schuster, 1997), 340.

61. Quoted in Kitfield, "To Halt an Enemy," 65. Scales's experiences led him to write *Firepower in Limited War* (Novato, Calif.: Presidio Press, 1995), which argues strongly for retaining traditional infantry maneuver skills to complement emerging firepower capabilities. See especially page 295.

Appendix

U. S. Army and U.S. Marine Corps
Active Duty Infantry Battalions
(as of 1 January 1998)

Airborne infantry battalions: 11

1st Battalion, 325th Airborne Infantry Regiment[1]
  2d Brigade, 82d Airborne Division, Fort Bragg, North Carolina
2d Battalion, 325th Airborne Infantry Regiment
  2d Brigade, 82d Airborne Division, Fort Bragg, North Carolina
3d Battalion, 325th Airborne Infantry Regiment[2]
  2d Brigade, 82d Airborne Division, Fort Bragg, North Carolina
1st Battalion, 501st Parachute Infantry Regiment
  1st Brigade, 6th Infantry Division (Light), Fort Richardson,
  Alaska[3]
1st Battalion, 504th Parachute Infantry Regiment
  1st Brigade, 82d Airborne Division, Fort Bragg, North Carolina
2d Battalion, 504th Parachute Infantry Regiment
  1st Brigade, 82d Airborne Division, Fort Bragg, North Carolina
3d Battalion, 504th Parachute Infantry Regiment
  1st Brigade, 82d Airborne Division, Fort Bragg, North Carolina
1st Battalion, 505th Parachute Infantry Regiment
  3d Brigade, 82d Airborne Division, Fort Bragg, North Carolina
2d Battalion, 505th Parachute Infantry Regiment
  3d Brigade, 82d Airborne Division, Fort Bragg, North Carolina
3d Battalion, 505th Parachute Infantry Regiment
  3d Brigade, 82d Airborne Division, Fort Bragg, North Carolina
1st Battalion, 508th Parachute Infantry Regiment[4]
  Southern European Task Force (SETAF), Vicenza, Italy

Air assault infantry battalions: 11

1st Battalion, 187th Infantry Regiment
3d Brigade, 101st Airborne Division (Air Assault), Fort Campbell, Kentucky
2d Battalion, 187th Infantry Regiment
3d Brigade, 101st Airborne Division (Air Assault), Fort Campbell, Kentucky
3d Battalion, 187th Infantry Regiment
3d Brigade, 101st Airborne Division (Air Assault), Fort Campbell, Kentucky
1st Battalion, 327th Infantry Regiment
1st Brigade, 101st Airborne Division (Air Assault), Fort Campbell, Kentucky
2d Battalion, 327th Infantry Regiment
1st Brigade, 101st Airborne Division (Air Assault), Fort Campbell, Kentucky
3d Battalion, 327th Infantry Regiment
1st Brigade, 101st Airborne Division (Air Assault), Fort Campbell, Kentucky
1st Battalion, 502d Infantry Regiment
2d Brigade, 101st Airborne Division (Air Assault), Fort Campbell, Kentucky
2d Battalion, 502d Infantry Regiment
2d Brigade, 101st Airborne Division (Air Assault), Fort Campbell, Kentucky
3d Battalion, 502d Infantry Regiment
2d Brigade, 101st Airborne Division (Air Assault), Fort Campbell, Kentucky
1st Battalion, 503d Infantry Regiment
2d Brigade, 2d Infantry Division, Camps Casey and Hovey, Republic of Korea
1st Battalion, 506th Infantry Regiment
2d Brigade, 2d Infantry Division, Camp Greaves, Republic of Korea

Mechanized infantry battalions: 24

2d Battalion (Mechanized), 2d Infantry Regiment
   3d Brigade, 1st Infantry Division (Mechanized), Vilseck, Germany
1st Battalion, 5th Cavalry Regiment⁵
   2d Brigade, 1st Cavalry Division, Fort Hood, Texas
2d Battalion, 5th Cavalry Regiment
   1st Brigade, 1st Cavalry Division, Fort Hood, Texas
1st Battalion (Mechanized), 6th Infantry Regiment
   2d Brigade, 1st Armored Division, Baumholder, Germany
2d Battalion (Mechanized), 6th Infantry Regiment
   2d Brigade, 1st Armored Division, Baumholder, Germany
2d Battalion (Mechanized), 7th Infantry Regiment
   1st Brigade, 3d Infantry Division (Mechanized), Fort Stewart, Georgia
3d Battalion (Mechanized), 7th Infantry Regiment
   1st Brigade, 3d Infantry Division (Mechanized), Fort Stewart, Georgia
2d Battalion, 7th Cavalry Regiment
   3d Brigade, 1st Cavalry Division, Fort Hood, Texas
1st Battalion (Mechanized), 8th Infantry Regiment
   3d Brigade, 4th Infantry Division (Mechanized), Fort Carson, Colorado
2d Battalion (Mechanized), 8th Infantry Regiment
   2d Brigade, 4th Infantry Division (Mechanized), Fort Hood, Texas
1st Battalion (Mechanized), 9th Infantry Regiment
   2d Brigade, 2d Infantry Division, Camp Hovey, Republic of Korea
2d Battalion (Mechanized), 9th Infantry Regiment
   1st Brigade, 2d Infantry Division, Camp Casey, Republic of Korea
1st Battalion, 9th Cavalry Regiment
   3d Brigade, 1st Cavalry Division, Fort Hood, Texas
1st Battalion (Mechanized), 12th Infantry Regiment
   3d Brigade, 4th Infantry Division (Mechanized), Fort Carson, Colorado

1st Battalion (Mechanized), 15th Infantry Regiment
   3d Brigade, 3d Infantry Division (Mechanized), Fort Benning,
   Georgia
3d Battalion (Mechanized), 15th Infantry Regiment
   2d Brigade, 3d Infantry Division (Mechanized), Fort Stewart,
   Georgia
1st Battalion (Mechanized), 16th Infantry Regiment
   1st Brigade, 1st Infantry Division (Mechanized), Fort Riley, Kansas
1st Battalion (Mechanized), 18th Infantry Regiment
   2d Brigade, 1st Infantry Division (Mechanized), Schweinfurt,
   Germany
1st Battalion (Mechanized), 22d Infantry Regiment
   1st Brigade, 4th Infantry Division (Mechanized), Fort Hood,
   Texas
1st Battalion (Mechanized), 23d Infantry Regiment
   3d Brigade, 2d Infantry Division, Fort Lewis, Washington
1st Battalion (Mechanized), 26th Infantry Regiment
   2d Brigade, 1st Infantry Division (Mechanized), Schweinfurt,
   Germany
1st Battalion (Mechanized), 30th Infantry Regiment
   3d Brigade, 3d Infantry Division (Mechanized), Fort Benning,
   Georgia
1st Battalion (Mechanized), 36th Infantry Regiment
   1st Brigade, 1st Armored Division, Kirchgons, Germany
1st Battalion (Mechanized), 41st Infantry Regiment
   3d Brigade, 1st Armored Division, Fort Riley, Kansas

Ranger battalions: 3

1st Battalion, 75th Ranger Regiment[6]
   Hunter Army Air Field, Georgia
2d Battalion, 75th Ranger Regiment
   Fort Lewis, Washington
3d Battalion, 75th Ranger Regiment
   Fort Benning, Georgia

Light infantry battalions: 18

2d Battalion, 1st Infantry Regiment
  1st Brigade, 6th Infantry Division (Light), Fort Wainwright, Alaska
1st Battalion, 5th Infantry Regiment
  1st Brigade, 25th Infantry Division (Light), Fort Lewis, Washington
2d Battalion, 5th Infantry Regiment
  3d Brigade, 25th Infantry Division (Light), Schofield Barracks, Hawaii
1st Battalion, 14th Infantry Regiment
  2d Brigade, 25th Infantry Division (Light), Schofield Barracks, Hawaii
2d Battalion, 14th Infantry Regiment
  2d Brigade, 10th Mountain Division (Light Infantry), Fort Drum, New York
1st Battalion, 17th Infantry Regiment
  1st Brigade, 6th Infantry Division (Light), Fort Wainwright, Alaska
5th Battalion, 20th Infantry Regiment
  1st Brigade, 25th Infantry Division (Light), Fort Lewis, Washington
1st Battalion, 21st Infantry Regiment
  2d Brigade, 25th Infantry Division (Light), Schofield Barracks, Hawaii
2d Battalion, 22d Infantry Regiment
  1st Brigade, 10th Mountain Division (Light Infantry), Fort Drum, New York
1st Battalion, 24th Infantry Regiment
  1st Brigade, 25th Infantry Division (Light), Fort Lewis, Washington
1st Battalion, 27th Infantry Regiment
  2d Brigade, 25th Infantry Division (Light), Schofield Barracks, Hawaii
2d Battalion, 27th Infantry Regiment
  3d Brigade, 25th Infantry Division (Light), Schofield Barracks, Hawaii
4th Battalion, 31st Infantry Regiment
  2d Brigade, 10th Mountain Division (Light Infantry), Fort Drum, New York

1st Battalion, 32d Infantry Regiment
  1st Brigade, 10th Mountain Division (Light Infantry), Fort Drum, New York
2d Battalion, 35th Infantry Regiment
  3d Brigade, 25th Infantry Division (Light), Schofield Barracks, Hawaii
1st Battalion, 87th Infantry Regiment
  1st Brigade, 10th Mountain Division (Light Infantry), Fort Drum, New York
2d Battalion, 87th Infantry Regiment
  2d Brigade, 10th Mountain Division (Light Infantry), Fort Drum, New York
5th Battalion, 87th Infantry Regiment
  United States Army South (USARSO), Fort Clayton, Republic of Panama[7]

Marine infantry battalions: 24

1st Battalion, 1st Marine Regiment
  1st Marine Division, Camp Pendleton, California
2d Battalion, 1st Marine Regiment
  1st Marine Division, Camp Pendleton, California
3d Battalion, 1st Marine Regiment
  1st Marine Division, Camp Pendleton, California
1st Battalion, 2d Marine Regiment
  2d Marine Division, Camp Lejeune, North Carolina
2d Battalion, 2d Marine Regiment
  2d Marine Division, Camp Lejeune, North Carolina
3d Battalion, 2d Marine Regiment
  2d Marine Division, Camp Lejeune, North Carolina
1st Battalion, 3d Marine Regiment
  3d Marine Division, Kaneohe Bay Marine Corps Base, Hawaii
2d Battalion, 3d Marine Regiment
  3d Marine Division, Kaneohe Bay Marine Corps Base, Hawaii
3d Battalion, 3d Marine Regiment
  3d Marine Division, Kaneohe Bay Marine Corps Base, Hawaii

1st Battalion, 4th Marine Regiment[8]
3d Marine Division, Camp Pendleton, California
2d Battalion, 4th Marine Regiment
3d Marine Division, Camp Pendleton, California
3d Battalion, 4th Marine Regiment
3d Marine Division, Camp Pendleton, California
1st Battalion, 5th Marine Regiment
1st Marine Division, Camp Pendleton, California
2d Battalion, 5th Marine Regiment
1st Marine Division, Camp Pendleton, California
3d Battalion, 5th Marine Regiment
1st Marine Division, Camp Pendleton, California
1st Battalion, 6th Marine Regiment
2d Marine Division, Camp Lejeune, North Carolina
2d Battalion, 6th Marine Regiment
2d Marine Division, Camp Lejeune, North Carolina
3d Battalion, 6th Marine Regiment
2d Marine Division, Camp Lejeune, North Carolina
1st Battalion, 7th Marine Regiment
1st Marine Division, Camp Pendleton, California
2d Battalion, 7th Marine Regiment
1st Marine Division, Camp Pendleton, California
3d Battalion, 7th Marine Regiment
1st Marine Division, Camp Pendleton, California
1st Battalion, 8th Marine Regiment
2d Marine Division, Camp Lejeune, North Carolina
2d Battalion, 8th Marine Regiment
2d Marine Division, Camp Lejeune, North Carolina
3d Battalion, 8th Marine Regiment
2d Marine Division, Camp Lejeune, North Carolina

Notes

Sources: The most up-to-date listings come from the World Wide Web. For more on these battalions, see the following web sites, all as of 8 February 1998: www-2id.korea.army.mil; www.army.mil;www.army.-mil/USARSO; www.bragg.army.mil; www.campbell.army.mil; www.-carson.army.mil; www.drum.army.mil; www.hood-pao.army.mil; www.hqusareur.army.mil; www.lewis.army.mil; www.mfp.usmc.mil; www.okr.usmc.mil; www.riley.army.mil; www.stewart.army.mil; www.-USARPAC.army.mil; www.usmc.mil; www.polarnet.com. All U.S. Army data was verified by Maj. Douglas E. McCallum, USA, "E-Mail to Daniel P. Bolger: List of MTOE Infantry Battalions," 8 February 1998. McCallum worked as U.S. Army Personnel Command's Infantry Branch, which assigns all infantrymen worldwide.

1. Under the 1957 Combat Arms Regimental System, U.S. Army infantry battalions are designated by regiment in order to maintain unit heritage. This reflected the transition from the old fighting regiments to the fighting battalions more common in modern warfare. Before that shift, each battalion had unique letter companies. (1st had A-D, 2d went with E-H, 3d used I, K, L, and M. American soldiers traditionally disdain the use of J to identify companies, batteries, or troops.) Since 1957, all Army infantry battalions have companies lettered A–C, with D and E used in some organizations.

By doctrine, Army battalions can move freely among brigades, although in practice most brigades keep their core of three assigned battalions except for specific tasks. The Marines and two Army armored cavalry regiments (2d and 3d) retain the fighting regiment and so kept the old lettering system. The Rangers also can and do fight as a regiment, but each battalion uses the letters A–C for rifle companies. Reflective of their strong veterans' lobbies, battle honors, and infantry-based tactics, the 82d and 101st also group their infantry into nominal regiments, with all three active battalions under the same brigade. Like the Rangers, though, the airborne and air assault divisions go with the post-1957 lettering, with rifle companies lettered A–C in all three battalions. For more on this, see James A. Sawicki, *Infantry Regiments of the U.S. Army* (Dumfries, Va.: Wyvern Publications, 1981), 26–30.

2. This battalion was known as 4/325th during Operation Just Cause in 1989.

3. The 6th Infantry Division (Light) has been deactivated. Its 1st Brigade remained active and was reflagged as the 172d Infantry Brigade (Light) in spring 1998.

4. Flagged as 3/325th during Operation Assured Response in Liberia in 1996, it changed designations shortly after that mission.

5. Although designated as "cavalry" to preserve the battle honors and lineage of famous units, these are standard mechanized infantry battalions.

6. The 75th Ranger Regiment reports to U.S. Army Special Operations Command for routine matters and serves under deployed special operations commands as required by the mission.

7. This battalion is scheduled to deactivate in summer 1999.

8. Although billeted at Camp Pendleton, the 4th Marines belong to the 3d Marine Division on Okinawa on execution of certain war plans. The 3d Marine Regiment in Hawaii will arrive under similar arrangements. The 3d Marine Division routinely commands three rotational infantry battalions from Pendleton or Kaneohe sent to Okinawa under the Unit Deployment Program (UDP). One executes short floats as part of 31st MEU (SOC). These normally range the western Pacific Ocean but have sometimes gone into the Indian Ocean or even into the Mediterranean Sea. This happened during the 1983 fighting in Lebanon.

Index